Josephine Butler

Josephine Butler

Patron Saint
of Prostitutes

HELEN MATHERS

The
History
Press

To Nigel,
who has supported this project throughout

Cover illustration: The official portrait of Josephine Butler as the leader of the LNA taken in 1870. (The Women's Library @ LSE Josephine Butler Society)

First published 2014
This paperback edition published 2021

The History Press
97 St George's Place, Cheltenham,
Gloucestershire, GL50 3QB
www.thehistorypress.co.uk

Typesetting and origination by The History Press
Printed and bound in Great Britain by TJ Books Limited, Padstow, Cornwall.

Trees for Life

Contents

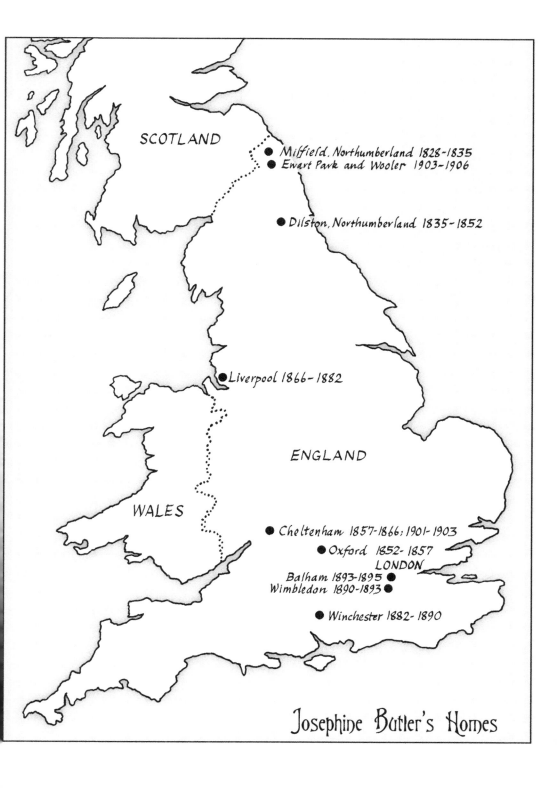

● Milfield, Northumberland 1828-1835
● Ewart Park and Wooler 1903-1906

● Dilston, Northumberland 1835-1852

SCOTLAND

● Liverpool 1866-1882

ENGLAND

WALES

● Cheltenham 1857-1866; 1901-1903
● Oxford 1852-1857
LONDON
Balham 1893-1895 ●
Wimbledon 1890-1893 ●
● Winchester 1882-1890

Josephine Butler's Homes

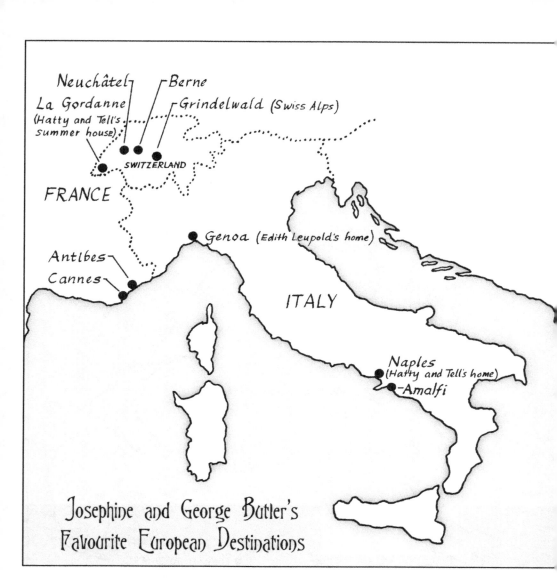

Neuchâtel
Berne
La Gordanne
(Hatty and Tell's
summer house)
Grindelwald (Swiss Alps)
SWITZERLAND
FRANCE
Genoa (Edith Leupold's home)
Antibes
Cannes
ITALY
Naples
(Hatty and Tell's home)
Amalfi
Josephine and George Butler's
Favourite European Destinations

THE GREY FAMILY

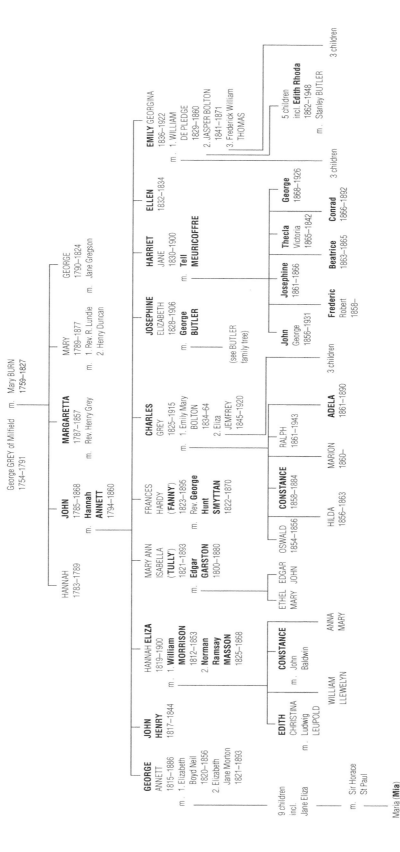

Note: **Bold** indicates people who appear in this book
With thanks to John Thompson, David Thompson and Claire Grey

THE BUTLER FAMILY

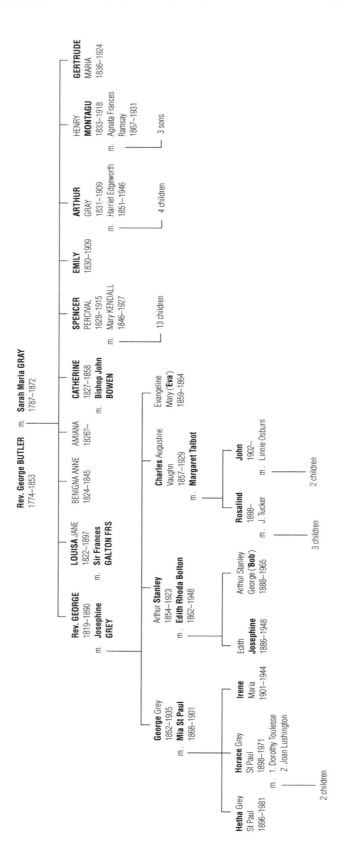

Introduction

I first heard about Josephine Butler when I was an undergraduate history student, and I began to research her writings in 1998 when I was a university teacher of religious and women's history. I was astonished by the power of her conviction and her personality, the range of her ambition and the extent of her achievements. I wanted to understand her, and I found that task to be long and complex – so long, indeed, that I put it aside several times in order to complete other books. Since I started my research, other books about Josephine Butler have been published, and yet it remains true that her name is not well known to the British public – but it should be. She was once described as 'the most distinguished Englishwoman of the nineteenth century'.[1] She was the leader of a national women's political campaign in Victorian England, at a time when women did not have the vote, and succeeded in repealing a law to which she and her followers strongly objected but which public opinion generally supported.

Josephine Butler's life spans the Victorian age – born in 1828, she was 9 when Victoria came to the throne, and died five years after the Queen, in 1906. She was tall and beautiful, with thick lustrous hair which she wore long, in ringlets tied with ribbon or secured with a plait. She was slim, and always dressed with care, choosing tactile fabrics like lace and damask, set off by dramatic beads and earrings. She played the piano with true skill and sensitivity, and loved animals, especially dogs and horses. She came from a comfortable family home in the countryside, and was a devoted daughter and sister.

She was happily married to a husband who adored her and they had four children. But at the age of 40, Josephine became obsessed with the needs of women who were completely unlike herself. While living in Liverpool, she began to care for imprisoned and ill prostitutes, even inviting some to live in her own home. After the Contagious Diseases Acts were passed, which allowed these women to be sexually assaulted by police surgeons on a regular basis, she went into battle with Parliament, the police and the judges to change the law.

This battle consumed her home life, and undermined her physical and emotional health. Many times she collapsed and was confined to bed for weeks, but she kept the campaign going and secured the change in the law. The Ladies' National Association for the Repeal of the Contagious Diseases Acts, which she led, was the first national women's organisation to score such a triumph in England. After this triumph she did not retire, but until the end of her life carried on trying to help abused women.

Why is Josephine Butler not as famous as Victorian heroines like Florence Nightingale? She achieved as much as Nightingale, probably more. But she was never celebrated by her country, never became a national heroine. Indeed, to many she was the reverse of a heroine, because she fought for women's rights, at a time when (with the single exception of Queen Victoria) men had all the power. Even worse, she fought for 'fallen' women, who were regarded as 'subhuman' by polite society. Prostitutes, she was told, were 'a class of sinners whom she had better have left to themselves' since they were the authors of their own destruction.[2] Josephine Butler never gave up, never backed down and forced society to face the sordid details of the abuse she was fighting. No wonder she was unpopular. Some of that rejection, that unpopularity, seems to have clung to her memory ever since.

This book aims to explain Josephine Butler's complex personality, motivated as she was by both feminism and her deep Evangelical Christian faith. The best way to understand this is through an account of her life and her relationships with her family, her supporters and her God. As a professional historian, I have sought to contextualise her campaigns with 'Interludes' between the chapters explaining the historical background. Other Interludes explore her most important writings.

Josephine Butler's dramatic life story is far more sexually graphic than any Victorian novel. She went into brothels, prisons and the 'lock' hospitals where women were examined and treated against their will. She stood up to cruel and coldly calculating authority figures such as the Superintendent of the Morals Police in Paris, the Minister of Justice in Rome and the Public Prosecutor in Brussels. It is also a great love story – the marriage of Josephine and George Butler was blissfully happy and an invaluable source of support to her.

'She chose a life which was a crucifixion' is the verdict of one contemporary.[3] Yet her achievements had lasting impact. Her name deserves to be remembered by all who value women's struggles to improve their lives.

Josephine Butler in Pontefract

The following story, in her own words, illustrates Josephine Butler's character. In 1872 she and her friends were trying to stop the election of a candidate they detested, a man who supported the ill-treatment of prostitutes and had pimps among his supporters. The scene of this tense by-election was Pontefract in West Yorkshire, where large crowds had gathered and passions had been roused on both sides by fervent speeches. The fact that women were among the campaigners enraged men who thought they had no business becoming involved. The welfare of prostitutes was, in any case, a topic which respectable women should never speak about.

Josephine was undaunted by this, and indeed determined to find as many public platforms as possible. She decided to stage a parallel meeting to that of the candidate she opposed, Mr Childers:

> On a certain afternoon, when Mr Childers was again to address a large meeting from the window of a house, I and my lady friends determined to hold a meeting at the same hour, thinking we should be unmolested. We had to go all over the town before we found someone bold enough to let us a place to meet in. At last we found a kind of large hayloft over an empty room on the outskirts of the town. You could only ascend to it by means of a kind of ladder, leading through a trapdoor in the floor. However, the place was large enough to hold a good meeting, and was soon filled.
>
> ... the women were listening to our words with increasing determination never to forsake the good cause, when a smell of burning was perceived, smoke began to curl up through the floor, and a threatening noise was heard below at the door. The bundles of straw beneath had been set on fire ...
>
> Then, to our horror, looking down the room to the trap-door entrance, we saw appearing head after head of men with countenances full of fury; man after man came in, until they crowded the place. There was no possible exit for us, the windows being too high above the ground, and we women were gathered into one end of the room like a flock of sheep surrounded by wolves ...[1]

Since the women were trapped, all they could do was stand firm in the face of the shouting, swearing thugs who were advancing on them. Some were obviously pimps. Josephine and her friend Charlotte Wilson were their targets:

... Mrs Wilson and I stood in front of the company of women, side by side. She whispered in my ear, 'Now is the time to trust in God; do not let us fear'; and a comforting sense of the Divine presence came to us both. It was not personal violence that we feared, as what would have been to any of us *worse than death*; for the indecencies of the men, their gesture and threats, were what I would prefer not to describe. Their language was hideous. They shook their fists in our faces, with volleys of oaths. This continued for some time, and we had no defence or means of escape.[2]

Their male supporters arrived but were unable to help, and indeed made matters worse:

... A fierce argument ensued. Meanwhile stones were thrown into the window, and broken glass flew across the room ... Our case seemed now to become desperate. Mrs Wilson and I whispered to each other in the midst of the din, 'Let us ask God to help us, and then make a rush for the entrance.' Two or three working women placed themselves in front of us, and we pushed our way, I scarcely know how, to the stairs. It was only myself and one or two other ladies that the men really cared to insult and terrify, so if we could get away we felt sure the rest would be safe. I made a dash forward, and took one leap from the trap-door to the ground-floor below. Being light, I came down safely. I found Mrs Wilson with me very soon in the street.

Once in the open street, these cowards did not dare to offer us violence. We went straight to our own hotel, and there we had a magnificent women's meeting. Such a revulsion of feeling came over the inhabitants of Pontefract when they heard of this disgraceful scene that they flocked to hear us, many of the women weeping. We were advised to turn the lights low, and close the windows, on account of the mob; but the hotel was literally crowded with women, and we scarcely needed to speak; events had spoken for us, and all honest hearts were won.

In pursuit of her campaign, Josephine was brave, determined, even foolhardy – in order to hold her women's meeting she risked violent attack, even rape ('what would have been to any of us *worse than death*'). Although she felt at that moment that she 'had stirred up the very depths of hell', she carried on.[3]

A Beautiful Home in an Ugly World

'The bright large family circle'

Josephine Butler was born on 13 April 1828, the seventh child of John Grey and his wife Hannah Annett. The Greys were country people, born and bred in the north-eastern borders, where the Cheviot Hills divide England from Scotland. The Northumberland border country of Glendale, along Hadrian's Wall, is remote and thinly-populated – Josephine described it as 'bleak and almost savage' in character.[1] Its people were tough, determined, combative and self-reliant, shaped by the clashes which scarred centuries of border history. John Grey's home was only a mile from the site of the tragic Battle of Flodden in which 'the flowers of the forest', the noble youth of Scotland, 'were a' wede away'.[2] Josephine remembered her father reciting these lines as she walked with him there; she loved 'border tales of tragedy and romance' and shared his love for 'sweet Glendale'.[3] Her Grey ancestors had lived there for centuries 'derived from a long line of warriors, who were Wardens of the East Marches' and governors of the border castles.[4]

By the time of Josephine's birth the Grey family had three branches with local estates. One distant cousin, Charles Earl Grey, whose estates were at Howick, has several claims to fame. As the Whig Prime Minister 1830–34, his administration passed the first Parliamentary Reform Bill (1832) and abolished slavery in the British Empire (1833).[5] In his youth he was the lover of Georgiana, Duchess of Devonshire whose husband the Duke forced her to give up the daughter, Eliza, fathered by Grey.[6]

Josephine's branch of the family had no such skeletons in the closet and its property was relatively small, consisting of farmland and a house, Milfield Hill, overlooking the River Tweed. Her grandfather, George Grey (1754–88), had cleared the land from wild forest and started farming, but he died tragically young leaving his wife Mary with four young children. She rose to this challenge magnificently, and succeeded in managing the farm and raising her children single-handedly. Josephine's grandmother was a 'very thoughtful and studious' woman, who educated her children while doing the household chores.[7] They were encouraged, for example, to learn epic poetry, such as Scott's *Marmion*, by heart and she borrowed books for them from the local lending library. Later she found the money to send both her boys and girls away to school. Mary Grey was herself a model of female independence and resilience, and an influence on Josephine's views about what women could achieve, even though she died before Josephine was born.

John Grey was 8 when his father died. Ten years later, as the eldest son, he took over the management of his 'patrimonial estate',[8] along with land which the family farmed as tenants. By all accounts he was an excellent farmer and land manager, an enthusiast for the agricultural reform which was transforming the countryside. Waste land was reclaimed and fenced off, turnips were grown to dramatically enhance the yield from crop rotation, and threshing machines efficiently processed the grain harvest. The animal stock was improved beyond recognition through selective breeding and better nutrition. John Grey also had a talent for making good relationships with both staff and tenants, and was highly respected among his neighbours.

Josephine's mother, Hannah Annett, came from nearby Alnwick; her ancestors were 'poor but honest' Protestant silk-weavers driven out of France, probably in 1685.[9] It was unusual for 'Huguenot' families in England to move so far north, however – the vast majority went to settlements in London and the south.[10] Hannah Annett met John Grey at a country inn where both had stopped for food and shelter during a long ride through snow. Her mother romantically recalled for Josephine the moment that John 'placed himself in front of her horse, held its rein with a firm hand, and, fixing his eyes on her, said some words ...' Her mother did not repeat the words, but they 'sent her on her way in such a frame of mind that her horse sometimes took the wrong turn in the road without her noticing it'.[11] They were married within the year, 'the bride riding to church dressed in a beautiful pale blue riding habit, richly embroidered'.[12]

John and Hannah took possession of Milfield Hill on their marriage. Mary Grey moved out, John's sisters were already married and, although his brother George stayed on, he too departed a few years later for London. There George died in sad and painful circumstances after a fall 'from a horse or carriage' – the details were never clear to the family because they were not contacted until several weeks later, when he was at death's door. A devastating postscript to a letter summoning John told him, 'His struggles have ceased exactly an hour.' Too late, John travelled to London by mail coach to be told the story of George's last days, and the many times he had called out for his brother and mother.[13]

John and Hannah had ten children in total; three boys and seven girls, of whom Josephine was the fourth girl. Her brother George, the eldest child, was 13 when she was born, followed by John (11), Eliza (9), Mary Ann ('Tully', 7), Fanny (5) and Charley (3). George and John were old enough to seem distant to a little girl, but Josephine was always close to her sisters and to Charley. The family were fortunate that their mother was so strong – at a time of high maternal mortality Hannah survived all her births and enjoyed good health for most of her life. The Greys celebrated their 45th wedding anniversary before Hannah died in 1860.

Dilston House

Both Hannah and John loved their Milfield home, but in 1833 John was offered an opportunity he could not refuse – the management of the vast estates belonging to Greenwich Hospital, totalling over 34,000 acres, which were scattered all over Northumberland. He was ideally suited to this new role, which gave him wider scope for agricultural reform and for educating the farmers. His conscientious work proved to be a 'model of estate management'.[14] Josephine adored her father and was proud that he was described as 'a good and wise and powerful man'.[15] Travelling around the county, overseeing work on the land and introducing improvements to the agriculture and the conditions of the tenants meant inevitably that much of his time was spent away from home.

By this time Hannah had nine children at home in Milfield, after the births of Harriet ('Hatty') and Ellen ('Ellie'). John missed them all deeply, and wrote to Hannah asking for news of them, especially the youngest, who was only 1 – 'How I should like to see little Ellie toddling on her own small feet'.

Shortly afterwards, the three younger children caught scarlet fever; Ellie then succumbed to typhus and died while John was away from home.[16] Like John, Hannah doted on their small children, describing her grief in a letter to him written several months later, '... in walking the street, if my eye rests on a little one with tottering feet and chubby hands, my heart sinks within me. Oh! How many darts pierce a bereaved mother's bosom which no one knows of!'[17] This tragedy cast a cloud over their plans to move to a new house.

John and Hannah were offered the chance to build a home on his employer's land, and selected a hilltop site at Dilston, dramatically positioned high above a river called the Devil's Water. This beautiful and secluded location even had the romantic ruins of a fifteenth-century castle in its grounds.[18] They designed a spacious family home – large enough for each child to have a bedroom, with plenty of room for visitors as well. They moved there in 1835 when Hannah was still mourning the loss of Ellie. Her eldest son, George, had also stayed behind to take over the management of Milfield, 60 miles distant over narrow lanes. For her there was 'a pleasure in the pathless woods' but sadness that 'our little group' was not complete, and never would be again.[19]

For Josephine ('Josey'), now 7, and her brothers and sisters, Dilston was perfect. This is Josephine's evocative description:

> Our home at Dilston was a very beautiful one. Its romantic historical associations, the wild informal beauty all round its doors, the bright large family circle, and the kind and hospitable character of its master and mistress, made it an attractive place to many friends and guests ... It was a place where one could glide out of a lower window, and be hidden in a moment, plunging straight among wild wood paths, and beds of ferns, or find one's self quickly in some cool concealment, beneath slender birch trees, or by the dry bed of a mountain stream.[20]

Clearly Josephine sometimes liked to escape from the company of so many brothers and sisters!

She was a studious and thoughtful child, reserved and 'shy', with delicate health after a premature birth – she described herself as 'a weak, wretched infant, hard to rear at all'.[21] If Josephine was difficult to rear, this might explain why she appears to have been closer to her father than to her hard-pressed mother. During games with her siblings she often felt faint if she ran around a lot. This did not stop her enjoying outdoor life, but she spent a lot of time in sedentary pursuits like reading, painting and playing the piano. As a pianist she had genuine talent, and Hannah encouraged her to practise seriously and to become a good musician, rather than simply a competent parlour performer.[22] Josephine took great pleasure in playing well and, as a teenager, was given a 'splendid grand piano' by her father which the family loved to hear her play. Her sister Hatty remembered in particular 'the magic of the Moonlight Sonata' – one of Beethoven's sonatas in a bound volume which Hannah gave to Josephine and which she treasured for the rest of her life.[23]

The Siblings

Hatty was two years younger than Josey and within the family they formed a pair. Closest together in age, they 'walked, rode, played and learned our lessons together'.[24] Hatty was robust, chubby, gregarious and cheerful, the perfect foil for Josey's introspection and occasional low spirits. Throughout her life Josephine relied on Hatty's good sense and unquestioning devotion. They both loved animals and had pets, including not only dogs but also 'ferrets, wild cats from the woods and owls'.[25] Hatty collected so many newts in jam jars on a shelf above her bed that it collapsed, flooding the mattress.

In the stables were ponies which all the Grey children learned to ride. Josey became a proficient and enthusiastic rider, but Hatty was the one who managed to stand upright on the saddle and wanted to run away to join the circus.[26] They trained horses for their father, and as teenagers enjoyed going hunting at Milfield with their brother George. Often they accompanied their father on his rides round the estate, as Hatty recalled:

> ... sometimes such merry wild gallops over high grass-fields in Hexhamshire, or above Aydon, bending our heads nearly to the horse's mane, to receive the sharp pelting hail on our hats, the horses laying back their ears, and bounding at the stinging of the hail on their flanks, and coming in with heavy clinging skirt, and veil frozen into a mask the shape of one's nose, revealing very rosy cheeks when it was peeled off ...[27]

This evocative description shows that Josephine was not the only inspired writer that the Grey family produced. Josey recalled Hatty's heartbreak when her pet dog, Pincher, was accused by local farmers (unfairly in her opinion) of worrying sheep. He 'was tried, condemned and executed ... wagging his tail to the last and offering his paw, in sign, my sister said through her tears, of forgiveness of his murderers'.[28]

Hannah gave birth to her last child, Emily, at the age of 42 in 1836. As the six daughters grew older, each was allocated a bedroom leading off the upstairs hall. Sometimes they would be summoned by a shout from their father's dressing room, because 'the tying of a necktie was a mystery he never could compass ... It always ended with the appearance of a piece of crumpled hemp'. All the available daughters would rush out of their rooms, 'anxious to help the old Dad' but some had to stand on a stool as he was so tall.[29]

This family scene was described by Josephine – others come from her parents' letters. On New Year's Day 1843, John wrote to Tully, 'some of the young folks are reading, and others chatting in the blaze of a Christmas fire in the drawing room. I hear Charley's voice overheard in discourse with mamma. He looks the little man in tails less gracefully than the tall boy in a jacket.'[30] Evidently Charley had been forced to adopt a man's tailcoat at the age of 17. As the youngest of the three sons, Charley seems to have been quite the favourite of his mother – once when absent from home to stay with her uncle Hannah wrote to John of how much she missed the family, 'It would be quite a treat to see Charley come in and throw his hat in a wrong place, and leave his books in a litter, as that would give life to the scene.'[31]

By this time John, the second son who had a punctured lung caused by an accident, had left home to visit his sister Eliza in Hong Kong in the hope of improving his health.[32] Josephine quotes touching letters to him on his voyage from their father: 'My very dear John, I am often thinking of you when the wind raves among our trees. But then I recollect that it may be calm in your hemisphere ... Be watchful, my dear boy, of your thoughts and actions, make good use of your opportunities of observation, take especial care of your health, and come back cheerful and strong and instructive. Ever your affectionate father, John Grey.'[33] The letter never reached John as he had 'died off the Cape', as the family discovered in a terse message from his boat while berthed in China. Months later they received a 'badly spelled and badly written' letter from a sailor-boy who had looked after John and reported that, on his deathbed, 'Mr Grey sang out for his mother ... [and] talked much about his brother George and thought he was coming to him'. Hannah took hope and comfort from this letter, happy that her son had had a friend to cheer him and to read him 'the word of life', the Bible.[34]

'It was my lot from my earliest years to be haunted.'

The Grey family was happy and idyllically cocooned in the countryside, but John and Hannah did not forget the outside world. John, in particular, more pessimistic and introspective than his practical and positive wife, could become obsessed with the horrors endured by less fortunate people. Josephine's father was a committed supporter of anti-slavery campaigns. He was horrified by 'a system in my mind repugnant to every principle of justice and to every feeling of humanity'.[35] John was 21 when William Wilberforce's campaign against the slave trade came to its triumphant conclusion in 1807; the battle moved on to the freedom of slaves in the British colonies. John spoke against slavery at election meetings, organised petitions and made the acquaintance of leaders of the movement. He was in close touch with his cousin, the Prime Minister, and rejoiced that he was able to lead this campaign to success in 1833. John went on to join the campaign to free the slaves on the plantations of the American South. Josephine remembered a visit to their home by one of its leaders, William Lloyd Garrison – a sign of how important her father's influence was. Garrison became one of her heroes; in her own campaigns she often used his catchphrase – 'I will be as harsh as truth and as uncompromising as justice. I am in earnest ... and *I will be heard*.'[36]

Like most anti-slavery campaigners, John Grey was inspired by religious conviction. He was an Evangelical, like Wilberforce, and believed that, as a born-again Christian, he should attack evil in the world wherever he found it. Slavery was an evil, a denial of the fact that God loved all men and women, of whatever colour, equally. Evangelical families like the Greys were on a mission against sin, and their children were caught up in it.

When John Grey became a father, he introduced his children to the family's mission and did not spare them the shocking details. So Josephine learned at a young age of whippings and brandings, and the separation of slave children from their parents. Her father told her of slave sales in which the 'merchandise' was poked, prodded and assessed like cuts of meat. The strongest impact on Josephine was made, she said, by the dreadful treatment of female slaves, who were 'almost invariably forced to minister to the worst passions of their masters'.[37] One story she never forgot was that of a slave woman:

> ... who had four sons, the sons of her master. The three eldest were sold by the father in childhood for good prices, and the mother never knew their fate. She had one left, her youngest, her treasure. Her master, in a fit of passion, one day shot this boy dead.[38]

The mother did not survive this final blow, but died distraught and despairing. Recalling these stories later, Josephine wrote that they 'awakened my feelings concerning injustice to women through this conspiracy of greed and gold and lust of the flesh'.[39] Her strongest feelings were for suffering women; she felt that they endured more because of their sex and had much less power to do anything to improve their situation.

Stories of slavery and suffering conjured up images which, she said, 'haunted' her.[40] When she was 17, this caused a crisis of doubt about the Christian faith she had learned and accepted as a child, questioning why God allowed this suffering and why the world seemed 'out of joint'.[41] She described it as 'one long year of darkness'.[42] She ran out into the woods and 'used to *shriek* to God to come and deliver'. Her sisters, not surprisingly, thought she was 'a little mad'.[43]

Josephine eventually found a measure of peace and acceptance, but her questions remained for many more years before she found the answers she was looking for. She also became seriously ill around this time when she 'broke a blood vessel in my lungs.'[44] Her family feared for her life, especially after a visit from her brother-in-law, the husband of her eldest sister Eliza, who was a surgeon. He pronounced her 'doomed'.[45] She recovered from this and similar attacks in the future. Her resilience in the face of serious health problems, which kept her in bed for weeks at a time, is one of the recurring themes of Josephine's life.

Until she was 19, Josephine's travels hardly extended beyond a 60-mile radius of her home. Although she was well informed about its existence, she had very little direct experience of poverty. A trip to Ireland in 1847 brought her a terrible enlightenment. In the Irish potato famine of the mid-1840s, hundreds of thousands of Irish peasants had starved to death. Many more had fled abroad, to England or America, to escape the terrible hunger and the barren land filled with rotting, useless plants. Those who were left behind were often the weakest and most desperate. When Josey and Hatty visited their brother Charles, who was staying in Ireland, the horror of what they saw was overwhelming. Josephine recalled that the gardens and fields in front of the house were:

> ... completely darkened with a population of men, women and children, squatting, in
> rags; uncovered skeleton limbs protruding everywhere from their wretched clothing, and
> clamorous, though faint voices uplifted for food.[46]

There was a 'strange morbid famine smell in the air'. This terrible experience was her first encounter with abject suffering. Josephine wondered once more why evil and pain were such dominant features of a world created by God.

Faith and Happiness

These unhappy experiences were powerful enough for Josephine to recall them in old age, but most of her teenage life was happy, relaxed and convivial. The Grey children enjoyed a lively social life with plenty of dressing up and dancing. They went to all the local balls where, Josephine recalled, she and her sisters 'were great *belles*, in our snowy book-muslin frocks, and natural flowers wreathed in our heads and waists and skirts'.[47] Emily, the youngest, accompanied them at the age of 15, 'her golden hair dressed like a crown'.[48]

The Alnwick County Ball attracted all the local gentry, and John was joined by his cousin Lord Grey, Lord Howick and Lord Durham 'all standing in a group in the very middle of the ballroom floor, regardless of the dancers all around them, deep in some Liberal political intrigue'. Josephine danced with the heir to Lord Tankerville, even though 'my father did not quite like my dancing with a Tory!'[49]

The Greys owned a family carriage, drawn by two horses, which they used for great occasions, like the trip to the County Ball. They also kept two carriages which seated four people and a 'high small open gig' in which John Grey often drove Josey and Hatty.[50] They usually made the journey to Milfield in an open carriage, with a one night stop. In 1839 the first railway from Newcastle to Carlisle opened, passing so close to Dilston that a private station was built. This gave easy access to Dilston for their wide circle of friends and relatives.

At Dilston the Greys entertained guests on an impressive scale. Hatty noted 'such a house full' in the summer of 1850 when at least eleven stayed at once.[51] Some friends and relatives remained for weeks at a time; Hatty preferred those who 'fitted ... into the family' and did not demand to be 'amused'. A favourite was Miss Sands, who 'thought it so nice to paint and practise with Josey'. There were many excursions to local places of interest, like the 'jolly little picnic to Stewart Peel and Langley Castle' when their sister Tully and her husband Edgar were visiting, evocatively recalled by Hatty:

> We had the open carriage with Mama and Mrs Morrison, Josey and Tully (with straw hats on) inside, Edgar on the back seat, and Mr Hill beside John on the box ... Emmy and I rode on Bobby and Undine ... We ... had the horses put up an hour at the Peel while we rambled about and gathered wild flowers ... the deep ravine [was] close on each side, with such a mass of wooded park to look down upon ... After a time we became so hungry we could admire no more, and returned to Langley, which we reached at 5 o'clock and didn't we set to with hearty goodwill to scramble up the long dark stairs to where our good dinner of cold lamb, and chickens, and ham, and hot potatoes, was spread out ... When dinner was over we were so tired and sleepy, we made pillows of our cloaks, and lay down on the flags, all in a row like sheep ... except Mama and Mrs Morrison who sat bolt upright on two uncomfortable chairs. But any attempt to go to sleep was vain, for Emmy crept quietly about from one to another ... whispering mischief in our ears and making us laugh.[52]

The Greys were relaxed and full of life because they believed in a version of Christianity which emphasised love. Other Victorian Christians, such as Calvinists, were oppressed by feelings of guilt and sin. The Greys were convinced of their forgiveness and redemption by Christ, which gave them confidence, hope and an immense compassion for others. Among Victorian families, they most resembled the so-called 'Clapham Sect', of which William Wilberforce was a member.

Like the Clapham group, the Greys were members of the Evangelical wing of the Church of England. The established church had a wide range of belief within it, from the Anglo-Catholics or ritualists, whose beliefs and services were very similar to those of the Roman Catholics, to the Evangelicals, whose beliefs were very close to Nonconformists like the Methodists and the Baptists. Evangelicals believed that human beings were innately sinful but that they could be forgiven through repentance and 'turning to Christ'. Christ had saved sinners through his death on the cross, and accepting Christ as Saviour (described as conversion or rebirth) would lead to new life.

Hannah Grey, although brought up as an Anglican Evangelical, had received some of her early education from a Nonconformist sect, the Moravians. It was said within the family that the founder of Methodism, John Wesley, had taken her on his knee as a young child, placed his hands on her head and pronounced 'a solemn and tender benediction'.[53] This was impossible, since Wesley had been dead for several years before Hannah was born, but the story does show the reverence the family had for John Wesley.[54]

Josey and Hatty's nurse, Nancy, who was a Methodist, sometimes took them to her own chapel.[55] There they would have sung great hymns, such as 'Guide Me, Oh Thou Great Jehovah' (*Cwm Rhondda*) and Charles Wesley's 'Love Divine, All Loves Excelling'. They would have sat through the long sermons delivered from the high and imposing central pulpit. Usually this would be delivered by the 'circuit' minister but occasionally a lay preacher gifted with powerful oratory would come to plead with sinners to repent and turn to Jesus.

In the 1830s and 1840s Methodism was gathering many new converts, who testified to their experience of 'rebirth' during the services and at class meetings. Josephine was so affected by this that she later insisted that she was 'brought up a Wesleyan'.[56]

In fact John Grey took his children to the local parish church in Corbridge every Sunday. Hatty remembered that she and Josey 'used to trot along to church, each with hold of one of Papa's hands, who took such long steps that we had to run like little dogs by his side'.[57] It was a long walk for children – almost 2 miles. The Grey children were taught Christian toleration. John and Hannah had learned to value the teaching of other churches besides their own, and were not hostile or disparaging of Christians from other denominations.

Throughout her life Josephine preferred not to identify herself with any one church. Her experience of attending Anglican services made her very critical of them. The preaching did not impress her at all. Referring to her religious crisis, she wrote that the minister 'taught us loyally all that he probably knew about God, but [his] words did not even touch the fringe of my soul's deep discontent'.[58] This was to be the pattern of her life; she rarely found that Anglican ministers understood her concerns and so she remained on the fringes of the Church.

What Josephine valued was 'vital Christianity' and the freedom to develop her own ideas about God. She also adopted millenarian beliefs that the world was entering a time of evil, war and unbelief from which it would be rescued by the Second Coming of Christ. The doctrine that this Second Coming was imminent was preached by Edward Irving, who gained many followers in the English border country during the years of Josephine's childhood. She and Hatty were taken to an Irvingite 'camp meeting' at Barmoor, 5 miles from their home, 'in a cart with straw in it and a sack to sit on and we used to sit and hear the words and "prophesyings" of ... those gifted men'.[59] The meeting would have featured miraculous healings and speaking in tongues, and its powerful effect on children is not hard to imagine. In adult life, especially when overwhelmed by problems and setbacks, the prospect of 'the great Deliverance' and 'the New Dispensation' gave her hope for the future.[60] The Second Coming was 'the advent of the Day which we long for'.[61]

Education for Girls

Josephine went to a boarding school in Newcastle which her sister Fanny had attended. Hannah used to visit by train and sometimes sent them tuck boxes.[62] It was run by a woman called Miss Tidy who became a friend of the family but had little to equip her for the task, beyond what Josephine described as 'a large heart and ready sympathy'.[63] She was 'not a good disciplinarian'. When Hatty joined the school she spent much of her time drawing, including humorous illustrations in her teacher's copy of the *History of the Italian Republics*.[64] Hatty did not like school and left after only two years; Josephine stayed longer.[65]

Apart from that, the sisters were educated at home by governesses and by their mother Hannah, who 'would assemble us daily for the reading aloud of some solid book, and by a kind of examination following the reading assured herself that we had mastered the subject'.[66] This was a typical education for girls at that time, and not a very satisfactory one. Among Victorians it was a common view that there was little point in teaching girls any academic subjects, since they would grow up to have a domestic role as wives and mothers. Even though Hannah insisted that 'whatever we did should be thoroughly done', Josephine had deficiencies in her education which she rectified herself (with great success) in adult life.

It is surprising that John Grey did not do more for his daughters, since his own mother Mary Grey sent both his sisters to school in London. There is a family story that his sister Margaretta, frustrated that women were not allowed inside the Houses of Parliament, dressed up as a boy in order to gain entrance.[67] John Grey also made sure that the children of tenants on his estates received an education. However, his high expectations of his daughters and the freedom he allowed them compensated a great deal for the gaps in their education. They were treated as equals within the home, and John discussed 'all matters of interest and importance, political, social, and professional, as well as domestic' with his wife and daughters.[68] This gave Josephine a wide knowledge of social and political issues, and also an unquenchable confidence in her own value as a woman. This was a great gift, since so many Victorian women were brought up to see themselves as weak and inferior to men.

Josephine would have adored the chance to go to university, but it was never offered. She was, in fact, born just in time to achieve that goal, since Bedford, the first women's college, opened in 1849, when she was 21. The campaigner Barbara Bodichon, born in the same decade as Josephine, attended.[69]

Margaretta Grey saw the dangers for the daughters of wealthy families of 'too abundant leisure' and activities like 'visiting, note-writing, dressing and choosing dresses ...' instead of having 'any real and important purpose' in life.[70] She criticised most female schooling as 'a broken, desultory education, made up of details, of which the secondary and mechanical often have precedence of the solid and intellectual'. It is no surprise that Josephine's own frustration, finally boiling over in her thirties, led her to direct her first campaigning efforts towards the higher education of women. But first came marriage and children.

Well-known Victorian Women – Who Were Josephine Butler's Contemporaries?

Born more than 10 years earlier	Born within 10 years of her birth (1828)	Born more than 10 years later than her
Harriet Martineau *Journalist and author*	Josephine Butler (1828–1906) *Feminist campaigner*	Millicent Garrett Fawcett *Women's suffrage campaigner*
Charlotte Brontë *Novelist*	Barbara Leigh Smith Bodichon (1827–1901) *Feminist campaigner*	Emmeline Pankhurst *Women's suffrage campaigner*
George Eliot *Novelist*	Catherine Booth (1829–1890) *Salvation Army co-leader*	
Florence Nightingale *Nursing reformer*	Isabella Bird (1831–1904) *Traveller and author*	
Elizabeth Gaskell *Novelist*	Frances Power Cobbe (1822–1904) *Feminist campaigner*	
Harriet Taylor Mill *Feminist campaigner*	Anne Clough (1820–1892) *Women's education campaigner*	
	Charlotte Yonge (1823–1901) *Novelist*	

Josephine Meets George

 George Butler

All the Grey daughters married, and Josephine wrote a touching account of the way they parted from their father:

> ... the visit paid in the morning to the bride's room, the long, tender, silent embrace, and the throbbing of his strong heart, which betrayed his emotion. 'Father, you have other daughters left,' it was sometimes remarked; the only reply was 'My child' and a moment's closer grasp to his heart.[1]

In some cases the daughters left home for the first time to live abroad. Hatty was to live in Italy after her marriage to a wealthy banker, Tell Meuricoffre. Their sister Eliza moved to Hong Kong with her husband, William Morrison.

Josephine herself, however, did not stray further than Oxford after her wedding, nor did she marry a rich man. George Butler, although in his late twenties, was still to make his career when she met him. He was not personally ambitious and appears to have been rather indecisive.[2] In his youth he was quite a disappointment to his father, the Dean of Peterborough, who had previously been the headmaster of a top English public school, Harrow. As a Harrow pupil, George did not distinguish himself (although he won a prize for Greek) and later recalled that 'he was considered to be extremely good at "shying stones" and could hit chimneypots far better than the other boys'.[3]

At Cambridge University, he enjoyed the social life, was 'attracted by music, art, outdoor exercises, and athletics', and neglected his studies.[4] George, in short, had a healthy love of life and revelled in sport, games and physical exercise. He enjoyed risky climbs and jumping into cold water 'hissing hot' which in his opinion 'helps one to resist the chill of the water, and brings about a speedier reaction, and that glow which is the bather's delight and reward'.[5]

His father intervened, and withdrew George from Cambridge. After a period of five months studying with a private tutor, he moved to Oxford to study Classics. George had decided to turn over a new leaf, and gained a first class degree in 1843. He, characteristically, later described this time as his 'owlish phase – read all day, spoke little, ate little, walked much, wrote Latin letters to my friends, and was generally very disagreeable'.[6] During the next four years he stayed in Oxford, studying, teaching and leading reading parties in the vacations.

He was also private tutor for several months to Lord Hopetoun, the son of an aristocratic family.[7] None of these activities amounted to a career, so he was relieved in 1848 to move to Durham University as a tutor in residence. He enjoyed teaching and was resisting pressure from his father to be ordained as a minister in the Church of England. He later explained some of his reluctance:

> I don't like parsons ... if I were like some of them that I know, I should cease to be a man. I shall never wear straight waistcoats, long coats and stiff collars! ... Great strictness in outward observances interferes with the devotion of the heart.[8]

George was a questioning, sceptical member of the Church of England. His experience of the Church was stifling, and his father's position as a Dean was not a beacon to follow but a shadow over his hopes of finding a different career. The Dean hoped that the 'clerical atmosphere' of Durham would have a positive effect on George, but he immediately disliked it, since Anglo-Catholicism, with its emphasis on ritual and ceremony, was popular. George much preferred 'inward conviction and fervour' to outward display, and he had also made many friends at Oxford who were liberal 'Broad Church' Anglicans.[9]

The Path of True Love ...

Even though Josephine wrote a biography of her husband, she never gave an account of their first meeting.[10] There has been speculation that Josephine could have met George in Durham, while on a visit to her brother Charles, who was a postgraduate student there.[11] However, Charles was awarded his MA in February 1849 and Josephine was absent from home (probably for medical treatment in London) for seven months that year.[12] There would have been a long gap before Josephine and George met again.

A recently discovered letter from George's sister, Louisa, suggests a later date – June 1850. Louisa tells her youngest brother Monty about George's passion for Josephine Grey, who 'lives north of Durham, is very beautiful, plays divinely, is clever, sensible and altogether one of those Phantoms of delight'.[13] George 'fell in love with her at a ball in June and ever since, his love has waxed warmer and more warmer [sic]'.[14]

We know that Josephine was the belle of many balls and that George was athletic and probably an excellent dancer. George must have told Louisa the story of how he met the beautiful Miss Grey, with whom he was now helplessly in love. He began writing love poems to Josephine in October 1850, after his first visit to Dilston.[15]

George's poems were written in his room at the top of Durham Castle tower. He transcribed them in beautiful copperplate handwriting and presented the volume to Josephine on the tenth anniversary of their engagement.

The Rose of Dilstone a Song

O twine for me no second wreath;
The jasmine, nor the eglantine.
I'd seek no broom, nor flowery heath,
Were the wild rose of Dilstone mine.

'Mid feathery ferns and liched rocks
Beneath the silvery birches shade,

Uninjured by the winds and shocks
How gracefully it rears its head!

Its beauty glads the passer-by
Its fragrance fills the vale of Tyne;
No other rose, no flower would I,
Were but the Rose of Dilston mine.[16]

A second poem, 'The Rose and the Primrose', is addressed to both Josephine and Harriet and contrasts the 'brilliant tints' of the primrose who 'everyone admired' with the modest 'loveliness and heavenly grace' of the rose.[17] Those early conversations and outings with the sisters must have been entrancing, and George felt as if he had come home. He instantly fitted into their family life, and enjoyed all their outdoor activities, especially horse riding and hill walking.

In a third poem, 'The Early Morn', written at Dilston, George celebrates the beauty of the landscape, but ends on a note of desolation:

And I am driven forth, alas.
To wander cheerless and forlorn.

In vain for me the words are drest
In autumn's hues, fair nature's pride –
The thoughts that rise within my breast
Will not be stifled nor denied

No more can nature give relief,
Nor art her treasures ope to me,
For all my joy and all my grief
Is centred, Josephine, in thee.[18]

Josephine had rejected his early advances – he had been too eager. Back in Durham, he recalled 'thy just reproof/and saw thy slow retreating form'. He 'cursed my faltering tongue' and resolved to take 'the path of duty – harsh and stern'.[19] To win Josephine, he would have to restrain his passion and move in step with her.

He was so successful that, less than three months later, Josephine accepted his proposal and they became engaged in January 1851. George had secured a new post, as Public Examiner at Oxford University, and would leave Durham at Easter. Although this post was part-time it was better than the 'drudgery' of the work in Durham and he had many friends and better prospects in Oxford.[20]

At this transitional stage of their lives, we can look not only into George's heart, but also into Josephine's since she used her correspondence with her sister Eliza in Hong Kong 'as a sort of safety valve' in which she could 'put down all kinds of things, bad as well as good'.[21] Her letters offer 'a rare insight' into the worries, fears and joys of 'a young Victorian woman about to be married'.[22]

The early months of their engagement were anxious ones for Josephine. She confessed to Eliza that although they wrote to each other a great deal, 'I feel rather a difficulty in getting on with him when he comes here first of all'.[23] Partly this was because she did not see him very often, so 'there is always some ice to be broken every time'. But she is frustrated that he seems to be 'very guarded always ... I don't see why he should not *come out* with his feelings to me sometimes. If I did not exercise a *childlike* faith in the existence and strength of his affection for me, I might sometimes doubt it.' Knowing the true strength of George's feelings, it is easy to see that he was afraid of another rebuff if he expressed them too strongly. Victorian conventions decreed that physical contact, even between engaged couples, had to be very limited. He was also nine years older than Josephine – an age gap of which they were both strongly aware. Josephine told Eliza, 'He is 32 nearly ... rather too old I think.'

When Josephine wrote this letter, in March 1851, she was anticipating a long visit from George over Easter. He was staying at Dilston prior to his departure for Oxford. A dressing room had been turned into a study for him so that he could read each morning in preparation for his new job. (Quite a daunting one, since the Public Examiners conducted oral questioning of candidates in front of an audience.) Josephine was full of trepidation: 'I hope we shall get over our fear of each other after he has been a few days in the house.'[24] Hatty was at Milfield Hill, and 'I feel so "friendless" without her, and I need her to back me up'.

Hatty's absence may well have been deliberate – Hannah also kept to her room, and John was out much of the time. In a move which was unusual and enlightened at the time, her parents deliberately made it possible for Josephine and George to get to know each other. George's stay lasted six weeks and proved, of course, to be 'a most delightful and happy time indeed', as Josephine told Eliza in the next letter.[25] 'I am so glad of this visit for we did not know each other well enough before ... George and I have had to keep house together – and I do so admire and like the domestic part of his character which has been thus drawn out.' Her fears about his age were banished now that he was 'so playful and merry ... he is just like a boy and confesses in such funny innocent ways how ... in love he is'. In fairness she had to confess this to Eliza since 'I wrote in rather a different strain last time'.

Strict convention and their own principles would have stopped them sharing a bed or having sex, but their closeness from this time onwards must have made the transition easy and happy after their marriage. Josephine was pregnant within a few weeks of their wedding in January 1852 and spoke of herself as 'the happiest of women myself in all the relations of life'.[26]

Prelude to the Wedding

Passionate letters passed between them after George's departure for Oxford. They regretted the delay before their wedding which, George said, 'there would have been no reason for had we been rich'.[27] During May and June, Josephine spent several weeks in London and they managed to meet up there. During this visit she sat for the fashionable London artist, George Richmond, who had painted the authors Charlotte Brontë and Elizabeth Gaskell.[28] The result is a beautiful study which captures the 'rapt, self-possessed expression of a woman in love'.[29]

Although she had told Eliza that 'I detest London', she enjoyed her visit and took music lessons from Sterndale Bennett, the composer, who she liked 'excessively ... I get him to play to me a good deal.'[30] She also made two visits to the Great Exhibition at Crystal Palace, first with Tully and her husband Edgar Garston, and second with her mother and a group of friends.[31] She was surprised and overwhelmed (as everyone was) by the size of the building, the sheer number of exhibits and the crowds. In a long letter to Eliza in

Hong Kong, she said little about the exhibits, but noted 'the Crystal Fountain, a fountain of white glass which throws up jets of sparkling clear water' and the 'mounted policemen, whose beautiful horses stand like statues in the very thickest of the crowd, arching their necks and looking so calm and dignified'.[32] They struggled to get out, 'It is a terrible place for weariness – Mama was nearly dead and wanted to come away by the front entrance again but that is not allowed, and so we had to make her walk nearly half a mile of the South Transept before we could get out. We came home in the Carrs' carriage very hungry and tired.'

They had dinner at Lord Mounteagle's, and went to Kensington Palace Gardens and on the Thames before George arrived. Josephine confided to Eliza that she contrived to spend the evening alone with him when everyone else went to church, 'we stood listening to a nightingale singing – actually a nightingale! ... It was *very* sweet and the distant sound of the organ in the church ... made it very delightful.'[33] By the end of June, she was 'delighted at the thought of getting away from hot London streets' and made her first visit to George's family home, along with Hatty, Emily and her parents.[34] It was 'a very jolly party' and Josephine declared herself 'delighted with the old Dean'.[35]

George had to spend the rest of his summer in Oxford, where the examinations were taking place. He saved the life of his friend Ralph Lingen when they went swimming in a river and he was caught by the strong current. It says much for George's physical strength that he not only battled against the current himself, but was able to pull his friend to the bank safely.[36]

George's sisters, Catherine and Emily, visited Dilston and were treated to one of the family's favourite outings – a visit to Queen Margaret's Cave, which involved a scramble down rocks, and lighting candles in the darkness to try to detect 'traces' of the Queen.[37] Needless to say, they found none.

The Wedding of Josephine and George

With the wedding set for 8 January, Hatty started to worry about life without Josephine, 'I really don't know what we are to do without her, sweet little body ... I am perfectly unfit to fill up even half the gap her departure will make.'[38] At the end of the year she decided to keep a diary, which records precious memories of her sister's last few weeks at home.[39] The first entry describes 'Josey the belle' of a ball at Newtown Hall, Durham, on 20 November. After the dancing, the girls went shopping for the wedding. Hatty and Josey left Durham on 24 November and 'met Mama in Newcastle, shopped all day'. They returned the following week, when their friend Meggy Carr joined them to choose bridesmaids' bonnets. (Hatty and Emmy were to be bridesmaids, along with Meggy and George's sister, Emily.)

George arrived at Dilston on 20 December and they 'put up the wedding cards' on 6 January, and held a dinner party for family guests, including George's younger brother, Spencer. George Grey arrived from Milfield with his wife and baby. Hatty did not fail to note the presence of attractive and eligible men like Spencer Butler and John Blackett, with whom she had a 'very nice chat' the following day.

On the day of the wedding, 8 January 1852, Hatty put her sadness aside and enjoyed herself thoroughly. After breakfast she 'pinned favours' on the four groom's men.[40] There were flags on the lawn and five wedding carriages to the parish church at Corbridge. 'Josey looked very lovely, in white, orange wreath, and long veil and behaved very well ... dear sweet bride.' The ancient parish church, with arches from Roman and Norman times, must have been a memorable setting.[41] The church's peal of three bells would have chimed to welcome the newly-weds.

The wedding party returned to Dilston for a wedding breakfast at one o'clock. The bride and groom left only two hours later, when the festivities had hardly started. Josephine and George missed the arrival of extra guests 'by the 5 train' and an evening dance, at which there was a bonfire and fireworks in the Castle.[42] Hatty enjoyed dancing with John Blackett and his brother Monty, but it was Monty with whom she had a 'delicious moonlit walk' after the party broke up at 2 a.m.

The Blacketts left the next day but many guests remained; charades were played and there was a ball for the servants. (There were six in residence at Dilston House, including a cook and a lady's maid.)[43] Hatty enjoyed long talks with Tully, her husband Edgar, and Spencer Butler, and they went out riding – 'galloped along in the fresh wind'.[44] She walked to the station with the final departing guests a week after the wedding.

Married Life in Oxford

Settling in at Oxford

Josephine and George's honeymoon probably included a visit to Peterborough, where George's parents lived. George later recalled bringing Josephine 'as his bride' to visit his father.[1] His father was not well and neither of his parents appears to have attended the wedding.

On their return, they set up home in Oxford. The fellows and professors of the university staff lived in the college, in spacious rooms attended by domestic staff. They dined at the 'High Table' in the college dining room and led a convivial life free of domestic responsibilities. George was attached to Exeter College, but as a married man he was not entitled to live in the college, so Josephine and George occupied a series of apartments during their time in Oxford.

Josephine's sketch of their first drawing room, at 124 High Street, shows 'an austere place' with a few pictures hanging on the walls and a 'very stiff sofa, with curled-up ends and hard cushions worked with beads'.[2] Later in the year they moved to 34 Beaumont Street, described by Hatty as having a 'remarkably pretty' drawing room 'with two wide windows down to the floor, and a veranda outside; pretty panelled paper, and blue curtains'. A china table, the wedding gift of their sister Eliza, looked 'so handsome standing opposite one of the windows' and Josephine's new grand piano took pride of place.[3] This was the wedding present from a rich great-uncle, Joseph Hardy, after whom she was named. It was a 'Broadwood' which had won a prize at the Great Exhibition, and Josephine treasured it until the end of her life. She said it 'responded to my soul more than any other piano'.[4]

Hatty's diary gives an account of the first year of George and Josephine's marriage, when she was a regular visitor. She packed up Josephine's clothes in Dilston and sent the boxes with the servants to Oxford on 21 January. The newly-weds must have arrived home that week, and scarcely had time to settle in before Hatty arrived on 10 February, travelling unchaperoned by train. Although Josephine loved her sister dearly, she must sometimes have had mixed feelings about this visit. Hatty would have been a constant presence in their new home. She was so much more vivacious than Josephine – the 'Primrose' of George's poem, with the 'brilliant tints' who 'everyone admired'. Would Josephine be overshadowed? On the other hand, Hatty oiled the social wheels for her in navigating a new and challenging social world, and supported her early experiments as a hostess.

The newly-weds were in demand, they dined out many times while Hatty was with them. George had a large number of friends in Oxford and Josephine was introduced to them all. She reciprocated with the first of her evening *soirées*, which were very popular, and a dinner party for eight. The guests included family friends like Montague Blackett ('very glad to see him', noted Hatty).[5] Monty was soon superseded by George's brother Arthur (Arty), then aged 21, who was an Oxford student. He took Hatty on some special walks and joined the Butlers for dinner and outings. Describing Josephine's arrival in their community, Arty later wrote: 'I can never forget the charm of her first appearance at Oxford. She took everyone by storm.'[6]

The Butlers and Hatty explored Oxford in walks to Christ Church Meadows 'full of water', the park of Magdalen College with its 'broad walk planted by Wolsey', and Ferry Hinxey, along the river, with friends and their two dogs.[7] They borrowed horses for what Hatty recalled as a '[m]ost delicious ride through Lord Abingdon's park ... splendid view of woods and rivers from the hill-top'. A considerable number of young men showed Hatty round Oxford, sometimes in the moonlight. The sisters attended lectures, including ones by George on sculpture and painting, which later formed part of a book. Hatty bade 'darling Josey good-bye' on 11 March and set off for their brother Charles's home in Ireland.

George's Career at Oxford

The newly-weds were not well off. In a letter to her father Josephine confessed that, 'We find housekeeping hard work, with small means and prices so high. I pay 22 shillings a ton for coals.'[8] Their marriage settlement included an annual income of £150 from his father,[9] but George's position as a Public Examiner was part time. He supplemented this income with extra work, such as writing reviews, cataloguing drawings by Michelangelo and Raphael and preparing a new edition of Chaucer's poems. They returned to Dilston during the vacations, to countryside which George had come to love as much as Josephine.

George had much to offer Oxford. The range of his intellectual interests extended far beyond the Classics, Latin and Greek, in which he had gained his degree. He was fluent in Italian and eager to promote the study of art and geography. However, his career did not prosper there. He had to rely on short term contracts for much of his income and failed in his attempt to gain more secure posts, such as Professor of Latin. Competition was fierce for such prestigious posts, while the far-sighted innovations in which George was interested did not attract kudos or income.

When George worked at Oxford, the university did not offer degrees in the natural sciences, physics, biology and chemistry, and had not a single laboratory in its buildings.[10] The introduction of science was seen by some as a threat to religious belief, but not by George, who supported a project to build facilities to display the university's scientific collections and provide premises for research and teaching. He became the project's Honorary Secretary, and oversaw the building of the beautiful 'Museum in the Parks'.

In pursuit of this objective he made influential friends, like John Ruskin the art critic, who advised on the neo-Gothic design of the building.[11] 'The entire design was intended to reflect the art of nature, with the wrought-iron ornaments supporting the roof designed to represent trees and plants, and the shafts of the pillars made from the "important" rocks of the British Isles, creating a geological exhibit.'[12] The court was to house life-size statues, including Bacon, Galileo and Newton, which were donated by Queen Victoria. George supervised the work of the young sculptor, Alexander Munro, who created some of the statues. Munro was a close associate of Ruskin and the Pre-Raphaelites, and his friendship with the Butlers and admiration for Josephine's beauty led him to produce a most striking sculpture of her. Inspired by Rossetti's poem 'The Blessed Damozel', Josephine appears in a loose off-the-shoulder blouse, with her hair flowing freely and adorned with stars.[13] For its time, this bust was unconventional and even erotic; Josephine was presumably encouraged by George to pose for it and agreed in order to help their friend's career.

George's enthusiasm and expertise in art were acknowledged when he gave a series of lectures in 1852 (attended by Josephine and Hatty), which were chaired by the Vice Chancellor and published in a book called *Principles of Imitative Art*.[14] But Oxford had no career posts in art or in geography, which George can fairly claim to have introduced there. At a time when the subject was 'entirely new', he gave geography lectures for which Josephine was his assistant. They drew maps together on the walls of the lecture room. Josephine was amused at the geographical ignorance of the dons, including one who, coming into the lecture room, could not point to Egypt on the map.[15]

She helped in his work on the Chaucer poems, sitting with him in the Bodleian Library 'puzzling out the old English black letter, which was sometimes partly defaced, and transcribing it in modern characters'.[16] In the evenings George encouraged his wife to improve her painting, as well as teaching her Italian. This was the start of Josephine's further education. She read widely and became fluent in French and Italian, skills which served her well during her future European campaigns.

The Birth of Georgie Butler

John Grey provided Josephine with a 'fine well-bred chestnut' so that she could continue riding in Oxford. On summer evenings, she and George saddled their horses and took long rides out towards Abingdon Park and Bagley Woods where they heard nightingale 'choruses of matchless song'.[17]

Josephine was pregnant with their first child, expected in November 1852, when in September they returned to Dilston for a holiday during which George enjoyed his favourite outdoor pursuits, including pheasant shooting. Hannah Grey was not well, as Josephine told Eliza, 'she is quite low and hysterical ... It is regular violent hysteria and very distressing to watch. She is just like 2 people. At one time calm and philosophical, and contented ... and then suddenly she takes a desparate [sic] crying fit.'[18] The transformation of their capable and calm mother must have been distressing for her children. More immediately, it meant that she would not be well enough to attend the wedding of her son Charles to Emily Bolton, or to help Josephine with the birth of her first baby. Hatty agreed to come to Oxford in her place.

Josephine was confident, 'everything about me seems to wear a cheerful hopeful aspect', and she continued to receive visitors and to go for walks right up until the birth.[19] Hatty described Josey as 'remarkably well, going about so light and brisk'.[20] At an evening party in the drawing room she 'looked so pretty with a white lace shawl (her wedding veil) over a white silk dress'.

She gave birth to a son, George Grey Butler ('Georgie'), on 15 November 1852. Hatty recorded that all went well:

Monday, 15th [November 1852]: Little Master George Butler born at 3.30 a.m. Darling Josey getting on well; nice little baby that can open its eyes and has curly dark hair, and only cries a little bit ...

Tuesday 16th: Wrote heaps of letters ... Josey and baby flourishing. I went to top of Radcliffe to see floods around Oxford. Water over railways and roads ...

Thursday 18th: ... First fine day for weeks ... Josey's baby flourishing.

Friday 19th: Arthur [Butler] came ... Took him to the nursery to see his little nephew who he nursed in a most knowing way ...

Saturday 20th: Dear Josey got on to the sofa in her own room; I read to her, and she had a capital night after the change ...

Saturday 27th: ... Josey and baby out.

Josephine refused to have a doctor in attendance at the birth. Years later, when both she and Hatty had given birth several times, she explained that she had followed the example of their mother – 'My beloved mother had twelve children and never had a doctor near her. I followed her example and was carried safely through every confinement. [Hatty] was the same.'[21] (However, if her mother did give birth twelve times she must have lost two babies, since there were only ten Grey children.)[22]

Their distrust of doctors was well-founded. Many middle- and upper-class families believed that the money spent on a doctor ensured the best outcome, but this was not necessarily the case. Doctors were more likely than midwives to intervene during childbirth, for example by using forceps during a difficult delivery, and interventions of any kind risked infection. The most dangerous result of this was puerperal fever, which hit the new mother just as she was recovering from the birth. It caused high temperature, delirium and, in most cases, death. Doctors and nurses did not adopt proper antiseptic practices until Joseph Lister showed the value of washing with carbolic acid in 1867.[23] Josephine's resistance, however, was mostly aroused by the invasion of privacy involved in consulting a male doctor. She once wrote to a male friend:

> How would any modest *man* endure to put himself into the hands of a woman medically as women have to do into the hands of men? And are women less modest than men? God forbid. They are *not*, and believe me, the best and purest feelings of women have been torn and harrowed and shamefully wounded for centuries, just to please a wicked custom.[24]

Georgie was christened a month later, on 18 December 1852, at St Mary Magdalene's church. Hatty (of course) was named godmother, and started educating Georgie straight away, giving him 'long lectures, which he listens to, looking up in her face all the time'.[25] Josephine's description of this scene, in a letter to Georgie's Butler uncles, was illustrated by a cartoon.[26]

Hatty left Oxford on New Year's Day, having thoroughly enjoyed the social whirl of Oxford. Josephine insisted, rather implausibly, that she had not become 'an admirer of *undergraduates* ... her friends and admirers are some of the first rate tiptop people in Oxford'.[27]

Georgie must have acquired a nursemaid, since Josey was free to attend communion on Christmas Day, and to see the procession of the boar's head up the Hall at Queen's College. George joined in the singing of the traditional Boar's Head Carol, and they heard Handel's

Christmas anthem 'Unto Us a Child is Born' in Magdalen Chapel.[28] By 28 December Josephine was again playing Beethoven duets in her drawing room.

George's Ordination

The Butlers spent the first week of 1853 in Peterborough, where George's father was 'very pleased with his new year present of a grandson, the first he has had'.[29]

In April, Josephine returned with Georgie and was, unhappily, a witness to the Dean's death, at a lunch party where there was 'conversation and merry laughter' with guests until the moment when he suddenly collapsed.[30] She telegraphed to George, telling him only that his father was ill, until he arrived. George was distraught, saying, 'Oh I wish I might have been in time to hear his last words!' It was Josephine who had walked with the Dean, just thirty minutes before he died, and noted that he was 'breathing rather hard'. She reproached herself for 'having perhaps walked rather fast for him' and also for having let him carry his grandson.

Georgie seems to have grown up believing that this had hastened his grandfather's death.[31] However, the Dean had a serious heart condition and, according to his daughter Catherine, had not expected to live through that year.[32] George wrote a beautiful tribute to his father in a letter to John Grey, 'we should be thankful for having been blessed for so many years with the love of so tender a father, and the converse of so highly-gifted a man and so true a Christian'.[33]

It had been his father's dearest wish that George should be ordained. It cannot be a coincidence that, after so many years of hesitation, he now decided to enter holy orders. He resolved his dilemma by deciding that he did not have to become a parish priest, but could instead be 'a Christian teacher, with authority to speak to [his pupils] as such'.[34] He was ordained by the Bishop of Oxford the following year, 1854, after a period of preparation at Cuddesdon College. Josephine described the service as 'very beautiful' but long – 'nearly four hours'.[35] 'George and I are so accustomed to doing everything together ... that when the bishop's hands rested on his shining curls I felt as if I was being ordained too.'

Double Standards at Oxford

Despite the happiness of her marriage, Josephine found it very hard to be separated from her 'large family circle', especially when Oxford was so different – 'a society of celibates, with little or no leaven of family life'.[36] The university was entirely male – there were no female lecturers or students since none of the colleges admitted women.[37] They met women who lived in their neighbourhood, as Hatty's diary attests, but Josephine's memories of Oxford were of an environment which was overpoweringly masculine. If George was away for a few days, she quickly became lonely.

At the *soirées* they held in their drawing room, Josephine entertained their guests on her new grand piano. She loved to play her favourite pieces and her skill and expression entranced her audience. Sometimes the dons played Mozart and Beethoven quartets with her. Josephine found that Max Muller, the double bass player, drove her mad 'by going faster and faster and swaying his head about, German fashion, till he nearly hit mine'.[38]

She was an attentive hostess. She wrote to her parents about one of her guests, George's friend Arthur Stanley, who hated music. Wondering how to entertain him, she noted that he loved buttered teacake. So 'I always provide a large stack of buttered teacake when he comes to tea. I do not offer it to him, but I stand guard over it to see that no one else eats it; and gradually he is attracted to it, and eats layer after layer of it to the end, while we are very careful not to notice the fact.'[39] Since there were very few women guests, all the talk was about male interests. Often it was also dauntingly intellectual, full of the concerns which Oxford men felt to be important, but of no interest to anyone else. Josephine had nothing to contribute. She later recalled that she 'sat silent' on many such occasions – not at all her normal instinct.[40] In later life Josephine would address large gatherings of men and give evidence to a Royal Commission, but as a twenty-something woman in the company of Oxford professors she struggled to express herself.

Often she found herself at odds with their opinions, especially on religion, a keen area of Oxford debate. Benjamin Jowett, the distinguished Professor of Greek, gave her the impression that basing her Christian beliefs on the Bible and private prayer was naïve.[41] She was outraged: 'the things which I believed I had learned direct from God … at that moment it seemed to me that the smile of contempt was directed at Him, my sole authority, in whom I believed all truth centred.'[42] Some of the dons tactlessly provoked her. One evening, they were discussing a painting by Raphael, and Josephine said that she found the woman's face 'insipid', or expressionless.[43] This brought the response that the face of a woman in prayer was always 'insipid'. She took this personally and in an angry outburst stressed that from her own experience of prayer, 'every faculty of the mind and emotion is called to its highest exercise'. This did not help her very much. At Oxford, emotion in relation to religion was thought to be unwise, and in the case of women to be positively dangerous.

She later carried on a correspondence with Benjamin Jowett on this subject, of which one letter has survived. Here Josephine writes about 'clever men who do not know intimately the hearts of many women', an exact description of the professor, and charges him with thinking:

> … that women generally accept Christianity without a thought or a difficulty; that they are in a measure instinctively pious, and that religion is rather an indulgence of the feelings with them than anything else.[44]

This sexism angered her. For herself, she says, 'to be guided by feeling would be simply dangerous'. Her own beliefs are founded on the 'practical test' of prayer. She stresses that she does not 'work myself into any excitement; there was much pain in such an effort, and dogged determination required'. She rejects the notion (popular at Oxford) that Truth can only be arrived at by a life spent on academic research. The existence of God cannot be proved, she argues, it can only be felt. It is like a mother who knows, through 'maternal feeling' that her children love her and that she loves them.[45]

This is a statement of her conviction that women have as much (if not more) to offer the world as men. But at Oxford she was powerless, and the weight of assumption and belief was entirely against her. Oxford men had attended male-only public schools before continuing their single sex education at university. Their experience of women would have been limited to female relations, and the 'lower classes' – servants and prostitutes. Their stereotyped views of lower class women shocked Josephine.

The conversation one evening turned to a newly published book by Mrs Gaskell. This was *Ruth*, the tale of an unmarried servant girl who falls in love, becomes pregnant and is deserted by the upper-class father of her child. Mrs Gaskell felt sympathetic towards a girl who was ignorant and unwise, rather than wicked. The novel does not condemn her, but powerfully depicts the weight of the burden Ruth shoulders in trying to keep her son and bring him up herself. The stigma of the 'fallen woman' makes it almost impossible for her.

The Oxford men adopted the conventional Victorian view – Ruth was far more culpable, more immoral, than the father of her child. She had brought an illegitimate child into the world. Josephine could not abide this view, the 'double standard' – 'every instinct of womanhood was already in revolt ... and I suffered as only God and the faithful companion of my life could ever know.'[46] George told her to pity them for their poor judgement in relation to women – 'they know no better, poor fellows'.[47]

Rescuing the Victims of Oxford

Josephine and George became conscious that there was a seamy, shadowed side to Oxford. Lower class women were exploited to maintain this 'monastic' society and a heavy veil of silence protected the perpetrators. Josephine plucked up the courage to speak to 'one of the wisest men ... in the University' about 'a bitter case of wrong inflicted on a very young girl', but was sternly told that nothing could be done – 'It was dangerous to arouse a sleeping lion'.[48]

Such a silence would, she knew, simply allow the double standard to continue and flourish. She came to hear of an appalling case, a young girl who had been seduced by a don, and abandoned when she was pregnant. In despair, the new mother had killed her baby and been imprisoned in Newgate Gaol. Despite her crime, Josephine and George felt sympathy for her. They saw that she was a victim of society's rejection, and of the 'morals' of Oxford, which allowed the father to go back to his easy college life with no questions asked. Josephine wanted to 'go and speak to her in prison, of God who saw the injustice done, and who cared for her'.[49] George came up with the more practical suggestion that they write to the chaplain of Newgate offering to employ the girl as a servant in their home when her sentence was completed.

This girl, whose name is not recorded, was the first of many 'fallen' women to be invited to live with the Butlers. Although she was officially a servant, she would have been treated kindly and Josephine would have 'spoken to her of God', as she did to so many others later.

Another woman (again unnamed) who aroused Josephine's strong sympathy at Oxford was an acrobat who the Butlers met, probably at church, after she had fled from the circus. By Josephine's account, she was little more than a sexually exploited slave, who was recaptured and forced to resume her old life. Although deeply distressed by her fate, it was impossible to do anything to help her. Josephine recalled that, as she sat at her window, 'It seemed to me that I heard a wailing cry somewhere among the trees ... It was a woman's cry – a woman aspiring to heaven and dragged back to hell – and my heart was pierced with pain. I longed to leap from the window, and flee with her to some place of refuge.'[50]

At that moment, Josephine herself needed a 'refuge'. There was a 'great wall of prejudice, built on a foundation of lies' all around her, and nothing was being done to address the problem.[51] She could not ignore it, as everyone around her did. It affected her happiness and even her health, which grew worse the longer she remained in Oxford.

A Victorian Obsession: Rescuing Prostitutes

The Butlers' decision to take the young mother imprisoned in Newgate as a servant was the start of their rescue work with vulnerable women. Rescue work was a particularly Victorian obsession. The aim was to persuade prostitutes to give up their self-destructive lifestyle. It was often (but not always) accompanied by the message of the Christian gospel – that all who repent of their sin can be saved, reborn, and lead a new life.

There are famous examples of prominent men involved in rescue work, including W.E. Gladstone and the writer Charles Dickens. Charles Dickens 'relaxed' from his hyperactive hours of writing by taking high-speed walks across London, seeking out the sights and sounds of the teeming slums, and frequently stopping to speak to the rough men and 'loose' women who thronged its streets. Many of these scenes and characters found their way into the pages of his novels, in which his compassion is demonstrated by violent denunciation of the social, political and legal system which created such inequality and such misery. Dickens was a reporter and novelist, but he was also a campaigner and practical philanthropist. He sponsored 'Urania Cottage', a house of help for prostitutes, which offered them refuge from the streets, and trained them for different kinds of work. Dickens hoped that they would emigrate and make a respectable marriage out in the colonies, and it appears that, for just over half the inmates, this objective was achieved.[52]

The majority of people (and there were far more women than men) who rescued prostitutes did so out of a sense of Christian duty. Many middle-class Victorians had direct experience of the dreadful conditions in which the poor lived. Philanthropy was a religious duty, and visiting the homes of the poor was popular, especially for Christian women. Every Victorian middle-class family also came into regular contact with working-class people through the live-in servants they employed. A caring employer talking to these servants learned a lot about the desperation of lives blighted by poverty. In church (which more than half the population attended on a typical Sunday)[53] caring for the poor was preached through stories like the 'Good Samaritan', who did not pass by the injured man lying in the road. Jesus taught that at the Second Coming the 'sheep' would be separated from the 'goats'. The 'sheep' would be blessed because 'I was hungry and you gave me meat, thirsty and you gave me drink, a stranger and you took me in, naked and you clothed me, sick and you visited me, in prison and you came to me'.[54]

Many of the rescuers believed that Christ had led them to such work through his own treatment of 'fallen' women. A favourite biblical text was 'the woman taken in adultery' to whom Jesus said, 'Neither do I condemn thee; go, and sin no more.'[55] This woman was believed to be Mary Magdalen, which is why prostitutes became known as 'magdalens' and rescue work as 'magdalenism'. The movement had its own magazine *The Magdalen's Friend*, which told its readers, 'If you would follow in the blessed steps of His holy life, you must not neglect your duty to your fallen sisters.'[56] This 'duty' was interpreted in different ways. In the earliest days of magdalenism, the emphasis was on the sin of the prostitutes, who must do extreme penance to achieve forgiveness and rehabilitation. They were confined in a 'penitentiary' with a harsh regime of punishment and deprivation.

This cruel system had largely been rejected by Josephine's time, in favour of kindness and loving treatment.[57] Rescue workers reminded themselves that Jesus had not condemned the 'women taken in adultery'. He had suggested that these women were more sinned against than sinning. Rescuers began to set up houses of help for them, whose names included such words as 'home', 'cottage' and 'mercy', to suggest caring and forgiveness. The women who ran these homes regarded themselves as a friend or mother to the inmates; some described themselves as their 'sisters'. A typical article in *The Magdalen's Friend* asked its readers, when they were at home, warm and in a comfortable bed, to:

> ... think for ten minutes of midnight streets, cold pavements, dreary doorsteps, dark corners ... filled with women, young girls, your Sisters, once fair and loved as you, now debased, and humbled, and degraded to the level of the brutes ... and then turn your head on your pillow and bless that gracious God who has kept you *unfallen* in the eyes of the world.[58]

The charitable women who set out to care for and to rescue prostitutes in London and the big cities usually came from respectable homes. Forsaking, or even foregoing, husbands and families, they visited women in prison, approached prostitutes soliciting on the street and went inside brothels in their quest for a woman who was unhappy, ill or exploited enough to be turned away from her 'life of vice' and persuaded to enter a refuge. The rescuers often approached the work with great trepidation. One woman remembered being violently sick after her first visit to a brothel.[59] The results of their work are impressive. By 1906, London could offer one place in a home for every six prostitutes; some other cities offered even more.[60]

Births, Illness and the Move to Cheltenham

A Brother for Georgie

Josephine was a relaxed and happy mother with Georgie, describing him as 'a dear little fellow ... healthy and good-tempered, and handsome and strong'.[1] He responded to strangers by burying his face in her neck, but 'I like him to be just so much exclusive in his affection'. She gave birth to her second son, Arthur Stanley (presumably named after George's friend, and known as Stanley or 'Cat'), in May 1854. Stanley's birth was more difficult than Georgie's; she felt 'weak and useless' afterwards and could not even look after her children.[2] Second births are not normally more difficult than the first, so perhaps there was an awkward presentation, such as a breech. Stanley's birth started a prolonged period of ill-health; she later recalled that she was 'laid up, scarcely able to walk about my house' for several years.[3] She consulted a number of doctors, including the first female doctor in England, Elizabeth Garrett. Josephine said she felt 'able to *tell* her so much more than I ever could or ever would tell to any *man*'.[4] This suggests a gynaecological problem.

When 'Cat' was 2 months old, and Georgie 20 months, she managed to take the children on a seaside holiday with the help of Mary, the nursemaid.[5] George, conducting exams in Oxford, was informed in a letter that 'Georgie rode on the donkey all across the beach by himself, Mary leading it ... Then we bathed in the sea. I took Georgie in with me. He did not cry when bathed himself, but when he saw me take a header from the machine, and disappear in the water, he screamed ... and held out his little arms to save me.'[6]

Hatty was married that summer to Tell Meuricoffre, a Swiss banker based in Naples. All the admirers she had lined up over the previous years were abandoned in what appears to have been a whirlwind romance – there is no mention of Tell in letters she wrote a year before the wedding.[7] She had stopped keeping a diary, so we have no account of their meeting, but it must have been through family connections. Edgar Garston, her brother-in-law, had known the Meuricoffres in Italy before his marriage to Tully, and he probably introduced the two families, since Tell's uncle and brother both visited Dilston.[8] Tell visited England after a business trip to the United States, so presumably that is when he met Hatty.[9]

The Meuricoffre family were wealthy Swiss Protestants who had established a thriving private bank in Naples which Tell and his brother had inherited from their grandfather.[10] The family home, Villa Meuricoffre, was so striking that it was described as one of the 'sights of Naples'.[11] Tell took Hatty to live in a hilltop palazzo with 'a marble terrace, built on lofty arches, in front, planted with orange trees, and then the woods slope down from the house – immense ilexes and pines, and far down a peep of the domes and towers of Naples skirting the shore of the Bay'.[12]

Despite the beauty and luxury, for Hatty it was a leap into the unknown, isolating her from her family. She and Tell visited Oxford on the way to their European honeymoon, and when Hatty gave birth to her first baby, John, she insisted on bringing him across Europe to visit the Butlers for Christmas, despite the snow.[13] Both she and Josey felt the distance between them very keenly, but letters kept them in close touch. Later, when they had more money, George and Josephine made frequent trips to Switzerland, where the Meuricoffres had a holiday home, as did other members of the family. John Grey made his last visit to Switzerland when he was 79.

A Powerful Spiritual Experience

George's reputation in the art world led to an invitation from the Taylor Gallery to catalogue their drawings by Raphael and Michelangelo. During the long vacation of 1855, he went to Germany to visit Passavant and other writers on art. Despite the absorbing interest of the trip, he missed Josephine and the boys so much that, he confessed in a letter, 'I do not like the wandering life as much as I did. I feel like the bird which had got so used to its cage that, after a day's liberty, he flew back and begged to be let in.'[14] He saw a sunset so glorious that, 'I shall never to my life's end forget [it], or my longing desire to have you with me'.

George embarked upon a long-term project that year, to provide facilities for young men to study at Oxford without entering any of the colleges. He and Josephine decided to invest their limited funds in renting a 'pleasant house in St Giles' as a combined family home and hostel for undergraduates.[15] This was 15 St Giles Street, known as 'Butler House', which had among its first students an artist, George Davies, who later exhibited at the Royal Academy. George was also invited to act as curate to the parish church of St Giles, an onerous job when the vicar decided to take a holiday. During a cholera outbreak, George loyally visited the sick, not telling Josephine of the risks but taking all the precautions he could 'for the sake of his little family'.[16]

Early in 1856, Josephine became seriously ill with 'attacks of chills and fever'.[17] She believed her illness was caused by the winter floods around Oxford, especially the 'horrible smell' from the meadows as the water seeped away. Housebound, she spent her time in prayer and meditation, seeking for 'a manifestation of God'. Her prayers were answered – Josephine had a powerful spiritual experience, of the kind which many Christians have described as conversion.[18] It left her with no doubt that God existed. She began a new diary to record this as 'A day ever to be remembered by me':

> Today about dusk, Christ revealed Himself to my Spiritual sight in a manner which I never felt before. I could not bear to tell this to anyone in whom there was not sympathy. These are not words of 'enthusiasm' so called, but words of sober truth. I saw no vision nor had I any sensuous perception. It was, I think, simply the fulfilment of the promise so little believed in 'I will *manifest* myself to him'. So overpowering was the sense of that Blessed presence that I ceased to pray or even to praise Him, but just kept silence before Him.[19]

This experience was formative, the moment when Josephine Butler's life took a turn which would mark her out as extraordinary. It provided the foundation of her belief from that time onwards, that God was with her and that the channels to Him were open through prayer. The Church had no part in this – indeed she thought that there was too much public religion and too little being 'thrown in solitude, upon God'.[20]

Forced to Move from Oxford

As Josephine's health remained precarious, it was decided that she, Georgie and 'Cat' should leave Oxford for the healthier air of Dilston. Josephine wrote to tell George:

> We arrived here very comfortably, and I suffered very little from the effects of the journey, which I managed more easily all the way from London than any journey for a long time. I felt well yesterday – only a little sleepy, had a ride in Mama's donkey chair, and sat out in the garden. Georgie rode the Donkey postillion* fashion, and Baby sat by me in the chair.[21]

'Cat' was now scarcely a baby, being almost 2, and Georgie 3.

Josephine's joy in her spiritual journey continued at Dilston: 'yesterday and this morning got up early and went into the garden, and spent an hour there in delightful communion with God.'[22] George too was inspired, he wrote to tell her that 'I spent an entire day, or the largest portion of it, in direct communion with God'.[23] But he ended his letter 'tell me stories of my boys. I have no greater joy than to know that my children walk in truth.'

He spent the month of July in London, working as an examiner for the India Board. His 'only earthly anxiety', he wrote:

> ... is that your health may be sufficiently restored to enable you to do the work for which you are so well fitted – the duties of a Christian wife and mother – and mistress of a house – without suffering from lassitude and pain ... But if this may not be, I must acquiesce in the decrees of Providence.[24]

George joined his family at Dilston after completing the examinations and stayed on until the end of October, standing in at the local church while the vicar of Corbridge took a break. The Butlers lived in the vicarage and Josephine helped with George's visits to the congregation. She could not resist recording that the church was 'well-filled' for George's services and that 'many Wesleyans' attended.[25]

On their return to Oxford, inevitably, the weather took its toll on her health. 'The autumn fell damp and cold' and Josephine became seriously ill again.[26] She was also pregnant with their third child. Even during the early months of this pregnancy she notes in her diary that, 'I am in a great measure unable to walk, combating daily with infirmities and languor; with child; and peculiarly disabled from physical effort'.[27] She had help with the children, probably from Mary, since she writes, 'I have days tolerably uninterrupted (except by illness) and long quiet hours'.

She felt frustrated that she could not continue the work she had done with George in Corbridge. She had 'a guilty feeling that I am not *doing* enough for God'.[28] She wanted to do as other Christians did – 'visit the poor and sick, and teach classes'. Physically unable to do that, she spent her time in 'study, thought and writing' and 'a prayerful study of the Word, laying up by fervent prayer and deep meditation material and experience which may either be communicated to others now, or be laid up in store for a future time'.

As Josephine's weakness continued, George seems at times to have feared for her life. But it was not consumption (tuberculosis), the dreaded chest infection for which

---

* Sitting astride the donkey rather than in the chair with Josephine.

there was no cure, and which tragically carried off many Victorians before their time. Josephine's chest and heart problems continued for the rest of her life, but it was a long and very full life and her ailments 'were so complicated with the spiritual and intellectual being'.[29]

That was the opinion of many doctors, including a London specialist, Sir James Clarke, to whom George took Josephine during that winter.[30] He also stated, with the certainty of a doctor who had little else to prescribe, that she must not return to 'the chilling influence' of the Oxford floods – not even for a day.[31]

Poor George had to find somewhere else for Josephine and the boys to live immediately. They could not return to the vicarage at Corbridge, and he settled on 'the sunniest part of Clifton', in Bristol. He asked his sister Catherine to join the family and to look after Josephine. Their third son, Charles Augustine Vaughan (Charlie), was born at Clifton on 16 May 1857.[32] George had to give up Butler House; 'all the hopes and plans my husband had cherished [were] abandoned', lamented Josephine.[33]

Security at Cheltenham

George had recently failed in his application to become Professor of Latin. A cartoon by Hatty (imagining the scene in far off Naples) shows George as a barefoot tramp with his possessions in a bundle slung by a stick over his shoulder, setting out into the wilderness with Josephine following, carrying both children inside her shawl.[34]

George was forced to fund the family by freelance writing while he applied for jobs. He was offered a temporary post by a friend in London, the charge of the chapel in Blackheath, and the family moved there for the summer. George had turned down an invitation to apply for the post of Rector (Principal) of Edinburgh Academy, a boys' school, in 1854.[35] Now he realised that his best chance of secure employment was to follow the family tradition set by his father and brothers, and look for posts in prestigious schools. He was intensely relieved, in the autumn, to be offered the post of Vice Principal of Cheltenham College. Cheltenham had a healthier climate and the salary was sufficient and, above all, reliable. At the age of 38, George at last gained some status and embarked on a satisfying career, one which he quickly grew to love. Cheltenham College was one of the first Victorian public schools designed to educate the sons of the growing urban middle class.[36] It was linked to the Church of England and built a chapel during George's time there, where he enjoyed the chance to preach sermons.[37]

The Butlers moved into the huge school house, The Priory, which had reception rooms on the ground floor totalling 16m in length, sufficient for a previous owner to hold a ball for 800 guests.[38] There was a large kitchen, larder, scullery, butler's pantry, wine and beer cellars, 'every domestic office' and of course the staff to service it.[39] The Priory was not only home to the Butlers, since its eight bedrooms included dormitories for school boarders.[40]

The move to Cheltenham marked 'the cessation of material difficulties and anxieties' and the chance to enjoy a beautiful home and the responsibilities that living and working there entailed. 'I think we shall like Cheltenham', wrote Josephine to her friend Mr Spring-Rice, 'It is pleasant being connected with so flourishing an institution'.[41]

A great joy was the birth of a daughter to Josephine and George in May 1859. She was named Evangeline Mary (Eva) after the heroine of the anti-slavery classic, *Uncle Tom's Cabin*,[42] and was an active little girl, with an engaging interest in everything around her. Her grandfather John Grey found her full of 'life, energy and merriment' when she visited

Dilston; caressing his dog, Tip, planting a little garden and gathering flowers.[43] There are glimpses of her early life in the few letters that survive from this period. At the time of her first birthday Georgie reported that 'Eva can stand on her own legs for a little time'. George remarked that 'Eva looked so pretty in her white dress and black ribbon'.[44] As she grew older 'she flitted in and out like a butterfly all day', was never ill and 'never gave us a moment of anxiety'.[45]

A month after Eva's birth, Josephine wrote, 'I am a "joyful Mother of children" and very happy.'[46] However, she was not strong and longing for 'a flight somewhere where pure air may be had'. Bronchitis was affecting her even in Cheltenham. Eva was Josephine's last child, although she was only 31 when her daughter was born. However, she may have been advised against having more children due to the state of her health.[47] She and George were opposed to the use of contraception, which was in any case very unreliable at that time, so the decision to avoid more pregnancies will have affected their sexual relationship.

Catherine Butler

Northumberland continued to be the location of most of the Butlers' summer holidays, but in 1858 they toured Ireland and visited Josephine's brother Charles in his Tipperary home.[48] Two years later they took Georgie to visit Hatty and her family in Switzerland. Josephine recalled that they travelled to the Rhone Valley and Chamonix, spending one night at the St Bernard Hospice, where she made the acquaintance of its famous dogs.[49] A 'veteran' among them, Bruno, attached himself to them. This was the beginning of her love affair with St Bernards; she loved all dogs but these enormous, selfless, companions were her favourite.

A great grief was the death of George's sister, Catherine, who had been Josephine's close companion at Clifton. Catherine was a devout Christian who had worked among the poor in London and felt herself called to the African mission field when she heard a sermon preached by the Rev. John Bowen. He had been appointed bishop to the colony of Sierra Leone and was calling for helpers. Catherine became his wife, after a very short acquaintance, in the autumn of 1857; Josephine recalled that her 'countenance was beaming with serene happiness' on her wedding day.[50] They set sail immediately and sent happy news after a few months that Catherine was pregnant. Tragically, her son was stillborn in August 1858, and she herself died a few days later. John Bowen was ill in the adjoining room with a tropical fever and could hardly crawl to visit her. He succumbed to another attack only seven months later. Josephine recalled that 'A sketch was sent home to us of the picturesque spot, under the burning sun of Africa, where stand the graves of the father, the mother and the little child'.[51]

The missionaries who ventured to Africa at this date knew the risks they were running; John Bowen spelled them out in the sermon which Catherine heard. Yet they were also foolhardy. Two previous bishops had died in the same way. Josephine was happy to record that, after this, 'a real black bishop', Oxford-educated and more likely to withstand the climate, was appointed and filled the role for many years.[52] Catherine's death may have been caused by fever or a lack of skilled help during the delivery. Her suffering must have been extreme. George was deeply distressed by her death and grieved for his mother, too, who had had no chance to bring help and comfort to her daughter. He wrote that Catherine was 'one of the most constant, true and devoted Christians I ever knew'.[53]

Josephine's Doubts

Josephine's diary is one of the few surviving records of their years in Cheltenham. It shows that her mysterious ailments continued. There is one terrible entry headed 'Cheltenham, Spiritual Night': 'Dear Lord, grant me a little oblivion – put me out of pain – If I take opiates, Thou knowest it is terror which drives me to seek oblivion in them.' She even seems to be contemplating suicide and asks God to 'keep me from open sin, from this desperate unrecallable act'.[54] Her pain was not only physical. She later spoke of this period (1858–62) as 'the years when my heart was in darkness on account of sin, the sin, the misery, and the waste which are in the world, the great and sad problems of life, the prosperity of evildoers, the innocent suffering for the guilty'.[55]

Her faith may also have been challenged by the publication of Charles Darwin's *On the Origin of Species* in 1859. She does not mention the book by name but talks about 'the multitudes who seem to be created only to be lost', which could be a reference to the cruel process of evolution which Darwin described. Darwin had found it hard to believe that a loving God would choose this method of creation, and Josephine may also have struggled. Later she linked this 'fearful valley of the shadow of death' to the suffering of child prostitutes.[56] Her doubts were terrible, 'I could see no God or such as I could see appeared to me an immoral God. Sin seemed to me the law of the world and Satan its master. I staggered on the verge of madness and blasphemy ...'[57]

Unlike Darwin and the many other believers who lost their faith, Josephine's survived and was even strengthened by this struggle. She eventually found peace and acceptance:

> Now I know, when my heart is strangely stirred by the sight of a vast multitude in some great city, that my heart's yearnings over them are but the faintest shadowings of His heart's yearnings over them; that my love, which would embrace them all, is but as a drop of water to the ocean of His love, which would embrace them all.[58]

Family Life

When the American Civil War broke out in 1861, Josephine and George supported Abraham Lincoln who was leading the fight against the southern slave states.[59] They were shocked to discover that many friends did not agree that the issue of slavery should have been pushed to the point of civil war. They only changed their minds after Lincoln was assassinated. Until then, the Butlers felt themselves to be part of a pariah group 'impelled to give up visiting, finding themselves out of sympathy with the persons they met daily'. She was filled with joy on the day in 1865 when the North won the war:

> God has heard the cry of the oppressed. I do solemnly thank God that I have lived to see the day when the Capital of the Slave States has fallen. It is a wonderful fact that the first who entered Richmond as conquerors were a regiment of freed negroes.[60]

Josephine's mother, Hannah, died in 1860. When Josephine arrived at Dilston she wrote to George of 'the mournful family' assembled there and her father's desire that he attend the funeral, but reluctance to ask since it was such a long journey.[61] 'You would infuse calmness and hope even by your voice and bearing. Do come, dearest', wrote Josephine and George went, of course, travelling through the night on his return trip to Cheltenham. He also went to see Josephine's elder sister, Fanny, who seems to have been too upset to go to the funeral. She had taken a 'little home' at Cheltenham. Her marriage was in a state of collapse, and she was 'an invalid and in anxiety'.[62] Her husband, Rev. Smyttan, attended Hannah's funeral and even chose the site for her grave, but appears to have left Fanny shortly afterwards.[63] A year after her mother's death she moved to Dilston to become her father's companion.

Josephine's oldest sister, Eliza, was also lodging in Cheltenham after returning from Hong Kong with four small children under very sad circumstances. Her husband, the surgeon William Morrison, had died there after a distressing illness in 1853. Eliza stayed at Dilston and with various family members until the move to Cheltenham. Josephine became very close to Eliza's daughters Edith, Constance and Anna, who were now teenagers. Eliza married again in 1861, to Norman Masson, and the entire family moved to Italy after Edith married Ludwig Leupold, a banker based in Genoa.[64] The close relationship between Josephine and Edith led to many years of sustained correspondence and visits by the Butlers to her home on the Mediterranean coast.

There are glimpses of happy family life at Cheltenham in a few surviving letters. Georgie, for example, wrote to 'Dear Darling Paps' when George was away from home:

> Dr Kerr says Mama has got a sharp attack of Rheumatics and must stay in bed a day but she will be all better soon. We are praying to be good boys and not to do mischief. Mama does love you so very much dear sweet Paps and we all love you.[65]

This was clearly dictated by Josephine, but the loving tone was constant in letters written by the boys to their father, who they always called 'Paps'. Josephine had a number of names, including 'Mauddie' and 'Meelchis', and they invented nicknames, such as 'Dear Fruit'.[66] When Josephine's sister Fanny stayed at The Priory she observed 'a good deal of amusing chafing and fun going on between her and the boys'.[67] George teased Josephine about her lack of appetite, in doggerel verse he wrote for the children:

> Poor Mama – she was a case
> That once had something in her
> Of stomach now she'd not a trace
> A sinner without a dinner.[68]

On another visit, Fanny observed 'two little happy faces and bright eyes very wide open, and noses flattened against a window pane, in grave childlike observance of my doings'.[69] This was Eva and Charlie. Eva made her aunt a pincushion and when Fanny gave her a present in return, 'her little face flushed all over with a pleased surprised glow, and she flew to my arms to hide the warm face against my heart'.

The Death of Eva

The Butlers had a happy summer holiday in August 1864 at Coniston in the Lake District, where they stayed in a house 'situated in a rising ground above the lake both the private grounds and the surrounding lake affording endless fields for exploring and outdoor life'.[70] Eva was 5, and the great tragedy of the family's life occurred a few days after their return to The Priory.

On the evening of Saturday 20 August, Eva decided that she would slide down the banisters, a game she had played with her three big brothers, in order to say goodnight to her parents in the downstairs drawing room.[71] She fell from the banister on the top floor, and landed on her head on the stone floor 40ft below. Neither George nor Josephine saw the fall, although many accounts have suggested that they did.[72] Only the butler, Eva's governess Maria Blumké and her brother Charlie actually saw it, but George heard the governess scream and ran out of the drawing room.[73] 'It was pitiful to see her, helpless in her father's arms, her little drooping head resting on his shoulder, and her beautiful golden hair, all stained with blood', lamented Josephine.[74] She was unable to describe in detail what followed until many years later.[75]

Josephine recalled that Eva was carried to a bedroom, where she suffered convulsions which 'were terrible to witness'. During the 'long hours of agony', she was unable to recognise her parents and never responded when they called her name. There was 'no word of farewell'. But 'at the end, a change came, a wonderful change. The convulsions ceased. She lay still, and an expression came over her face, so holy, so solemn, so beautiful that I can never lose the memory of it.'[76] Some of those present hoped that she was starting to recover, but Josephine knew that it was the prelude to Eva's death. She told the sobbing servants to be silent:

> I knew that the Lord was calling the child, and I could only say 'happy, blessed Eva, would to God that I might go with you my child' ... She opened her eyes and seemed to see some glory approaching, and her face bore the reflection of that which she saw. Her look was one which rebuked all wild sorrow, and made earthly things sink into insignificance. It was as if she said, 'Now I see God'. She gave one or two gentle sighs, not of pain, but of sweet relief and contentment, and her soul passed away.[77]

This moment was the only consolation for her agonised parents, who endured 'some weeks of uncomforted grief'.[78] Josephine found it almost impossible to accept that their beautiful, exuberant child had been taken from them so suddenly and needlessly. Josephine wrote to a friend, 'I don't think I ever had a thought of death in connection with her: she was so full of life and energy.'[79] The last conversation she had had with Eva was about 'a pretty caterpillar she had found; she came to my room to beg for a little box to put it in. I gave it her and said: "Now trot away, for I am late for tea". What would I give now for five more minutes of that sweet presence?'

Eva had been 'passionately devoted to her father' and had made him 'blue, pink, white and striped pincushions and mats, for which he had not much use! But now he treasures up her poor little gifts as more precious than gold.'

George was completely heartbroken and Josephine had to make strong efforts to pull herself together in order to help him. She wrote a special prayer 'for him who is as dear to me as my own soul' inscribed 'for the dear Father of my Saint in heaven'.[80] They were both consoled by the visits of family and friends and they received some beautiful letters of sympathy. John Grey, who endured the deaths of several grandchildren, consoled them with the thought that 'your beloved child had a joyous existence here and is now in the presence of a living Saviour'.[81] George's friend the vicar of Blackheath wrote: 'Your little Eva's image rises before me as I had last seen her, clinging round your neck and her bright hair streaming over her shoulders; and it turned my heart cold to think of your and her mother's anguish ... She impressed a stranger at once. What must she have been to her parents? ... When these little ones are taken, I always think of the words, "Jesus called a little child unto Him". He calls, and they go, suddenly or slowly, but in each case it is to Him.'[82]

Frederick Denison Maurice, the founder of the Christian Socialists, wrote to reassure them of the truth of the Afterlife:

> You cannot think that your child is really severed from you. The yearning you feel for her is the pledge and assurance that it is not so ... If you ask me whether I can say that it seems reasonable to me that this love on both sides should be immortal ... I can answer 'no other option appears to me reasonable'.[83]

This belief comforted many Victorian parents, and did eventually sustain the Butlers, but their struggle to accept Eva's death left permanent scars.

Parents never truly recover from the death of a child, and Josephine certainly did not; she later told Stanley that 'for twenty-five years I never woke from sleep without the vision of her falling figure, and the sound of the crash on the stone floor'.[84] The tragedy affected the lives of Eva's brothers, particularly Charlie. Aged only 7 when his sister died, his mental health may have been permanently affected by the shock of witnessing her fall. Certainly Josephine thought so. She tried to help him (and herself) by taking him out for drives and encouraging him to pick wild flowers in memory of his sister; a habit he continued for many years.[85] Throughout their lives all three brothers found it difficult to talk about Eva's death, even with their own children. Stanley's son, Bob, recalled that 'My sister and I grew up with the shadow of the disaster still there'.[86]

A Traumatic Sea Voyage

Josephine's father, John, had retired the previous year at the advanced age of 77, although 'he retained the vigour possessed by some men only in their prime'.[87] His son, Charles, took over his work running the Greenwich Hospital estates, and he and his family moved into Dilston House. John, accompanied by Fanny, had found a retirement home nearby, Lipwood House. Eva must have visited her grandfather there, for when Josephine returned in the autumn of 1864, she wrote to George, 'This place is haunted by a fairy form. Every walk, and tree and flower recalls her. I went under the trees today and prayed constantly to God to support me in my grief and to show me how happy she is now.'[88]

At the end of October Stanley was taken seriously ill with diphtheria. 'For some days he hovered between life and death' but Josephine and George 'were spared the added sorrow we dreaded'.[89] They decided that both Josephine and Stanley needed a holiday to recuperate and they set off for Italy. Josephine wrote to George regularly to tell him of their journey over Mont Cenis in deep snow and on to Genoa in north Italy where they stayed with their newly married niece Edith Leupold.

In Genoa at the end of November it was warm enough to sit out all day. Josephine told George that 'we walked about among the orange and lemon trees, which are loaded with fruit'. She rejoiced that she could 'breathe freely', but this summer scene renewed her grief. 'It all seems to put my lost darling further off. It seems like a year since she lived among us, chasing the butterflies.'[90] Hatty, with some of her children, joined them there, very concerned about the 'terrible nervous shock' Josephine had sustained, in losing her child in such a traumatic way.[91] Edith showed them a packet of letters written by their mother, Hannah, at the time of the death of their sister Ellie. 'Josephine was deeply touched by these letters, feeling how she had been treading in the same path, mourning for her child.'[92]

Josephine had never visited Hatty's home in Naples, and now she proposed to travel there by sea, a three-day voyage down the long leg of Italy, since the railway and roads were flooded.[93] They embarked on the mail ferry against Harriet's better judgement, knowing how fragile her sister was. Hatty's worst fears were realised when a severe storm blew up. Josephine became seriously ill, first with sea sickness and then with terrifying convulsions, 'her face was grey, and her hands rigid and blue like those of a corpse'. Hatty was desperately alarmed to hear her say, 'I think I am going. Dear George; Dear George!' Hatty offered 'all that I possess' to the captain if he could bring them in to land, but that was impossible.

Josephine's life was saved, she believed, by the fact that he was able to hail the mail steamer returning north, whose captain (aptly named 'Fortunato') agreed to take her on board. On this ship there were willing helpers, and a professional gentleman who confidently diagnosed 'congestion of the heart' and prescribed 'warmth at the extremities'. She was dosed with ether and mustard, rolled in blankets and surrounded by stone hot water bottles. Her arms, hands and feet were steadily rubbed, but for a long time, Hatty recalled, they remained 'as stiff and as cold as marble'. At last, after more than an hour, 'with trembling joy I felt her feet less stiff, and watching her face I saw it unlock as if something melted. Such an indescribable difference! ... I could not help laying my face on the blanket and crying as I went on with the rubbing.'

As the ship lay off port, a doctor came on board to examine Josephine. Sailors improvised a stretcher to transfer her to the captain's own rowing boat for the journey to the shore. Finally she reached a hotel, and was able to rest. 'The anguish had been so great', Hatty wrote, 'that I felt almost ten years older that night, but, oh, so full of thankfulness.'[94] Her greatest dread, never absent during those hours, was 'the despair of having to tell George' that his wife had died.[95]

This drama, described in such compelling detail by Hatty, shows her great resourcefulness in demanding, often through charm, the help that she needed. The family were surrounded by the kindness of strangers – the two captains, the doctors, the assistants on the boat, and finally by one Pietro who, when they reached the hotel, produced 'two gorgeously embroidered nightgowns, stockings and night caps'.[96] Their luggage was still on the first boat, bound for Naples, and he 'had been to his home and rifled the wardrobe of Mme Pietro' – an offence against English standards of decorum which Hatty decided to overlook, in the circumstances.

Josephine later said that this collapse was caused by heart trouble and that during her recovery she consulted nine doctors about it. 'They all said *rest* and quiet were the only things; they *all* said I would *never* be strong, and they all said that the medical art could do nothing for me.'[97] All the treatment she received was 'slight palliatives and soothing things'. Today the most likely diagnosis would emphasise the severe traumas she had experienced in the previous few months. This combined with sea sickness to cause a psychogenic paralysis, which produces this dramatic physical manifestation of the patient's emotional suffering.[98] When Josephine was on dry land she recovered quickly, especially when George arrived to look after her.[99]

Josephine never reached Naples on that holiday. Instead, she and George took their first holiday in Florence in 'lovely winter sunshine', returning via Pisa and the Carrara mountains, where George took great delight in inspecting the quarry where Michelangelo found his block of marble for the statue of David. Then they collected Stanley in Genoa, and returned home to Cheltenham, hoping profoundly that the new year would be happier for their family.

Victorian Prostitutes by Day and Night

It's impossible to know exactly how many prostitutes there were in Victorian Britain as they did not come forward to be counted. The Metropolitan police estimated that there were 8,600 prostitutes in London in 1857, of which 921 were 'well-dressed, living in brothels', 2,616 'well-dressed, walking the streets' and 5,063 'low, infesting low neighbourhoods'.[100] The numbers in other cities were just as high.[101] The vast majority of these women eked out a meagre living and struggled with the threats of pregnancy and venereal disease. Many ended their lives tragically early and in dire poverty. If they were too old or too ill to prostitute themselves they risked ending up in the workhouse.

Although the popular image of a prostitute is 'the good time girl', the overwhelming majority of prostitutes never drank champagne or entered a casino. Even fewer became kept women in a fashionable home. It was not even usual for prostitutes to operate from a brothel – in Victorian Britain, 'only a minority' did so.[102] One hard up 'soldier's woman, past her prime' refused to work from a so-called 'house' because 'you ain't your own master and I always like my freedom'.[103] Like most of her fellows, she preferred to solicit on the streets and work from rented lodgings, which were often shared with two or three other women. These private apartments made up 63 per cent of the 'brothels' listed for London in 1857.[104]

> The average age at which women become prostitutes is from fifteen to twenty. The average duration of women continuing prostitutes is, I think, about five years. The most common termination of the career of prostitutes is by death, and this is to be accounted for by the extremely dissolute life they lead. For the most part they live in a state of great personal filthiness – they have most wretched homes – they are scarcely ever in bed till far in the morning – they get no wholesome diet – and they are constantly drinking the worst description of spirituous liquors. In addition to those evils they are exposed to disease in its worst forms; and from their dissolute habits, when disease overtakes them, a cure is scarcely possible.[105]

This description refers to prostitutes in Glasgow in the 1840s, but it could apply just as well to the prostitutes of other cities. They led wretched lives in the poorest slums, and were driven to prostitution by desperate poverty.[106] Either they could not get any other work, or the pay for the work they did was so abysmally low that they were forced to supplement it by soliciting. Desperate women turned to prostitution because they did not receive a living wage. Seamstresses, for example, were appallingly exploited in both their pay and working conditions. They became a *cause célèbre* for their suffering. One seamstress told the social investigator Henry Mayhew that no girl could make a living from the piece rates they received for work in their own homes:

> It stands to reason that no one can live and pay rent, and find clothes, upon 3 shillings a week, which is the most that they can make clear, even the best hands, at the moleskin and cord trowsers work.

I am satisfied there is not one young girl that works at slop-work [piece work] that is virtuous, and there are some thousands in the trade. They may do very well if they have got mothers and fathers to find them a home and food and to let them have what they earn for clothes; then they may be virtuous, but not without.[107]

Low wages led to temptation – graphically depicted in J.E. Millais' famous drawing 'Virtue and Vice', which shows Virtue, a poor seamstress, being tempted into taking up prostitution by Vice, the Devil.

Most of the so-called 'dollymops' who supplemented their income by prostitution eventually abandoned what little work they had for a full time life on the streets.[108] Once there, these women were easily identifiable to Victorians by their clothes which (superficially at least) were better than other girls on the back streets. They wore 'dirty white muslin and greasy cheap blue silk' or 'a gaudy hat and feather and a fashionably made skirt and jacket of some cheap and flashy material and nothing besides in the way of undergarments but a few tattered rags'.[109] Few wore shawls, which would have hidden the shape of their figures, and all wore cosmetics. This was the greatest giveaway since only actresses and prostitutes used make-up.

Nancy in *Oliver Twist* is not identified as a prostitute,[110] but Charles Dickens' description of Nancy and her friend Bet 'with a great deal of colour on their faces' and 'a good deal of hair' was sufficient for Victorian readers to identify them. Dickens also described them as 'being remarkably free and easy with their manners'. On another occasion Bet is 'gaily if not gorgeously attired, in a red gown, green boots, and yellow curl-papers'.[111]

A 'dollymop', aged 19, interviewed by Mayhew said, 'I've hooked many a man by showing my ankle on a wet day.' She had been brought up in the workhouse and had a job as a typesetter, but went to the Haymarket to pick up clients in order to supplement her income. 'I long for certain things ... and I must have them by hook or by crook ... when I can I live in a sumptuous manner.' She had a fiancé who, she believed, did not suspect her of being unfaithful; she planned to marry him and give up the streets.[112] Such women were to become Josephine's regular companions within a very short time.

The Butlers in Liverpool

‿‿ 'I often feel as if my heart were breaking.'

The only record of the Butlers' lives in the year after Eva's death, 1865, is Josephine's spiritual diary. She laments the 'long drought – long drought in my soul – long drought on the earth'.[1] Josephine was spending many hours in private prayer, which sustained her and granted her joy when, 'today I stood before the Lord. He granted me an audience. He had in His hand the petitions which I desired of Him. To pray thus is *my life*. This is my true, my only life. What is life to me without it?'

On Easter Sunday she felt too weak to go to church or to visit Eva's grave, but wrote in her diary:

> I often feel as if my heart were breaking – not with misery, but with its heavy burden of desire, love, and sorrow ... I long to have a hundred voices, that with all of them I might pray without ceasing that Christ will come quickly, and deliver for ever the poor groaning world: the slaves from all their woes, the victims also and slaves of lust in our own land, the poor women who are driven as sheep to the slaughter, into the slave market of London; prisoners, captives and exiles. My heart is bruised and crushed every day, in going its rounds through the suffering world.[2]

These 'rounds through the suffering world' seem to be a metaphor for her sustained and urgent prayers. In Cheltenham 'the suffering world' was far away. Why did she begin now to think about the 'slaves of lust in our own land'?[3] Possibly she was trying to save them, since she could not save her daughter. She may have felt a degree of subconscious guilt over her accidental death.[4] There is no obvious reason, but the time was fast approaching when the world of the 'slaves of lust' would, in reality, take over her life.

‿‿ Liverpool College

George's career at Cheltenham College had gone well, apart from a bizarre controversy when one Principal, Rev. H. Highton, impressed by his expertise in Latin and Greek, invited George to teach the top Classics class. This was supposed to be the job of the Principal, and there was a tense standoff with the college governors and staff, which even reached the local newspapers. Highton resigned over this and other areas of contention.[5]

The boarding houses were said to be overcrowded and insanitary, and putting boys aged 7–18 together resulted in bullying. The Priory, over which the Butlers presided, was no different from the others.[6]

It was time to move on.[7] In the autumn of 1865 George was offered a new appointment as Principal of Liverpool College, a public school designed like Cheltenham for middle-class boys.[8] With bluff honesty, the directors told him, 'You will find it an arduous post, involving contact with some rough and rude characters.'[9] But George was ready for the challenge, and the role proved to be ideal for him. The great diversity of his gifts suited a school where sport, Classics and languages, not to mention the Church of England, were all important. His friends were delighted for him. Mr Powles wrote from Blackheath: 'Only the other day Froude and I were lamenting that you were not at the *head* of a Foundation, whatever good you might be doing as second in command. We had no idea how soon we were to rejoice in the fulfilment of our wishes.'[10]

Georgie, Stanley and Charlie were enrolled at the college and, in January 1866, the Butlers moved to Liverpool. This great port on the north-west coast served towns and cities created by the industrial revolution, supplying raw materials from around the world, especially cotton from the American South and the West Indies for the mills of Lancashire. The finished products returned to Liverpool in huge bales and boxes for export overseas. Liverpool built many of the cargo ships, and the docks were the ever-changing centre of its activity, as each tide brought new vessels to unload, and the departure of others. The dockyards provided most of the employment, so that the predominant culture was of casual labour and a semi-skilled workforce. Foreign sailors thronged the cheap boarding houses and made the most of their time ashore in pubs and gambling dens. There was great wealth to be made, but it coexisted with desperate poverty. Josephine was conscious that, only a generation before, many of Liverpool's cargoes had been the product of slave labour. She was living in a port which, before the success of the anti-slavery campaign supported by her father, had been a conduit for the slave trade.

Instead of the school house in Cheltenham, they were now to live in a private rented house in an area known as The Dingle, not far from the docks. It had no direct connection with the school; an enormous change for Josephine, in particular. Her life was no longer to run to the rhythms of the school day or facilitate her personal contact with the staff and schoolboys. She had never lived in a northern city, apart from her time at school in Newcastle, and the port of Liverpool was a noisy, urgent and raw environment. There was 'no greater contrast' she wrote, between Liverpool and 'the academic, intellectual character of Oxford, or the quiet educational and social conditions at Cheltenham'.[11]

Josephine soon found herself lonely and dissatisfied, with much time on her hands. She had few friends and many thoughts of Eva, 'how sweet the presence of my little daughter would have been now'.[12] Her grief returned in a second wave, almost more powerful and debilitating than the first. Her usual pastimes, music, reading, art, could not console her. It was then that she decided to take up the 'active work' which she had previously been unable to do. She did so now as a means of survival:

I became possessed with an irresistible desire to go forth and find some pain keener than my own – to meet with people more unhappy than myself ... I had no clear idea beyond that, no plan for helping others; my sole wish was to plunge into the heart of some human misery, and to say (as I now knew I could) to afflicted people, 'I understand. I, too, have suffered'.[13]

She chose the most abject human misery she could possibly find – that of women who had been incarcerated in the 'Bridewell' in the Liverpool Workhouse on Brownlow Hill. The Victorian workhouse provided last-ditch accommodation for the poor who could no longer support themselves even by begging. Having to go into the workhouse was feared and dreaded because family members were separated, the food was scarcely enough to live on and every waking hour was spent in exhausting, degrading, 'task work'.

The Liverpool Workhouse stood on a hilltop ironically known as 'Mount Pleasant'. It was so large that it housed around 5,000 inmates, in buildings which included workshops, hospitals and endless dormitories. These buildings were often inadequate, unventilated and badly drained. Infectious diseases like typhoid, cholera and even smallpox broke out with appalling frequency. Agnes Jones, a Nightingale nurse known to Josephine, who undertook the herculean task of improving nursing standards there, succumbed to typhoid contracted from her patients after scarcely more than two years.[14]

Josephine chose to volunteer there after discussions with Charles Birrell, a Liverpool Baptist minister who was her cousin by marriage.[15] She wrote a graphic account of her early visits there.[16] The women incarcerated in the prison, known as the 'Bridewell', had 'most frequently been convicted of fighting or brawling, on the quays and docks, of theft or drunkenness' and been 'sent to "do a week" or a month there'. They joined other poor women, 'driven by hunger, destitution or vice, begging for a few nights' shelter and a piece of bread', who were required to 'pick oakum' in the vast 'oakum sheds'. These were housed underground, in 'huge cellars, bare and unfurnished, with damp stone floors'.

Oakum picking was a popular form of 'task work' in workhouses, especially those in ports, since it involved unpicking old ropes to obtain loose fibres which were then sold to the navy or shipbuilders. The work required no tools, and was very hard on the fingers. Josephine went alone to the vast, dark, oakum sheds, where she found more than 200 women and girls. All she did on her first visit was to sit down on the floor with them and pick oakum. Not surprisingly, they laughed and told her that her fingers were of no use for the work. The laughing broke down a barrier, allowing her to suggest to the women that they 'learn a few verses [from the Bible] to say to me on my next visit'. She succeeded in persuading one girl to recite from St John's gospel, 'Let not your heart be troubled, neither let it be afraid.' In Josephine's view this message was the most powerful gift she could give them.

She had never done anything like this before, but the power of her personality and Christian conviction, forged by her countless hours of prayer and Bible study, shone through. By her account, the women 'listened in perfect silence' and 'every one of them' fell down on their knees 'reverently' when she prayed.[17] Perhaps, in reality, some did not but this account, the first of many she told about outcast women, is typical. Josephine always focuses on the good in them. She knew that the public wanted to believe that their characters were blackened beyond the chance of redemption, so she very rarely gave any ammunition which could be used against them. In this account she insists that many of the women 'prided themselves on their virtue' and 'earned a scanty living, by selling sand in the street (for cleaning floors), or the refuse of the markets to the poorest of the populations'. Even the female prisoners had 'stuff among them to make a very powerful brigade of workers in any active good cause'.

Josephine needed all the power of her personality and conviction in this situation – a matron had recently been beaten to death by a group of inmates. The new matron was so afraid of her charges that she often refused to accompany Josephine.[18] She was literally thrust inside and left to fend for herself. Her strategy was to speak lovingly to them, as a contrast to the rejection and abuse they encountered. The proof of her success is the fact that she not only survived but created lasting devotion among these women. One of them, Catherine Lynch, told her that the matron had punished some inmates by excluding them from Josephine's visit. One 'poor creature was broken-hearted and wept all the day', as a result.[19]

On her way to the Bridewell, Josephine dropped into other parts of the workhouse. In the orphan wards she was attracted to a 3-year-old girl, Polly, 'because she so strongly resembled our Eva in the face'.[20] She found a way to rescue Polly from the workhouse and place her with a woman she knew in Clifton, Bristol. Apparently Polly hoped that she would one day become Josephine's maid. Josephine visited the workhouse infirmary as well, where many of the women were dying from tuberculosis. The staff was overwhelmed and glad of any help; she sat with many dying patients, praying for them and reassuring them. Ellen Lambert, 'a girl with a most beautiful smile and white teeth' clung to her when she was leaving, asking her not to go. When Josephine returned the next day Ellen was dead, but the nurse reported that she had consoled herself by saying, 'she loved me, Mrs Butler loved me'.[21]

Rescuing Outcast Women

The next step was forced on Josephine by her success. The women she met in the oakum sheds, and in the hospital and on the quays, saw her as a potential saviour from their distress. When they emerged from the workhouse, they sought out her home and gathered round it, pleading for help. This was a new situation – the invasion of her private space. When she was out on the streets she would meet girls who refused to let her go, like the young prostitute with 'toes coming out of her ragged shoes' whose story Josephine could scarcely hear 'for the rattle of the buses'.[22] She was an orphan who 'was longing to go to a Refuge'. Josephine handed over her card, drove home and 'was taking off my hat at the window, when I saw the poor lost thing, running up and down the road looking first at my card, then at all the houses, and not knowing which gate to go in at. How she must have *run*, poor child, to get up so soon all that way.'

She could not ignore these pleas and send desperate women and girls away. In Liverpool there were a number of refuges. Josephine had already visited one with 'thirty poor rescued girls' after she met the proprietor, Mrs Cropper, who listened to her tale of loneliness and grief and advised her that 'there were disinherited hearts waiting for the overflow of that motherly love'.[23] Another was the Benediction House near the Butlers' home, which had space for up to forty women.[24] Josephine was able to place some of her 'penitents' there, but could not find sufficient places in refuges she approved of. The Protestant penitentiary was old-fashioned and 'prison-like'.[25] She wanted 'love and gentleness' to be 'the chief power' and the religious instruction to be 'very wide and simple and unsectarian'.[26] Most of the rescue homes in Liverpool were Roman Catholic, and Josephine disliked the fact that the inmates were taught to pray to Mary. She could not conceal her satisfaction when one girl in the workhouse infirmary prayed to Jesus, rather than Mary, as she died.

The outcasts for whom she had the greatest pity were the offspring of 'intemperate and criminal parents – who were humanly speaking, useless, not quite "all there"'.[27] She and George agreed to take some into their own home. Josephine found space for them in a 'dry cellar ... and a garret [attic] or two' and helped to care for them herself.[28] The women she chose were ill and needed special care. The very first was Mary Lomax, who Josephine encountered in the workhouse infirmary, dying from tuberculosis. She caught Mary's 'wistful haggard look', went over to her and began to stroke her hair. As Mary responded to her touch, Josephine impulsively promised, 'you shall come with me dear, and I will nurse you in my own home and you shall be my daughter'.[29] She hired 'an easy car' and took Mary home where George was waiting to greet her – 'giving her his arm, he led her gently upstairs as he would have led any lady visitor, speaking courteously to her'.[30]

Mary joined their household in November 1866. Once Josephine had crossed this Rubicon she proved unable to stop taking in destitute women. George was soon commenting that she had 'very nearly fill[ed] the house as full as it will hold of the dears'.[31] They were treated with the greatest respect, but even his tolerance and generosity was stretched. The accommodation on offer spread from the cellar and attics into some of the bedrooms. The patients were living in rooms next to the schoolroom used by the Butlers' adolescent sons. This has been seen as a danger to their 'moral well-being' and it was certainly risky, both for the boys and for George's career.[32] However, it was not uncommon for Evangelical families to involve their children in philanthropy. It was seen as part of their Christian upbringing. The Butlers had decided to treat these women as welcome members of their family, which of course included their three sons.

It satisfied something very deep in Josephine's nature not only to offer tender practical care to these women, but also to minister personally to them. The word 'minister' is important: it means the offer of spiritual help and consolation. Josephine believed that salvation was a gift offered to all sinners who repent, and it was her job to deliver this message, especially to the dying who could depart in peace and in the hope of heaven. She once said, 'it is really for their *souls* that I wish to do it.'[33] Although George was the official chaplain to these women, and took his role seriously, Josephine was just as keen to act in that office – we are reminded of her statement, 'I felt as if I was being ordained too'.

Mary Lomax

Josephine Butler wrote two pen portraits of Mary Lomax, who affected her in a unique way. The first was in a long letter to her niece, Edith Leupold, in March 1867, in which she exclaimed, 'O I do so wish you could see her and talk to her. She is just like one of us.'[34] This is an astonishing thing for Josephine to say about a woman she had found dying in the workhouse hospital, but Mary had fulfilled all her hopes. When Josephine said, 'I will nurse you in my own home and you shall be my daughter', Mary replied, 'O you don't know what a wicked girl I have been or you would not even *look* at me.' This was a sign that Mary was a repentant sinner, whom Josephine could 'make a present of to *my* Saviour'.

When Mary arrived in the Butler household, she was 'unacquainted with the Scriptures' but under George's tutelage she 'mastered the New Testament so thoroughly ... that her acute questions and pregnant remarks were a source of wonder to [him]'.[35] She asked, for example, about the origin of evil and why God did not prevent it.

Josephine and George did not talk to her about her previous life because they 'felt that *human* kindness and loving action should come first and last'.[36] Mary recognised that Christian faith and compassion was the motivation for her treatment in their home. She told George that he did not need to tell her about Jesus, as she had already met Him, 'Sir, you have brought me to your own beautiful home. You have treated me as if I were your own daughter, as if *I had never done anything wrong*. That is what I mean. I have *seen* Jesus.' After a few months, Mary 'was so clean taken out of all memory of sin', said Josephine, 'that one feels as if talking to a being of angelic purity'.[37]

Mary's life story emerged slowly. She was the daughter of a Derbyshire farmer who, sent into service in Liverpool, took up with a sailor who seduced and deserted her.[38] In her despair, she 'became reckless', stayed out late one evening and lost her job. Mary's parents were horrified and refused to see her again 'till she had redeemed her character', but the result of this rejection was that she 'fell lower' and ended up in the clutches of a brothel-keeper, Mrs Mandeville. Josephine knew this madam, who 'goes about covered with diamonds, and has 50 or 60 fine girls in her house, over whom she places several slave drivers, who bully them, and make them drink drugged spirits'. Mary suffered greatly in her house as she was 'always a favourite and asked for by gentlemen'. When Mary's uncle tracked her down and tried to reclaim her, Mrs Mandeville hid Mary in an empty boiler and threatened her life if she made any noise. She escaped the brothel only after she developed consumption. Mrs Mandeville threw Mary out on the streets, saying 'you are of no use to me now'. She 'crawled' to the workhouse, in a suicidal state, but the next day was found and rescued by Josephine.

As she lay dying in the Butlers' home, Mary received visits from their friends and became close to the boys; Stanley copied a poem she had written.[39] Mary's father visited and 'sat for two days holding her skinny little hand, and she talked to him about Jesus and heaven'. George spent an hour with her every day studying the Bible. On the last day of her life Josephine sat with Mary all day, holding her hand, until she died in the evening.[40]

INTERLUDE

The Dark Side of English Life

Josephine's second account of the sad life of Mary Lomax was one of five stories she published in 1877 with the graphic title The Dark Side of English Life.[41] These record the lives and deaths of five 'fallen' women – 'Marion', 'Katie', 'Emma', 'Margaret' and 'Laura'. 'Marion' was the alias for Mary Lomax.[42] Josephine said that she wrote this story as 'a trophy of the Saviour's grace and goodness', meaning that it was a successful rescue case.[43] Mary's story would prove to her readers that Christian salvation was available even to prostitutes.

Josephine uses lurid and melodramatic language, very popular at the time she was writing. About Mrs Mandeville's brothel, she says that 'Marion':

> ... was literally kidnapped, and for several years brought great gains to the slave owners in that mansion, where there are satin-damask curtains and every adornment of the gate of hell ... When she first became ill, her 'mistress' turned her out into the streets on a cold November night, to 'get her own living', saying, 'You are useless to me now'.[44]

That night 'Marion' tried to commit suicide, but was rescued the next day when Josephine found her in the workhouse hospital. When invited to live at the Butler home, 'Marion' 'replied with a gasp of astonishment, grasping my hand as if she would never let it go again'. She died after a 'long death struggle, lasting twelve hours', described in graphic detail:

Her long black hair thrust wildly back, was like the hair of a swimmer, dripping with water ... Towards sunset she murmured: 'Oh come quickly Lord Jesus', and then she became speechless. During that long day she continually moved her arms like a swimmer, as if she felt herself sinking in deep waters. Then her poor little head fell forward, a long sigh escaped her ghastly parted lips, and at last I laid her down flat on her little bed.

Josephine's husband and sons 'returned from college, and stood round her corpse a few minutes'.[45] Josephine was convinced that she was at peace, and dressed 'Marion's' body 'as a bride for her Lord', filled her coffin with white camellias and summoned her parents to attend the funeral. Her grieving mother blamed her seducer and said, 'What a difference there is in English gentlemen's households! To think that this child should have been ruined in one and saved in another.' Josephine then explains that:

Marion was not fifteen when [an English] gentleman sent her up to his room to fetch a cigar-case, and followed her and shut the door ... Then followed child-bearing, shame, concealment, in which the parents, strong in north-country virtue, treated their child with a harshness of which they afterwards bitterly repented. She came to this city [Liverpool] to try to redeem her poor little character.

There is no mention of Mary's sailor boyfriend. Josephine censored this story and substituted a fiction in order to make it more acceptable to middle-class readers.[46] The rape of a young girl by a worldly aristocrat allowed for greater sympathy for the 'fallen woman' since she was an unwilling party. It comes as something of a shock to discover that Josephine changed a true story.[47] But for Josephine literal truth was less important than emotional truth. Mary/Marion's story demonstrated her conversion and forgiveness and her 'good death', secure in the knowledge of salvation. The chief purpose of the story was to witness to this.

Josephine's own role in *The Dark Side of English Life* stories has been described as 'omniscient narrator, stage manager and supportive grieving mother'.[48] She is the successful Evangelist, bringing near-death souls to God. She is an 'avenging mother' in the story of 'Margaret', when she takes a 'poor starved infant', the child of an unnamed seamstress, to the hotel where its father was staying for the hunting season:

'Look at him', I said, 'Ay! Look at him well, he resembles you, he is your son. Look well at him, for you will not see him again till he faces you at the last dread day.' The man was glad to pay a pound or two to get rid of the annoyance, and then, springing into his 'drag' with cigar in mouth, he lashed his horses off to the 'meet'.[49]

This is melodramatic, and may have been influenced by other tales of seduced seamstresses, such as Mrs Gaskell's *Ruth*.[50] However, there are convincing human touches in Josephine's story as well, such as when she says that the seamstress found it hard to sew because her baby 'tore away at her threads and cuttings and hindered her work as it lay on her knee'.[51]

The story of 'Katie' is so highly coloured that it is impossible to believe in. Josephine also added important elements of Mary Lomax's story to 'Katie's', as Jane Jordan has shown.[52] We have no other source for the story of 'Margaret', but Josephine here shows that her compassion extended even to a starving mother who had murdered her 3-month-old baby in despair, when the father refused to acknowledge his child.[53] 'Margaret' is full of self-condemnation, which was eased in the Butlers' home after an 'old and dear' family servant read her the biblical story of Manasseh, who had 'prayed to the Lord' after murdering his own children and received forgiveness. Josephine condemned the real author of her crime:

> Was Margaret the real murderer of that child? How does God, looking from heaven, judge of this matter, and others which occur every day? If the murdered infants, now hidden beneath the soil of England, were to rise today, and, spectre-like, stand face-to-face, not with their mothers, but with their fathers ... would these fathers be able to face this infant army of spectres?[54]

In 'Margaret's' story, Josephine quotes from a poem by Elizabeth Barrett Browning, a lurid tale of a black slave raped by her white master, who kills the white child she has borne.[55] This horrific story is told sympathetically from the black mother's point of view. The poem spoke directly to concerns dating back to Josephine's girlhood, when she first heard of the rape of black women by white men. Now anger at the suffering of the 'white slaves' of her own country was stronger even than the urge to condemn a child murderer. Margaret 'crept to the feet of the Saviour and received his pardon'.[56]

Josephine crafted these stories to persuade her readers 'of the approachability of outcast women and of the practical efficacy of rescue work'.[57] Increasingly, she saw her role as that of a campaigner and teacher, as well as a rescuer.

The Birth of a Feminist Campaigner

Hatty's Family Tragedy

In September 1866, Hatty and her husband Tell came to visit the Butlers in their new Liverpool home. Their 2-year-old daughter Beatrice (Bee) had died the previous year from cholera in Naples. Her older sister, 5-year-old Josephine, 'seemed to droop' after this death but was healthy enough to travel to visit her grandfather at Lipwood.[1] On the way to Liverpool, however, she was taken ill and Hatty and Tell were forced to stop at Ormskirk in Lancashire, where anguished letters passed between them and the Butlers. George wrote to Tell:

> Even if your darling should sink after this revival, it must be a comfort to you to think of that look of recognition she gave you and her mother ... I cannot help praying that He who has given you a glimpse of His power to save may give you back your precious child ... And if He does not answer our prayers in the way we should choose, may He bring His power and His love home to our hearts in some other way, so that we may say: 'The Lord hath been with us even in the deep waters of affliction'.[2]

Little Josephine did not recover and, desperate for the support of the Butlers, Hatty and Tell arrived in Liverpool carrying the body of their daughter. Hatty later recalled that 'the pretty guest chamber [was] ready for her, in spite of all the unhealed wounds the sight must have opened in your hearts' – the painful memories of the death of Eva at exactly the same age.[3]

Hatty and Tell had a third daughter, Thekla, who survived into adulthood along with four sons.[4] While in Liverpool, Hatty visited hospitals and refuges with Josephine, neither of them disguising their grief, but sharing it by showing photographs of Bee, Josephine and Eva to 'the poor ruined girls', some of whom were very young.[5] They 'seemed to sympathise with us in the loss of our darlings, as much as we did with them in the destruction of their own childhood and youth', said Josephine. These visits consoled Hatty, and for Josephine they confirmed that her new work was God-given. 'I have a certain feeling that the love and the sacred souls of these poor girls are given to us in return for the loss of little Eva and Josephine and Bee. *Nothing* can repair *that* loss. Still, it seems as if God would give us souls while he gives us sorrows.'[6]

～⊗ The House of Rest and the Industrial Home

In 1867 Josephine told her niece Edie that, through all the years when she was ill:

> I did hold fast my secret convictions, especially about certain things in society, and at last
> God enabled me to *act* them out. The last year or two has been, through his mercy, a kind
> of harvest of which the long years before were the seed time.[7]

She was busy and fulfilled, visiting the workhouse, finding rescue placements for the women there and running her 'little hospital' at home. In February 1867 she received 'another *hint* from Heaven' when her doctor made a home visit to treat Georgie for headaches. Josephine took the chance to ask Dr Moore 'what palliatives to give the poor girls for pain and sleeplessness'.[8] He not only examined them and advised on their treatment, but said that if she ever set up a hospital of her own he would treat her patients, free of charge.

Josephine immediately set about looking for a suitable property and before the month was out had found one, at a rent of £25 a year. Some of the money came from friends, but Josephine turned her hand to fundraising and persuaded some 'young unmarried men of means' to guarantee £100 towards the costs.[9] She told her friend Mrs Myers that the hospital was to be a 'House of Rest' for 'dying magdalens' who 'want a place to *die* in'.[10] She had five patients ready to move in, and three girls living in her own home.[11]

So far Josephine had managed with the help of her servants, especially her housekeeper, Jane Taylor, who was 'a silent woman with rare good sense and much graciousness'.[12] Now she needed extra help and thought of Fanny, the sister to whom she had already confided her plans and who was living with their father at Lipwood. She wrote to her in dramatic terms, telling her that she and George were overwhelmed with 'poor penitent women swarming up from the town'.[13] She asked her to come to Liverpool to help, not with nursing but assistance in finding placements for these women by corresponding with other refuges. This is the first time that Josephine had needed a secretary, but she was now running a considerable enterprise. She did not cease to write letters herself, either. Her new life released a flow of words which was almost unstoppable. From now until the end of her life she was to spend several hours every day writing letters.

Apologising for 'abruptness' while writing to one potential matron, Josephine wrote, 'I hope you are not an extremely bigoted protestant. Here in Liverpool, two-thirds of our poor women are Catholics, and I intend my House to be *wholly* unsectarian.'[14]

She was soon writing to her friends about the patients there. One was a young unmarried mother, Margaret Winstanley, whom Josephine had found living in a cellar with her baby. Margaret was emaciated and suffering from consumption, but her child entranced Josephine, 'a most beautiful baby of 6 months who gurgled and crowed at me and seemed to think life full of joy and fun. It kept putting my [feather] boa to its little nose and smiling when it tickled it and then grinning at me.'[15]

While setting up the House of Rest, Josephine was making progress with another project, to help the oakum pickers by providing them with work so that they would not need to go on the streets. Many of these were the Irish Catholic women who 'prided themselves on their virtue'.[16] She wanted to set up a 'lodge' where they could both live and work, and the Workhouse Committee initially guaranteed £200 towards the cost. Her disappointment was great when they withdrew this offer, offering to support it only once it was successful.[17]

She had enough money to set up 'a very small temporary lodge, just a workroom for poor destitute girls to work in'.[18] By Easter, however, Josephine had secured enough funding from Liverpool merchants to move to 'a very large and solid house, with some ground around it'.[19] Here she created the 'Industrial Home for the healthy and active, the barefooted sand girls, and other friendless waifs and strays'. George became the chaplain of both homes, visiting in the evenings and on Sundays. Under the supervision of a matron, the women at the Industrial Home learned laundry work, and later made envelopes which could be sold to well-wishers and tradesmen.

All this happened very quickly – within a year of the Butlers' arrival in Liverpool. Josephine's life had become a whirlwind of activity. By Easter 1867, she was well known as a rescue worker and had established two rescue institutions, as well as caring for dying women in her own home. Josephine's mission was established, and she was now presented with new challenges.

Campaigning for Women

During the years 1866–67 it became possible, for the first time, to propose female suffrage. A political cataclysm was taking place in Britain. Working men were demanding the vote and the government was rocked to its foundations by the Reform League's enormous Hyde Park rally. The Liberal Prime Minister, W.E. Gladstone, resigned when his reform bill failed to pass in the Commons. The Conservatives, led by Disraeli, introduced a more ambitious scheme, the famous 'leap in the dark', which awarded the vote to all male householders and even to some lodgers.

In this mood of revolutionary change, a small group of campaigners organised a petition proposing votes for women, which secured 1,500 signatures. John Stuart Mill MP used this support to propose an amendment to the 1867 Reform Act to substitute 'persons' for 'men' in the extended franchise. It did not pass, of course, but received more support in the House of Commons than might have been expected – seventy-three votes. Josephine was one of the signatories of this historic 1866 petition. She would not have been known to the organisers, so she probably answered an appeal in the press. She always believed that enfranchising women would make it far easier to achieve reforms that benefited them. Policies would have to be framed to attract female voters, and there would be women MPs to sponsor them in Parliament. 'We cannot *always* depend on the self-sacrificing efforts of noble men ... to right our wrongs,' she told her friend Charlotte Wilson.[20]

Josephine went over to Manchester for the day, in February 1867, to talk to other like-minded women. She met Elizabeth Gloyne, the head of a large girls' school, and Lydia Becker, who had just become the secretary of the first women's suffrage committee, which was based in Manchester. Josephine had an immediate rapport with Lydia, who she found of 'especial help' in understanding the problems of her rescue work in Liverpool.[21] This was the first time Josephine had met a female leader of a campaign and realised what women could achieve by working together and forming committees.

Shortly afterwards, Josephine met another female campaigner, when Anne Jemima Clough knocked on the Butlers' door.[22] She did not know Josephine, but had come to enlist George's support for her campaign. Anne Clough's family came from Liverpool and she had a passion to improve the quality of girls' education. Middle-class girls, she said:

... were like caged birds, with their strong passions intensified by the want of action ...
living together in dull contracted surroundings, in homes where there was not enough
occupation ... [they] were restless and unhappy ... Many suffered grievously, some fell into
ill health, many were soured and spent their lives in foolish and useless complaining.[23]

She had run her own successful school in Ambleside, despite her complete lack of
appropriate experience, since she herself had been educated at home by her mother and
the sum total of her 'training' was a period of three months observing schools in the
London area.[24] Anne had become convinced that specialist teaching for girls, at both
school and university level, was needed and she had returned to Liverpool to conduct a
pilot project with the schools there.

This was another cause close to Josephine's heart. During that first conversation she
agreed to give practical support to Anne, and in that moment embarked on her first
feminist campaign. She did this despite the fact that she was already very busy with her
work rescuing prostitutes. Campaigning involved a range of skills which she had never
needed before, including writing pamphlets and making speeches. It also pushed her into
the 'public sphere' in which conventional Victorian society believed that women should
not operate. But Josephine accepted the challenge with enthusiasm. She realised that real
changes in women's lives would have to be achieved by political action, by challenging the
laws and conventions of the country.

The Education and Employment of Women

Josephine quickly proved that the skills of networking, writing, speech making and
campaign organisation came naturally to her. Anne Clough encouraged her to focus on
female education and employment. This was a classic feminist cause, then as now. Poor
women were confined to unskilled, low paid jobs and there were hardly any working
opportunities available for middle-class women, since their closest male relative (usually
husband or father, but sometimes a brother or an uncle) was expected to support them.
Almost the only option for a middle-class woman if this support failed was to become a
governess in another family's home. This job was frequently thankless and lonely as many
accounts by governesses, such as those by the Brontë sisters, have shown.[25]

Josephine's first contribution to Anne Clough's campaign was a pamphlet, *The Education
and Employment of Women*, published in 1868. It reads like a serious newspaper article,
and is bolstered by facts and statistics drawn from census data. But Josephine leavens
this dry information with individual anecdotes, like the shocking fact that 300 desperate
women replied to one advertisement for an unpaid nursery governess. Even when paid,
the salary of a governess was rarely more than £1 a week, and she was expected to dress
smartly and find the costs of travel home out of this pittance. Josephine included case
studies, based on the experiences of a number of women she had met, which showed that
they were often inadequately fed and felt miserably lacking in education. One governess
told her, 'Worse than the bodily privations or pains are these *aches and pangs* of ignorance,
this unquenched thirst for knowledge ... this depressing sense of a miserable waste of
powers bestowed on us by God.'[26]

With these personal stories, Josephine created a powerful indictment of the lack of
training opportunities available to governesses, and a system that ensured that the young
girls they taught would grow up just as unprepared for any role outside the home. She was

equally critical of the fact that no other employment opportunities for unmarried middle-class women existed – even though there were 2½ million of them.[27] The few jobs available offered pitifully low wages. When women did secure jobs, the men they worked with could make their lives impossible. The female china painters of Worcester, for example, earned higher wages than their male colleagues for the fine painting at which they excelled. In a rage, the men 'forcibly deprived [them] of the maulsticks on which it is necessary to rest the wrist while painting'.[28] Without this tool they could no longer paint finely, only do 'coarser kinds of painting'.

Something had to be done to combat male hostility and open up the job market. 'There is work on every side waiting to be done by women – the work of healers, preachers, physicians, artists, organisers of labour, captains of industry &c.'[29] The fact that Josephine mentioned such high status jobs shows how radical she was prepared to be – no woman was, or had been, a 'captain of industry' at that time. She was convinced that women had something of unique value to offer society. This was:

> The maternal character [which] is rooted in almost all women, married or unmarried ...
> It will always be in her nature to foster, to cherish, to take the part of the weak, to train,
> to guide, to have a care for individuals, to discern the small seeds of a great future, to
> warm and cherish those seeds into fullness of life.[30]

This special character would be enhanced, she argued, by entry into the world of work.

This pamphlet, Josephine's first publication, was attacked in ways which were hurtful then and are incomprehensible today. She received 'the most *horrible* letter from F. Harrison ... He says *no* occupations ought to be open to women, not even light trades, they ought *never* to work nor have the *means* of working.'[31] Josephine had known Frederic Harrison since her Oxford days, when he was a Fellow of Wadham College, and he was influential, as a leading Positivist and member of the Royal Commission on Trades Unions. She replied, telling him that the views of the Positivists on women were 'the rotten part of their system'. Unmarried women had little choice about working, and not all could marry when women outnumbered men in the population. She concluded, 'I have written indignantly. I cannot help it. You can be angry with me, or despise all I have said. It does not matter the least. I have spoken the truth. *I am ashamed of my countrymen.*'[32]

This letter, and the need to reply so forcefully, made her so angry and upset that she fell ill with terrible headaches, followed by delirium. To a close friend, Albert Rutson, she wrote, 'I believe it is difficult for friends to believe how my spirit can be darkened ... until it ends in an illness like this. I suffered more for four days and nights than I have done for several years.' In this state, 'I used to cry out for some way of escape for starving women and saw thousands of them being swept up with a broom and hidden like ashes under a huge grate, by political economists'.[33] This disturbing image shows both the intense strain Josephine felt and her complete identification, in body and mind, with the women she had chosen to campaign for.

INTERLUDE

A Victorian Brand of Feminism

The word 'feminism' was not used in Victorian times and it is easy to exaggerate its incidence.[34] Although support for women's rights dates back to the publication of Mary Wollstonecraft's *A Vindication of the Rights of Women* in 1792, very few Victorian women accepted its radical views. There was enormous pressure on them to conform to the so-called 'spheres', in which women kept to the private sphere of home and family, while men could operate in the public sphere of work, commerce and politics. Women who challenged these boundaries risked rejection and contempt, of the kind Josephine suffered from Frederic Harrison.

However, her brand of feminism differs from the one familiar since the 1960s. In some ways it can be misleading to use the same word. Josephine supported Christian teaching about marriage and the family, believing for example that sexual relationships should be confined to married (heterosexual) partners. She was opposed to abortion and contraception. Other aspects of her feminism are more familiar. Josephine passionately believed in the equality of all women before the law. She supported the 'votes for women' campaign, tried to increase employment opportunities for women and helped to organise the Married Women's Property Committee. She was an early leader of the campaign to extend higher education to women and, through her own life, she showed that a woman could petition Parliament, negotiate with politicians and rouse public opinion to achieve the repeal of an unjust law.

Josephine put women's interests first and refused to accept that men were entitled to rule the world. How did she become so radical and unusual for her time? Partly it was the effect of her upbringing, by a father who regarded his daughters and his wife as intellectual equals and discussed social and political issues with them. The Grey girls were allowed a great deal of freedom. By contrast, many a Victorian *paterfamilias* saw it as his job to keep his female relatives innocent – that is, ignorant. Their reading was restricted, their companions strictly vetted and opportunities to see life beyond their home were very limited. Empty headedness and conformity was a natural result. Josephine's aunt, Margaretta Grey, wished that she could take her share of the family work by presiding in 'the dairy, the confectionary, the store-room, the still-room, the poultry-yard, the kitchen-garden, and the orchard'.[35] She regretted that women were banned from pursuing professions like medicine, and she passed on these views to Josephine.

Even more important, Josephine was married to a man who agreed with her views. Most Victorian husbands revered the domestic role of their wives but treated them as intellectually inferior. It was Josephine Butler's supreme good fortune, and evidence of her excellent judgement in choosing a husband, that George was not like that at all. Indeed, he helped her to develop her ideas. 'But for him' she wrote, 'I should have been much more perplexed than I was. The idea of justice to women, of equality between the sexes ... seems to have been instinctive to him.'[36] George wrote Josephine an extraordinary promise before they were married:

> I should think it undue presumption in me to suggest anything to you in regard to your life and duties. He [i.e. God] who has hitherto guided your steps will continue to do so ...
> I must not ... fancy that I have within me the power of judging and acting aright which

would alone authorise me to point out to you any path in which you ought to walk. I am more content to leave you to walk by yourself in the path you shall choose; but I know that I do not leave you alone and unsupported, for His arm will guide, strengthen and protect you.[37]

Almost all Victorian husbands expected their wives to obey them, as they promised to do in the marriage ceremony. But George does not value his own 'power of judging and acting aright' above Josephine's. He knows that she will be guided by God through her prayers and Bible study, as he will be. Their marriage will be a three-way partnership between husband, wife and God.[38]

Josephine took guidance from George, but ultimately only from God. Her feminism, above all, was derived from her Christian faith. 'I never sat at the feet of any man', she said, 'nor on churches and creeds had I ever leaned.'[39] Even at Oxford, she rejected the opinions of high ranking male clerics, because 'the things which I believed I had learned direct from God'. Her perception of God was both her motivating power and her source of supreme confidence in herself as a woman.

Victorian feminists found support in the Bible, especially in St Paul's letter to the Galatians – 'There is neither male nor female: for ye are all one in Christ Jesus'.[40] St Paul, however, was a problematic guide since he also taught his followers that women should be treated differently in church, saying in another letter: 'I suffer not a woman to teach, nor to usurp authority over the man, but to be in silence.'[41] That teaching dominated the Victorian Church's view of women, and Josephine tackled the issue directly in her second book, *Woman's Work and Woman's Culture*.[42] Jesus himself, she argued, had always treated women as of equal value, and had never himself suggested that they could not become preachers and teachers. Those who came after him, even St Paul, were capable of error.[43]

The examples she noted from the Gospels included Mary Magdalen, one of Christ's most devoted followers, 'the most stupendous announcement ever made to the world ... – the resurrection of Christ – was first made to women'.[44] Mary Magdalen is named in all four gospels as being one of these women, and in John's gospel as being the sole witness to the Resurrection.[45] She goes to the garden, finds the empty tomb and, weeping, does not recognise Jesus standing before her. During Josephine's Christian revelation in 1856, she believed that 'He met me and called me by my name, as when He called "Mary" in the garden'.[46] Josephine identified with her and was inspired by the important role Mary was given and the respect she received from Jesus.

Josephine was equally affected by the considerate way in which Jesus treated 'fallen' women, like the 'woman in the city', described in the gospel of St Luke, who washed Christ's feet with her tears, wiped them with her hair and anointed them with precious ointment.[47] Jesus took the tears as a sign of her penitence and forgave her sins, despite the objections of his disciples. Josephine's conclusion is a powerful and radical statement:

> Search throughout the Gospel history, and observe his conduct in regard to women, and it will be found that the word liberation expresses, above all others, the act which changed the whole life and character and position of the women dealt with, and which ought to have changed the character of men's treatment of women from that time forward.[48]

In the 1970s feminism was called 'Women's Liberation'[49] but here we see that this word has powerful Christian roots. Josephine Butler believed that Christ had liberated the women he met and therefore that Christian faith should liberate all women.[50]

Education and Employment for Women

~~George and the Boys

Liverpool College suited George very well.[1] The school had been left in good shape by the previous Principal, so he was able to concentrate on developing his pet subjects, science, art, modern languages and geography. While George was Principal, Liverpool boys won most of the medals awarded to school pupils by the Royal Geographical Society. He taught far more frequently than most heads – twenty hours a week. He could be very firm, and was 'naturally of a quick and hasty temper', but he was often kind to the pupils.[2] Remembering his own school days, he said, 'I am never hard on boys on account of mere mischief' and he could not restrain a smile when the report of one of his sons described him as 'playful in school'.[3]

He changed the college's homework rules after he found a boy sobbing because he was overwhelmed by study. He persuaded the parents that it was good for the boys to have time off for games, improved the playgrounds and installed a cricket ground.

The only fly in the ointment was the state of Liverpool's trade – it had lost many valuable raw cotton cargoes due to the American Civil War. Unemployment affected even the middle classes, and some pupils were withdrawn. George was employed at a lower salary (£850) than that of the previous Principal, and had to find ways to increase the income or save costs. He was keen to introduce boarding, and encouraged masters who provided boarding places in their own homes.

The three Butler boys thrived at the college and generally did well academically. Glimpses of their school life appear in letters. When Josephine was in London staying with her niece in December 1867, George wrote:

> The boys did justice to their provisions, and had a good play in my lecture room afterwards. They seemed very happy ... The cat [Stanley] is much pleased at his chemistry gas light and shelf being put up ... With a triple bouquet of love from your boys. Your loving husband, G Butler.[4]

George tried to take the family out of Liverpool as much as possible; they all felt happier in the countryside. Josephine lamented that Liverpool was 'far from being a beautiful town; some portions of its outskirts through which he had to pass daily on his way from our home to the College were almost squalid in appearance'.[5] Moreover, there was no open countryside close by, so 'our half-holidays were sometimes used up in a desperate effort to snatch a few hours of country walking between two railway journeys'. They could not yet afford regular foreign holidays. They returned to Northumberland in the summer, where John Grey could still guide them on walks 'over the breezy moors' near his retirement home.[6] In the summer of 1867 they spent a few weeks in St John's Parsonage on Lake Derwentwater.

The Lake District was near to Liverpool and George knew it well from his summers spent taking student reading parties there. He loved swimming in the cold water of the lakes, and was sometimes able to take climbing expeditions with friends like J.A. Froude, 'the most perfect companion imaginable', and his brother-in-law Francis Galton, the leading scientist and geographer, who was Charles Darwin's cousin.[7] He had trekked in south-west Africa, then 'largely unknown to Europeans'.[8] George would have been fascinated to hear about this journey, and the meteorological investigations he undertook on his return.

University Education for Women

In November 1867 Josephine Butler and Anne Clough formed another organisation, the North of England Council for Promoting the Higher Education of Women (NECPHEW).[9] This was the next stage of their campaign to create job prospects for women by improving their education. The standard of teaching in girls' schools was very low and could not be improved unless women received higher education to become specialist subject teachers. Thoughtful and intelligent women were also crying out for the knowledge offered by university lecturers. In the North of England there were very few higher education colleges, and none offered lectures or courses for women. Most people had no notion that women's higher education was possible.

NECPHEW set up committees in four northern cities, Liverpool, Manchester, Leeds and Sheffield. Josephine was the first President and Anne was Secretary. The twelve-member council included nine women, most of them closely connected with the world of education, like Elizabeth Wolstenholme, who was the headmistress of a girls' school.

Josephine, Anne and the NECPHEW council promoted the idea of 'University Extension' – public lectures given by specialists from Oxford and Cambridge. The first lecturer they employed was James Stuart, a young fellow at Trinity College, Cambridge, who was 'a raw Scotch youth ... of great promise', according to a supporter of university extension who knew him there.[10] James said he was motivated by 'the widespread and real desire for some form of higher education which existed throughout the country' and 'the obligation there was on the two ancient universities to come forward to supply that demand'.[11] He decided to offer a course in the History of Science, since his expertise was in mechanical sciences.[12]

The audience for the first lecture was 'entirely composed of women' and the arrangements for it were quaint. It was thought improper for the audience to put questions to a young male lecturer, so Stuart distributed a printed list of questions with the offer to correct answers sent to him by post. Around 300 women took up his offer – an enormous extension to his workload. However, both these elements, the printed syllabus and the written work, were to become indispensable features of the extension classes which developed from these initial lectures.

The first lecture courses were held in Leeds, Liverpool, Sheffield and Manchester. We can imagine the satisfaction with which Josephine and George attended the Liverpool lectures. George himself also gave lectures in all four cities, stating that to deprive women of higher education was to deprive half of society.[13] In Sheffield he said, 'so take courage, ladies, struggling now at this day for the right to cultivate to their full extent the faculties and gifts which God has bestowed upon you'.[14]

Within a few years the courses spread to other parts of the country, with more lecturers being employed. There were demands for lectures for working men and James Stuart was again a pioneer, travelling to lecture to railwaymen at Crewe in 1867. James Stuart, Josephine Butler and Anne Clough were the pioneers of University Extension.[15] The movement proved to have limitless potential. In 1873 James persuaded the University of Cambridge to sponsor Extension work, with the result that by 1876 there were about 100 courses operating in various centres throughout the country. The universities of London and Oxford joined the movement in the 1880s.

The impact of these courses was so great that several northern universities can trace their origins back to the Extension movement. Sheffield is one example, where Firth College was built in 1879 to accommodate the lectures, and expanded from there. From the earliest days of Firth College, women students were taught alongside men and allowed to study every subject except medicine.[16] One woman spoke for many when she described University Extension as 'a gift from heaven'.[17]

The Death of Josephine's Father

Josephine and George visited Lipwood House only once more, to attend John Grey's funeral in January 1868. On his last morning, John stayed in bed longer than usual and his daughter Fanny asked if there was anything he needed. He replied, 'No, I thank you my dear; *my wants are very few.*' Shortly afterwards she found him on the stairs where 'he raised his forefinger as if … he heard someone calling him' and 'died without a struggle, and apparently without pain, in the eighty-third year of his age'.[18] He was the fortunate possessor of good health until that moment, and had been on horseback a day or two previously.

The tributes that followed were for a good man who had lived an energetic life devoted to his work and family, an agricultural reformer and a good employer, and an enthusiastic supporter of liberal causes. Josephine wanted him to be remembered for 'the gentle purity of his nature' and his desire 'to repress inclinations to self-indulgence'.[19] He was a model, she thought, for all men to follow, an example of what men could achieve.

From Lipwood, Josephine wrote to her sons at home in Liverpool, 'poor dog Tip goes every morning to grandpapa's room, as usual, and waits for him to come out … Think of us tomorrow at midday in the churchyard where grandpapa took you to see grandmamma's grave.'[20] John was buried next to Hannah, and within a month Josephine had accepted her brothers' invitation to write a biography of their father. Her *Memoir of John Grey* is based on family letters, from which she compiled a vivid account of his Northumberland heritage and the valuable extent of his agricultural and public work. She gives us the story of his parents and sisters, of his meeting with Hannah, and their family life at Milfield and Dilston. The *Memoir* leaves a powerful impression of John Grey's outstanding personal and moral qualities.[21] It is no surprise that his daughter was also morally and personally exceptional.

Albert Rutson, Black Prince and the Visit to Cambridge

In the month after her father died Josephine had 'an attack of rheumatism' and confessed that from this and her heart problems 'my sufferings are very great at times: so great that I cannot wish much to live'.[22] She poured out these worries in letters to Albert Rutson, who was a barrister eight years younger than her, and had been a student at Oxford when she and George lived there.[23] She accepted his urgent appeals to rest, but would not agree to see a doctor; she had consulted so many already who had told her 'it was not a case for an earthly cure!'[24]

Albert, and other 'kind promoters of my health' offered her a horse, and Josephine decided to accept, 'being able to ride daily will be quite a blessing to me'.[25] Discussing the choice of mount, she told Albert that:

> I can do with any amount of spirit, but I like a business-like horse, who does not make a flourish and a splash ... as park horses do, but who will leave the stable at a walk and walk steadily five miles if one wants it ... I like the colour of black or dark brown very much.[26]

The arrival of Black Prince thrilled her. By May, he grew 'handsomer every day' and on May Day she rode him 'with long wreaths of daisies and spring flowers hung about him, which Charlie made'.[27]

Albert Rutson supported Josephine's rescue work in Liverpool, both financially and through emotional support. She sent him graphic descriptions of the women in the Bridewell, and he visited Mary Lomax before she died and took an interest in the House of Rest. When he sent her some money she 'hired an old shabby large open carriage twice on some warm spring like days we had, and packed five or six of [my sick people] in, and ... drove round Smith Down Cemetery which is pretty. They enjoyed it so very much.'[28]

Despite her continuing weakness, Josephine involved herself in the campaign, started by Emily Davies, to make it possible for young women to enter Oxford and Cambridge universities. Emily Davies had already persuaded Cambridge to open its entrance exams to girls and had begun a campaign to build a women's college there.[29] However, a split developed between NECPHEW and Emily Davies.

Anne Clough believed that women needed a different examination, with a modern curriculum suited to their strengths, while Emily Davies insisted that women should take the same degree exams as men, even though the Classics-based Cambridge curriculum was 'acknowledged to be archaic and in need of change'.[30] Josephine strongly disagreed with her, predicting that 'these masculine aiming women *will* fail ...'[31] She thought that Emily's attempt to set up a women's college was too ambitious, and suggested 'taking a boarding house merely, within reach of Cambridge and working up for examinations given by Cambridge Syndicate'. This vision was too limited, but on the other hand Josephine supported the idea of mixed classes, while Emily Davies wanted the women in her college to have an education entirely separate from men.[32] Her hard-line stance was 'controversial and lonely' in the 1860s.[33]

Relations with Emily Davies broke down completely after Josephine and Anne Clough, supported by a Cambridge professor, Henry Sidgwick, decided to campaign for special examinations for women.[34] They had the help of Albert Rutson, who was a close associate of H.A. Bruce MP, a leading Liberal and supporter of women's suffrage.[35] Bruce endorsed the idea of special examinations and suggested that its supporters organise a statement of their case, to be 'signed by a few Oxford and Cambridge men'.[36] James Stuart helped Josephine to send out circulars and petitions in May 1868, since she herself was still very ill – 'for a month past I have been strangely sad ... I suffered more for four days and nights than I have done for several years ... George has been much alarmed.' She agreed to see a doctor who 'said at once he saw the sadness of heart which had brought it on'.[37]

Josephine went to Cambridge with Charlie in late May armed with petitions signed by 800 women, including 500 teachers. She interviewed forty-eight Cambridge students and dons, and probably made a greater impression on them because of her obvious suffering. Fresh petition forms were continually arriving during her stay, and the Senate was impressed that the signatories included well-known women like the wives of Gladstone, Tennyson and the historian J.A. Froude. Albert urged her to go to Oxford as well but she resisted, saying that it was 'so full of sad and painful associations to me and I had almost rather never go back to it'.[38]

Although George liked Oxford, she felt that very few people cared for her there, whereas at Cambridge 'the people are all so lovingly and loyally disposed to me that my heart is quite melted towards them ... they only want to see a *living* woman to convince them that it is a living scheme.' As she stayed on there, she heard from George that '*all* our servants fell ill in one day of diphtheria'.[39] He engaged a nurse for them and sent Georgie and Stanley to The Mount, outside Liverpool, the home of their aunt Tully and her husband Edgar Garston.

Josephine's health fluctuated, but was eased by opiates which helped her to sleep.[40] She told Albert that she 'had a very happy Whitsunday, and there was a beautiful anthem in Chapel. It is a very favourite anniversary of mine. I love the thought of the gentle unseen influences of the Holy Spirit.'[41] The next day, however, she wrote: 'The neuralgia is the severest I ever had' and 'I lose heart about Oxford'.[42] She stayed on another four days, rousing herself to address the university Senate, a novel experience for this assembly of men which must have been a crucial factor in gaining its support. Albert generously paid for her to return home to Liverpool in a first class rail carriage. She felt pleased that she had aroused 'new sympathies and awakened energies and friendliness', and done as much as she could.[43]

It proved to be a great deal. The result of this campaign was the inauguration of the Cambridge Higher Examination for women over 18, which examined its first students in 1869. Most of the credit for this is due to Anne Clough, but she acknowledged that Josephine's Cambridge mission 'drew to the cause many friends'.[44]

When lectures for women began in Cambridge, Anne Clough moved from Liverpool in order to establish a house where young female students could stay. It opened in 1871 and was oversubscribed immediately. Anne was soon negotiating with St John's College for land on which to build a new women's hall, which opened as Newnham Hall in 1875. This became a women's college, with Anne as its first Principal. Emily Davies managed to build a women's college in the village of Girton, outside Cambridge, which opened in 1873. For many years Girton and Newnham were the only women's colleges at Cambridge.

ᘰᕲ Resistance to 'Coverture'

Despite the state of her health, Josephine found it impossible to resist the lure of feminist projects. While campaigning for women's higher education and maintaining her rescue work, she had become involved in a third issue, the rights of married women. In 1868 a wife had no legal existence, but was regarded as being one person with her husband under the doctrine of 'coverture'. By law, she had no separate identity. Her property became that of her husband's on marriage and she was at his mercy – if he abused her, it was almost impossible to obtain a divorce. If she did, a separated wife risked losing the custody of her children, since by law they belonged to the husband.[45]

Married women were slaves to their reproductive system – ten pregnancies were not uncommon and the rates of infant and maternal mortality were tragically high. Only the richest wives could afford a household staff of servants, so most managed with one young girl's assistance, the untrained 'maid-of-all-work', and obviously without labour saving appliances.[46] This was all that women had ever known, and the Victorians invented a way to make it not only bearable, but actually desirable. The role of the wife within the middle-class home was idealised into a 'mission'. Within the 'domestic sphere' the wife became the 'queen' and was in control, teaching moral and social values to her children and the servants. She was 'The Angel in the House', the title of a popular poem by Coventry Patmore extolling the domestic virtues of his own wife. This idea seems to have satisfied many wives.

Josephine, however, rejected the notion that wives could be 'superior beings, for *worship* (a thing which every sensible and honourable woman rejects with scorn), because she knows that God alone is to be worshipped'.[47] The myth was a convenient smokescreen to legitimise the oppression of women. She knew men who '*talked* about women as divinities' while actually 'treating the women who are most closely connected with them with cruel injustice, ruling over them like tyrants, despising them and silencing them'.[48]

Barbara Bodichon and the ladies who worked at her London office in Langham Place had been leading the fight for marriage reform since the mid-1850s, and had succeeded in making small improvements to women's divorce rights. However, they had made little headway on the issue of property. A married woman could not own any goods in her own name, even her possessions and money at the time of her marriage, nor could she earn money in her own right. There had been several petitions for married women's property and earnings rights, including one which John Grey signed a few months before his death. Josephine recalled that, having signed it, he said to her, 'Stay, my dear, let me put *J.P.* after my name. Maybe if they knew what an old magistrate I am they would think my signature had more weight.'[49]

In April 1868, a Married Women's Property Committee was formed by the leaders of the Manchester Society for Women's Suffrage, including Lydia Becker, Elizabeth Gloyne and Elizabeth Wolstenholme.[50] The latter two were working with Josephine on the campaign for women's higher education, and they naturally asked Josephine to join their new committee. She agreed to take on the role of joint secretary. This committee quickly became more active than the Langham Place Group – the main 'driving force for a married women's property bill'.[51]

However, all the women were grappling with the demands of several campaigns at once. Josephine's surviving correspondence from 1868 shows that her greatest commitment was to women's education and employment, in addition to her rescue work. Lydia Becker urged her to recognise that women's suffrage was the key to every other reform 'for every woman you rescue another falls into the pit ... what I want you to do is to leave educational matters, and mere philanthropic efforts to alleviate individual misery ... and to devote your own efforts ... to obtaining political power for women'.[52] She even told Josephine that, 'If you had worked as hard, and begged as much, for the franchise movement in Liverpool as you have done for your Industrial Home perhaps Liverpool would have had a committee equal to that in Manchester.' Although Lydia saw it as 'a great proof of friendship that I have dared to write this letter', it is unlikely that Josephine saw it in the same way. We do not have her reply, but she never regarded women's suffrage as the only important cause. Lydia Becker, on the other hand, increasingly adopted this 'narrow' approach, especially after she became a leader of the national movement.[53] Elizabeth Wolstenholme eventually took sole charge of the Manchester Married Women's Property committee.

Woman's Work and Woman's Culture

It is no surprise that Josephine told Albert Rutson in June that she felt 'overworked'.[54] He had suggested that she form yet another organisation, 'an association to help women into employment', and she could see the value of it, but did not eventually do so. At the time, however, she organised a meeting about it with her contacts, including Elizabeth Wolstenholme, Miss King and Jessie Boucherett in London, and generally kept up a ferocious level of correspondence concerning all her projects. By 26 July, 'crushed by severe headaches', she retired to Gilsland, in her beloved Northumberland, where she rode Black Prince 'who is the admiration of everyone'.[55]

Josephine sold Black Prince to a stable in London later that year; we next hear of him in January 1869 when Josephine hired him from the stable while on a visit to the capital. On an early morning ride in the park accompanied by Frank Galton, 'I got nice and warm. My poor old pet knew me, but he is in such high condition that he is rather furious and does not understand the paces of Rotten Row, and wants to be off on his cross country pace.'[56] Perhaps she could not afford to maintain him in Liverpool, but the sale of his gift may have angered Albert. The frenzied rate of their correspondence began to diminish in the autumn of 1868, and the following year she found other confidantes. Josephine advised Albert to go into Parliament and he took her advice, becoming Private Secretary to H.A. Bruce, who in December was appointed Home Secretary in Gladstone's government.[57] In that office he followed his master and when Josephine clashed with Bruce in 1871, Albert gave her no support. She concluded, 'It seems like many men in office he has given over his conscience to his chief.'[58]

Josephine's widening circle of contacts, together with the success of her pamphlet *The Education and Employment of Women*, gave her the idea for her second book. She drew up plans for a volume of essays on all the current 'women's issues', with contributions from many of her new friends. This was her own project, for which she approached the publisher Macmillan in London in January 1869. She asked Frances Power Cobbe and Elizabeth Wolstenholme to contribute essays on the education of girls. Jessie Boucherett and Sophia Jex-Blake, one of the first female doctors, agreed to write about women's employment prospects. George Butler offered his expertise on working opportunities in education and James Stuart on the teaching of science. Further essays explored suffrage, family life and the legal effects of marriage. Josephine, as editor, made sure all the essays were completed on time.

Josephine's concern for prostitutes comes to the fore in her Introduction, when she writes about 'the wholesale destruction which goes on from year to year among women – destruction of bodies, of consciences, of souls'.[59] 'There are 1,500 women who are pursuing this calling ... [in] one of our great seaports [obviously Liverpool] who are under 15, with a third of those under 13.'[60] She gives the example of a French girl who was 'bribed from her home by fair offers of honest employment and success in England' and was then forced into a life of 'deepest ignominy'.[61] This is the first time that she writes about child prostitution and trafficking, issues which dominated her later campaigns.

Turning to marriage reform, she addresses men and women who believe that 'woman's sphere is the home'. These are:

> ... mocking words to women who are not wives and mothers and cannot hope to be.
> [In any case, marriage should not be] ... the one end of a woman's life, when it is degraded to the level of a feminine profession, when those who are soliciting a place in this

profession resemble those flaccid Brazilian creepers which cannot exist without support, and which sprawl out their limp tendrils in every direction to find something – no matter what – to hang upon.[62]

This image of marriage is damaging for both parties, it should be 'a free and deliberate choice – a decision of the judgement and of the heart'.[63] Unmarried women have so much to offer society 'when they cease to be soured by disappointment or driven by destitution to despair'.[64]

John Stuart Mill's book *The Subjection of Women* was published just before Josephine's. His views on marriage (and those of his wife Harriet Taylor) were far more radical than hers. He compares it to slavery, describing marriage as 'the only actual bondage known to our law'.[65] Josephine had made a clear distinction between freely chosen marriage and arranged marriage, and stressed that she herself was very happily married. *Woman's Work and Woman's Culture* was more practical in its suggestions about employment for both middle and working-class women than Mill's book, it had a 'wider social vision'.[66]

The expanding breadth of Josephine's vision is demonstrated by her next move, into the international arena. She wrote to some of the most prominent and influential women in Europe to gather information about female education and employment in their countries. Crown Princess Victoria of Prussia, the eldest daughter of Queen Victoria, replied in a long letter, supporting the opening of professions to women 'accompanied by the appropriate training places' as teachers, nurses, stenographers and book-keepers.[67] She rather spoilt this, though, by adding that these plans could only be implemented 'with the advice and assurance of men of standing in the social and political world' and advising Josephine to look to 'wise and experienced *men* for answers'. She also stated her opposition to female suffrage.

Josephine had replies from Princess Victoria's sister, Princess Louise, and from as far afield as Russia. All applauded her idea of launching a periodical to review the international state of women's work and education. She also had a supportive letter from John Stuart Mill.[68] The name of the review proved contentious, Princess Louise suggesting that it 'would be tactful to avoid mentioning women in the title'.[69] Josephine selected *Now-a-days*, the first edition of which appeared in July 1869. That edition was probably the only one ever published but 'it showed quite remarkable self-confidence to take on such a project'.[70] *Now-a-days* was abandoned for the same reason that Josephine gave up all her other feminist concerns. In the autumn of 1869 a new project took over her life entirely.

INTERLUDE

Dr Acton and the Lock Hospitals

Victorian morality had created the myth of two kinds of women – the pure and the fallen. The myth of the pure woman was given pseudoscientific credibility in a book by Dr William Acton, a surgeon specialising in genital disorders. Acton prided himself on his research. On the basis of the observation that female animals 'will not allow the approach of the male except when in a state of rut', he believed that marriage, motherhood and domesticity were the main drivers of normal female sexuality.[71] The depraved prostitute, or indeed any woman who engaged in sex for other reasons, was therefore 'unnatural'. He described the pure, respectable, 'normal' woman as asexual:

> I should say that the majority of women (happily for society) are not very much troubled with sexual feeling of any kind ... She submits to her husband's embraces, but principally to gratify him; and, were it not for the desire of maternity, would far rather be relieved from his attentions.[72]

Acton (in common with most Victorian doctors) believed that the male body possessed only a limited quantity of semen; it was therefore important that the woman should not be too exciting as this would lead to health damaging 'excesses'. A wife who became sexually excited was on the way to nymphomania and no better than a prostitute.

Prostitutes were uniquely threatening in the eyes of most Victorian men. They lured married men away from their pure wives, depleted their semen and harboured venereal infection. They were 'sub-human' and beneath contempt – 'Miserable creatures who were mere masses of rottenness and vehicles of disease'.[73]

Before antibiotics were invented, there was no cure for syphilis or gonorrhoea.[74] Gonorrhoea ('the clap') caused a profuse and unpleasant genital discharge in both sexes, and could lead to infertility. It was actually a more serious disease for women, but this was not recognised in Victorian times when doctors thought it was a mild infection of the vagina. The primary site was in fact the cervix, uterus and fallopian tubes, and if left untreated the infection could cause severe pelvic pain and sterility. Syphilis was a particularly nasty disease, which was transmitted during sexual intercourse. It caused painless lesions, a widespread rash and emotional depression, which could go on for months. The disease could reappear many years after the original infection, and in its most serious third stage could attack the bones or the liver, lungs, brain, joints and muscles and even cause insanity and paralysis. The unborn children of syphilitic mothers could develop fatal congenital syphilis.

Prostitutes, themselves at the most risk of infection, tried to prevent their vaginal wall being infected by rubbing in oil. If prostitutes became infected, their prospects were chilling. The only treatment offered was in the so-called 'lock hospitals', special facilities which were opened because so many hospitals refused to admit 'fallen' women. Confusingly, the name does not mean the wards were actually locked; it derives from the word 'loke' meaning a house for lepers.[75] Infected prostitutes were treated like lepers, outcast from society.

Dr Acton had learned about the most advanced theories of treatment and diagnosis of venereal diseases from his training in France.[76] It was important to catch a primary syphilitic infection early to stop it spreading, because the later stages were so hard to treat. The speculum, a cold metal probe which was expanded inside the vagina to allow inspection of the cervix, allowed early diagnosis. Dr Acton was enthusiastic about its use for this reason, but it had hardly been used in England because so many doctors were concerned about 'propriety'. Acton promoted the use of the speculum, and described its use for prostitutes at the London Lock Hospital:

> The patient ascends the steps placed by the side of the [raised] bed, lays down, places her feet in the slippers [stirrups] arranged for the purpose, and the house surgeon separates the labia to see if there are any sores. If no suspicion of these exists, and if the female

is suffering from discharge, the speculum is at once employed. In this institution several sizes are used, and they are silvered and covered with India-rubber. The head nurse after each examination washes the speculum in a solution of permanganate of potash, then wipes it carefully, oils it ready for the next examination, so that the surgeon loses no time, and the examinations are conducted with great rapidity. In the course of one hour and three-quarters I assisted in the thorough examination of 58 women with the speculum.[77]

Acton criticised the regime at St Bartholomew's in London, where 'the indecent system of exposing females before the whole class of students is still pursued'.[78] He favoured a treatment which involved 'vaginal injections' of lotion by syringe and examination with the speculum 'at least twice a week'. He recommended the application of lint dipped in lead lotion (a poison) a few hours beforehand. For women with uterine and cervical infections it often proved necessary to apply nitrate of silver through the speculum. Despite its caustic nature he insisted that there was 'rarely any pain' caused by using such astringents.[79]

Acton did have the excuse that he was trying to prevent secondary syphilis setting in, and the treatment for that was certainly much worse. For centuries the only remedy available was mercury, which was administered in the form of pills, vapour baths and ointment, but the treatment could be 'unpleasant, long drawn out, and causing noticeable physical stigmata'.[80] These stigmata included gum ulceration, tooth loss and bone deterioration. Mercury is, after all, a poison and doctors found it hard to agree on a dose which would be helpful rather than lethal. Some patients undoubtedly died, slowly and in agony, from the treatment. In the most severe cases there was little treatment available, and some doctors believed that it was divine retribution – syphilis was 'intended as a punishment for our sins and we should not interfere in the matter'.[81]

Dr Acton stated that treatment in the London Lock Hospital lasted, on average, for twenty-three days, but that readmissions were 'unfortunately too frequent'.[82] Some women returned as much as six or seven times a year. In the hope of stopping this revolving door, the lock hospitals took on a reforming role. In addition to training their patients in habits of personal hygiene, the staff imposed a strict regime of harsh discipline and religious training. They expected them to work for nothing, usually in the hospital laundry. The attitude of the staff and the harshness of the treatment made the hospitals very unpopular. Women would not go there unless they were desperate for treatment, or confined there by the force of law.

'This Revolt of the Women'

~~A Holiday in Switzerland

Josephine was suffering severely from a lung condition in February 1869 – wracked by coughing, she was 'choked with phlegm and blood' at night.[1] George, she said, had to sleep in his dressing room, 'a long way off, so that he cannot hear me cough'. The doctor told her that only one of her lungs was still working and suggested moving to a warmer climate, but Josephine knew from Hatty that even Naples could sometimes be cold, and refused to move from her warm house or separate herself permanently from her family. She told her mother-in-law, 'I think I am wonderfully tough, though I suffer a good deal.'[2] Mrs Butler responded by sending her a 'bright shawl' which Josephine loved; 'the colour is *much* admired' she told her, 'and it is so clinging, and warm'.[3]

The family planned a summer holiday at La Gordanne, Hatty and Tell's home in Switzerland. Hatty had decided to hold 'quite a family gathering' there in August and September, inviting several of her sisters and their families. George's mother contributed towards the cost of the trip, and both George and Josephine tried 'to save or make a little to help as we are a large party to go'. She put her money from the sale of Black Prince towards the holiday.

In June, Josephine made her first attempt at public speaking, a lecture at Liverpool College which delighted George.[4] The Butlers hosted a meeting of NECPHEW in Liverpool, and Josephine corresponded regularly with Anne Clough, informing her on 7 July that Emily Davies 'shortly and not courteously declines to have any connection with us'.[5] But in between these bursts of energy, Josephine remained extremely ill. On 13 July she wrote twice to Anne Clough, once to advise her about the drafting of an appeal for funds, and later in the day to tender her resignation as President of the Council, due to the state of her health.[6] She later changed her mind, and remained President until 1873.[7]

Josephine and the boys left for Dover on 20 July, where they were joined by George after a visit to his mother. He kept a diary of the trip for her. They went first to Lucerne for a few days' rest and then George introduced his boys to the pleasures of climbing in the Swiss Alps. After 'a most beautiful walk by the Wengern Alp', George made a sketch of the Jungfrau 'seen through pine forests. I never saw anything more beautiful than the sunset as we returned.'[8] George was in his element; climbing and sketching were the pattern of many Swiss holidays to come. At Rolle, the Meuricoffres' carriage was waiting for them and 'we had a joyful meeting'. La Gordanne, on the shores of Lake Geneva, proved to be 'elegant and comfortable. The grounds are extensive, and reach down to the lake, where there is good bathing. There are vineyards above the house, and beyond, high grass fields commanding extensive views of the lake and Mont Blanc.' They were joined there by Eliza, her daughters Edith and Constance, and Maud, the wife of Tully's son Edgar.

'Healthy Whores' – By Act of Parliament

During Josephine's stay at La Gordanne, she and Hatty were invited to address a meeting of ladies from Switzerland, France, Germany, Italy and Russia who were opposed to the system of regulated prostitution on the Continent. In each of these countries, an oppressive morals police force registered prostitutes, checked on their activities and often arrested them. The ladies immediately decided to form an international women's association to oppose the legalised activities of the morals police.[9]

Josephine already knew about this system, and had been horrified by a law passed by the British Parliament in 1864. Its name, the Contagious Diseases (CD) Act, sounds innocuous. It could have referred to any infectious disease. Many of the MPs who voted for the Act in a sparsely populated House of Commons apparently thought that it dealt with animal diseases, and no effort was made to tell them the truth. In fact it dealt with sexually transmitted infections, syphilis and gonorrhoea in particular. The government, urged on by doctors and the sanitary authorities, had decided to confront the problem that soldiers in barracks and sailors in port were consorting with prostitutes and picking up sexual infections in increasing numbers. In a desperate attempt to limit this epidemic, they decided that the solution lay in serving up disease-free prostitutes to the troops.

The CD Act should have been called the 'Healthy Whores' Act, as then everyone would have known what it was about. The government and the military were not interested in the welfare of prostitutes; their only concern was the health of their fighting men. The army had collected statistics which charted a steadily rising graph of infected soldiers. By 1864, one in three sick soldiers had gonorrhoea or syphilis.[10] Their proposed solution was simple and 'sanitary': to ensure that every prostitute hired by a soldier or sailor had been certified free of venereal infection. To create this disease-free nirvana, the 1864 Act was followed by two more, in 1866 and 1869, which enshrined a failsafe system to take infected women out of circulation. By 1869, police officers in a total of eighteen British port and garrison towns (such as Portsmouth, Southampton, Plymouth, Colchester and Aldershot) were required to round up all the women they suspected of being prostitutes on a regular basis. The women were to be taken to a police station or certified hospital to be examined by a doctor for sexually transmitted disease. If any woman objected, magistrates were informed and could make an order to examine her by force. If she proved to be infected, she was kept in a lock hospital or workhouse ward for up to nine months, deprived of her liberty until she had recovered. She was then free to walk the streets again, brandishing her certificate of health.

Most Victorians supported the government's decision. There was very little that doctors could do about infectious disease, so if isolation was a means of preventing it, then, through this cold logic, the drive was on to find these 'vehicles of disease' and remove them from society. Some Victorians, however, were horrified. The CD Acts enshrined the double standard in law – prostitutes were to be arrested and detained purely because of their sex and their 'profession', not because they had committed any offence. Opposition to the Acts had already been mobilised, led by a group of doctors and by Daniel Cooper of the Rescue Society.

Josephine heard that the 1869 Act had been passed when she returned from Switzerland and received a letter at Dover from Daniel Cooper.[11] Only after she had checked the truth of this information with James Stuart could she quite believe it. She was horrified in particular by the extension of the detention period to nine months – 'A small clique in Parliament had been too successfully busy over this work of darkness during the hot August days, or rather nights, in a thin House'.[12] Before she left Dover she had also heard from Elizabeth Wolstenholme and from two Nottingham doctors opposed to the Acts, Charles Bell Taylor and Thomas Worth.[13] All urged her to lead a women's campaign against the Acts – 'these women must find representatives of their own sex to protest against ... the Parliament and Government which had flung this insult in their face'.[14]

Josephine may have been singled out because she was a married woman and the doctors were reluctant to push an unmarried woman into a spotlight where she would be forced to discuss sexual matters openly. But the dangers for a married woman were also daunting. In the years to come, the press would insinuate that she had taken up the campaign because of marital unhappiness. One Member of Parliament referred to her as 'a woman who *calls* herself a lady', and another said, 'I look upon these women who have taken up this matter as worse than the prostitutes.'[15]

When the invitation came, Josephine immediately saw that it might be a call from God, 'the very work, the very mission, I longed for years ago and saw coming, afar off, like a bright star'.[16] But, repulsed by the prospect of the campaign, she tried to run away. It seemed to her that God wanted her to 'run my heart against the naked sword which seemed to be held out'. This dramatic language is biblical – Mary the mother of Jesus was warned that 'a sword shall pierce through thy own soul also'.[17]

For three months Josephine was 'very unhappy', because of 'the villainy there is in the world, and the dread of being called to oppose it'.[18] She tried to appease God with other work, but the appeals continued to arrive. She knew what the campaign would mean. She would have to speak and write about the topic of sexually transmitted disease, explain the horrors of the lock hospital, and alienate a great many people, including friends, who regarded the CD Acts as a 'sanitary' solution to the problem of providing a sexual outlet for soldiers and sailors. Her final decision to accept the call was made in solitude, for she found it impossibly difficult to discuss with George.[19] She knew that if she took on such a mission it would impact heavily on his own life. Eventually she wrote him a letter and gave it to him to read privately. George must have been dreading this, and the depth of his unease is shown by the fact that several days passed before they talked about it. Then Josephine told him, 'I feel as if I must go out into the streets and cry aloud, or my heart will break.' George foresaw the anguish ahead, but accepted that a call from God 'is man's highest honour to obey'. In later life, Josephine spoke of 'my own and my husband's first call to this great work', but it was Josephine who was called and George who followed.[20]

By then a campaigning organisation, the National Anti-Contagious Diseases Acts Association (NA) had been formed by a committee of men, including Dr Worth. The formation of a Ladies National Association (LNA) was well under way, and Josephine agreed to become its leader.*

Why did Josephine do it?

Josephine had sufficient work for several women by 1869, but she cast most of that aside in order to take on a cause which she regarded as 'so dreadful, so difficult, so disgusting'.[21] She cared deeply about the campaigns for women's higher education and employment,

---

* This men's campaign will be known as the NA; the women's campaign as the LNA.

and for marital reform, but this one was different. In some ways her entire life had led to this moment. The plight of fallen women had always been closest to her heart. She was magnetically drawn to them by the conviction that these women were her suffering sisters and that she was called to care for them. Josephine believed that Jesus had liberated the 'woman in the city', a prostitute, just as he had liberated her. They were of equal value in His sight. In later life she described her feelings:

> Looking my Liberator in the face, can my friends wonder that I have taken my place (I took it long ago) – oh! with what infinite contentment! – by the side of her, the 'woman in the city which was a sinner'.[22]

In addition, the CD Acts angered her beyond all other injustices to women. They were 'this great wickedness' which filled her with 'such an anger, and even hatred'.[23] By then she had discovered that, for her, it was better, and even easier, to take action than to burn with anger and do nothing. In the book she later wrote about the campaign, *Personal Reminiscences of a Great Crusade*, she reflected that its rigours were 'for me light and easy to bear in comparison with the deep and silent sorrow, the bitterness of soul of the years which preceded it'.[24]

Even though the campaign involved persecution, ridicule, threats, even violence, she had at last received 'a call to action'. This was 'a welcome sign that the battle is set in array, and that the enemy is roused to bitterest hatred because his claims are disputed and his sovereignty is about to be overthrown'. The language is again biblical, and the imagery of the battle was a powerful spur. Her fight was against a sin, 'the shameful inequality of judgement concerning sexual sin in man and woman', and her mission was from God.

This was also a cause which she could lead. Other women, Anne Clough, Lydia Becker and Elizabeth Wolstenholme, were the leaders of the campaigns she had so far been involved with. In this new campaign she had a unique voice, and she knew from her brief apprenticeship that she had the skills, the impact, the enterprise and the confidence to take on the role of leader. She may not have consciously known how much she would revel in being the focus of attention, but her personality drew her to the centre of the stage. In a twenty-first century context she would tour television studios, beautifully dressed and made-up, and write regular articles for the national press. She would launch high profile websites and send thousands of emails. Her conviction that she was right was impregnable and her energy proved to be enormous.[25]

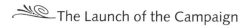 The Launch of the Campaign

Main Points of the Women's Petition (published *Daily News*, 1 January 1870)

1 The Acts remove every guarantee of personal security from women and 'put their reputation, their freedom, and their persons absolutely in the power of the police'.
2 The Acts 'punish the sex who are the victims of a vice and leave unpunished the sex who are the main cause'. These punishments are 'of the most degrading kind'.
3 By offering to provide healthy prostitutes, the State is 'legalising a revolting vice'.
4 It has not been proved that the Acts have led to a decline in disease.
5 The Acts are making it more difficult, not easier, to tackle the 'moral evil' which is the real cause of the problem.

Josephine's first public engagement, as the new leader of the Ladies National Association, was surprising. Instead of gathering an audience of ladies, she took the train to Crewe, where James Stuart had made arrangements for her to make a speech to working men. The topic proved to be familiar to some of them, who had been in Paris and knew of the laws designed to regulate prostitutes there. Encouraged by their support, she went on to Leeds, York, Sunderland and Newcastle, where the response 'exceeded our utmost expectations'.[26] She encouraged her audiences to form committees, with the result that local repeal societies sprang up in the places she had visited.

At the same time the LNA was organising a petition and a press campaign. This was timed for the turn of the year and began with the publication in the *Daily News* of letters from the author and campaigner Harriet Martineau, who signed herself 'An Englishwoman'.[27] Harriet had criticised the Acts as far back as 1863, and was succinct and devastating in her arguments. She pointed out that the most recent Act had been passed almost in secrecy, and with no press coverage. Women had lost their right to protect their own bodies – 'Any woman of whom a policeman swears that he has reason to believe that she is a prostitute is helpless ... She is subject to the extremity of outrage under the eyes, hands and instruments of the surgeons.' In this process the woman has no means of trial or defence, which is 'contrary to all precedent and the whole spirit and method of the British penal law'.

Harriet Martineau also showed that the goal of the Acts, the reduction of venereal disease, could not be achieved. In France, where regulation had been in force for years, prostitute encounters had simply increased because men were not afraid of catching disease. The idea that the women were healthy was an illusion. Since syphilis and gonorrhoea could be latent for years and could have invisible symptoms, the result of regulation was actually an increase in disease. In addition, the French system (like any form of prohibition) encouraged evasion. Women were held as prisoners in secret brothels, where no one could help them. The most pathetic victims were their children, who 'disappear as if through a trapdoor in the streets, or who are sold by vile parents'.

Harriet summarised her argument: 'The national vitality of France is dwindling and sinking under a system of licence of vice which breaks all its promises, and destroys the health and vigour which it engages to save.' Having written in more explicit language than any woman had done before in a public newspaper (although under a pseudonym), Harriet asked, 'What of this Association of Ladies? ... How can women speak or act on such a subject as this, while society supposes that the very existence of prostitutes, and of the horrors of their trade, is unknown to educated and modest women.'[28] Her answer was couched in the language of the Christian home, 'they are striving to save home itself, and to preserve the most sacred of institutions ... the Family', but a feminist argument had been made, and had been heard. It shocked the Establishment to the core. One leading MP famously responded, 'this is very awkward for us – this revolt of the women. It is quite a new thing; what are we to do with such an opposition as this?'[29]

Harriet Martineau's articles were followed by the publication of the women's petition on New Year's Day 1870. This had 2,000 signatures, including those of Florence Nightingale, Lydia Becker and Elizabeth Wolstenholme. Josephine had written to ask Florence Nightingale for her support in November. She replied with a request for specific details about the wording of the petition and the aims of the LNA campaign, and must have been satisfied by Josephine's reply since she returned her signature in December.[30] Josephine rejoiced that the petition was 'flashed by telegrams to the remotest parts of the Kingdom' and reproduced extensively by the local press.[31]

This was the best newspaper coverage they received for several years, however. That may be because the subject was taboo and readers reacted with shock. But most newspaper editors were themselves supporters of the Acts and had no incentive to alienate their readers. Josephine noted that the press was happy to print statements in favour of the Acts.[32] Harriet Martineau suggested to George Butler that they try to see the silver lining to this cloud: 'The extraordinary violence and ill manners of the *Pall Mall Gazette* and some other papers seem to me to indicate that they think our cause is gaining ground.'[33]

The *Pall Mall Gazette* published a letter from Elizabeth Garrett, the only British woman qualified as a doctor at that time, who supported not only the CD Acts but also their extension to civilian areas. She was commended for this support by the *British Medical Journal*, which argued that only doctors could really understand the crying need to contain syphilis. 'Miss Nightingale and her coadjutors' should leave well alone, since only men, with 'the rarest exceptions' (such as Elizabeth Garrett) had 'any hope of understanding it'.[34]

Dr Garrett's attitude was a blow to Josephine, who had believed women doctors would support female causes. She had also consulted Elizabeth Garrett herself two years earlier and felt able to confide in her.[35] She never trusted her again.

Such disappointments were mitigated by the many letters of support the LNA received, including from opponents of regulation on the Continent who were delighted at the British campaign. The novelist Victor Hugo, for example, wrote from Paris, 'I am with you, Madame and ladies. I am with you to the fullest extent of my power ... The slavery of black women is abolished in America but the slavery of white women continues in Europe'.[36]

INTERLUDE

Steel Rape

The CD Acts allowed doctors to assault women in the name of the law. The women rounded up by the British morals police could refuse to submit to an internal examination, but an appeal to the magistrates was almost always refused. In practice, they had no choice. Josephine learned many of the horrific details of their treatment through prostitutes who had been detained in Liverpool, and from Garth Wilkinson, a homeopathic doctor who opposed the Acts and wrote pamphlets full of passionate invective against them. He had become 'an increasingly shrill Cassandra against the dominant intellectual and social trends in medicine'.[37]

In his 1870 pamphlet with the uncompromising title *The Forcible Introspection of Women*, Wilkinson described the examinations as 'steel rape'. The doctors were 'opening women's bodies with large glass instruments, or with large expanding steel instruments'.[38] Resistance to insertion made this operation extremely painful; even prostitutes, inured to unwelcome penetration, still hated it with passionate intensity. Wilkinson quotes a letter he received from Josephine, using capital letters for the following story from a Liverpool prostitute:

... the attitude they push us into first is so disgusting and so painful, and then these monstrous instruments, – often they use several. They seem to tear the passage open with their hands, and examine us, and then they thrust in instruments, and they pull them out and push them in, and they turn and twist them about; and if you cry out they stifle you with a towel over your face.[39]

Other witnesses endorsed these stories. Mrs Kell, the wife of a Unitarian minister, said that she had personally seen young girls 'with bursts of tears declaring that they would not be examined, and they have been kept in the examination house hours before they would submit, and then they submitted under various threats, threats that they would be ... sent to prison'.[40] Garth Wilkinson reported one additional, horrific, detail: 'To one menstruating girl violated, the doctor said that if she did not comply, he would declare her diseased, and send her to the Lock Hospital.'[41]

Women were sometimes able to avoid the examination by telling the magistrate that they were menstruating, but even this loophole was closed by an amendment to the CD Act in 1869. This allowed the authorities to keep them incarcerated for five days 'so as to prevent women escaping examination by claiming that they were menstruating'.[42] By the time this amendment was passed, even MPs who had misunderstood the purpose of the Acts could scarcely have had any doubt what they were about.

When diagnosed with the disease, the treatment they received was often excruciatingly painful and involved the regular application of astringents, as recommended by Dr William Acton. Garth Wilkinson was horrified by this and reported:

I have before me depositions of girls violated three times a week, and others every day. Syringed six times a day. Exposure before three doctors, one a young student. The injection used too hot. Exposure before four doctors. Injections principally of alum; this contracts the passage very much and so it is most painful: the girls cry out dreadfully and bleed profusely.[43]

None of this was talked about in polite society, of course, and few respectable women knew anything about the regime in the lock hospitals. Those who did were shocked by the idea of the internal examination, even though it had recently been adopted by some gynaecologists (administered, of course, in a much gentler way).[44] Josephine herself said, 'I had much rather die than endure it.'[45] Another opponent of the Acts, Mrs Lewis, said that she personally would prefer to go to prison rather than be examined, and that she advised threatened girls to do the same:

My Bible says 'Do unto others as ye would have them do unto you' and I would not have my person outraged in that way, I would rot in prison first, and I would not have my daughter outraged so.[46]

The police were integral to this 'outrage', since the CD Acts gave them unfettered power to pick up women from the streets. They did not have to justify their choice, and there was no guarantee that a woman arrested and subjected to 'steel rape' was a prostitute. The opportunities for policemen to exploit their new powers corruptly were legion. Garth Wilkinson spoke of 'the police lust of hunting and persecuting women'.[47]

Magistrates also colluded in this corrupt system, and one of Josephine's favourite anecdotes was about a prostitute who told her: 'It did seem hard, ma'am, that the Magistrate on the bench who gave the casting vote for my imprisonment had paid me several shillings a day or two before, in the street, to go with him.'[48]

One example of a girl who fought back was Ellen Vokes. She was a servant living in her employer's house in Farnborough who 'kept company' with a soldier.[49] This was apparently enough for the police to start a campaign of sustained harassment, telling her employer that she was a 'common prostitute', following her, and summoning her to the police station for the dreaded inspection. Luckily, she had the intelligence and knowledge to insist on her legal rights. She was able, with the help of her employer and a solicitor, to persuade a magistrate that she was not a prostitute. Her only apparent fault seems to have been that, in her limited free time, she enjoyed the company of soldiers. She was able to give evidence of several jobs as a servant and argued in court that 'it was most improbable that a prudent, honest and industrious girl, as I was proved to be ... would so soon sacrifice a well-earned, honest character by leading a life of infamy'.[50] She avoided the examination, but the vast majority of girls arrested by the police did not.

The Constitution Violated, 1870

~~~ Josephine Rouses the Country

During 1870 Josephine travelled 3,700 miles (mostly by train) around the country and addressed ninety-nine meetings.[1] She continued to give speeches to audiences of working men, as she had first done at Crewe. In going to the working class, she was following her instinct that the vast majority of ordinary family men would be horrified by Acts passed in their name. She roused them to condemn pimps, and the 'profligates' of high society, who would personally benefit from them. In Liverpool in March 1870 she told a men's meeting that:

> A friend of mine at an evening party overheard two gentlemen conversing in a low voice about the probable extension of this Act. One said to the other with evident delight – 'We shall now have the same facilities in London as we have in Paris'.[2]

So it was no surprise that her campaign aroused furious resistance from such men:

> I heard from a high authority in London that when our opposition was first made known the excitement was great. 'It is as if the depths of hell have been stirred', he wrote, 'so fierce is the passion of young men – and of some who are not so young – at the thought of being turned back from a career of vice which they had promised to themselves would be made safe and easy'.

She used these examples to underline her message that regulation was as much a man's issue as a woman's: 'The legislation we oppose secured the enslavement of women and the increased immorality of men.'[3]

At this Liverpool meeting 'men only, and of a respectable and steady class' were invited.[4] Josephine Butler was the only woman present, accompanied by George and a few leaders of the NA. It is easy to imagine the sensation she must have caused and the effect of her words, even though she made no explicit references to 'steel rape'. Some of the impact Josephine Butler made on male audiences can be attributed to the thrill of witnessing a beautiful, impassioned woman speak about an illicit sexual topic. John Addington Symonds, who encountered her in Oxford, even admitted that 'his reproductive equipment swelled'.[5]

At women's meetings her comments were less guarded and more personal, and the audience's response was more openly emotional. Her speech to more than 1,000 women at Nottingham in March was reported as follows, with the audience reaction in brackets.

(They would have known that the word 'outrage' was code for the forced examination by speculum.):

> [Mrs Butler] thought the supporters of the measure had been alarmed from the first at the resistance offered by the women. They knew that no law on earth could morally compel a woman to submit to an indecent and horrible outrage. ('Shame, shame' and deep moans.) ... Women were going to prison rather than submit to this shocking outrage. ('Quite right.') ... There were now girls in gaol who were sent there for a month because they would not submit to the outrage. At the end of that month they would still be liable to be outraged, and if they refused, they would have to go back to prison again, and might thus be kept in prison all their life. ('Shame, shame' and great sensation.)[6]

As she became aware of her impact, Josephine used it to dramatic effect, sometimes dressing entirely in white, so that it was said 'on the platform she is like an angel of light'.[7] She learned to use humour and sarcasm, as well as passion, to make her point. 'As an orator she touched the hearts of her hearers as no one else has done to whom I have listened', said James Stuart.[8]

Some of the women Josephine addressed were ready for her call, like her Quaker friends living in Clifton, Bristol – Mary and Anna Maria Priestman, their married sister Margaret Tanner, and friend Mary Estlin. Quakers were deeply committed to philanthropy and to women's rights, and were horrified by the CD Acts. On a visit to Mary Priestman and Margaret Tanner, Josephine discussed the 1869 Act with them. 'You can picture these two ladies and myself, sitting face to face, in gentle consultation', said Josephine, '"What shall we do?" One of them replied, "Well, we must rouse the country".'[9] Josephine was touched by their determination. 'So gentle, so Quakerly, yet convinced that we three poor women must rouse the country.'

Josephine became nothing short of a religious leader to these devout ladies. Mary Priestman and Mary Estlin went to Birmingham in 1870 to 'find for ourselves whether she was really one whom we could fearlessly follow in the dark path upon which we had entered'.[10] Addressing the meeting, Josephine appeared:

> ... slight, graceful, almost young and very beautiful. As she moved to the table she raised her eyes, weighed down with a look of inexpressible sadness, as if the weight of the world's sin and sorrow rested on her innocent head. Surely here was a Christ sent to save us from despair, was the involuntary thought that came into my heart.[11]

In an earlier draft of this account, Mary Priestman called her 'A woman Christ':

> Josephine's message was eminently one of deliverance: it was so that day, and it has been so whenever I have heard her speak: – she opened the prison doors of the soul, inspired her hearers with her own strong faith, and gave them Courage and Hope.[12]

At the Bristol branch of the LNA, the ladies gathered regularly for prayer, guidance and mutual support since 'the influence of religious fellowship and acquaintance is of great value, in overcoming the natural shrinking from a painful subject which cannot but be felt by everyone'.[13] It was often impossible to describe this 'painful subject' to others. Josephine told her mother-in-law only that she had been 'on a sort of preaching tour on behalf of a question of social importance of a rather sad and painful kind'.[14]

The Strength of the Opposition

Within a few months, all the major cities had NA repeal committees and many had ladies' committees as well. The early impact of the petition was so great that it was possible to believe that repeal might be achieved almost overnight. In March Dr Hooppell began publishing a weekly repeal journal, *The Shield*, in which speeches and papers were reprinted, along with correspondence from supporters. In April, Sir Henry Storks, an ardent supporter of the Acts, was forced to withdraw as a candidate in the Newark by-election after Dr Bell Taylor, Dr Worth and Dr Banks publicised his lurid views on posters round the town.

However, the strong current running in their favour soon encountered obstructions. There were a great many supporters of regulation. The political climate was also unpromising, since it was going to be difficult to change minds in a Parliament which had just passed the 1869 Act. However, an MP who opposed regulation, William Fowler, agreed to introduce a repeal bill into the House of Commons in May 1870. This was an early opportunity for the repealers, which they grasped with both hands, lobbying MPs and organising more petitions. They faced opponents of repeal under the strong leadership of Dr Lyon Playfair MP, who argued that, since the government wanted to stop 90 per cent of the forces from marrying, 'certain sanitary safeguards' were essential.[15] This was his description of the compulsory detention and examination of large numbers of women. He dismissed the idea that the Acts were an attack on liberty, saying that every progressive measure infringed liberty to some extent.

The debate had scarcely got any further when the Liberal government moved an adjournment, promising a Royal Commission on the Acts. The repeal campaign had caused a dilemma for the Liberal government, since the party was split. It opted to set up the Commission as a classic political delaying tactic, 'kicking into the long grass'. On the positive side, the Royal Commission could be seen as a genuine attempt to allow both sides to put their case. But Josephine and the repealers reacted with disappointment, since there could be no more repeal bills while the Commission was sitting. They realised that the campaign would have to prepare itself for a prolonged battle and feared the political stalemate that did, in fact, ensue.

Josephine went to London in May to meet the Home Secretary, H.A. Bruce, as part of a repeal deputation. She concluded that repeal would be 'a great struggle'.[16] The first ever Female Suffrage Bill was going through Parliament, and Josephine was in the Ladies Gallery of the House of Commons when the second reading was passed by a majority of thirty-three. She wrote to tell George that she had watched the vote with her friend Lydia Becker, who was leading the campaign. They 'came back early in high spirits'.[17] It was a great day for the suffrage campaign, even though the bill was defeated at a later stage.

Storks 'shot dead'

Sir Henry Storks tried to enter Parliament again in October, this time as the Liberal candidate for Colchester, a garrison town. The CD Acts were in force there, and Storks was an ardent supporter. He had previously commanded the army in Malta, where he had enthusiastically enforced a regime of prostitute registration and examination. Josephine hated him for his 'actual tyranny over the women' there.[18] The NA decided on the risky tactic of sponsoring its own candidate, Baxter Langley, to stand against him.

Josephine went to Colchester with James Stuart to campaign for Langley. The atmosphere at the election rallies turned very ugly, with NA speakers threatened by a mob led by 'keepers of houses of prostitution in Colchester'.[19] Josephine witnessed attacks on James Stuart and Dr Langley in which chairs and benches were flung at them, their clothes were torn and they were 'covered with mud, flour, and other more unpleasant things'. She herself was advised not to try to speak, and the police proved hostile, refusing to give her adequate protection.[20] Undaunted, she managed to get into a women's meeting by disguising herself. 'I had no bonnet or gloves – only an old shawl over my head – and looked quite a poor woman.'[21] The women 'listened most attentively' to her speech, but 'threats and groans' from the crowd of men outside could be heard and she was advised to leave through a back door.

Walking alone through the streets, she was turned away from several hotels and had to leave the one which did give her a room after the landlord received threats to set fire to the house. This was the first time she had encountered personal danger and she comforted herself with this biblical text:

> Thou shalt not be afraid for the terror by night; nor for the arrow that flieth by day; nor for the pestilence that walketh in darkness; nor for the destruction that wasteth at noonday. A thousand shall fall at thy side, and ten thousand at thy right hand, but it shall not come nigh thee.[22]

Her faith gave her a 'quality of fearlessness' which had also been natural to her from a young age.[23] Her grandson linked it to her experiences of the hunting field.

Josephine told the story of her escape in a letter to her sons, who were probably not reassured about her safety. Her husband, however, shared her conviction that she would come to no harm. Once, when her train was severely delayed George told her that he had not been anxious because 'I believe that no evil will happen to you, so long as you are engaged in this mission.'[24] He met her at Liverpool railway station 'at all hours and in all weathers' and during every speaking tour was 'careful for her health and strength, anxious lest she overtax herself, and offering her continual assurance that, should she ever need him, he would immediately come to her'.[25] Both Josephine and George hated being separated, something which had not happened before in their marriage, but their love, and the letters they exchanged, enabled them to endure it.

Storks was defeated ('shot dead') in the election, but the candidacy of Baxter Langley caused a split in the Liberal vote, with the result that the Conservative candidate won. As a loyal Liberal, this might have worried Josephine, but it did not. However, it gained few new friends for the repeal campaign in the Liberal government. The whole tactic of intervening in elections was of questionable value. Focussing on the issue during a by-election gave supporters of the acts just as much publicity as opponents, and there was a real risk that a Liberal seat would be lost.

A striking feature of the elections is the degree to which women were involved, despite not having the vote. Josephine Butler spoke at election rallies, the LNA held special women's meetings, and at an individual level women made full use of their influence on the men in their life. Josephine recounted an 'amusing' conversation between 'an immense workman' and his 'fragile' but determined wife:

> She was shaking her little fist in her husband's face, and I heard her say 'Now you know all about it; if you vote for that man Storks, Tom, I'll kill ye.' Tom seemed to think there was some danger of her threat being put in [sic] execution.[26]

The newspapers carped about 'electioneering ladies', but they may have been afraid of their political influence.[27] Women were refusing, more and more, to be shut out of the 'public sphere' inhabited by men. By modelling a woman's role in politics Josephine laid crucial foundations for the future. Her example inspired many women to become politically involved for the first time.[28]

The Garrison Towns of Kent

Josephine Butler proved to be not only the most powerful speaker, but the most powerful writer that the repeal campaign possessed. She found time to produce repeal publications from the very earliest days. We can imagine her train journeys being occupied with constant writing – speeches, letters and pamphlets. The first of these, *An Appeal to the People of England*, came out in the early months of the campaign and was republished in 1870.[29] Like Harriet Martineau, she wrote anonymously, calling herself 'An English Mother'. She held up the terrible example of the French system of regulation which had brought in 'wholesale and legalised indecent assaults upon women'.[30] She reported French officials as saying that 'the women betray strong emotions at first, but very soon they care *not a sou* for anything'. The system had unlooked for effects – prostitution in Paris had increased because 'men, finding a greater security, are less restrained'.

She proved the truth of this for herself, on a trip to the garrison towns of Kent. Her report gave indispensable ammunition to repealers, in words which they often quoted. In Chatham she noted that prostitution had become:

> ... more respectable, a recognised trade, having its legitimate quarters and sanctioned hours and appliances.
>
> I see now, as I never saw it before, how clearly it is in the interests of the profligate man ... to have this outward decency, this 'closing of the streets', this seclusion of certified women in certain quiet localities ... It is much more convenient to have these women kept out of sight.[31]

Josephine was appalled that Dr Sloggett, who was in charge of the lock hospitals, had informed the War Office with satisfaction that the '*under*-garments' of these certified women were now 'so clean, so well-mended, their persons so well washed! Those who consort with them need fear nothing ... These women never have the itch now, as they used.'[32]

When their examinations proved them to be free of disease, they were given a paper signed by the surgeon, and called it their 'licence'. Men asked to see their 'licence' before they went with them, and she had been told that 'there is a great rush on the first day'.

This system offered novel ways for men to intimidate and betray women. 'Some young and very boyish soldiers were overheard laughing and joking about having "diseased" such and such a one, and sent her to hospital.'[33] Josephine was incensed by the story of a soldier who had seduced his girlfriend (a virgin), tired of her, and informed the police against her. She had never been a prostitute, but was treated like one:

> She [S.J.] was taken up, signed the submission paper, in complete ignorance of its meaning, and was degraded in her own esteem to the last degree. Her father could scarcely get over it. Her mother was weeping. S.J. said she must now never venture out of doors, or she would continue to be treated as a 'common prostitute'.

The girls with whom soldiers formed 'attachments' were equally at risk, especially if they lived together. Soldiers were not allowed to marry, and so the woman was seen as unchaste. Josephine was told that they were frightened by the idea that 'a new law has been made and *every girl who goes with a soldier* must be taken up'.[34] These 'clandestines' were often hunted down by the police or the government spies who patrolled the streets. Josephine spoke out in their support – these women were faithful to one man and therefore no more likely to convey a sexual infection than a married woman. '[T]o my mind it is a horror, a shame and an injustice that they should be included among the prostitutes, professedly dealt with by the Acts.'

James Stuart accompanied her on this visit to Kent, along with other repealers, but she often went into brothels alone. In Chatham, she found 'a dull place, with more than a hundred women sitting round the walls and no form of entertainment going on. A crowd of soldiers were talking to the girls and selecting such as they found attractive.'[35] Some were hanging back and told her that they were expected to go to this place in the evening, but did not really want to. This was a new concern, reluctant young men and the peer pressure on them to accept the only entertainment on offer.

On a visit to the Chatham Lock Hospital, she discovered that the 'lady workers' (volunteers) were excluded and not allowed to give comfort to the female patients who were suffering in there. 'What work is more properly and entirely women's work than that of ministering to her fellow women ...?' she asked.[36] One of the inmates had complained, bitterly:

> It is men, men, only men, from the first to the last that we have to do with! To please a man I did wrong at first, then I was flung about from man to man. Men police lay hands on us. By men we are examined, handled, doctored, and messed on with ... We are had up before magistrates who are men, and we never get out of the hands of men till we die!

Josephine thought, 'and it was a Parliament of men only who made this law which treats you as an outcast'.[37]

She visited Dover Prison, where five women were kept in solitary confinement for most of the day, because they had refused 'the ghastly indecency, the shame and the pain which the Act commands them to endure'.[38] One woman had resisted because:

> When she went through the process the first time she had not been three weeks risen from childbed, and she suffered so terribly from the instrumental violation that she could not go again. She said, 'The man might have known that a woman in my state was not fit to go through all that horrible business.'

Josephine Butler concluded her account with this story, stating:

> I think it is right that the women of England should know distinctly whether the law makers of our country have enacted that women shall periodically be violated while pregnant, up to the time of delivery ... and as soon as possible again after delivery.

The Constitution Violated

The visit to Kent included 13 April, Josephine's birthday, when George wrote to say that it was 'hard to be long parted' from her.[39] He was about to join her for a meeting in Birmingham, at which he was a platform speaker, and suggested that they could go on to

Cheltenham and 'put a fresh wreath of immortelles [everlasting lilies] on darling Eva's grave'.[40] In June, Josephine was in Plymouth on George's birthday and was tempted 'to travel all night in order to reach home earlier', but he discouraged her.[41]

In Chatham, Josephine heard the story of Caroline Wyburgh, a 19-year-old girl who lived in one room with her mother, keeping them both 'by working at the most menial form of domestic service – scrubbing doorsteps and basement areas for a penny or two a time'.[42] Unfortunately she had been observed 'walking out' with a soldier.

Inspector Wakeford of the Metropolitan police roused her in the middle of the night and required her to go with him 'voluntarily' for an inspection. When she refused, saying she was 'not one of that lot', he threatened her with three months' hard labour in Maidstone prison. Her mother then pleaded with her to go. At the station she was tricked into signing a 'voluntary submission' to inspection, but took one look at the instruments laid out in the examination room and absolutely refused to go any further. She was strapped to a bed for four days and given only black tea and dry bread. On the fifth day she agreed to be examined if no instruments were used. However, as soon as she entered the room she was forced into a straitjacket and her legs were clamped apart. She struggled so hard that she fell off the bed and was badly injured. The doctor confirmed that she was, as she had said, a virgin – 'You have been telling the truth'.

After hearing this story (which was well authenticated) Josephine sat down to write a 180-page book, *The Constitution Violated*. In it she argues the case for victims like Caroline in language which was designed to influence every politician and lawyer in the country – it is unemotional, logically argued and carefully referenced. Even Benjamin Jowett, who thought women could not be intellectual, might have been impressed! The book is a careful examination of the way in which English law had, over centuries, developed a system for protection of the innocent and vulnerable which the CD Acts violated completely.

The 'violation' of the title has a double meaning. It is the violation of women detained under the Acts, and the violation of the original constitution of England, *Magna Carta* (which she calls 'Magna Charta'). The violation of women is a violation of the constitution, because Magna Charta forbids 'any proceeding on the body of an accused person unless after trial by jury'.[43] The CD Acts, of course, allowed a woman to be forcibly examined not only without trial by jury, but simply on the opinion of one policeman or police informant. She could be forced to agree to a 'voluntary' examination in the way that Caroline Wyburgh was. She could also be recalled periodically for re-examination and imprisoned for up to nine months if she refused to attend. These Acts, wrote Josephine, 'virtually introduce a species of villeinage or slavery. I use the word not sentimentally but in the strictest legal sense. Slavery means that condition in which an individual is not master of his own person [i.e. body].' If so, then all the arguments against slavery (which was abolished in 1833) could also be used against the CD Acts.

The Acts presumed that prostitutes are easily identified, but Josephine showed how difficult this was in practice – 'every degree of shade [exists] between the absolutely virtuous woman and the most degraded and evident harlot'.[44] The result was:

> The policeman and justice of the peace ride rampant at their pleasure throughout all
> that immense border land of humble society which lies between the confessed prostitute
> and absolute virtue ... The whole operation of the law degenerates into a mere hunting
> in the streets by policemen of women suspected by them of unchastity.

It was not just the streets – young women could be tracked to their homes simply because they had a soldier boyfriend, like Caroline Wyburgh. The most vulnerable were poor women whose families were dead or far away. There was a class issue here. 'Ladies who ride in their carriages through the streets at night are in little danger of being molested.'[45] Josephine pointed out that a poor woman's honour could be the only 'property' she had – once she lost it, she would be unable to get 'respectable' work or attract a 'decent' man as a husband. The most vulnerable of all were girls as young as 12 who, at that time, were legally old enough to give their consent to intercourse. Josephine quoted a case which had come before the courts, a servant girl of 14, who was sexually assaulted by her master, a man of 30. His defence was 'consent'. In this case the judge (unusually) found in favour of the victim and commented that:

> He had had to try a great many cases of this kind, especially where girls were servants, and where their masters, instead of protecting the poor children under their charge, had corrupted them; he hoped that ... outrages upon these little ones would be made an offence against law without any question of consent.[46]

The age of consent was swiftly becoming the most embarrassing aspect of the set of laws which enabled the men of England to indulge their sexual whims without fear of prosecution. As Josephine showed, these laws all stemmed from 'tender regard for the erring man, which is by no means extended to either the frail or the virtuous woman'.[47] They had been passed by a Parliament of men who were protecting their own. So husbands owned the bodies of their wives, making rape within marriage legal, and indifference to the suffering of young girls kept the age of consent as low as 12. Whenever Parliament had to deal with issues concerning sex and women's rights, its members thought first of the impact on themselves and their sons. During a debate on raising the age of consent, one member of the House of Lords said, 'very few of their Lordships ... had not, when young men, been guilty of immorality. He hoped they would pause before passing a clause within the range of which their sons might come.'[48]

The Constitution Violated was written at the end of 1870, during what she described as 'several weeks of bodily suffering'.[49] It is astonishing that she could produce a serious study of the law and politics in such circumstances, and even more amazing that she wrote it in such a short time. She must have done some of the background reading on her train journeys, and called on George's expertise in Latin for her definition of legal phrases. Even so, the publication of this book demonstrates Josephine's complete immersion in the cause, and her unique ability to fight it on all fronts – from writing, to speech-making, to administration, to networking and 'rousing the troops'.

She accomplished so much in that first year of the campaign that she had little time for her family, though she often longed to be at home. George's letters told her about their daily doings. In June he reported that 'George and Stanley are in the town for the Oxford Local Examinations. George has done well again today in mechanics and hydrostatics. Charlie has so got into the habit of bringing your afternoon tea that he has just brought me some, and is very loving.'[50] When Josephine was at home, Charlie sometimes helped her, as when he 'stood by my side busily stamping the many letters which I had to write'.[51]

Liverpool College was flourishing under George's leadership. According to the college's historian, the period from his arrival in 1865 until 1872 was 'perhaps the most distinguished, academically, in the whole story of Liverpool College'.[52] Flags and bunting were put out in 1870 when a former pupil won the title of 'senior wrangler' for the best mathematics degree at Cambridge. The Mayor of Liverpool boasted that he was the 'son of a Liverpool tradesman', and George produced a pamphlet describing the boy's career. It was a huge boost to the academic status of the college.

The campaign being conducted by the headmaster's wife, however, was an embarrassment, especially after a repeal meeting was held in the college.[53] Even though 'the Liverpool press treated us quite respectfully', according to Josephine, the governing body was concerned and George decided to adopt a lower profile and confine his own campaigning to the holidays. Josephine's frequent absences were blamed for the fact that the Butler boys often went to school untidily dressed – odd stockings were noted one day. She tried to make up for this by making a contribution at important times. She played the piano at college concerts, choosing popular pieces such as Mendelssohn's Wedding March and joining with a teacher to play organ/piano duets.

These were brief times of relaxation, when she could retreat into her family life and the comfort of George's protection. She was under severe stress, caused not only by her workload but also by the constant, wounding, attacks on her personal integrity.

INTERLUDE

Speaking on Public Platforms about Unmentionable Subjects

An indecent maenad, a shrieking sister, frenzied, unsexed, and utterly without shame.[54]

This was a journalist's description of Josephine Butler, one of the attacks on her modesty and respectability which targeted her deepest fears about the campaign. It was unusual for women to speak on public platforms on *any* subject, due to the culture of 'separate spheres'. A woman who breached those barriers in order to speak out about such subjects as sexually transmitted disease, prostitution and the 'outrage' performed on women had placed herself beyond the pale in the eyes of most respectable opinion.

Josephine took these insults to heart, writing in 1870, 'To a sensitive soul, already enduring much in such a cause, it is an added grief to be looked upon by the good and gentle as one who is wanting in the feminine attributes of delicacy and refinement.'[55] Her critics did 'not see the pain endured', did not realise that, as a 'tender woman', she was suffering even though she refused to give up the fight. 'The charge of immodesty' was, she said, particularly hard to bear. For Christian women, words such as 'indecent, prurient, shameless' were arrows pointed 'straight at the clefts in our armour'. But, she added bravely, 'we are not going to die of these wounds'.[56]

Her enemies, of course, saw the clefts and targeted them mercilessly. A typical attack claimed that 'the subject is a very unsavoury one for public discussion' and blamed the repealers who had 'dragged such ghastly matters to light, and paraded them before the eyes of the young and pure'.[57] It was as if she and her followers had created the offence, just by talking about it.

Josephine relied on George, and her prayers, to maintain her sanity. She was driven to the 'edge of despair', what she called the 'darkness' of the soul, by 'an inability to communicate the fundamental principles governing her attitude towards the Contagious Diseases Acts, combined with a terrible empathy for the exploited, the destitute, the outraged ...'[58] She was beset by a double bind – the need to speak about a taboo subject which directly concerned women, and the certainty that she would be howled down as a result.

At this time, and often in the future, she took comfort in recalling Christian women of the past who had suffered and endured. Marie de Pollalion, the wife of a count in seventeenth-century France, boldly demanded entrance to a brothel, 'rebuked some men of the Court who were there with a [terrible] severity' and rescued a young girl. Later, through 'constant prayer', she persuaded eight young women to abandon their 'profession of infamy'.[59]

Mary, the mother of Jesus, had kept silence after the angel Gabriel visited to tell her that she would bear a son, even though as an unmarried woman she had to endure the stigma of being thought 'unchaste'. 'Has any *man* ever tried or dared to think what those months were to her?' asked Josephine.[60]

There were times, she told an audience in Croydon, when women should speak out boldly and fearlessly. The CD Acts had been passed without public debate and middle-class women had 'been systematically drilled into silence' on the subject. Their menfolk wanted them to remain ignorant, and yet the topic 'more intimately and terribly concerns the whole of womankind than any other'.[61] When the House of Commons was debating the repeal of the CD Acts, she wrote to an MP demanding the right of women to be present. The 'propriety and modesty' urged upon respectable women, she told him, had been 'the cause of outrage and destruction to so many of our poorer fellow women'.[62] She saw the danger of the 'separate spheres' – and rejected them.

Speaking on the 'Duty of Women' to an audience of ladies in Carlisle, Josephine tried to sustain their fight for the LNA. She recognised the social pressures on them and the 'long strain of one painful topic'.[63] She told them that the struggle was bound to be long and punishing, since 'the crusade we are engaged in is for the liberation of our fellow-women from the darkest, cruellest slavery the world has seen'. She quoted an Anti-Slavery pioneer, who said, 'Only love enough and all things are possible to you.' She reminded them that Jesus had allowed Mary Magdalene to kiss his feet even though his disciples had told Him to send her away. She appealed to their maternal instincts, describing several examples of girls of '14, 13, and even 11 years of age who had been entrapped into signing the fatal paper and put on the register of public prostitutes'.

In these speeches we see Josephine developing the art of rhetoric – speech-making with rhythm, power, vivid language and a stirring climax. Even though we can only read them and can never hear her voice, it is easy to imagine the effect on her hearers. To an audience of women she spoke as a sister, knowing that they would empathise with her feelings just as she understood theirs. At the same time, she was also the reliable, trustworthy leader urging them forward.

Whenever she spoke, Josephine was careful in her choice of language; she did not refer directly to internal examinations and rarely used the word 'rape'.[64] Instead she chose words like 'forced', 'violating', 'outrage', 'degrading' and 'brutalizing', which conveyed her meaning and were sufficiently graphic. She was angry with repeal speakers who did not exercise her restraint, feeling that too much salacious detail would alienate audiences. The worst offender was Dr Hooppell, who was in the habit of holding up a speculum when he addressed meetings and 'minutely describing' its use. Josephine told her friend Charlotte Wilson that this was 'needlessly and grossly indecent. *He* says it rouses men against the Acts more than anything. On the other hand I know it has annoyed and repelled many good men. Surely our *moral* arguments are strong enough without us using means as coarse as this.'[65]

The Royal Commission, Bruce's Bill and the Pontefract Election (1871–74)

The Royal Commission on the Contagious Diseases Acts (1871)

In December 1870 the great inquiry into the operation of the CD Acts finally began its work. Josephine felt 'so miserable and angry' about it. To her, the facts were already clear and the Commission was 'a number of men ... in deliberation to consider whether it *answers* to violate women by hundreds!'[1] There were only three opponents of the Acts among the twenty-three Commissioners, and the LNA resolved to have nothing to do with its enquiries.[2]

The Commission heard evidence for six months and, for the most part, simply gave a platform for supporters of the Acts to air their views. The early witnesses formed an interminable parade of the Metropolitan police inspectors, doctors and nurses given unfettered power to detain, examine and treat women under the Acts.[3] Almost all of them denied that detained women had ever been treated harshly or unfairly. The common claim was that the internal examination was conducted kindly and that women never objected to it, appeared shamed by it, or cried out. A superintendent of the Metropolitan police at Portsmouth, Mr MacDonald, actually said what many other witnesses implied:

> He does not think the women have the slightest sense of degradation in being subjected to the examination. It is difficult to see how women should object to being examined in presence of one of their own sex, in the kindest manner by a medical gentleman, when that very night they perhaps allow a half-drunken ruffian to do anything he likes with them for a shilling.[4]

When witnesses were questioned about the examination of pregnant women, their accounts varied: an Inspector at Devonport said that women in advanced pregnancy were not examined, while the surgeon there simply said that he examined them 'with extreme delicacy'.[5] Most dismissed the claims that 'respectable' women were being examined by mistake, like Inspector Anniss from Devonport, who denied:

> ... a statement that had been made by women that the metropolitan police came into their rooms, dragged the bedclothes off them, and used obscene language to them ... he stated that it was an absolute falsehood, utterly without foundation ... such a mistake as going to the house of a respectable woman believing her a prostitute never occurs.[6]

One policeman, Captain Harris, admitted a mistake, but said that the woman 'brought it on herself by her levity of conduct'. The constables appointed to this work were 'selected with the utmost care' from married men nearing retirement (which may have been the aspiration, but was not true in practice).[7]

Many witnesses claimed that the Acts had reduced prostitution by closing down brothels and that they led to the 'reclaiming' of many of the women detained in lock hospitals. W.H. Sloggett, the Inspector-General of the certified hospitals, said that the number of prostitutes in Devonport had reduced from 2,000 to 500–600.[8] These figures were disputed, but both chaplains and matrons of the lock hospitals agreed that it was much easier to persuade women to give up prostitution while they were under their control. A matron at Portsmouth Hospital said that she tried to encourage the women to move into a home where they could receive training as a domestic servant. Detaining them by force was necessary because they got restless, especially when a ship or regiment arrived in town.[9]

The LNA maintained its policy of non-compliance with the Commission until it became clear that the voice of repealers might be drowned out by the flood of supporters. Among the first sixty witnesses, only twelve spoke against any aspect of the CD Acts. The LNA's barrister intervened to ensure that repealers were called to give evidence, including Josephine herself on 18 March 1871. She was buoyed up by the success of a 'Monster Petition', launched by the LNA, which was gathering thousands of signatures by the day. Letters from supporters, including a large number of working men, told her of mass meetings 'totally opposed to those low, grovelling, licentious, and harlot-manufacturing Acts'.[10]

When she appeared before the Commission, Josephine was subjected to several gruelling hours before a panel of harsh cross-examiners. Despite stating that the moral principle was the only aspect that interested her, she was drawn into debating the practical details, where she was sometimes on treacherous ground. The Commission objected to her description of policemen as 'hired spies' and she was unable to substantiate her charge. She stated that the LNA had 'abundant suggestions' for how the State could check male sexual 'profligacy' but when challenged could not produce one.[11]

The LNA had not gathered enough statistical and factual evidence. They relied on statements from individual women about their maltreatment which their opponents could dispute. Police witnesses had checked the women's stories and sometimes found them inaccurate. Josephine was presented with the case of a girl named Mary Hagar who had become a test case for the repeal campaign. Mary and her mother denied that she was a prostitute, but she had been arrested, forcibly examined and detained in hospital. Josephine had alleged 'gross misconduct on the part of the police' in a letter to the Secretary of State for War. However, an inquiry by Dr Sloggett had found '10 or 12 persons' who all testified that Mary Hagar was a prostitute, and a surgeon who had 'found her diseased'.[12] Sloggett himself had seen her 'sitting on the step of a low public house, half-clothed, dirty, and to all appearances a prostitute of a low class'. Josephine was forced to state that she regretted writing the letter to the War Secretary. However, she defiantly refused to concede that Mary Hagar's story was false, saying, 'I believe the woman and the girl in preference to Mr Sloggett.'[13] When asked for a further statement, Josephine bravely denounced the whole Commission:

> All of us who are seeking the repeal of these acts are wholly indifferent to the decision of this Commission ... [we] consider it an absurdity, a mockery, that any tribunal of gentlemen, however wise and conscientious, should be set to inquire into a moral question like this.[14]

Little wonder that James Stuart told her 'not to charge the Enemy in that bold way'![15] Josephine rejected the justification that the CD Acts helped to persuade prostitutes to leave their way of life, insisting that, even if 90 per cent of the women were reclaimed, '... you are stimulating the vices of men'.[16] It was impossible for the Acts to 'serve two masters' – their main objective was not to reclaim prostitutes but 'the providing of clean harlots for the army and navy'. She succeeded in getting the chairman's assent to that and his damaging admission that 'the object of the Acts is the maintenance of public servants in a state of health'.

In most evidence heard by the Commission, 'fallen' women were presented as the authors of their own fate. Josephine challenged this picture with a different, shocking, scenario: the rape of girls through incest. She had learned from girls who had sought refuge in her home in Liverpool that 'it was a common thing that their own fathers, in a fit of intoxication, had violated them'.[17] She painted a picture of 'five or six of one family' having to sleep together. Some girls were even sold into vice by their parents.

She argued fiercely that women needed work and training as an alternative to the streets and brothels. Here she was not aided by the otherwise sympathetic Commissioner, Robert Applegarth. He was a trade union leader who felt bound to question whether women should be allowed to work, since their lower wages destroyed the opportunity for some men to become breadwinners for their families. This was the common view of working men at the time, and it aided the supply of prostitutes.

Josephine's evidence has been criticised by one historian as 'overwrought, even hysterical'.[18] She may have floundered in the witness box at times, but she was kept there for much longer than she expected, and had not been told in advance to produce some of the evidence requested. Josephine told George afterwards that: 'It was an even severer ordeal than I expected ... I felt rather like [St] Paul before Nero, very weak and lonely.' Her support had come from God. 'I almost felt as if I heard Christ's voice bidding me not to fear.'[19]

Her fellow repealers produced convincing evidence for the Commission. R.B. Williams of the Rescue Society produced a notebook full of quotes from women on the streets – often ones who had tried to solicit him. They said that their 'tickets' (the certificate of examination) made it easy for them to attract clients. One talked about herself and her friends as 'government women' who went regularly for their examination even though it was a 'beastly affair ... you got to show your private parts to a drunken old beast in the presence of another woman, who must be a d–d sight worse than we are to stand by and see it all ... It's made a drunkard of me, for I can't never stand it until I gets half drunk.'[20]

Williams asked another woman what the difference was between 'exposing themselves to any man who came to have connexion with them, and showing themselves to the doctor'. He received a disdainful response – 'I should have thought you'd have known better nor that. Ain't one in the way of natur', and the other ain't natur' at all.' This was on the forty-fifth and last day of evidence in May 1871. Little wonder that the Commissioner, A.J. Mundella, spoke of 'six weary months on the Commission such as I hope never to pass again'.[21]

At the end of March, Josephine took the Monster Petition, which she called her 'dear fat baby', from Liverpool to London.[22] It had gathered 250,000 signatures from women calling for repeal. The petition was so large, reported Josephine, that 'its railway ticket cost me 17.6. [17s 6d] and it required 2 or 3 men to get it hoisted on the top of a cab at Euston'. MPs had been notified to expect its arrival and there was 'a great crowd of them waiting in the Lobby and about 100 inside the House'. Both sides of the folding doors had to be opened to let it in.

Josephine was thrilled to be 'allowed to stand quite at the door, almost in the House, directly facing the Ladies Gallery (which was crowded with ladies)', but not overawed. Boldly she told Cowper Temple, one of the Commissioners, that when she appeared before them 'my soul was deeply troubled at the sight of so many men with so base and low a moral standard as you seem to have'. She later apologised to him when the final report showed that he had been convinced by repeal arguments.

The Aftermath of the Royal Commission

Josephine was back at the House of Commons in July, after the Commission reported. She had prayed that 'God would be pleased to "confound their deliberations", and make the result like the confusion of tongues at the building of the Tower of Babel', and so it proved.[23] The Commission had found it impossible to agree. A majority report accepted the evidence of the police and medical officers 'that the Acts have operated beneficially on the health of the men'.[24] Its text was loaded with such double standards, calling prostitutes 'miserable creatures who were mere masses of rottenness and vehicles of disease'. It dismissed the idea that the men should be examined as well, since the motives of the women were so much worse. For them, 'the offence is committed as a matter of gain', while for men 'it is an irregular indulgence of a natural impulse'.[25]

However, the graphic evidence about 'steel rape' led the majority to recommend the ending of the compulsory fortnightly examination. Women should instead be encouraged to attend voluntarily, and those found to be diseased should be detained in hospital, as before, until they were cured. Shocked by the exploitation of young girls, they recommended that the age of consent should be raised from 12 to 14, and that girls under 16 should be sent to a home or industrial school with the aim of rehabilitation.[26] There was a sting in the tail, however – if voluntary examination was useful for 'naval and military stations', then it should also be available in any district 'peculiarly liable to sanitary disease'.[27] They recommended establishing hospitals and police regulations in those areas.

The minority reports dissented from some of these recommendations, but everyone supported raising the age of consent. With hindsight, the Liberal government should have immediately introduced a bill to deal with this issue, since it was the only one on which there was consensus. However, the main issue for the repealers was abolition of the compulsory examination. Josephine was taking advice from the Liberal MP James Stansfeld, a strong supporter of repeal, who urged the LNA to seize their moment and 'deluge the Government with memorials, protests and demands'.[28]

In July, a deputation of more than 200 repealers processed down Parliament Street and crowded into the office of the Home Secretary, H.A. Bruce, causing him to declare angrily that it was not a public meeting.[29] *The Times* claimed to be horrified by the presence of women in 'these disorderly and indecent proceedings'.[30] The women themselves, who of course were not unruly or 'indecent', saw this as a chance to put their point of view to Britain's 'Parliament of rich men'.[31] Bruce felt himself backed into a corner by the conflicting demands of the Commission, the repeal campaign and the government, which was bitterly divided on the issue of repeal. He took no decisive action for six months.

The Vigilance Association for the Defence of Personal Rights

Josephine's experience of the House of Commons convinced her that Parliament could not be relied on to legislate for women, since they did not represent them or even the majority of working men. A new association was needed, she believed, to keep a 'vigilant' watch on its activities. Ideally, it would employ a parliamentary agent to scrutinise proposed acts of Parliament and check 'what is done *after midnight* and in a nearly empty House'.[32] She never forgot that it was in this way that the first CD Act was passed.

Parliamentary committees 'composed entirely of men' examined issues about which women knew far more, such as the causes of infanticide.[33] Josephine noted that, 'a gentleman giving evidence before a Baby Committee, while dictating the precise sum which a poor woman ought to be made to spend on her infant weekly, did not know, when asked, the price of milk in London!' She was also very concerned about 'that tide of legislation on sexual matters now strongly settling in, which is so oppressive to women and so degrading to men'. The Vigilance Association* was founded at a meeting in Liverpool in November 1871 with Josephine and Elizabeth Wolstenholme as co-secretaries. She used it to remind 'our legislators of the old constitutional defences of personal freedom, which have of late been in several instances recklessly set aside' and to continue her fight for women's causes.[34] Women should be entitled to work, and Parliament was exercising 'despotic power' if it tried to forbid them to do so.

Bruce's Bill, February 1872

The repealers had appointed William Fowler MP as their leader in Parliament, but he had a daunting task, struggling with two opposing forces – the weight of support for the Acts within the House and the pressure from the opposition outside it. Josephine was not impressed by his efforts, warning one of her committees that 'Mr Fowler may be a little apathetic and he must be kept up to the mark'.[35] The first repeal bill he proposed, in the autumn of 1871, fell by the wayside.

However, the Home Secretary was finally convinced that 'it is impossible to maintain laws which have not the sanction of public opinion'.[36] Bruce introduced a government bill in February 1872 which appeared at first sight to offer most of what the repealers wanted, even though he had not (as events were to prove) given up any of his personal support for the CD Acts. He proposed to suppress brothels, to raise the age of consent to 14, and to crack down very severely on the prostitution of girls under 16. 'Bruce's Bill' also called for the repeal of the three CD Acts, which Josephine hailed as, 'a triumph ... a confession of weakness, an admission that something must be done to quiet the "wretched fanatics"'.[37] 'Fanatics', of course, were the repealers.

The text of the bill, however, destroyed those feelings of triumph. It introduced a new rule that any woman convicted under the Vagrancy Act of soliciting or being a common prostitute should be inspected while in prison. If found to be diseased, she was to be detained in a lock hospital or prison for up to nine months. This was a milder requirement than the CD Acts, since it applied only to women who were convicted prostitutes, but it was to extend to the whole country and not just the port and garrison towns. Josephine

---

* Please note this is not the Vigilance Association formed by others in 1885; see p. 159

rejected it straight away. The bill 'so far transcends in indecency the present Acts, as to give these powers to men for the surgical violation of women in every part of the United Kingdom'.[38] She explained in a long letter to repealers why this part of the bill must be rejected: it embodied the double standard since its object was 'to protect men from the physical consequences of their vices'.[39]

In her letter, Josephine was scathing about 'our faltering friends in Parliament [who] have descended to the wretched position ... of beseeching us to accept a compromise'.[40] At this moment, she burnt her boats. She could have supported the clauses in the bill which she liked and fought against the clauses she disliked. This was the line taken initially by the leaders of the NA, and even the LNA was split. All the MPs who favoured repeal voted for a second reading of the bill, and were angered by Josephine's attitude – one refused to speak to her.[41] Josephine was not swayed. She called on 'True Hearted Women' to petition against Part 1 of the bill.[42]

This was the first serious split in the repeal movement, and the strain on Josephine was immense. She poured out her heart in a letter to her sisters Hatty and Fanny, 'after wearing out our lives, in a 3 years' struggle ... we find ourselves *not* in prospect of victory – *not* advancing to overturn the Acts where they have taken root – but driven back to the position of trying to prevent their extension all over the country'.[43] Her prayers were 'dark hours which seem to take one near to Gethsemane – hours when I have scarcely know[n] how to endure the terror which seizes my spirit'. Gethsemane was the moment when Christ was alone before his arrest and pleading with God.

She took comfort from the company of Quakers at their annual gathering in London, 'a very solemn soul stirring meeting'.[44] She often found their silent prayer suited her best.

'The advancing horror which is gaining on us step by step' was averted.[45] Bruce's bill was too unpopular with supporters of regulation.[46] Realising the impossibility of passing the bill, Bruce withdrew it, with the support of the Prime Minister, W.E. Gladstone. Thereafter, the balance of opinion among repealers swung towards Josephine, but damage had been done. She worried that, 'our ranks have been paralysed. Our coffers are empty.'[47]

Josephine produced another very effective pamphlet during this battle. In *The New Era* (1872) she examined the system of regulation in Berlin, which had been used as the basis for Bruce's bill.[48] Despite being imposed with typical Germanic efficiency, so that almost 30,000 women were being periodically examined, the incidence of syphilis had actually risen. Regulation could be shown to have failed, and to be doomed to failure elsewhere as well.

The Pontefract By-election, August 1872

As the Bruce bill was foundering, William Fowler was about to introduce a repeal bill on 9 July when his wife died in childbirth and, grief-stricken, he temporarily abandoned the fight. Josephine refused to take a summer holiday; George, Stanley and Georgie went to Ireland without her while she went to Pontefract in West Yorkshire.[49] Erskine Childers, a Liberal who had administered the CD Acts as part of his job as First Lord of the Admiralty, was seeking re-election and the repealers had decided to launch a high profile campaign.

Among those gathered in Pontefract were Henry Joseph Wilson and his wife Charlotte. Wilson was a businessman and Liberal Town Councillor in his native Sheffield and a devout Nonconformist who, like Josephine did not like identifying himself with one church, and often attended Quaker meetings. When asked why he did not go to chapel more often, he replied, 'I so often want to move an amendment to the sermon!'[50]

An enthusiast for moral causes such as repeal of the CD Acts, temperance (anti-alcohol) and non-sectarian education, he was unflinchingly prepared to take up unpopular issues and defend them against all comers. 'A man of war, full of fight to his fingertips', said his Conservative opponents.[51] Josephine told his wife Charlotte, 'What a treasure your husband is to us and to the cause: his activity seems to be unceasing.'[52] Charlotte was herself another 'treasure' who became, for a time, a political aide to Josephine as well as a personal friend. She organised a women's meeting in Sheffield in 1871 to protest against the CD Acts and made her first political speech. Later she recalled, 'how appalled I was at the sound of my own voice – the first time I had heard it in a public hall'.[53]

Josephine, James Stuart and the Wilsons travelled to Pontefract with another new friend, the Quaker Joseph Edmondson.[54] They found out how unpopular their cause was when they attended a public meeting in an inn yard addressed by Childers.[55] When Henry Wilson tried to ask a question he was immediately shouted down by supporters of Childers. The chairman even approached him wielding an umbrella to force him to be silent. The violent and intimidating atmosphere increased in intensity, culminating in a serious incident the following day in the hayloft where Josephine and Charlotte were holding a women's meeting.

This is the incident Josephine describes so vividly in the prologue to this book: 'We women were gathered into one end of the room like a flock of sheep surrounded by wolves.' When the hayloft was set on fire, they received no help from the police, and James Stuart was almost thrown out of a window when he tried to intervene. Josephine later claimed that the Pontefract campaign had 'stirred up the very depths of hell', since the attackers were pimps and brothel-keepers – men who 'had a personal and vested interest in the thing we were opposing'.

Josephine and her friends carried on. During the night before the poll, the men hand-delivered a printed appeal to every house, and at dawn they all left the town. One helper, Algernon Challis, a 'working man of Leeds', walked almost 20 miles back home in darkness in order to work the following day.[56] Although Childers was re-elected, his majority was reduced from 233 to eighty, allowing the repealers to claim that their intervention was a success. Childers himself was shaken by the campaign, and tried to prosecute the men responsible for the hayloft incident. He even contacted Josephine to ask if she knew their names. In a parliamentary debate in 1875 he voiced his first criticisms of the CD Acts, and eventually voted for their repeal in 1886.

The Northern Counties League

At the end of August, Josephine travelled to Sheffield and stayed at the Wilsons' home for the launch of a new organisation, the Northern Counties League (NCL).[57] Another by-election, in Preston, was imminent and Wilson wanted to improve on their efforts in Pontefract. That had been a last minute campaign, but had proved successful in gaining press coverage for their arguments. A proper electoral organisation, with agents working in many constituencies, could deliver much more. Wilson decided to focus his efforts on the Northern Counties and became Secretary of the new League. He found a chairman, Edward Backhouse, who generously provided the bulk of its funding, and was supported by Joseph Edmondson, who took over as secretary in 1873.

Another 'electoral union' was formed in the Midlands, led by Harriet Martineau's nephew Robert, and the NA itself appointed two new agents. Josephine was delighted, telling Hatty that 'the quickened zeal of *men*, and the new electoral agencies have given us more hope than we ever had yet'.[58] The NCL became an important, but draining, extension of Josephine's activities and, after going to Preston, she became ill and was under doctors' orders to rest at home for at least three weeks.[59]

The majority of repealers supported intervention in elections, but by no means all. Some other 'moral issue' campaigns had abandoned these tactics because they split the Liberal vote.[60] The strategy which eventually succeeded for the repeal campaign was the more subtle one of working on Parliament directly, through supportive MPs. However, there was no doubting the publicity value of elections: throughout the autumn Josephine heard of people who had become 'convinced of the wickedness of the Acts' due to 'the disgraceful conduct of those men at Pontefract'.[61]

George's Rejection by the Church

Looking back on her campaign, Josephine Butler once commented, 'It seems strange that I should have been engaged in taking up the cudgel against men when my father, brothers, husband and sons have all been so good.'[62]

During its 1872 Congress, George attempted to address the Anglican Church on the subject of the CD Acts. Even though all the members of his audience were church ministers, some of them had 'been carefully trained by evil advisers to consider the recent legislation as an excellent thing', according to Josephine, who witnessed George's ordeal from the gallery.[63] His colleagues howled down his speech.

After standing in dignified silence for some time, the 'uproar' did not diminish and George was forced to abandon his paper. He later commented that the Congress had refused to face up to 'the great social evils among us ... It struck me as a grave omission on the part of congress that there was little, if any, reference to rescue work, and still less to the grand necessity of repressing male vice.'[64]

He published his intended speech with a preface reminding his fellow clergymen that Jesus did not turn his back on a prostitute, but said to her, 'Go, and sin no more.' They should recognise:

> ... their duty to look things evil fairly in the face; and not to reject a certain class of subjects as 'tabooed' because their existence conveys a reproach and a sense of uneasiness. It is their want of courage which has caused women to step forward and do the work which men should have done.[65]

Those displaying 'want of courage' included the Archbishop of York, an old friend of George, who wrote to criticise his speech. This episode reinforced Josephine's lack of respect for the established church. In an address to the LNA entitled *Sursum Corda* she pointed out that churches often failed to take the lead on moral issues and even supported corrupt systems. For example, the Church in America had supported slavery, just as the Church of England supported the CD Acts. 'What beautiful language, what subtle arguments have men brought, in all ages, to the support of the recognised indulgence of their own selfish interests and degraded passions!' she wrote.[66]

George himself was upset, but probably not surprised, by his reception. He remained on the periphery of the Church, as an ordained headmaster without a parish. To gain promotion, he would have had to place his career prospects higher than his conscience and his wife. There was no dilemma in his mind. Josephine depended on him and, with his support, pushed herself to the limit and beyond. Fortunately, George was not a driven personality, but enjoyed life in a balanced and relaxed fashion. He loved travelling and enjoyed fishing so much that once, on holiday in Germany, he 'forgot it was Sunday and went out to fish'.[67] He regarded the wine store in his cellar as among his most prized home comforts, and had many close male friends, who found him excellent company.[68] James Stuart said that he was 'a man of great good humour, and a very excellent teller of a story'.[69] He and George played badminton and practised archery together. He had 'the quality of stillness which Josephine so conspicuously lacked, and it was this which made him so necessary to her'.[70]

The 1872 summer term at Liverpool College was crowned with prizes for all the headmaster's sons, and in the autumn, Georgie went to Trinity College, Cambridge, with an Exhibition award. During his first year he won the Bell's Scholarship, writing out the entire notice in a letter to his father and sending him a telegram as well.[71] Josephine was away from home and saw the news first in *The Times*.[72] Apart from the academic honour, the scholarship was badly needed as George's income was only £800 a year and the expenses of a Cambridge education potentially ruinous.[73] Family help was also forthcoming: Georgie received small legacies from his grandfather John Grey and from George's mother (who died in 1872) and gifts from his Butler uncles.[74] James Stuart was delighted to contribute, since Georgie was attending his own university.

In letters signed 'Your Loving Goat', Georgie thanks his parents for a cheque for his bicycle and reports that his sports include sculling, rowing, walking, swimming, tennis and 'fives'.[75] He fears his father may be 'a little too hopeful' about his Classics result. He is concerned for his mother's health: '*Please* Melchis, don't write too much. If you are ever tired and doubting whether to finish a letter to some Birmingham worthy or not, think of *us* who want you to reserve your strength.'[76]

Meeting Gladstone

In December 1872 George Butler invited the Prime Minister, W.E. Gladstone, to speak to the boys of Liverpool College and attend a reception afterwards. George knew him well, as Gladstone lived at Hawarden Castle, near Liverpool. Gladstone was a devout Christian, involved in prostitute rescue and prone to taking up moral causes and campaigning as fervently as even Josephine could wish.

Josephine had hoped that he would champion repeal and was dismayed by his support for Bruce's bill.[77] During the reception, she took Gladstone aside and 'led him as *close* as I possibly could' to the subject of the CD Acts without directly talking about it.[78] However, she did mention marriage, domestic life, 'Christ's law of purity as binding on all' and even 'certain modern designs for alleviating physical evils' – by which she meant contraception. It is scarcely surprising that he was taken aback. '[H]is surprised look,' she said, 'makes me feel, rather sadly, what a loss he has in not being surrounded with sensible women.' Josephine never had a high opinion of Mrs Gladstone.[79] She had to stop talking to him in order to be polite to other guests, but his lack of positive response led her to conclude, 'hope *nothing* from Mr Gladstone as Prime Minister in respect of our Cause'.[80]

The position was more complicated than that, however. Gladstone actually shouted 'hear, hear!' when, in his speech, George candidly admitted that he was 'the husband of the President of the Ladies' National Association' and said that it was 'a great honour' to have his name associated with hers.[81] Gladstone privately supported their views, but was not prepared to speak out against the CD Acts in Parliament, because it was not politically expedient at that time to do so, and he had many other pressing concerns.

1 John Grey, Josephine's adored father. His support for the anti-slavery campaign inspired her with the desire to fight against social injustice to women. (Northumberland Archives)

2 Hannah Grey, *née* Annett, Josephine's capable mother. Her grandson noted, 'I remember seeing her at Dilston long ago and this gives very much the expression she had then.' (Northumberland Archives)

3 Milfield Hill House, where Josephine lived until she was 7. Hunting was the passion of her brother, George, who took over the tenancy of the farm. (Claire Grey)

4 This study by the fashionable artist, George Richmond, captures Josephine's beauty and radiance during her engagement. It was painted in London during the family's visit to see the Great Exhibition, 1851. (© National Portrait Gallery, London)

5 Dilston House, Northumberland, the happy childhood home built by Josephine's parents. The grounds were surrounded by 'pathless woods' and contained the romantic ruins of Dilston Castle and Chapel. (A.R.C. Bolton)

6 George Butler, Josephine's devoted husband and a great athlete in his youth. We have no photograph of him at that age. This one was taken in Liverpool when he was in his late forties and the Principal of Liverpool College. (Northumberland Archives)

7 Josephine's younger sister Hatty looking gorgeous in a photograph taken in Naples after her wedding to Tell Meuricoffre. (Northumberland Archives)

8 This bust of Josephine Butler was sculpted in Oxford in 1855 by Alexander Munro. It is strongly influenced by the Pre-Raphaelite style. As a friend, Josephine agreed to pose for Munro wearing an off-shoulder blouse. (Photograph Tate Images © Tate, London, 2013. Image by permission of the Mistress and Fellows of Girton College, Cambridge)

9 Eva Butler holding a dove, by Alexander Munro. It was sculpted after her death, using the 'death mask' which Munro took while Eva's body was lying at home. Josephine told Hatty that the mask showed 'the thick eyelashes still clotted with the gummy tears which were squeezed out when she was dying from the poor broken head'. Munro's marble bas-relief is understandably sentimentalised, but George described it as 'the most perfect *likeness* of our dear child'. (Conway Library, The Courtauld, London. Photo © The Courtauld)

10 The Priory, Cheltenham, where Eva died after she fell, aged 5, from the top banister rail. The Butlers moved there in 1857 after George was appointed Vice Principal of Cheltenham College. The Priory housed the school's boarding pupils. (Cheltenham Local and Family History Library)

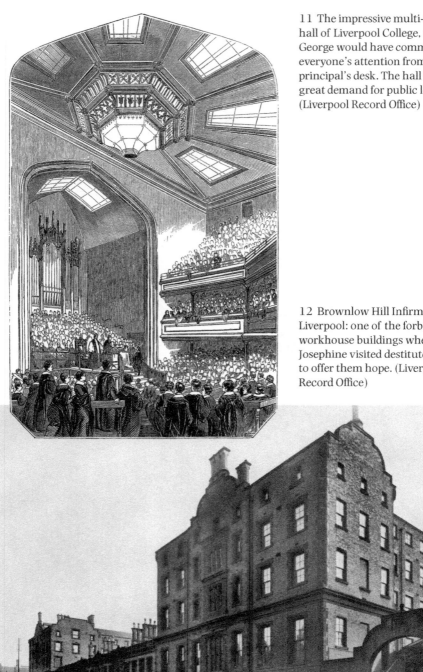

11 The impressive multi-tiered hall of Liverpool College, where George would have commanded everyone's attention from the principal's desk. The hall was in great demand for public lectures. (Liverpool Record Office)

12 Brownlow Hill Infirmary, Liverpool: one of the forbidding workhouse buildings where Josephine visited destitute women to offer them hope. (Liverpool Record Office)

13 The official portrait of Josephine Butler as the leader of the LNA, taken in 1870. Her clothes are elaborate and she adopts a serious pose, eyes downcast reading a book. This portrait conveyed the striking impression of a woman in a public role who was both intelligent and beautiful. (The Women's Library @ LSE/ Josephine Butler Society)

14 Harriet Martineau launched the LNA campaign against the CD Acts with her 'Women's Petition', published in the *Daily News* on 1 January 1870. She was a Unitarian and a highly experienced writer on political, economic and social issues, who used her journalistic skills to great effect in the service of the campaign. (Mary Evans Picture Library)

15 & 16 The men who supported Josephine Butler throughout her campaigns. *Above*: An informal photograph with Henry Wilson (centre) and James Stuart. (The Women's Library @ LSE) *Below*: James Stansfeld, who in 1874 became the leading MP championing repeal of the CD Acts. He expected to become the 'best abused man in England' as a result. (*Vanity Fair*, 10 April 1869)

In 1883 he voted in favour of suspending the compulsory examination of women under the Acts.

In these situations, Josephine quite openly made use of her femininity, beauty and charm. It is typical of her that she described Gladstone as 'certainly loveable. I felt, if I had the opportunity, I could *with ease* carry him to the deepest questions and plead with him as a woman can with a sensitive refined man, of intense feelings and keen intellect.'[82]

Josephine continued to be unwell in the new year, 1873, but toured the country from north to south, paying particular attention to Bath, where an election was due in June. The repeal campaign of speeches and letter-writing began early and she sent 5,000 letters to clergymen. Josephine had to warn Mary Priestman that she often lost her voice and could not make 'a popular speech such as one makes to a vast crowd'.[83]

In London James Stansfeld was so alarmed by her appearance that he would not let her speak at all.[84] Josephine's doctor had advised her to go to a warm country to cure her 'congestion of the lungs' and her friends rallied round to help. Robert Martineau, Henry Wilson and Joseph Edmondson collected £200, in £10 donations, to pay for the Butlers to holiday on the Continent.[85] Josephine was overwhelmed by their generosity. 'I feel as if I could hardly write about it, I feel your kindness so much', she wrote to Henry Wilson.[86]

In July Josephine, George and their sons travelled to Bavaria and the Tyrol, where they enjoyed drives and walks in the mountains and bathing in the lakes.[87] Josephine was entranced by the religious culture of the Tyrolese:

> Though their creed differs, they reminded me very much ... of Northumbrian or Scotch people ... The old women going to church on Sunday carried in their hands a prayer-book, a pocket handkerchief tightly folded, and a bunch of southernwood (old man), mint and marigold, just as we used to do when we were children, and went to the Methodist meeting-house at Milfield with our nurse Nancy.[88]

George and Charlie returned to Liverpool for the start of the college term, while Josephine, Georgie and Stanley lingered. Stanley was about to become a freshman at Exeter College, Oxford, his father's college when he was Public Examiner there.

The Defeat of the Liberal Government

Before their holiday, Josephine was in the Ladies Gallery on 21 May, when the House of Commons voted on a repeal bill introduced by William Fowler. The words of a venerable and respected MP, Mr Henley, greatly affected her:

> In this matter women have placed their feet upon the 'Rock of Ages', and nothing will force them from their position. They knew full well what a cross they would have to bear, but they resolved to take up that cross, despising the shame. It was women who followed Christ to His death, and remained with Him while others forsook Him, and there are such women amongst us now.[89]

She was 'full of thankfulness' that 128 MPs voted in favour of repeal. Forty-five MPs had changed their minds and only seven MPs in the Cabinet supported the Acts. Gladstone was one of those who abstained.[90]

This was progress for the repeal campaign, but it was nowhere near the top of the government's agenda and was never to get there. The Liberal government was struggling for survival and was defeated in the General Election of February 1874. Despite herculean efforts in their constituencies, at least sixty supporters of repeal lost their seats, including Fowler, the parliamentary leader. As Disraeli, the Conservative leader, took office, Josephine tried to find a replacement for Fowler and quickly fell ill in London. She had to be nursed by 'a family of "Good Samaritans"' before she could retreat home to Liverpool.[91] She lamented to Mary Priestman, 'the air is full of heaviness. This shade of Toryism is depressing in every way.' She knew that the struggle would now be long and, under the Tories, almost certainly fruitless.

The Attack on Women's Bodies

Although Josephine tried to restrain herself in public, she blurted out her true feelings in letters to friends, both men and women. The speculum was a 'hideous instrument of hell', she told Joseph Edmondson. She could not abide the 'terrible aristocratic doctors' who had increasing political power and imposed the vaginal examination:

> No words can tell what I and other women suffer at the sight of this violent desire on the part of certain powerful men to legalise by one means or another this hideous personal outrage ... It is coming to be more and more a deadly fight on the part of us women for *our bodies*. If these doctors could be forced to keep their hands off us, there would be *an end* to laws which protect vice and so many other evils.[92]

This horror of vaginal invasion lay at the heart of the campaign – every woman campaigner could empathise with it, even if she had never personally been examined with a speculum. This empathy made the campaign unique, and made women's leadership of it crucial. Josephine wrote in 1874, 'there are comparatively few men who have the strength of motive which women have to assail this particular form of evil'.[93] She understood what the prostitutes to whom she talked had gone through:

> ... simply because I am a woman. I know my own make ... in merely listening to their accounts I have pain in my back and loins from the very sympathy I feel.[94]

Josephine made no distinction between 'respectable' and 'fallen' women. This issue was about 'justice to one half of the human race'.[95] Her personal identification with 'the threatened woman, the endangered body' was 'something entirely novel' in British political debate.[96] For the first time, threatened women were fighting back.

By 1872, Josephine was openly writing about 'surgical violation' and the 'medical lust of indecently handling women'.[97] Victorian medicine had developed an obsession with the female reproductive system, believing that most women's health problems were linked to it in some way. Women's emotional problems and mental states were ascribed names like 'hysterical mania' (derived from the Latin word for the womb). Masturbation was seen as dangerously harmful to women's mental equilibrium, and was thought by some doctors to cause conditions like epilepsy. Clitoridectomy, the surgical removal of the clitoris, became a recognised treatment for this, and for other conditions like infertility until 1867, when medical opinion accepted the lack of any evidence for its value and Dr Baker Brown, its most outspoken practitioner, was expelled from the Obstetrical Society of London.[98]

The climate of medical opinion in which Dr Baker Brown could function was not erased so easily, however – there is no doubt that many doctors regarded women as dangerously emotional and in need of strict control.[99] One Victorian doctor who opposed this viewpoint wrote, 'the modern and multitudinous disorders attributed to the uterine system are wicked inventions, put forth to sanction unnecessary interference'.[100] He meant, in particular, 'this constant and general use of the speculum', to which some wealthy women had become accustomed by their private doctors. He questioned their motives, especially as they charged high fees for their examinations.

Doctors' supervision of childbirth had also become accepted practice. Mary Catherine Hume-Rothery, a supporter of Josephine's campaign, spoke of the 'corrupt and revolting practice of male midwifery' in her book *Women and Doctors*.[101] She was also opposed to compulsory vaccination of babies, enforced by the Vaccination Act of 1867. As a mother, she wrote, 'the preposterous and unnatural character of the operation flashed upon me by intuition. "Lacerate the skin of a healthy babe to infuse into its veins matter taken from a suppurating sore!"'[102] Josephine herself joined the Mothers' Anti-Vaccinationist League, a natural consequence of her dislike of medical intervention and possibly prompted by Garth Wilkinson, who opposed vaccination.[103] Like him, she also rejected experimentation on animals.

There were many doctors Josephine liked, and some who were her friends. Over the years, she consulted doctors for her heart and chest problems, but she was always happiest when she could manage without them. She had been brought up to believe in faith healing. A family story she told was that her mother, Hannah, once drank prussic acid by mistake for her normal medicine and sought help from their governess, who 'repeated to her the words "and if they drank any deadly thing it shall not hurt them"' from the gospel of Mark.[104] Hannah vomited up the poison and recovered quickly. Throughout her life, Josephine preferred to rely on strength of character, faith in God and the power of the body to regenerate itself, both for herself and the women she tended. At the Winchester Lock Hospital, for example, she prayed with girls who were threatened with inspection by doctors, and reported that they 'got well without any examination'.[105]

The New Abolitionists (1874–75)

Rallying the Christians

In 1874 the American revivalist Dwight Moody was turning the heads of congregations across the country. In civic halls, crowds gathered for meetings at which he claimed thousands of new converts. The atmosphere in these meetings was electric, built by the prayerful preparation of the audience, the hymn singing led by a massed choir and the stirring sermons, with the call to sinners to enter the 'enquiry room' for further advice and prayer.[1]

Josephine welcomed this 'Pentecostal breath of heaven', but demanded that it was used 'to bring down the strongest of Satan's strongholds to the ground'.[2] In a pamphlet which challenged Moody's limited horizons, she compared him unfavourably with the leaders of 'deep and fruitful religious movements', such as John Wesley, who were not afraid to 'speak the sternest truths, and to rebuke princes and leaders of society ... We want a far more stern, searching and uncompromising religious work ... [which will] boldly attack the gigantic sins of the day.' A successful revival, she wrote, should lead to 'the casting off of national evils and the overthrow of great instituted abominations', like white slavery.

Moody was quoting biblical texts to preach against women's activism, such as: 'Let the men pray, and let the women stay at home, adorning themselves with modest apparel.'[3] Josephine urged women, as well as men, to protest and asked why 'houses of infamy' were 'allowed to remain, and to exercise their contaminating influence, for a day, while thousands of people are assembling for daily prayer, asking "what must we do to be saved?"'

In this way, she challenged the conservative thinking of conventional Christianity and criticised a preacher who attracted thousands to his meetings. For her, Christianity had to be active and critical of the status quo. Christian missionaries should lead the way:

> It is on the religious sense of the nation that we must depend to counteract the wickedness of the governing class ... Nothing, I am persuaded, will save the nation but a revival of such fierce and God-like earnestness and intensity as shall make the present efforts small and insignificant in comparison.

The Vanguard of MPs (1874)

The 1874–80 Parliament came to be dominated by the clash of the titans, Disraeli and Gladstone, over the Eastern Question. Gladstone, now the opposition leader, toured the country speaking to huge audiences about the 'Bulgarian Atrocities' and the wickedness of a Conservative government which refused to condemn the Turks who had savagely assaulted an innocent population. Moral fervour animated the Liberal party – crusades were the fashion, and evil was in the rifle sights. Evil took the form of drunkenness, or the opium trade, or compulsory vaccination, or the CD Acts. Each had its campaign and its representation within the House of Commons. To unsympathetic MPs, these campaigns were 'fads' or 'crotchets' and their champions were misguided, rather pathetic, obsessives – certainly not 'men of the world'. The crusaders, for their part, carried on making their presence felt and planning for a better future.

After her initial despair following the election of Disraeli's government, Josephine was heartened by the support of these reforming MPs. Prominent among them was James Stansfeld, who was the most senior and experienced politician to become involved in the campaign.[4] As a member of Gladstone's cabinet, he had been unable to give active help whilst the Liberals were in office. Even so, he had 'been like a kind helpful brother' to Josephine in 1871, when the report of the Royal Commission was published.[5]

Stansfeld had been brought up as a Unitarian, a church with a strong commitment to social reform through political action. He had been trained as a lawyer but never practised, preferring to make his living from running a brewery, The Swan, in Fulham. This made him part of the 'drink trade' which was despised by many Liberals for encouraging the poor to spend their limited money on alcohol. The party as a whole, however, was more broad-minded and Stansfeld became MP for Halifax in 1859. He quickly secured junior government posts and was appointed to Gladstone's cabinet in 1871 as President of the Poor Law Board (later the Local Government Board). He made the decision to appoint the first woman Poor Law inspector, Mrs Nassau, despite fierce opposition.

Stansfeld had many enthusiasms in common with Josephine – both, for example, had passionately supported Mazzini and Garibaldi, the leaders of the Italian independence struggle in the 1840s and 1850s.[6] In June 1874 he agreed to become a Vice President of the NA and, at the LNA's Annual Meeting at Bristol in October, he made a public declaration of his passionate support for their cause, despite its unpopularity:

> I have made my choice – I have cast in my lot with these men and women ... who hitherto have led a hope which too long has seemed forlorn, and never will I desist and never will they desist from this sacred agitation until these degrading laws are blotted out from the Statute Book for ever.[7]

This was a wonderful moment for Josephine, which she celebrated by taking her son Charlie for a picnic at Avon Gorge.[8] Charlie was now attending Clifton College in Bristol. He had been rather homesick to begin with, but wrote to tell 'dear Meelchis' that 'I am changing my mind now'.[9] He missed their Liverpool garden, though, and sent Josephine detailed instructions for the care and planting of bulbs. He clearly saw himself as the expert and his mother as the novice in this matter.[10]

The press treated Stansfeld savagely. The Times, for example, deplored the 'defection' of a senior Liberal and his identification with 'such an hysterical crusade, in which it is impossible to take part without herding with prurient and cynical fanatics'.[11] Most objective observers thought Stansfeld had sacrificed any hope of a government appointment in the future. He himself had few illusions, and told Josephine that he 'hoped to be the best abused man in England within another twelve months'.[12]

Stansfeld proved his value to the cause immediately, by finding an MP to take over Fowler's role as leader of the campaign within the House of Commons. A long-list of candidates had, one by one, declined the honour.[13] Even Stansfeld did not offer to become leader himself, but persuaded Sir Harcourt Johnstone, a Whig baronet, to take on the role. Together they masterminded the Parliamentary campaign, but Stansfeld was their best orator, often making the most telling speeches in the House.

The Policing of Prostitutes in Europe

With little to do for the campaign in England, and reliable deputies in place, Josephine took the momentous decision to branch out into Europe. The ambition of her attempt to tackle the issue of prostitute management, in a range of different countries, makes this the most significant step she ever took. The regulation of prostitutes in Europe engaged her for the rest of her life, and consumed a great deal of her energy.

It seemed natural to Josephine, however, because she had a European outlook from a very early age. Visitors from Europe had frequently arrived at Dilston, and two of her sisters, Hatty and Eliza, lived in Italy. Josephine was a natural and enthusiastic linguist with a good command of both French and Italian. She loved warm weather, often complained of the cold in England, and had 'much faith in the restorative power of heat' when she was ill.[14] Her life from 1874 onwards was punctuated by regular trips to Europe, when holidays were combined with work.

Josephine had heard a great deal about the system in France, with its licensed state brothels and tight police regulation of prostitution. The CD Acts had been inspired by it. The *Police des Moeurs* (Morals Police) spied on suspect women and ensured that every prostitute was regularly examined and registered.[15] The Paris police were particularly brutal, terrorising the women they chose to suspect. On several occasions, public round-ups of women led to their incarceration in the dreaded St Lazare prison. In France (as well as Belgium and Italy), prostitutes were only allowed to solicit in the evening, between 7 and 11 o'clock. If they were seen on the streets at other times, they risked arrest by the heavy handed '*agents des moeurs*', whose pay depended on reaching a quota of women apprehended.

One licensed woman out shopping at 9 o'clock in the morning was arrested when she spoke to one of the stallholders at Les Halles market. The *Police des Moeurs* regularly broke down the doors of lodging houses and accused the female tenants of being prostitutes. One seamstress who had never prostituted herself was so terrified when the police reached her door that she threw herself from the window and fell through a glass roof. Despite her terrible injuries, she was not taken to hospital but to St Lazare prison, where she died two days later.

In her first *Appeal to the People of England* (1869), Josephine described Paris as 'ordered, bright and beautiful, like a magnificent whited sepulchre; but what a Golgotha within'.[16] In the first Ladies' Petition against the CD Acts, Harriet Martineau described the child prostitutes in Paris, who 'disappear as if through a trapdoor in the streets, or who are sold by vile parents'.[17] The repealers knew that state licensing of prostitutes extended to Belgium, Switzerland, the Netherlands and Italy, and that many admirers of the CD Acts in England wanted them to follow the European model more closely. Perhaps it would be impossible to resist the extension of the Acts in England if the system on the Continent continued unopposed. This worry intensified when a European congress of doctors in

1873 proposed the extension of regulation to every country and sea port under an internationally binding law.[18]

By June 1874, at the annual meeting of the LNA, Josephine was ready to declare that, 'this conflict is not for England alone. The eyes of Europe are upon us.'[19] She proposed that the LNA 'commence operations with a view to stimulate public opinion in continental countries.'[20] The LNA authorised her to begin correspondence with opponents of regulation, to set 'a spark to the smouldering embers' of opposition in Europe.[21] They soon discovered that there was scarcely any organised opposition on the Continent, and that Josephine would have to build the fire herself.

Investigations in Paris

In September all three Butler sons, now young men aged 21, 20 and 17, took a holiday in Switzerland. Josephine confided her anxieties about Georgie and Stanley's departure in her diary: 'Dear boys started for Geneva. I trust them to God. My fears cannot be quiet unless I trust *wholly*.'[22] When Charlie left two weeks later to join them she endured a 'sad night' when no telegram arrived. Then, '*relief at last*. How good God is. Letters and telegrams, and all in one day. All three are safe and well and full of affection.' She never wanted her private diary to be quoted in print, but such glimpses of family life are revealing. So often she seems superhuman, but here she is like every other mother who has no particular need to worry about her children's journey abroad, but cannot stop herself doing so.

This diary records her dilemma about Europe, 'to go, or not – tried to leave it all to God. Perplexities gradually pass away.'[23] Answers to her foreign correspondence 'come beyond all my expectations'. She had the names and addresses of possible contacts, and one of her letters yielded a response from Aimé Humbert of Neuchâtel in Switzerland, who was not in fact the person she had intended to write to. He encouraged her to visit. 'Bring among us ... the fire of that faith that can move mountains.'[24] Humbert and his wife were elderly and had fought many battles for social reform. At this stage of their lives they would have liked to rest but could not ignore 'an exceptional mission'.[25] Encouragement like this resolved her dilemma. She decided to leave for Europe in December 1874, despite the onset of winter.

To the LNA, her decision 'fell like lead on our already heavy hearts'.[26] They anticipated that Josephine's energies would be divided and drained, and that she would no longer be able to give day-by-day leadership to the CD Acts campaign. However, there were willing deputies for administrative tasks, in particular Mary Priestman to whom she entrusted her role as secretary. The Quaker Association for Abolishing the State Regulation of Vice paid Josephine's expenses, and she kept in close touch with them through letters (particularly to Joseph Edmondson) while she was abroad. The Quakers held a prayer meeting which helped her to relax:

> During those calm silences which I so much love in Friends' meetings, when God seems even more present than when any voice of prayer is breaking the hushed stillness, I did not think any more of the cold winter, long journeys, cynical opposition and many difficulties I knew I was going to meet.[27]

She arrived in Paris on 11 December, with Stanley for company.[28] Josephine had set out to conquer Europe single-handed, recalling her famous phrase, 'God and one woman make a majority.'[29] On the Channel crossing she found that George had written a 'Prayer for protection and help during a Foreign Mission' for her and placed it in her Bible.[30]

She had some contacts in the Protestant community in Paris, but otherwise was armed simply with letters of introduction – including one from the Foreign Secretary, Lord Derby, to the British Ambassador in Paris. She had discovered very few Parisian opponents of the 'Police des Moeurs' system, but put her trust in her own powers of persuasion and her ability to find dedicated supporters who could lead the fight in Europe.

On this first visit she made no speeches, but tried to meet as many people as possible. Shortly after her arrival she visited the novelist Victor Hugo, who had told English campaigners in 1869 that 'the slavery of white women continues in Europe'.[31] His support was helpful to her in opening other doors, but he was too old to be of practical help. The British Ambassador in Paris, rather surprisingly, introduced her to opponents of regulation, such as Jules Favre, a former government minister. Favre advised her that, to have any chance of success, she must win over influential leaders of the majority Catholic Church. However, Josephine had few Catholic contacts, since she could not overcome her dislike of their Church. She hated its hierarchal dictatorship, its doctrine of Papal infallibility and the fact that the Church had often supported organised prostitution. One of its medieval theologians, St Thomas Aquinas, had likened prostitution to a cesspool – a necessary fixture in order to drain away uncleanness.[32] Her first encounter with the only French Catholic priest she knew, Father Rogerson, was not encouraging.

In Paris, it was bitterly cold and melting snow clogged the streets. She had to 'insist on having good fires' in her three-room apartment on the Boulevard Magenta.[33] She reported to George that Cat (Stanley) was 'very loving and companionable' but a distraction rather than a help to her work, since he had to go sightseeing without her. 'I don't much like his being here in Paris, while I am at my work all day ... It is a horribly demoralised place this – we saw signs of it at every turn.'[34] She did not tell George that Stanley had been invited to a 'Bal de Nuit ... simple orgies where people dance nude'.[35]

Josephine's letters detail the meetings she held and the calls she received. 'The interest my little mission has excited is far beyond anything I had dared to hope ... It acts like fire', she told Stansfeld.[36] She was able to gain the support of people in a position of influence, such as Pastor Theodore Monod, who accepted her 'as a messenger from God'.

At drawing room meetings she spoke in French, forcing herself to make careful preparations, looking up words in the dictionary and memorising her arguments.[37] Persuading aristocratic ladies to listen to talk about prostitutes was difficult, but the support of Mme André Walther, who was 'quite a Queen' of Parisian society, helped a great deal, especially when she sat next to Josephine while she spoke.[38]

Josephine visited a house for former child prostitutes, which wrung her heart:

> I was shown a house full of some hundreds of little girls from 5 to 11 years old (400 I think) who were prostitutes FORCED to be so by bad men, victims, and my guides said, 'now is this not good. All these, housed.'[39]

The implication was that these children, though licensed prostitutes, were at least not on the streets. Josephine said very little more about this visit, writing to Edmondson: 'I dare not recall the horrors I have seen glimpses of today.'

Josephine wanted to confront the architect of this vile regime, the 'Prefect' of the Police des Moeurs, Charles Jerome Lecour. Her encounter with him is one of the great set piece stories of her campaign, and in her *Personal Reminiscences of a Great Crusade* takes up six pages, the transcript of an immensely long letter she wrote to her supporters.[40] On her arrival, she was struck by 'the grandeur of the externals of the Prefect's office, and the evidence of the political and social power wielded by that man Lecour'. She was ushered into 'an audience chamber ... more imposing than the room of any Minister of State I have yet seen in England', from which she could observe Lecour while he dealt with other visitors. She concluded:

> The man Lecour appears to me – and I tried to judge without prejudice – very shallow, vain, talkative; his arguments are of the weakest; he has a certain dramatic cleverness, and acts all he says with face, arms and legs. His countenance is to me very repulsive, although his face ... might be called handsome as to hair, eyes, eyelashes, etc. He has a fixed smile, that of the hypocrite, though certainly he is not exactly a hypocrite. He is simply a shallow actor, an acrobat, a clever stage-manager ... intoxicated with the sense of power.

He used this power to dismiss the claim of an elderly man who had come seeking mercy for a young woman in his family. Then he turned to Josephine:

> By this time anger had made me bold. I stood up before him, declining to sit. I told him who I was, and why I had come to Paris. He said he knew very well who I was. His manner became rather excited and uneasy. I continued to look very steadily, but not rudely, at him ... He became more and more talkative, as if to drown me with words ... he surely said much more than was prudent ... I asked if vice and disease were diminished or increased the last five years in Paris. He answered promptly, 'Oh, increased, they go always increasing, continually increasing' (in French, he does not speak a word of English).

He did not seem to realise that this admission damned his system. On the contrary, he blamed the increasing 'coquetry' of women, and even acted out a scene for her:

> An 'honourable young man' dining out, partaking *un peu généreusement* [a little too generously] of wine; a girl meets him, marks his unsteady gait – and then he acted out how she would place her arm in his and tempt him. There was no comparison, he said, between the two: the man was simply careless; the woman a corrupter.

Josephine asked him what the woman's motive could be, and suggested that it was poverty or because she was:

> ... a slave in one of your permitted houses ... He smilingly denied this and said 'No, no, it was not poverty, it was simple coquetry'. Then he said in a pompous and would-be impressive manner, 'Madame, remember this, that women continually injure honest men, but no man ever injures an honest woman.'

She could not convince him that his regime was both unjust and ineffective, and left feeling 'very sad'.[41] However, his encounter with Josephine made a strong impression on Lecour. He was 'clearly taken by her beauty and her charm' and invited her to visit him again when she was next in Paris. (She did not.) For ten years afterwards he sent her complementary copies of his books, pamphlets and magazine articles.[42] He also gave her *carte blanche* to inspect all the brothels under his control, as well as the St Lazare women's prison. She left his office carrying 'a splendid letter of recommendation, signed and stamped officially, which will gain me admission into every place I wish to see in connection with his horrible work'.[43] It seems he was so proud of his regime that he believed she would be won over.

In the South of France and Italy

George Butler and James Stuart arrived in Paris on 21 December, the day of her visit to Lecour, to take her away for Christmas.[44] She had confessed in a letter to George that 'this work in Paris is certainly the most difficult I ever did'.[45] She had been homesick enough to write, 'How is our very dear dog? I regret that I left home without a parting hug, the dear heart!'[46]

In a letter to Hatty she had complained of the terrible cold. Hatty warmheartedly responded that she had longed 'to be with you, that I might at least run after you with spirit-lamp and tea-caddy, or muscat wine, cloves and sugar to cheer you'.[47] Hatty was ever the homemaker. She had been afraid for Josephine, since 'every one out of England to whom I told your mission said you would be insulted and outraged in Paris and could not do any good'. Now she rejoiced that God had protected her 'with His shield' and 'laid your enemies under your feet!'

Josephine was so relieved to leave Paris and move south that she even enjoyed the eleven hour train journey to Lyons:

> It was the first real warmth and rest I had had for eleven days – with the large rug wrapped round me from head to foot, foot warmers, and an easy-running smooth express, kind fellow-travellers and no responsibility, I almost laughed to myself with joy![48]

The Butlers and James Stuart spent Christmas and New Year at the holiday home of their friends, the Closes, at Cap d'Antibes, where the weather was so warm that they were able to picnic on Christmas Eve. Then they moved on to Edith Leupold's home in Genoa, where a letter from Emilie Venturi told Josephine of a possible recruit to their European cause, Giuseppe Nathan. They met Nathan when they travelled to Rome, where George proved himself a delightful guide. 'He seems to know every stone of it, at first sight, and all about that stone, even to the disputes historians have over it!'[49]

While George and James lingered in Rome, Josephine went to Naples to stay with Hatty – a rare and precious opportunity for her to spend time with the sister to whom she was closest. Although she intended simply to 'see my darling Hatty and rest awhile with her in her beautiful home', she could not refuse a request to address a meeting about her mission.[50] However, most of her time was spent relaxing: her letters to George describe 'the most beautiful drives' in Hatty's carriage, followed by afternoon tea served by the butler, Giovanni.

In Italy and Switzerland

Taking reluctant leave of Hatty, Josephine went back to Rome in mid-January 1875. James Stuart was waiting for her, but she missed George's 'comforting and strengthening presence', now that he had returned to his work at Liverpool College.[51]

In Rome, the activities of the Italian Morals Police, although not as ruthlessly well organised as the French, were widely accepted. The 'Cavour Law' requiring prostitutes to register with the police, live in licensed brothels and submit to two examinations a week, had been passed in every state by 1870. Josephine bravely went alone to see Signor Vigliani, the Minister of Justice and Police, but was coldly received and felt helpless to influence him. 'It was clear to me from the first moment that nothing was to be gained here.'[52] Her failure to arouse support hurt her particularly because of her romantic view of Italy, derived from her father's enthusiasm for Garibaldi and Mazzini, the leaders of the liberation movement. Garibaldi had celebrity status with European Liberals, and both Josephine and Hatty idolised him. He actually wrote to Josephine in December 1874 to support her campaign.[53]

Although Josephine was disappointed by the response to her efforts in Rome, she had attracted the undying support of Giuseppe Nathan who, to judge from his letters, was a kindred spirit. 'I long to be of some slight comfort to these poor fellow-creatures of ours, whom cowardly man has taught even to despair of the salvation of their souls ... without purity and morality no nation can possibly advance.'[54] Nathan was 27, and grieving deeply for the loss of his wife after a few months of marriage. Josephine told him that there was 'work for his broken heart' and he saw this as 'a call from Heaven'.[55] A powerful speaker, 'full of Italian fire', according to Josephine, he travelled around the country to address audiences of working men and women, and established a committee to promote the campaign.[56]

As Josephine and James Stuart travelled on to Turin, Florence and Milan, they were continually aware that government regulation was corrupting the public sense of morality. It was 'a legal sanction' which 'produces public shamelessness', she wrote to Hatty. 'Fathers themselves introduce their sons to the houses of infamy, looking upon them as safeguards against imprudent marriages ... and all look upon them as institutions of public usefulness.'[57] To Hatty she admitted her despair:

> Going from city to city, tired and weary, always to meet with sharp opposition and cynicism, and ever new proofs of the vast and hideous oppression, is like running one's breast upon knife points, always beginning afresh before the last wound is healed.[58]

Josephine was consoled by the beauties of Florence and its Christian history. On a visit to the convent of St Mark's she spent a long time in the cell of the monk Savonarola, the scourge of church corruption in his day. In the Duomo, which was 'full of worshippers', she noticed 'several dear familiar cats, who rubbed themselves up against people's legs; pious well behaved cats!'[59] On this occasion, the devotions and traditions of the Catholic Church came closer to matching her mood, and offering her solace, than her own Protestant faith. The difference was starkly evident when she reached Geneva.

 In Switzerland

The theocratic regime of Geneva was the most moralistic in Europe, founded in the sixteenth century by John Calvin who believed that he and his fellow Protestants were the 'Elect', uniquely chosen by God for salvation. It was highly organised and deeply puritanical, since Calvinists believed that a sin such as prostitution, or even seduction, proved that the sinner was not one of the Elect. Such rejection left no room for repentance or rehabilitation. It was, Josephine remarked, a regime of 'cold, heavy Old Testament repression'.[60]

'Fallen' women were feared for the moral contagion they might spread. At the same time, the fathers of the Church were pragmatic about the need for male sexual outlets, and set up a highly organised system of brothels. In these the girls, often very young, were 'shut out from the world, without occupation, without interest in anything, cloistered in the twilight of filthy and infected rooms, reduced to a social intercourse consisting only of quarrels, or obscene conversations; and at the first appearance of revolt are beaten like slaves by the mistress or her bully'.[61] Their constant confinement, Josephine thought, made their situation even worse than the prostitutes of Paris. She was deeply angered to be told by one 'religious man' that 'they have *chosen* that profession, they are *determined* to follow it; they cannot be regarded any longer as women'.[62] She did not want to shake 'the ends of his cold fingers' but tried 'to remember that the heart may be changed, and that the man may yet repent'.

Her efforts in Geneva on this visit (she was to return many times) were devoted to meetings with potential supporters and a men's rally at which, it was reported, 'the pallor of her countenance, which bears the traces of earnest labour, the intensity of her convictions, the emotion of her accent, and the greatness of the aim she has in view, combined to produce a profound impression upon the audience'.[63] She made several lasting friends, including Mme de Gingins and a priest, Père Hyacinthe, who offered his services to her cause and 'spoke beautifully'.[64]

Her pallor suggests exhaustion, but Josephine had other Swiss cantons to visit, since the Genevan system was spreading. It was established at Zurich and 'they are fitting up their horrible examination houses at Lausanne', she told Edmondson. In Neuchâtel, fortunately, 'the tone was very different' and she had the support of Aimé Humbert, who lived there.[65] After Humbert's correspondence with Josephine, he and his wife and daughters had decided to devote themselves to the cause. Mme Humbert accompanied her to Chaux-les-Fonds, high in the Jura, which they approached through deep snow on horse-drawn sledges. The cold was so piercing that Josephine had to steel herself to endure it, but the meetings were well attended and supportive.[66] Neuchâtel was more receptive to her message than any other Swiss canton.

The Horrors of St Lazare

Before returning home, Josephine had unfinished business in Paris. Her journey from Neuchâtel was delayed by snow drifts, which she described in a letter to George, but she told him very little about her destination, the women's prison of St Lazare.[67] In fact she never wrote much about it, even in her *Personal Reminiscences of a Great Crusade*. Evidently it was too painful to record.

St Lazare combined the functions of a lock hospital and a prison for female convicts of all kinds, including those who had infringed the impossible rules of the *Police des Moeurs*.[68] Their offences were often slight, she told Edmondson, such as 'walking in streets which are forbidden and at hours which are forbidden!'[69]

As she approached the prison gates to inspect 'the whole world of misery contained within the walls', she saw a large prison van with high wheels and 'apparently no window at all ... like an immense hearse'.[70] Inside were 'only a few poor, weak, helpless girls, guilty of the crime of not ministering to impurity in accordance with official rules'. They were just like 'trembling caged linnets'. She had to beat on the gates with a stone to get in, but Lecour's letter of entrance smoothed the way and she visited 'every part of the building' and was there for 'a long time'. Most of the girls she saw taking recreation in the yard were 'fresh from nature's hand', not 'the heartless, artificial or hardened women of Paris'. Presumably the latter, indoctrinated in Lecour's regime, were at less risk of landing up in St Lazare.

The true horrors of St Lazare were described by Yves Guyot, who served on a commission of inquiry with the senators Edmond de Pressensé and Louis la Caze.[71] His overwhelming memory was of the smell, since the yards were covered in slops and sewage, and the hospital wards were badly overcrowded. The girls did not wash, since the nuns in charge would not allow them to undress for modesty reasons. Their treatment for gonorrhoea and syphilis involved the use of syringes which were never cleaned – an effective way of transmitting the infection. The prisoners' diet was tasteless and meagre, but the worst aspect of the regime was the punishment cells, where girls were held in straitjackets in windowless rooms with only a seldom emptied bucket for company.

Unregistered women were kept there until they accepted the licensing regime. Guyot also visited a dormitory for children who were kept in cages to keep them apart during the night. Lecour informed him that children whose parents or guardians could not be located were apprenticed to a licensed brothel on their release (such as the child brothel visited by Josephine).

Another visitor to the prison, Pauline de Grandpré, recounted in her diary (which Josephine saw) that when she visited the punishment cells 'the floors were deep in filth in which these noxious creatures crawled' and that she found workmen flooring over 'a large vault filled with innumerable skeletons'. The skulls were clearly those of young people 'whose despised corpses had been flung promiscuously there'.[72] This was the regime of which Lecour was so proud.

When Aimé Humbert joined Josephine in Paris, he visited the Inspector of Police, and was so depressed by his meeting that she sent him to the Louvre 'to look at the wonderful painting of St Marguerite, the patron saint of purity, trampling down the hideous dragon and looking so calm and peaceful'.[73]

Josephine herself found consolation in visiting a school, hospital and refuge run by deaconesses. The 'poor girls they rescue from misery and vice' were assembled to hear Josephine described as 'our friend: she has come to Paris to say that our bonds shall be broken'.[74] Josephine said 'a few words' and 'spoke only of hope' while being conscious all the time of 'the hidden agony of the heart' among the girls. She was encouraged by the support of Archbishop Manning, of the English Catholic Church, who was visiting Paris. He gave her a letter of introduction to the Catholic clergy stating that: 'This lady has undertaken a needful and difficult mission ... No Catholic who fears God can refuse to give his allegiance to the sacred cause which she has espoused.'[75]

In time, she received support from the Archbishops of both Orleans and Paris. She met Senators Le Caze and de Pressensé, who had already begun a campaign against the St Lazare regime, with the result that they became allies and leading opponents of state licensing of vice in France.

It was snowing again when she crossed the Channel on her way home. She wrote to Hatty, 'I suffered very much ... from violent headache, and cold, and sickness and cramp in my stomach and bowels but felt better after going to bed.'[76] She had often longed for Hatty on this trip and, having arrived in London, felt 'a long way away from you now'. But she was relieved to have left Paris.

~~The New Federation

Hardly pausing for breath, Josephine set to work to convince her supporters in Britain to create a new organisation, a federation of the committees formed in the countries she had visited to campaign for reform of the sex laws. She circulated detailed accounts of her meetings and activities abroad and spoke to a conference of supporters, organised by the Friends in London. She gave the hard message that repeal of the CD Acts was not enough – 'We should be merely lopping off a branch of the poisonous tree, so to speak. We should still have the old parent tree, with its deep roots and strong trunk standing in neighbouring countries.'[77] It was impossible for committed campaigners to resist such an appeal, although many assented with a heavy heart, knowing that they had embarked on the task of attacking a hydra-headed monster far more virulent than the CD Acts.

Delegates from Europe were invited to a meeting in Liverpool on 19 March which agreed on an unwieldy, unmemorable title, 'The British and Continental Federation for the Abolition of Government Regulation of Prostitution'. (On the Continent it was later shortened to 'International Abolitionist Federation'.) Josephine took the role of Secretary jointly with Henry Wilson, who reluctantly took the post until someone 'with more time' could replace him.[78] In truth, he had no personal experience of the European issues.

James Stansfeld, who had close ties to the radical Italian leader Giuseppe Mazzini, was elected as President and James Stuart as Treasurer.[79] Josephine ensured Aimé Humbert's appointment as the salaried 'Continental Agent', although she had first to deal with Wilson's characteristically picky demands that she provide a formal application with 'written testimonials'.[80]

'Sitting in Liverpool with a finger on each part of Europe', Josephine set about organising European branches and an international conference.[81] However, the enormous new workload, combined with the strain of the previous months, quickly began to tell. By April she had 'a painful cough, deep down, and spitting of blood and am so tired, I can hardly hold up my head'.[82] In May she told Henry Wilson that she was suffering from 'sleeplessness and bad headaches ... I found the preparation of the address from churches of Britain to churches on the Continent, in French, German and Italian, a heavy piece of work.'[83] Dr Carter had ordered her to stop work:

> I feel as if I was doomed ... I am filled night and day with terrors – among the worst terrors is that all my friends will blame me for dragging them into this foreign work ... I am not even to OPEN letters for a while.[84]

The nightmares of this breakdown are similar to ones she had endured before, for example in Cheltenham when she experienced 'abject terror and fear'. This time, it was clearly brought on by overwork, anguish about what she had seen abroad, and the fact that her friends could not share, indeed could scarcely believe in, her experiences. This was partly because she did not tell them all the details. She admitted to Edmondson that:

> If I were to tell you now what I saw in Paris, and what was the nature of things which were the real cause of my breaking down, you would not believe me.[85]

She was alone in a way she had almost never been before. She had been supremely courageous in going to St Lazare on her own, but perhaps she had needed not only a companion but also a witness to what she had seen. Deeply concerned, her friends now rallied round; James Stuart came to Liverpool to take over her correspondence. (By July she had acquired a secretary, Mr Llewellyn, with beautiful copperplate handwriting.) Josephine scribbled a pathetic pencilled note to Charlotte Wilson asking for her prayers. 'I long to be well for the sake of my beloved outcasts who few love as I love them.'[86] Charlotte travelled from Sheffield by first train the next morning to help her. Henry Wilson and Joseph Edmondson organised another whip-round to give the Butlers some money for a holiday, which touched Josephine so much that she could 'hardly help crying'.[87]

She was seriously ill, but so anxiously involved in the campaign that she never gave up work entirely. Nor was she free of other worries – Charlie was ill with a 'bad abscess' and was sent home from Clifton College in the middle of June.[88] Josephine had to arrange for him to travel lying down all the way from Bristol to Liverpool. Even though she was writing, 'I am ill and darkness sometimes comes', she took him on holiday to the Lake District.[89] The Butlers did not holiday on the Continent, as originally planned, but Josephine spent most of the summer away from home – three weeks in her beloved Northumberland in July with George, and a trip to Derbyshire and the Lakes in late August and early September.

A Voice Crying in the Wilderness

During her illness, Josephine carried on correcting the proofs of a collection of the speeches she had made, in French, during her European tour. This was published on the Continent in July under the title *Une Voix dans le Désert* (it was not published in English, as *The Voice of One Crying in the Wilderness*, until 1913).[90] In the opening paragraph she powerfully states that this voice is 'a woman's voice and she cries among the multitude in "this vast wilderness of men"'.[91] She thus links herself, a woman, to the prophets, including Isaiah, John the Baptist and Jesus, who were exiled to the wilderness before returning to proclaim their mission.[92] In the Bible the wilderness is a potent symbol of temptation and alienation from God. In Paris, Josephine felt alone in the wilderness, but she was convinced of her own prophetic power and proclaimed it in all her meetings. Her voice was 'the cry of women, crushed under the yoke of legalised vice'.[93] 'Oppressed women have needed to find this voice in one of their own sex. She is here, and she comes to proclaim uprising and deliverance.'[94]

To imagine Josephine saying these words to a rapt audience is to come close to understanding her power, and her readiness to assume the role of the prophet. She believed that this task was 'to show forth the mind of God on any matter', and that prophets could be women, as well as men.[95] God had chosen her to deliver fallen women from their tormenters, just as Moses was sent to lead the children of Israel to the Promised Land. No wonder she was, at times, overwhelmed by the responsibility. At the same time, she identified with the suffering of these women, to the point of saying that she, like them, had been dishonoured:

> The degradation for these poor unhappy women is not degradation for them alone; it is a blow to the dignity of every virtuous woman too, it is dishonour done *to me*, it is the shaming of every woman in every country of the world.[96]

Josephine Butler was both the prophet and the victim – just as Jesus was. She quotes his words: 'Inasmuch as ye have done it unto one of the least of these my brethren, ye have done it unto Me.'[97] This was a powerful motivation for Victorian philanthropy, but few took its message quite as much to heart as she did. Even fewer recognised that its implications were worldwide.

The first conference organised by the new Federation was held in London in May 1875. It was attended by Humbert and de Pressensé, whose speech greatly impressed the discriminating President, James Stansfeld. Within eighteen months there were branches of the Federation right across Europe, and active planning for an International Congress.

INTERLUDE

The Hour Before the Dawn

From 1875 onwards, Josephine Butler's time and energy was split between Britain and Europe. She was a leader of both the LNA and the Federation, and determined to do her best for both. However, the work on the Continent was both more demanding and more stimulating – there was so much more to engage her, while at home Parliament ritually debated the repeal of the CD Acts every year, and rejected the idea by large majorities. The Continental issues ranged widely across 'the horrors and hypocrisies of the sexual double standard'.[98] Josephine's campaigns gradually extended beyond the regimes of the morals police to include child prostitution, trafficking and the repressive social purity seen in its most repulsive form in Geneva.

Josephine was instinctively repelled by puritanical legislation. James Stuart painted a vivid picture of a discussion he had with her in the summer of 1875, 'while sitting out on the moors', about the punishment of fornication under civil law.[99] Josephine was opposed to pre-marital and extra-marital sex from a personal and Christian point of view, but believed it could not be enforced by law. Proof that it was taking place, she said, would require spies among the local community, and almost certainly the woman would suffer more than the man. The need for evidence might even lead to 'those hideous physical explorations which I consider in themselves to be an immorality'. In addition, the inflexibility of the law did not allow for forgiveness and, in cases of adultery, many husbands and wives decided to forgive one another. Purity was only possible through love, faith and morality, not legislation.

Josephine produced a pamphlet on this subject, anonymously, in 1876. *The Hour Before the Dawn, An Appeal to Men* is an impassioned sermon which pulls no punches in its excoriating attack on the mores of respectable middle-class men. She tells them that they are hypocrites if, after 'years of shameful wallowing in sin', they accept 'the comforts of home life ... smiled upon by pure women and loving children'.[100] It is unjust that society accepts such men as respectable, while rejecting their sexual partners:

> The lapse of a woman of the humbler classes, though that lapse has been induced by the pressure of poverty or the allurements of love, is made the portal for her of a life of misery and shame. Society drives such a one out of bounds, sets its hell-hounds on her track, and makes recovery all but impossible.

Josephine suggested that these women were more virtuous than the men because they, at least, were not leading a double life. Jesus Christ had said, 'The publicans and the *harlots* enter in the kingdom of heaven before you.'

She deals sympathetically but rigorously with men who are repentant and truly wish to change their lives. Their task will be impossible if they rely on their own will power, but with the help of God 'it is possible to be new created'.[101] The greatest of sinners, such as St Paul, became the purest of souls through knowledge of their own sin, and deep sorrow and repentance for it. Josephine had pondered and prayed about this subject – 'I speak to you as an equal, not a superior: as a fellow-sinner, a fellow-sufferer ... I hate your sins with a perfect hatred, but I love you: I claim you as brothers: your souls are precious to me.'[102] She recalls the 'years when my soul was in darkness on account of sin' – those years described in her Cheltenham Spiritual Diary.[103] Her published account here is as vivid as the diary, and just as personal. It concludes:

> The doubt, the dark misery, growing out of the sorrows of earth and the apparent waste of souls, are no longer able to drive me into sullenness and despair; for I have found the door of hope. I do not say ... that the perplexity is solved, that the worry is gone. Sorrow is with me still, the enduring companion of my life ... But I have found the door of hope.[104]

'The hour before the dawn', she explains, is the hour in which 'the powers of evil' will make one last overwhelming effort to overcome the forces of good. They will be eliminated by the arrival of the 'Son of Righteousness' and the dawn of a new day.[105] This is a vision of the millennium, often called Adventism, which anticipates Christ's return after a period of great evil, conflict and suffering.[106]

There are many examples of Josephine's belief in Adventism in her writings. Now that her sons were older, she shared with them her belief in the 'latter days', the final days before the reappearance of Christ on the earth, and the 'New Dispensation', the new rule of Christ:

> Dear sons, I hope you will learn to feel all that the Scripture says about the latter days, and wisely to compare it with the signs of the present times. To feel that the End of the world is not far off, is far more inspiring than looking forward to one's own death. When we can see the great truth that all evil, war, commotions, unbelief, as well as all noble effort, all pangs of heart endured by the faithful are ushering in the New Dispensation, or are signs of the rapid decline of the old, it raises you above the world, enables you to bear and do all things ... This is the secret of the hopefulness of believers, at a time when others, even thoughtful men and philanthropists, are almost in despair.[107]

Her own crusade, she stated in *The Hour Before the Dawn*, was one of the signs that the 'latter days' had come in her time – 'Throughout Europe there is the sound of the restless shaking of long-worn chains.'[108] The depths of evil she had plumbed, and the strength of the opposition to cleansing it, were symptoms of:

> ... A time of tempest ... for the dawn will not be ushered in calmly ... There is every sign around us of a preparation for a stern and bitter conflict ... But the bitter battle will be won: the light of day will fall upon all the dark places of the earth, now full of the habitations of cruelty, and there shall come forth, at the call of the Deliverer, the thousands and tens of thousands of the daughters of men now enslaved in all lands to cruelty and lust.[109]

In this new millennium, men and women would be truly equal.

The European Slave Trade (1875–80)

Mrs Percy and Government by Police

Shortly after Josephine returned from Europe in the spring of 1875, the English repeal campaign was handed a story which, though tragic, was a publicity gift. It attracted the attention of national newspapers and highlighted all the anomalous effects of the CD Acts.

It started with a dramatic letter to the *Daily Telegraph*, written or dictated by Mrs Percy, 'a professional singer and actress'.[1] She complained that she had been harassed by the Metropolitan police in Aldershot because she and her 16-year-old daughter had been seen in the company of soldiers. When two soldiers were observed to have stayed at her house till midnight, she was asked to attend the lock hospital, with her daughter. This step, she said, 'would have completely disgraced me in the eyes of all my acquaintances'. She had given up her job and left the town rather than submit.

Eighteen days later, Mrs Percy's body was found floating in the Aldershot Canal. At the inquest it transpired that she had returned to Aldershot and found work at the Queen's Tap, but was dismissed after the landlord was visited by police. A date was set for her examination and she had died the previous day, having told her friend Harriet that 'before she would go to the hospital she would drown herself'. She was deeply upset by the police campaign to label her a 'bad character', since there was no proof that she was a prostitute.

This evidence underlined the problem so often identified by repealers – that once a woman was stigmatised by the police, there was little she could do to escape them. If she left the neighbourhood she would forfeit her home and her job, which a widow like Mrs Percy depended on to support her children. Thus in order to survive she could actually be forced into prostitution as a direct result of the Acts. Mrs Percy became a martyr to the cause. Josephine even declared that she thought it 'a noble act ... to drown herself rather than be forced into infamy'.[2] The NA arranged care for her young sons, and Josephine and George offered a home to her daughter, Jenny.[3] In Liverpool, Josephine heard Jenny's story and published it in the *National League Journal*, while George read out her statement at one of the 'Indignation Meetings' which were held across the country.[4] Josephine also sent her agent Henry Bligh down to Aldershot. Bligh was a soldier who Josephine had bought out of the army in 1873 in order to work for her.[5] She thought his contacts would make him useful as an informer on the activities of the police in the regulated towns, and he proved his worth with his detailed reports on the Percy case.

Josephine's outrage at the activities of the police led later to the outspoken invective of her pamphlet *Government by Police* (1879).[6] Like *The Constitution Violated*, it argued that age old freedoms of the British people had been taken away by laws which gave the police far too much power. She contrasted local police forces, run by local police boards, with the Metropolitan police, which was answerable only to the Home Secretary and yet had 'vast police machinery' with a dangerous level of power. Her observations of the police in Europe highlighted the danger of giving them the task of regulating prostitution, which had 'so deeply corrupted the *personnel* of the police'. The Metropolitan police, charged with implementing the CD Acts, had become 'an organized body of women hunters, with the most frightfully arbitrary and irresponsible powers'. In particular, the power of the 'sanitary police' amounted to 'the forcible doctoring of the people'.

The Metropolitan police Commissioner made annual reports to Parliament, arguing the benefits of the Acts. In 1872, for example, the Devonport Division had reported: '142 women and girls were during the year saved from a life of prostitution by being led to give up immoral practices.'[7] These statistics of 'rescue' were meaningless, however, since no one could check whether these women really did give up their 'immoral practices'. The only hard statistics were examinations – '18,265 examinations of common women took place', for example, in Woolwich Dockyard. This was the reality of life in the subjected areas – not rescue, but regular appointments at the lock hospital and constant harassment. The daytime visits meant that women were labelled; one woman despaired that 'it was no use trying to reform now, she was registered as a prostitute and everybody would know what she had been doing, and what she was'.[8] The Acts locked them into a way of life which might otherwise have been a passing phase. Some women were hounded even though they had given up prostitution and had found a man to support them. There were so many of these in Devonport that for a time the courts were overwhelmed by women resisting the inspection.[9] The Inspectors were remorseless. Inspector Gregory in Aldershot terrified Mrs Percy, and Inspector Anniss of Devonport identified so completely with his role that he actually lived above the examination house in Plymouth. Government by police was a reality.

Work for the Federation, 1876

Josephine's health continued to be precarious, and she became ill again in October 1875, while organising a major conference to be held in Sheffield, for the Northern Counties League (NCL). She warned Charlotte Wilson that she was 'not equal to speaking at length'.[10] Despite herself, she delivered the annual report to the LNA, but then caught a cold and fever, with the result that George most untypically put his foot down, insisting that she attend no further ladies' meetings. His ban evidently upset Mary Priestman; Josephine had to explain that George 'naturally felt that if I was to pay with such suffering for every effort I now make, he must use his influence to keep me at home'.[11]

However, this did not prevent her speaking twice at the NCL conference in Sheffield's Albert Hall, the largest in the city. She also addressed an overflow meeting of women. Confident in her role as a public speaker, she made jokes about the weakness of her voice and provoked 'tremendous cheering' with the request: 'If prostitution is a necessity, I call upon Mr Cave, Colonel Alexander, and Mr Gathorne Hardy each to contribute a daughter.'[12] These Conservative MPs were prominent supporters of the CD Acts.

In December, Josephine had to respond to the difficulties created within the women's movement by her old friend Elizabeth Wolstenholme, a leading member of the Married Women's Property Committee. Due to her opposition to conventional marriage, she had decided to live unmarried with Ben Elmy, but the disapproval of her feminist friends, especially when Elizabeth became pregnant, caused her to agree to marry Ben in October 1874 before the baby was born.[13] However, Elizabeth's reputation was damaged, and her plan to return to her public roles in 1875 was opposed by leading feminists like Millicent Fawcett and Lydia Becker. Josephine became involved as a committee member of the Vigilance Association, of which Elizabeth had been the paid Secretary since 1872. Josephine did not join Millicent and Lydia in speaking out against Elizabeth, but she did decide it would be best, for the sake of the cause, if Elizabeth stood down quietly and voluntarily.[14] Her attitude has not always been understood and at the time there were rumours that she was 'making every effort to put Mrs Elmy into some prominent position'.[15] The truth is clear from her letters and the fact that Elizabeth did resign, to be replaced by Mary Priestman, who was recruited by Josephine.[16]

By April 1876 Josephine's work for the Federation was so 'heavy' that she was forced to take an office near to her home. A volume of her European speeches, *The New Abolitionists* edited by James Stuart, had been published, prompting new interest. Both Josephine and James worked hard to organise the first international conference of the Federation, held in London in May, with delegates from across Europe. Henry Wilson was in America promoting the Federation. Josephine boasted in a letter to him that she had dined with 'half the Cabinet' while in London, and that moral reform was 'the one question before them'.[17]

She was delighted that all her sons were able to attend the meeting. Stanley was still an Oxford undergraduate and Charlie was about to follow Georgie to Trinity College, Cambridge. Georgie had not quite fulfilled the astonishing promise of his first two years, when he topped his year group; in his final year (1876) he achieved a first class in mathematics but second class in Classics, a result he feared would be a disappointment for his Classicist father.[18] He decided not to try for a fellowship and took a post as a permanent examiner to the civil service commissioners in London, where he was lonely. He had few friends and missed his family. After seeing Josephine, he wrote to her asking for a photograph, giving minute instructions:

> Wear exactly the same clothes and hat as when I was with you at Euston station (with your black thing on over your dress) and get photographed like that ... I may not get so much out of spirits again, but if I ever should, I would look at your photograph and think of you, not as an agitator or anything great and grand, but as *my own dear mother*.[19]

The final comment shows Georgie's ambivalence about his mother's campaign.

After *The Hour Before the Dawn* was published in June 1876, Josephine returned to Switzerland with George 'to seek among the mountains the calm of spirit which we wished to possess'.[20] When George had to return to Liverpool in August, Josephine gratefully retreated to La Gordanne, the summer home of Hatty and her family on the shores of Lake Geneva. The next day, however, she was asked to give a speech to a mass meeting of the working people of Geneva – a daunting invitation. Josephine was fearful about her reception and terrified by the prospect of giving a speech in French at such short notice. Hatty spoke French fluently and promised to stand by her and interpret if necessary, but was ill on the day. Josephine did, however, have the support of Aimé Humbert and James Stuart. The meeting was packed, with many people standing outside, but she had a sympathetic hearing and 'was able, by God's grace, to deliver my message with comparative ease'.[21]

On their way home, Josephine and James visited Frankfurt and Brussels, where they were given disturbing information about the 'trade in girls'.[22] Josephine shocked the annual meeting of the LNA at Hull in October with news that the 'licensed houses' of Paris were supplied by girls brought forcibly from Belgium. Young girls, many not more than 13, had been 'crowded like cattle' into railway trucks at Liège station, and when they cried and refused to go, had their hands manacled behind their backs. 'They were thus taken *as slaves in chains from one brothel to another in Christian Europe*.'[23] This was Josephine's first report on trafficking, an issue to which she returned three years later.

Guyot's Campaign in Paris

That autumn the *Police des Moeurs* system in France came under unprecedented scrutiny and attack.[24] Josephine had stirred the embers of opposition and her contact, Yves Guyot, played a crucial role. As the editor of the radical journal *Droits de l'Homme* (The Rights of Man), in 1876 he began to publish terrible stories, including that of a respectable girl who was waiting for a train in Lyons when she was approached by three *agents des moeurs*, who dragged her screaming to a police wagon. She threw herself from it, crushing her legs under the wheels. A crowd gathered, demanding that she be taken to a doctor, but the wagon dragged her along the street to the nearest police station, where she was left lying on the floor. A doctor contacted by the crowd called a cab to take her to hospital. The police insisted on going in the cab with her, and as it passed along the banks of the Rhône, the girl pulled open the doors, fell out, and crawled to the river, where she threw herself in.

There was an immediate response when Guyot published this and similar stories. Humbert reported to Josephine that the furore was like 'a mine bursting under our feet'.[25] Guyot demanded that Lecour be called to account for arresting innocent women. However, Guyot was cleverly set up to make a false accusation. A man who appeared to be an *agent des moeurs* attempted to arrest an actress, who was a friend of his, as she left the theatre. She escaped by unceremoniously kicking him in the groin, and Guyot defended her reputation with high flown rhetoric in *Droits de l'Homme*. When the man was proved to be an imposter and not an *agent des moeurs*, however, Guyot was accused of 'having published in ill faith news which was false, and of a nature to disturb the public peace'. Summoned before a tribunal, the chief witness for the prosecution was Lecour, who put on his own theatrical performance. He assured the judge of his deep regret at the appalling treatment of 'a young lady of irreproachable reputation' and burst into tears as he lamented the slanders which he and his honest staff had been subjected to. Josephine's response was scathing – his agents 'were recruited from the very scum of society'.[26]

Guyot was sentenced to three months imprisonment and fined 3,000 francs plus costs, a debt which Josephine paid by making an appeal throughout the Federation. James Stuart personally took the money to Paris. Guyot's incarceration did, as he hoped, rebound on the unpopular right wing government. Growing political opposition led to the appointment of a Commission of Inquiry into the *Police des Moeurs* system. The Butlers, together with James Stuart and James Stansfeld, returned to Paris to give evidence to the Commission in January 1877.[27] Josephine believed that this inquiry, unlike the 1871 Royal Commission in England, was a genuine search for justice and truth. She and George addressed the first public meetings in Paris on this question, invited by 'red radicals' who were nervous about the possible response. Josephine received 'touching letters' afterwards 'from working men, from students and doctors, and from poor honest women who were there'.[28] George's involvement, however, was criticised in the British press, including the *Liverpool Mercury*, which accused him of betraying his position as a 'Liverpool schoolmaster'.[29] George contained his anger and responded with dignity, publishing his speeches to show how they had been misrepresented. However, he was now in his late fifties and feeling the strain of his multiple commitments. In Liverpool, he was deeply involved in planning the launch of the first College of Higher Education.

Guyot continued his publicity campaign after his release from prison, and the constant revelations about the excesses of the *Police des Moeurs* had their effect. Inspector Lecour was dismissed from his post in 1878, and satisfyingly demoted to the role of chief bell-ringer at Notre Dame Cathedral. However, the forces supporting the *Police des Moeurs* were very strong. Guyot and the Abolitionists succeeded in keeping their activities on the agenda throughout the 1880s, but 'in practical terms the gains were few'.[30]

The First Federation Congress, 1877

Progressive members of the Paris Town Council visited London on a 'mission of enquiry' in May 1877, when Josephine was distracted by her concern for her son Georgie's 'trying state of health, mentally and physically'.[31] She was also very busy preparing for the first Federation Congress, to be held in September in Geneva – a brave choice of location. This Congress was a far more ambitious affair than the London conference of 1876, since it aimed to agree resolutions for the achievement of moral reform across Europe. Its scale was enormous – 510 delegates representing fifteen nations, 120 papers and reports, and five separate sections (Hygiene, Morality, Social Economy, Preventative and Reformatory Work, and Legislation).[32]

Before the Congress started, Stansfeld discovered to his alarm that a significant number of delegates were in favour of Prohibition – making prostitution illegal. This was dangerous, in the view of the British delegates, because it would inevitably mean that prostitutes would work 'underground' and be far more difficult to help. Prohibition would hand the police even greater powers to persecute women, through the threat of arrest and imprisonment. Josephine took typically decisive action to prevent votes in favour of Prohibition. She recruited a number of extra delegates, from the LNA, to 'pack' the sections of the Congress most likely to cause trouble. The debates were long and heated, and at one point Josephine physically barred the door to prevent anti-Prohibition delegates leaving before a vital vote was taken. The LNA delegates moved between the sections, some ladies having to be prodded to stay awake when the voting lasted from 6.30 a.m. till midnight. But the objective was achieved – thirty-three resolutions were carried, and Prohibition was headed off.

The proceedings of the Congress were published, with its demands for the abolition of all forms of prostitute regulation and the creation of an international system to prevent trafficking.[33] Most tellingly, the Congress had highlighted the desperate inequalities for women in the workplace and the exclusion from so many trades that prostitution became the only option. The fact that delegates from so many countries had come together to debate these issues and agree a way forward was a source of immense satisfaction to Josephine.

The Repeal Campaign during Disraeli's Government

This progress was in wonderful contrast to the repeal campaign at home, which was becalmed and fruitless. Each year Stansfeld and Johnstone introduced a repeal bill in Parliament, in the hope that the speeches and publicity surrounding its presentation would keep repeal in the mind of both public and politicians. This bill became the focus for LNA and NA campaigners, who logged the commitment of MPs.[34] They were heartened, for example, by the fact that Gladstone and several other leading Liberals voted for the second reading of the 1875 bill. But it was still heavily defeated; a result which, Josephine said, 'tried me more than any illness'.[35]

At each subsequent annual vote the number of Liberal MPs voting in favour of the CD Acts went down, so the repeal argument was making progress, but the Conservatives were immoveable. One Tory MP, Henry Lucy, distilled the scorn with which the repealers were regarded when he defined an empty House as one in which 'Stansfeld was on his legs delivering his annual speech on the rights of his fellow-women'.[36] Stansfeld was a good speaker, but Johnstone was boring and neither could match the pithy brilliance of J.W. Henley, who told the House that 'it was no business of the state to provide clean sin for the people'.[37]

In 1877 Johnstone refused to introduce a bill because Parliament was preoccupied with the Eastern Question and a heavy defeat was inevitable. The repeal campaign struggled to cope without this focus and subscriptions fell. The only diversion was 'exciting Parliamentary by-elections', like Oldham, where the repealer John Hibbert was elected.[38]

When the repeal bill was restored in 1878, the LNA responded with a new petition which gained over 10,000 signatures. It is debateable how much such efforts influenced MPs, but petitions did indicate strong support in their constituencies. At elections this was important, but in the meantime repeal was an issue which most MPs could comfortably ignore.

A Time to Retreat, 1878

Josephine put a lot of effort into raising money in 1877–78: she told Hatty that most of it came in the form of small sums – five or ten shillings.[39] She was also delighted to have acquired a shorthand writer and wished she could lend him to Hatty for an hour a day. Early in 1878, Josephine took a break from fundraising and campaigning when she went on a long holiday to the South of France. Initially she had the company of George and Georgie, and hoped to begin a spiritual retreat after they left. She kept a diary which records her prayers and her frustration when she could not find 'sufficient privacy' in the places she visited.[40] Then she succumbed to a fever in Genoa and by 4 March was 'very ill. Prayed that I might live. Telegraphed to George. Edie [Leupold] came.'[41] Her telegram brought George within two days, accompanied by James Stuart. Josephine made a gradual journey home, with James as far as Mâcon, and George until Amiens.

On the boat to Dover Josephine read the psalms George had selected 'for comfort in separation'.[42] She was delighted to see all her sons when she reached London but, ironically, did not begin to recover until she reached her home in Liverpool. There she had 'a fortnight of most blessed retirement', the retreat which had eluded her before.[43] On Easter Sunday she and George were at Milfield where, instead of going to church, she prayed in the garden, 'my native place, full of hallowed memories'.[44]

On the anniversary of Eva's death in August, George re-read their condolence letters and said, 'I cannot understand how those who believe not in immortality can bear such trials.'[45] Josephine noted in her diary in September that they endured 'a long week of unmitigated mental suffering. I thought my brain would give way', when all three sons were in Switzerland and Stanley had gone climbing leaving 'no clue to his whereabouts'.[46] Josephine and George heard stories of accidents every day, including the loss of a Harrow teacher on the mountains, and could hardly sleep. George hovered near the post box and 'when the cards came at last, his eyes were quite juicy with thankfulness and relief'.[47]

⚘ Bouquets in Liège

By January 1879 Josephine was restored both mentally and physically. She wrote to the Federation committee to apologise for having done 'a minimum of correspondence' due to illness and to report that she was ready to 'recommence our work with vigour'.[48] The annual conference of the Federation was to be held in Liège, Belgium, in August so there was much to be done.

On a visit to London in March, Josephine attended a meeting of the Working Men's League for Repeal to support the election of Benjamin Lucraft in Tower Hamlets.[49] On another memorable day, she travelled on the underground with Charlie and James Stuart to attend a matinée performance of the comedy *She Stoops to Conquer*. Charlie took her to 'a little tea and coffee shop' opposite the House of Commons, before she watched the debate on women's suffrage from the Speaker's Gallery. Queen Victoria's view, 'we women are not fit to govern or to manage public affairs', was quoted as a reason to oppose women's suffrage. Josephine was disgusted:

> These words I consider neither queenly nor womanly, if the Sovereign can declare herself *unfit to govern*, her duty is clearly to abdicate at once! ... Her words were a sleight upon the English law, which permits a woman to govern.

The debate lasted until 1.30 a.m.; Josephine was so hungry that she did not wait for the division (which rejected women's suffrage by a majority of 114) but ran to her hotel where Stanley, who was staying with her, had left out a bun and some water.

The Butlers spent July in Coblenz, Germany, before going to Liège, in a heavily industrialised part of Belgium. The conference here proved, in Josephine's opinion, to be one of the Federation's most 'brilliant successes'.[50] Since the contentious Geneva Congress, delegates had accepted that the essential principle of their cause was 'the defence of individual liberty and right'. She knew that 'absolute principles' like this were the best means of uniting a widespread movement: they were 'our best security against inconsistency'. At public meetings the citizens were warned 'you are not free ... Paris, Brussels and your fine city of Liège are not free so long as any woman can be deprived of her civil rights at the caprice or tyranny of a police agent, or through the denunciation of a scoundrel'.

Josephine visited the Maison Hospitalière, which she called 'a true child of the Federation', because it was modelled on her own Industrial Home in Liverpool.[51] One of the women's meetings was addressed by four female speakers representing different nations. They prepared their speeches together in their hotel with Madame de Morsier correcting the French.[52] The hall was packed, with an extra audience listening outside the windows, and the speakers struggled to leave at the end, due to women asking questions and holding their hands.[53]

On the last night of the conference, there was an audience of 700–900 for a public meeting chaired by Aimé Humbert. Afterwards, Josephine remembered their visit to Seraing, the largest foundry in Europe, where English delegates addressed the workmen, and the friendly atmosphere at Chenée where they sang hymns together in chapel. The experience of 'uninhibited friendliness' among a group of men and women from different nations and religions was unprecedented and inspiring.[54] Lasting friendships were formed and Josephine received a bouquet of roses every day.[55]

The following year, at Josephine's request, Cardinal Manning informed the Pope that an International Congress of the Federation would be held in Italy. As a result, the Catholic press publicised the Congress and backed the principles of the Federation.[56] Organised by Giuseppe Nathan and the Italian committee, the Congress was held in September 1880 in Genoa's magnificent Opera House. On the final morning, the city's huge central piazza was thronged with delegations from across Italy. The resolutions of the Congress were read from a balcony and 'greeted with deafening cheers', as Josephine reported with delight.[57] Brusco Onnis, 'the oldest living friend of Mazzini' addressed the crowd and Garibaldi himself, disabled with rheumatism, drove through the city and stopped outside the Butlers' hotel. 'I think he is asking for you, mother', said Charlie and as she approached the window, Garibaldi raised his hand to her.[58] Giuseppe Nathan died a few months after the Congress, aged only 33; Josephine concluded sadly that he 'wore himself out in the cause'.

Social Purity

Nathan had told Josephine that he regarded the work of the Social Purity Alliance (founded in 1873) as 'noblest among the noble. To talk of purity is well, to lead a pure life is better, but it is best of all to oppose impurity with all the powers of heart and intellect bestowed on us by God.'[59]

Male purity became an increasing feature of Josephine's own writing and speeches after she had published *The Hour Before the Dawn*. She made a speech on purity to Cambridge undergraduates in 1879, when Charlie was studying there. It cannot have been easy to address young, single men on this subject, but she wanted them to experience 'moral enterprises' and become active members of the Purity movement.[60] It is unlikely that these students had previously heard a woman speaker, demanding that 'the woman's voice should be heard in this matter'.[61] A few might have read *The Hour Before the Dawn*.[62]

Josephine launched straight into a demolition of the idea that 'sowing wild oats' was acceptable for young men. On the contrary, a cruel double standard was created because 'a large section of female society' had to be reserved 'to minister to the irregularities of the excusable man'.[63] She pointed out that men who behaved like this were less likely to make good husbands and even mentioned the danger of bringing 'the hideous morbid fruits of his former impurity' (syphilis or gonorrhoea) into the marriage bed. It is impossible to know how many of them took her advice, but she forced them to consider the feelings of the 'fallen' woman. They may also have been ignorant of the long-term dangers of sexually transmitted disease. She was probably preaching mostly to the converted, but her suggestion that students should spend less time chatting to their friends and more time 'in communion' with God still seems impossibly idealistic.[64]

On a later occasion Josephine bravely went to Oxford to canvass support among the professors and clerics there, including some who 'displayed venomous hostility' to her arguments.[65] They included Professor Jowett, who banned the formation of a branch of the Social Purity League.[66] She told a startled Dr Talbot, the warden of Keble College, that she received letters from his students 'beseeching me to give them instruction ... on this great social problem', with the result that he took action to educate them in social purity. Talbot had begun by saying to her, 'but do you really think the sin is equal in men and women?' She felt that many of these men 'thought of me like Canon Liddon as "that dreadful woman Mrs Butler"'.

ᴺᴱᴼ English Girls Trafficked to Belgium

In 1879, Josephine became deeply involved in the issue of trafficking, 'the white slave trade', when her young Quaker publisher, Alfred Dyer, secured proof that young English women were being lured to Brussels with the promise of employment, and then incarcerated in brothels.[67] British girls were regarded as fair game because the law allowed them to become prostitutes once they had reached 13, the age of consent, while on the Continent prostitution was illegal under the age of 21. British girls over 16, unless they were heiresses, had no legal protection against abduction with intent to seduce. Girls under 16 without a parent or guardian had no protection at all. Josephine commented, 'Thus the most helpless of orphans ... are not considered proper objects for the legal protection of the State ... Who can wonder that a brisk trade is driven in their bodies and souls?'[68]

The first girl Dyer heard about was Ellen Newland, who had been lured to Brussels on the promise of marriage and then imprisoned in a brothel. She had been given a false name, registered as an official prostitute, and was 'forced continually to submit her person to the last indignity that can be inflicted on a woman'.[69] Believing that 'she was as much a slave as any negro upon Virginian soil', Dyer told her story to Josephine, who put him in touch with one of her Brussels contacts, the lawyer Alexis Spingard.[70]

He managed to find Ellen at 22 rue St Laurent, but was unable to rescue her. When Ellen was moved to hospital to be treated for syphilis, she secured the help of Pastor Leonard Anet in escaping to London. Dyer met her, corroborated her story and published it in a letter to London newspapers on 2 January 1880.

Dyer's account was attacked as sensationalist and false, and the Brussels police strongly denied that any girl could be registered as a prostitute against her will. Dyer decided to seek further proof by making his own investigations in Brussels. Together with Josephine's friends Benjamin Scott, who was the Chamberlain of London, and the Quaker banker George Gillett, he formed a London committee to campaign against the 'Traffic in British Girls, for Purposes of Continental Prostitution'.[71] Dyer and Gillett set off for Brussels in February 1880 to join Alexis Spingard.

Posing as potential clients (which Dyer found difficult, especially when, as a total abstainer, he was offered wine) they visited a number of licensed brothels and met English girls there. They quickly discovered a common pattern – English women were being tricked by attractive job offers into going to Belgium. Some may have known they were going to be prostitutes, but not about the conditions, which kept them in virtual slavery. A girl's clothes were removed on arrival and she was given 'a *peignoir*, a piece of tulle' to wear instead.[72] In this translucent nightgown she could not go outside, and was charged 60 francs for it, far more than it was worth. She also had to pay for a daily hairdresser and her washing – expenditure which exceeded her earnings. Thus her debt tied her to the brothel forever. If she tried to escape, she was charged with theft. The brothel-keeper enticed her into registering as a prostitute with a false name and birth certificate; this ensured that her identity was destroyed, so it became almost impossible for friends to find and rescue her.

In the lock hospital of St Pierre, Dyer and Gillett found Adeline Tanner, terrified and in horrific pain from vaginal surgery performed by the doctors there.[73] The terrible facts of her case gradually emerged. She was the 19-year-old daughter of a commercial traveller, well brought up, but forced to go into domestic service after her father died. Her head was turned by a chance encounter with two traffickers, John Sallecartes and Edouard Roger, who offered her the chance of a better life in Paris.[74]

Once on the boat she was in their hands, and found herself imprisoned in Roger's Brussels brothel, 3 rue des Commerçants. Two other girls, Emily Ellen and Lydia King, were abducted there at the same time. The following day they were tricked into registering as prostitutes, using false ages and names. Adeline, however, was physically unfit for prostitution owing, as Josephine later explained in a letter to her friend Dr Carter, 'to the exceeding smallness of her person and to some defect'.[75] She could not be penetrated sexually and so 'endured the most indescribable brutalities from men (the visitors) *assisted* by Madame the mistress'. When these efforts failed, *'torn*, and ill with the violence' she was taken to the hospital. There, without anaesthetic, doctors attempted to enlarge her vagina surgically, while medical students looked on and clamped her arms and legs. Because this 'treatment' failed it was repeated daily. Adeline later recalled that 'my screams and appeals to my tormenters for mercy were heard ... over the whole building'.[76]

Dyer and Gillett could not remove Adeline, but shortly afterwards she was taken from the hospital to prison, since the police had charged her with signing a false name (at the time of her registration). Dyer's London Committee had made contact with Adeline's family and sent her sister, accompanied by Mrs Mary Steward of the LNA, to Brussels, where they managed to gain entry to the prison. When she saw her sister, Adeline 'broke out into wild cries'.[77] The following day she was released and returned to London.

Adeline's story became the centrepiece of Dyer's book, *The European Slave Trade in English Girls*, which he published under his own imprint after failing to persuade the English press to report his discoveries. His stories were seen as scarcely credible and the details were hardly publishable in newspapers. They were also inflammatory in their charges against the Brussels police. In May Josephine joined the campaign, writing a letter to *The Shield* alleging that 'the official houses of prostitution in Brussels are crowded with English minor girls'.[78] She did not restrain her language, but described a house where 'there are immured little children, English girls of from twelve to fifteen years of age, lovely creatures ... stolen, kidnapped, betrayed ... and sold to these human shambles'.[79]

The Belgian Public Prosecutor (the *Procureur du Roi*) was sufficiently concerned by the allegations to invite English policemen to conduct their own investigation of the Brussels brothels. However, the policemen's tour was led by the chief of the Morals Police, Schroeder, who arranged that they saw nothing illegal. We know this for certain because, later that year, Josephine was contacted by a Belgian detective, de Rudder. He had decided to turn 'whistle-blower' and told her that Schroeder had personally instructed an English girl in a brothel to tell the visiting police that she was content to remain there.[80] This girl had been beaten into compliance by the brothel-keeper. Schroeder had also arranged for the English and underage girls who were in brothels at the time of Dyer and Gillett's February investigation to be sent into the country, so that they could not find them. De

Rudder had evidence to show that the police were involved in the sex trade up to their necks – the deputy, Lemoine, had inherited two brothels from a grateful owner whose business he had protected. The son of Lenaers, the police chief, ran a flourishing business from the family home supplying wine to the local brothels. All de Rudder's statements were verified by Spingard.

In the autumn of 1880, Josephine visited Brussels to see Spingard. She met the city's council leaders and made charges of police collusion in the traffic of underage girls. She was 'filled with horror. Surely Sodom and Gomorrah will rise up in judgement against the Belgian capital.'[81] But to expose evil greater even than that of 'Sodom and Gomorrah', she took great risks. 'Do you know that you are walking into the jaws of Hell?' she was asked by a gentleman in London.

On her return to Liverpool, she found that the Belgian Public Prosecutor had sent a demand to the Home Secretary, under the Extradition Act, that Josephine withdraw her allegations against the police or make a deposition (a witness statement under oath).[82] If her deposition was false she could be charged with perjury and if she refused to make one she would be open to libel action.

Writing to Hatty, Josephine told her that she was unsure what to do. She had been woken to knocking before 5 a.m., by a courier who had travelled by overnight train from London. He had been sent by Benjamin Scott with a packet of letters, including a coded telegram from Belgium warning of a 'trap being laid for us'. As her maid Jane made tea for the courier, Josephine lit a candle and pondered the telegram, which suggested 'some collusion' between the British and Brussels police. Josephine thought this unlikely. She was also unconvinced by Scott's letter, which 'implored me to refuse to give evidence' since 'it would be worth everything to the cause for you to suffer the full legal penalty of refusing to answer'. Josephine disagreed, reasoning that this would allow her opponents to claim that her charges could not be substantiated. Her instinct was to tell all. She had prayed that New Year, 'Oh God, I beseech Thee, send light upon these evil deeds! Whatever it may cost us and others.' Her resolution was shared by Humbert, who advised 'advance courageously, even into the jaws of the dragon if need be'.

Josephine's deposition, made to a magistrate in Liverpool on 8 November 1880, had to be based on firm evidence in order to save herself from prosecution.[83] She set out to substantiate, systematically, every charge she had made in her letter to *The Shield*, giving the addresses of at least ten brothels where young girls were kept out of sight but supplied on request, with detailed evidence and signed statements from gentlemen offered underage girls. Her first case was a brothel in rue St Jean Népumucène, identified by Spingard in February with the help of a local landlady. A remorseful client of this brothel had confessed to her that he had been offered a 12-year-old English girl there. When he was left alone with her, she had thrown herself into his arms 'in an agony of crying and weeping, and asked his help to get away. She said she was never allowed out of that room – never – never.' The client had been too afraid for his reputation to tell the police, but Spingard had reported the brothel.

Josephine prepared an additional voluntary statement containing case studies, in heartbreaking detail, of a further nine girls, and the names of two traffickers. She had alleged the existence of 'padded rooms' and proved this through witness testimony to a room:

> ... padded all over, walls and floor, so that a girl might be flung violently about the room,
> or dashed on the floor, without any serious bodily injury: (for she is valuable property to

the brothel-keeper so long as she continues to have any personal attraction). The sound of any noise outside would thus be deadened.

Methodically she listed the purposes of the room as: '(1) Indecent and unnatural orgies ...; (2) Girls are sometimes beaten, and are subjected at times to cruel and indecent torture, which I shall not further particularise.'

The magistrate refused to include Josephine's voluntary statement as part of the deposition, but it was later published in full by the courageous editor of the Brussels paper *Le National* who had asked Josephine to send it to him.[84] She had not expected him to publish it, but could hardly be sorry about the effect, since 60,000 copies of the paper's first edition were sold, and light poured in upon the activities of brothel-keepers, all named, including keepers of 'official houses of prostitution [which] are *schools for the teaching and practice of Sodomy*'.

Lenaers, the police chief, was alleged to be condoning a regime which imprisoned prostitutes indoors, and Schroeder, the chief of the Morals Police, to have obstructed enquiries by English detectives. The accusations were so specific that the editor's life was threatened and he was sued for libel by Lenaers and Schroeder. But, as a lawyer, Spingard had been waiting for such an opportunity.[85] At the subsequent trial, Lenaers broke down under Spingard's cross-examination, and both he and Schroeder were dismissed from office.

The Public Prosecutor put twelve prominent brothel-owners on trial, including Lemoine, the police deputy. 'The evidence brought against them,' said Josephine, 'was of the most awful kind, showing that the exaggeration with which we were sometimes charged had had no existence.'[86] She did not attend the trial herself, but arranged for abused girls to give evidence, including Emily Ellen, who had escaped from Brussels with the help of Pastor Anet and arrived at the Butlers' house in Liverpool as a 'refugee'. She had been imprisoned by 'the brutal creature, Roger' in an underground room, starved, and scourged with a leather thong when she refused to take part in 'some exceptionally base proceedings'. She still had the scars on her back and shoulders, which Josephine likened to those of slaves in the cotton plantations.[87]

Her reward was a telegram from Spingard on 15 December 1880 – 'All condemned' with sentences of up to three years, some with penal servitude.[88] Thirty-four English girls were released from brothels. The result was a triumph, but while rejoicing Josephine could not forget the girls who had been lost. Writing to Hatty, she mused, 'I do not find anything in Evangelic teaching which meets this mystery of wrong and pain, this woe of the murdered innocents.'[89] She concluded that 'God is above all human teachings. If *He* would reveal Himself more clearly to me, I feel sure I should be stronger to act ... Someday I believe He will tell me Himself what He has done, and is doing for them.'

The Aftermath, 1881

Josephine had sent her evidence to the Home Secretary, Lord Harcourt, who dispatched a lawyer, Thomas Snagge, to Brussels to investigate.[90] He confirmed the details of the system reported by Dyer: 'The girls who have been registered with false birth certificates live in constant terror.'[91] The trafficking of Englishwomen to Belgium and France was a 'fact established beyond all doubt'. He cited cases going back as far as 1874, and made recommendations, including restrictions on the issue of birth certificates to British women aged 20–30, and that the British consul should be informed of the registration of a British woman as a prostitute.

Josephine's preferred solution was a change to English laws on abduction and the age of consent. She began a campaign for this by writing a pamphlet, *A Letter to the Mothers of England*, which came out in April 1881. It begins with an emotional appeal: 'Listen to me, while I plead for the children.'[92] She tells the stories of these victims in heartrending detail, and asks mothers to imagine their own daughters in such a situation. She explains the lack of legal protection against abduction and the need:

> ... to act, in order that our fair England shall not continue ... to present the most tempting field to these kidnappers and slave-drivers. English mothers need to know that the latest fashion in vice is for the destruction of childhood. Libidinous devourers of human flesh and destroyers of souls prefer ... to devour the flesh of infants ... The younger, the more tender and innocent, the more helpless and terrified the victims, the greater their value in the eyes of these accursed beings. [In the face of this situation] If we women – mothers – should hold our peace, the very stones would begin to cry out.

Josephine also secured the signatures of 1,000 ladies, for a 'Memorial' to the Foreign Secretary, Lord Granville, asking him to enquire into the traffic in young girls.[93] She wrote to Lord Granville to warn him that she would wait outside his door for three days, if necessary, until he either heard her petition or ordered her removal. He replied immediately that there was no need for this, since he was in sympathy with her request and would arrange for a select committee of the House of Lords to take evidence, as a first step to changing the law. This committee met during June and July 1881, and heard from witnesses including Snagge, Scott, Gillett and Dyer. The latter read a statement from Adeline Tanner denouncing the continued trafficking of girls from Britain to the Continent as 'the cruellest thing that ever existed'.[94] It emerged that Dyer and his wife had cared for Adeline in their own home for more than a year.

The select committee took a year to report, but it endorsed the demands of Josephine's petitioners. Its recommendations included raising the age of consent to 16, and making attempts to solicit English girls to enter foreign brothels a 'serious misdemeanour'.[95] It took three more years and another campaign, however, before the law was finally changed.

INTERLUDE

Catharine of Siena

During Josephine's 'year of retreat' in 1878, her diary records that she 'read St Catharine' in Liverpool and 'wrote St Catharine' while in London, Cheltenham and Cambridge.[96] At first sight it is surprising that Josephine, a nineteenth-century Protestant, should write a substantial biography of a fourteenth-century Roman Catholic saint. However, this whole demanding enterprise answered very personal needs, and followed naturally from her time of prayer in Europe.[97] Josephine identified strongly with 'the combination in Catharine of the practical reformer with the contemplative mystic'.[98]

Catharine, an Italian nun, was chosen to negotiate a peace agreement between warring parties in Florence after a riot. As a result, she became a trusted adviser to the Pope. The fact that she was a woman was an advantage, 'at the present time the pride of man has become so great ... I will send to them *women*, unlearned, and by nature fragile, but filled by my grace with courage and power.'[99]

Like Catharine, Josephine was 'fragile' in health and 'unlearned'. Her descriptions of Catharine could often stand for herself:

> There are evidences that at times, when the strong claims of active duty were relaxed, she incurred a danger of being carried away by excess of feeling, in the exaltation of her spirit, and the intense communion of her soul with the unseen. This latter danger was controlled, however, by the deep, strong, human affection which ever impelled her to impart to others all that she had received of God, and to see in every human being who needed help the image of Him, whom her soul adored.[100]

Josephine also identified with Catharine's lonely search for knowledge of her Creator: 'He whom she loved gave her neither an angel nor a man to be her director, but appeared to her himself in her little cell, and taught her all that was most needful for her to know.'[101] It seems that Josephine is offering a guide into her own inner spirituality as she recounts Catharine's story.[102] Some episodes recall Josephine's own life experiences, such as when Catharine is taunted by university professors and publicly vilified for her unpopular views.[103]

In fact, Josephine plays down the role of the Catholic Church and its sacraments in Catharine's life, since it did not suit her purpose.[104] But in identifying both herself and Catharine as mystics, she was placing herself in a historic Christian tradition. In emphasising that she and Catharine were born to be leaders, of both men and women, she made a profound contribution to feminism.

Josephine confided to her diary that she wrote this biography for her sons, 'for them alone'.[105] They rarely came home to Liverpool and their spiritual outlook concerned her greatly. They did not have the habit of prayer and had not adopted the beliefs of their parents. Some of Stanley's ideas were 'heathenish', she thought, and she recommended the Quaker practice of silent worship to both him and Georgie.[106] Her one desire was 'that they may be saved and have *light*'.[107] Somehow she had failed to pass on the greatest gift she possessed, and this was her remedy.[108] From this time onwards, she wrote her private diaries with the idea that her sons might read them; often copying them out for this purpose.[109] These diaries, and *Catharine of Siena*, show how much she wanted them to share her faith, to understand her better, and to know that she was not unique. Catharine was another woman called by God to exercise leadership and influence the highest levels of government.

Despite Josephine's efforts, it seems impossible that her sons could have understood her, and sympathised with her, in the way their father did. *Catharine of Siena* is testimony, above all, to Josephine's personality and her identification with a saint who, she insisted, would have sided with Protestantism if she had lived during the Reformation![110] It shows her extraordinary self-discipline and capacity for work, completing extensive research and writing a volume of 338 pages within a few months. It was published so quickly (by Alfred Dyer) that she was able to present a copy to George in September.

As if to balance her output, in 1882 she published the life of a Protestant pastor, J.F. Oberlin from Alsace. She started writing it after returning from Geneva in 1880, when she was confined indoors with a bad cough.[111]

Oberlin ministered to 'scattered villages in the Vosges' during the French Revolution, and defied Robespierre's decree that all religious worship must cease.[112] He was arrested and threatened with the guillotine, but maintained his faith through prayer and was released when Robespierre died. Josephine was attracted not only by his heroism but also by his life among uncivilised peasants. Like her father, he introduced efficient methods of agriculture and transformed their prospects. He spent many hours in prayer, which his parishioners knew to be the foundation of his faith. The parallels with her father's life made the task of writing this book enjoyable and relaxing for her.[113]

Success for the Repeal Campaign (1881–83)

～The Butlers Move to Winchester

The year 1880 brought contrasting academic news from the Butler sons. Stanley was appointed to the post of professor in natural philosophy (sciences) at Scotland's most ancient university, St Andrew's. He was to stay there for the rest of his long career. Charlie, on the other hand, faltered in the final year of his Cambridge studies and opted out of the degree examinations.[1] This must have disappointed his father, in particular, but not a trace of this survives in his letters. Charlie spent the following months in Italy with the Meuricoffres, but his poor career prospects were a worry to his parents for years to come.[2]

George too was considering his future. Liverpool College had become less successful, due to competition from public schools which offered boarding.[3] Liverpool University College, into which he had put so much effort, opened its doors in 1881 – another of George's major contributions to English higher education. Initially these colleges, although founded to offer degree-level courses, took students from age 15 and thus overlapped with the education offered by schools like Liverpool College.[4] Josephine regretted this and was concerned about how tired George had become with all the extra work.[5] She did not see how George could retire when they had so little money – his salary was dependent on college fees and had declined along with the pupil numbers.[6] They had spent their meagre savings on putting their sons through university, and on donations to the many charitable causes in which they believed.[7]

Josephine told Hatty that she resented the fact that she herself had worked without pay for ten years, as Secretary to two and sometimes three associations – 'Why should I not work for money as well as anyone else?'[8] It would be lovely to have 'a country living in a healthy place' in contrast to their home in 'a street, with a pork butcher opposite!' which she felt their sons did not enjoy returning to. 'No country near, no walks' and she was convinced that the bad drains made them ill. Hatty wrote to tell George that she was incensed, on his behalf, that he had been 'kept waiting so long for preferment' in the Church. 'I fancy I see that there is something more than chance in it, when men of much less real worth climb up fortune's tree far before you.'[9] Josephine thought so too, writing to her niece Rhoda Bolton:

No church preferment is offered to him, though livings are falling vacant every week. We have lately been told that his want of success in this respect is plainly owing to the part we have thought it our duty to take in opposing those wicked and cruel *Acts*. No doubt it is so; I am sorry that Uncle George has to be passed over because of that, and all his hard labours in teaching unrecognised ... I don't know what we shall do to get our bread when we leave here.[10]

In the summer of 1881 the Butlers enjoyed a memorable holiday in the Engadine, a beautiful hidden valley in the Swiss Alps with wonderful opportunities for walking. George took temporary charge of a little 'church on the rock'. Georgie, Stanley and James Stuart joined them, and Josephine's letters and diary overflow with the happiness they shared.[11]

It was harder than ever to return to the smoke of Liverpool after 'the pure snow and light' of the Alps.[12] The following March, still without definite prospects, George informed Liverpool College of his intention to resign. As on previous occasions, the Butlers' good friends came to their aid. Henry Wilson and Robert Martineau established the Butler Fund to support them. The aim was to provide them with an annuity of £200 for the rest of both their lives – a remarkable act of generosity.[13] Several of their friends donated £100 each and they were to receive this money even if George was appointed to a Church position. Josephine, in her letter of thanks to Martineau, said that their hearts were 'filled to overflowing with wonder and gratitude'.[14] George believed that the money was due to her, for her work 'on behalf of justice and purity', and 'humbly puts aside any recognition for *himself*'.

W.E. Gladstone was now Prime Minister, with the power of nominating successors to vacant posts in the Church. He had recently congratulated George for his work at the college, 'a striking testimonial to your powers and your successes'.[15] In June 1882 Gladstone offered George the post of Canon at Winchester Cathedral – an ideal retirement role. He would join the clergy team, with a house in the cathedral close. 'How faithfully God answers prayer!' was George's response.[16] Hatty, writing to congratulate him, confessed that she had 'burst into tears' of relief on hearing the news.[17] Winchester was 'a very pretty place, and I think your artistic taste will feel at home with the cathedral architecture and its surroundings'. Josephine envisaged a new ministry for them both; Winchester was, she told George, 'a new sphere, a new stage of our earthly course and it is my longing that we both may be baptised with the Holy Ghost at this time, that the rest of our lives may be consecrated *fully* and thus we shall have a power to win souls and to glorify God, as we have never yet had'.[18]

George seems to have been unwell in the autumn, after a happy summer spent standing in for the vicar of Cornhill-on-Tweed in Northumberland, only a few miles from Josephine's childhood home, Milfield. They visited her eldest brother, George Grey, and George went out fishing on his favourite river, the Tweed. Josephine took charge of moving from their home of sixteen years, a task which involved not only packing up their possessions and selling furniture, but closing down the House of Rest as well. She had to tell 'our poor hangers-on that we would find for them friends in their own town, but that we could not continue absolutely to support them'.[19] There were few friends like the Butlers, however. Josephine was plagued in Winchester for years afterwards by letters from one of the 'hangers-on', Mrs Gelling, demanding 'regular supplies'.

This story 'gives some idea of the scale of the charitable claims upon the Butlers' and explains why they often had to rely on friends for financial support.[20] In October, Josephine told Hatty, she packed 'a little cabinet of Eva's' and found 'the *first* plaster caste of her dear face taken straight off as she lay dead, which no one saw ... it brings back the cruel nature of her death. The caste is so soft that to preserve it I must pack it in cotton wool and put it in my own box among my bonnets and best gowns: and it looks *so* pitiful.'[21] She longed again for a daughter to share her daily life and, at this moment, to help her move home. 'It is such a business turning out the accumulations of 19 years.' Their dear dog, Bunty was, she felt, too old and blind to leave their garden and the trees on which he 'has scratched himself for 12 years'.[22] She obtained chloroform from a chemist to put him down, but the task was beyond her and Bunty went to Winchester where he died naturally the following year.[23]

In November, at The Close in Winchester they found 'plasterers, plumbers and mess' and had to resort to lodgings until the house was ready. It was 'a ruin ... as old as King Ethelwulf'.[24] Josephine's dejection turned to joy once they took possession, later describing it as 'the beautiful old house, with its thick walls, its picturesque gables, its antiquity ... its ample accommodation ... and its surroundings of fine ancestral trees and flowering shrubs, gorgeous in spring!'[25] They could be as hospitable as they wished. Members of the family and friends of many nationalities visited them there; indeed, Josephine's description recalls her parents' home at Dilston. Constance and Adela Grey, the daughters of Josephine's brother, Charles, by his first marriage, stayed for long periods with them, becoming surrogate children.[26] The Butlers made friends within 'the society of the Close', especially with Dean Kitchin, who arrived shortly after George, and Mary Sumner, the Bishop's daughter-in-law, who was to found the Mothers' Union.[27]

The cathedral became, to both Josephine and George, 'a place of repose to which one could resort at any and all hours for moments of silence and rest, or for the enjoyment of its inspiring music and services'.[28] A retreat was needed, for Winchester was not a rural backwater. It contained a military headquarters and was one of the towns regulated under the CD Acts. There were plenty of young women in need of their help and Josephine lost no time in setting up a House of Rest in Canon Street, just a few minutes' walk from The Close.[29] Known as Hamilton House, it served as a hospital as well as a refuge. George held an informal service there on Sunday evenings. Amelie Humbert came to Winchester to act as Josephine's secretary, and helped her to open Hamilton House. During the first year, she recalled, they received forty sick women there. The 'little hospital' cost them 'much expense' over the years, often met by appeals to their friends.[30]

Working-Class Support

Although Josephine remained the Hon. Secretary of the LNA and kept an office in Liverpool, Margaret Tanner and Mary Priestman had taken over most of her day-to-day work. This left Josephine free to inject 'energy and ideas' whenever she thought it necessary and to make speeches and write pamphlets.[31] Speaking was not easy, however – she feared that audiences, especially female ones, were now wary of what she might say about the 'white slave trade'.[32] When she spoke to the Christian Women's Union in October 1881, she asked Charlotte Wilson to support her and 'reassure the ladies'.[33] The need to moderate her words was frustrating; she told the LNA that they needed to develop 'just anger' and 'well-governed indignation' to sustain and motivate them in their task.[34]

In many ways she was more comfortable with the working class, since she believed that 'poor working fathers and mothers whose children are stolen' instinctively opposed the CD Acts.[35] The Percy case had stirred working-class outrage at the actions of the police and led to the formation of the Working Men's National League (WMNL), after a meeting in Liverpool organised by the LNA's agent, William Burgess.[36] Henry Wilson opposed this because he did not believe in separate workers' organisations, but Josephine gave the WMNL her full support. Politicians now had to listen to the views of working-class men, since many had been enfranchised by the Reform Act of 1867, and more were to receive the vote in 1884. Leading Liberals like Wilson hoped that their party could represent working-class voters, and for a time this strategy worked, but Josephine was more far-sighted, less tribal, in seeing that separate organisations were crucial. The Trade Union Congress regularly condemned the CD Acts and over one third of its delegates in 1884 were members of the WMNL.[37]

Josephine and Wilson consulted regularly about their paid election agents, who often caused considerable trouble.[38] The worst incident was the death of Henry Bligh, the soldier who Josephine had recruited in 1873. His contacts made him very useful as an informer on the activities of the police in the regulated towns. Bligh's life ended tragically after he accused William Burgess of embezzling funds. Burgess counterattacked disgracefully by telling his LNA employers that Bligh had contracted syphilis while serving in the East Indies and infected his wife and child. Although he denied the claim, Bligh was so distraught that he cut his own throat with a penknife. Henry Wilson and James Stansfeld investigated, dismissed Burgess, and managed to keep the story from becoming public.

Wilson kept the agents on a tight rein, demanding daily reports, and dismissed several who did not meet his standards. Josephine sacked an agent herself for smoking and drinking. They expected their agents to visit three or four areas a week, calling on supporters, holding meetings and distributing publicity material. Josephine also wanted them to fundraise and was annoyed when they did not. About one agent, Fothergill, she wrote, 'He won't even *ask* for money; he says it would "do harm". So I have to do *every bit* of that myself.'[39] In 1882 she considered dispensing with paid agents, but decided they could not manage without them.[40] Josephine is here revealed in other roles: as employer (a woman employing men), and as fundraiser. This work was crucial as the campaign against the CD Acts finally reached a climax.

Another Parliamentary Inquiry, 1882

In 1882 Josephine was called to give evidence to a Parliamentary select committee into the workings of the Acts. This had been set up unexpectedly by the Conservative government in 1879, thanks to the efforts of James Stansfeld and Harcourt Johnstone. Both were appointed to the committee, together with William Fowler and another leading repeal supporter, Charles Hopwood MP. The majority of the committee members were supporters of the Acts, but both the NA and LNA seized the opportunity to make their case. It was a long and exhausting haul – the committee met for sixty-eight days spread over three years, and interviewed seventy-one witnesses.

The doctors and policemen called as witnesses almost unanimously maintained that the Acts had reduced the incidence of sexually transmitted disease in the regulated areas. In response, Stansfeld went to great lengths to prove that their statistics were highly suspect. He showed, for example, that doctors double counted patients initially treated for primary syphilis if they returned with secondary syphilis. His cross-examination of Surgeon-General Lawson destroyed much of his evidence.[41]

The repealers scored another triumph when they persuaded the local Plymouth and Devonport police to testify against the Metropolitan police.[42] They also invited witnesses with personal experience of the harmful effects of the Acts to testify. They presented a bizarre contrast to the official witnesses. Three days of the committee's time were taken up by Eliza Southey, who had been repeatedly harassed by the Dover police because her boyfriend, Bates, was a soldier.[43] After she had stayed at the barracks for over two hours on Christmas Day, Inspector Witney had instructed her 'to attend the examination'. She had refused and sought the help of a local repeal campaigner, Rowland Rees, who got her discharged in the magistrate's court. Although Eliza claimed that there had been 'no impropriety' between herself and Bates, the special police presented testimony that she had been observed 'having connection' with an artilleryman in a timber yard commonly used by local couples. However, there was no evidence that she was a prostitute, and her landlady testified that she had regular work washing and 'charring' (cleaning). Eliza's evidence was another success for the repealers, since it was clear that she would have been registered as a common prostitute without their assistance.

Josephine's appearance took place on 5 May 1882. She prepared her testimony very carefully for this return visit to the 'Lion's Den', telling George that she had learned the details by heart.[44] Her nerves showed at the start, when she muddled dates she knew very well and said she had been working with prostitutes 'since 1851' and that this was 'from within a few years after' her marriage.[45] However, she was sympathetically questioned by Charles Hopwood, and gave a confident account of the history of the campaign, explaining how painful it had been.[46]

She described her 1870 visit to the brothels of Chatham as a night in which 'my heart was well-nigh broken'. She had spoken to young men there who were 'extremely youthful in appearance'; some said they had no other amusement and that the soldiers were expected to enjoy the 'government women' provided for them. These girls had tickets (clean bills of health) pinned to their dresses. A few soldiers had confessed shame at their actions to her. Osborne Morgan, a supporter of the Acts, suggested that her evidence was out of date, since she had not been to Chatham since 1870. Hopwood had to remind her that she had visited Woolwich in 1879. She refused to accept Morgan's suggestion that lock hospitals could rescue women. In her opinion, the attempt to offer them religious teaching was 'a mockery of God' and any reclamation counted 'as nothing in comparison to the evil done'. Josephine had herself prayed with women in lock hospitals, but this comment shows that her opinions had changed. By now it was clear to her that the chance of rescue was a respectable smokescreen obscuring the sordid reality of the CD Acts regime.

The Liberals Return to Power

By this time the government had changed. 'The shade of Toryism', which Josephine had found so depressing, had gone.[47] When a general election had been called in 1880, the repeal campaign had changed its tactics. Henry Wilson and James Stansfeld insisted that repealers should not undermine Liberal candidates who favoured the Acts. The aim was to elect as many Liberals as possible. Josephine and the LNA saw the wisdom of this; the NA was reluctant, but the line was held and the result was a triumph. A high number of repealers were elected and the Liberals formed the largest party, with W.E. Gladstone as Prime Minister once again. Stansfeld was left out of the Cabinet, to his great disappointment. Leadership of the Parliamentary repeal campaign was hardly a consolation prize, and he agreed to accept it only if he was left entirely free to act according to his 'own judgement and conscience'.[48] His energy, commitment and experience proved vital, and he handled the parliamentary situation to perfection over the next three years.

There were still plenty of Liberal MPs who supported the CD Acts, but many of the newly elected MPs, known to their detractors as 'Faddists', were believers in moral reform. They were crusaders with Christian commitment, MPs after Josephine's heart. This new government was a great opportunity, but a tantalisingly brief one. It is perhaps just as well that the repealers did not know that their window of opportunity was only six years. The Liberal Party was overwhelmed by Gladstone's conversion to Home Rule for Ireland in 1886, subsequently split, and did not form another government until 1906.

Two of those six years disappeared while the select committee interviewed its interminable parade of witnesses and wrote its reports. While it was still deliberating, Stansfeld introduced a repeal bill which was defeated without a division in July 1882. His wife was seriously ill and he may have had no heart for it.[49] When the majority report of the committee finally appeared, it was a huge disappointment to the repeal campaign. Although most of the evidence presented by witnesses was in support of repeal rather than against it, the majority of commissioners were not persuaded.[50] Their report was 'a complete endorsement, indeed almost a eulogy, of the Acts; it found no fault and only regretted the impossibility of extension'.[51] Stansfeld's minority report, signed by six, probed the evidence, analysed the statistics and made the case against the Acts in lengthy and precise detail. His hard work was to prove crucial, because the majority report was too glowingly positive in the face of Stansfeld's mountain of contradictory evidence.[52] But in 1882 there was little sign that the tide was turning. *The Shield* described the majority report as 'a declaration of war' by the government.[53]

The report reopened the split within the repeal movement over support for the Liberal party. The NA was refusing to work with it, but Henry Wilson, though disappointed, was convinced that their only hope was to support the government and to persuade individual Liberal MPs to commit to repeal.[54] Ignoring the protests of William Shaen, the leader of the NA, Wilson created a 'Political Committee' in November 1882 with the aim of working on the Liberal Party from the inside. Josephine was in full support, believing that this would make Stansfeld feel less isolated.[55]

With typical energy, Wilson, James Stuart and other members of the Political Committee began going 'in and out of the House of Commons stirring people up', as Josephine put it.[56] Leading backbench Liberals such as Joseph Chamberlain (the chairman of the National Liberal Federation) declared for repeal. The support of figures like Chamberlain was important not only in convincing their colleagues, but in indicating to the national press that repeal had a real chance of success. Stansfeld worked on the Cabinet, telling them that they risked the disintegration of the party if they stonewalled on repeal. It is hard to believe that the party could really have collapsed over the repeal issue (it was hardly as crucial as Irish Home Rule), but Stansfeld's tactic was to persuade the government either to sponsor a repeal bill itself or, at the very least, to allow a free vote on the issue.

The Suspension of the CD Acts (1883)

The year 1883 began with a repeal conference organised by the Quakers, which they described as a 'Christian Convention'. Josephine and George were among the committee members.[57] True to their principles, the Quakers insisted that members of all Christian denominations should be invited, whatever their church background. Some repealers, like Mr Shaen of the NA, resisted the invitation to join in prayer with other sects. This upset the Priestman sisters, themselves Quakers, and it was in the context of showing that she personally hated 'narrowness' that Josephine made a surprising statement in a letter to them:

> I am *not* of the Church of England and never was. I go to the Church once a Sunday out of a feeling of loyalty to my husband – that is all. I was brought up a Wesleyan, but my father was allied with the free church of Scotland, and my mother was a Moravian.

I imbibed from childhood the widest ideas of vital Christianity, only it *was* Christianity. I have not much sympathy with the *Church*.[58]

Although Josephine went to the Wesleyan chapel with her governess, her parents took her to the Anglican church in Corbridge and she was married there. It is not true that she 'never was' of the Church of England. But her rejection of Anglican orthodoxy had been obvious for many years and the emphasis she places is on her non-denominational Evangelicalism – that is what she meant by 'vital Christianity'.[59] Attendance at church, support for its teaching, and communion with fellow believers is at the heart of the Christian experience for most people, but not for Josephine Butler. The church circle was too comfortable a place for her. But her attitude had some disadvantages – because she deliberately stood outside the Evangelical churches, it has been argued that she did not utilise their 'circuits and networks' to their best advantage in the campaign.[60] The Evangelical denominations (including the Methodists) had all declared for repeal. The Christian Convention was a chance to come together with other Christians, which she embraced and found inspiring. Prayer meetings became a political strategy, as part of the assembly of techniques to rouse support and influence Parliament.

The Christian Convention was well publicised and many influential people were invited. Male and female supporters gathered separately during the day, for sermons and prayer, with a public meeting in the evening.[61] Speaker meetings were arranged for those who did not want to join in 'anything of a devotional character'.[62] The prayer strategy tested the loyalty of Christians, like Stansfeld, who did not like communal prayer, and his sister Emilie Venturi, the editor of *The Shield*, who was an agnostic, but Josephine was sure that it would have a positive influence on MPs.[63] She wrote to Stanley: 'There is a distinct change of tone in the House, and your father and I believe that it dates from the time that we came forward publicly to confess God as our Leader.'[64]

In February, Charles Hopwood secured time to move a resolution against the compulsory examination of women in the House of Commons. Now the work arousing support in the country, so ably mobilised over the previous decade, came into its own. Petitioning reached new levels and MPs were swamped by letters demanding repeal.[65] One MP told Josephine that 'the amount of pressure brought to bear at this moment by the country was "unprecedented in the history of any agitation"'.[66] The result of a by-election held in Newcastle at this time was very encouraging: all three candidates declared for repeal and the new MP, John Morley, immediately offered his services to Hopwood.[67]

More prayer meetings were arranged for the day of the debate, 27 February, including a ladies' meeting at the Westminster Palace Hotel. Josephine reported that:

There were well-dressed ladies – some even of high rank – kneeling together ... with the poorest, and some of the outcast women of the purlieus of Westminster ... I felt ready to cry, but I did not, for I long ago rejected the old ideal of the 'division of labour', that 'men must work and women must weep'.

She wondered 'how long women will be refused a voice in the representation of this country'.[68]

Josephine was determined to watch the House of Commons debate from the tiny Ladies' Gallery. MPs often asked for the gallery to be cleared if the debate was thought 'unsuitable', so Josephine's plan was confrontational. Parliament had always tried to limit debate on the CD Acts and to exclude outsiders. Even some of her friends urged her to stay away, but she refused to give up, remembering how the CD Acts had been passed in the first place. In an open letter to MPs, she wrote, 'I cannot forget the misery, the injustice and the outrage which have fallen upon women simply because we stood aside when men felt our presence to be painful.'[69] MPs were objecting to the LNA's presence because 'it would be so very painful to ourselves to hear what must be said concerning the foul outrage. I say that as long as any woman is obliged to *suffer* that outrage, I should be ashamed to speak of the pain to myself of *hearing* of it.'

In the end, no debate took place on 27 February. Josephine went between the gallery and the prayer meeting several times, but Hopwood's resolution was forced out by other business. Deeply disappointing though this was, the tide was running in their favour. The MPs who supported Hopwood's resolution were frustrated, and no fewer than ten of them balloted for a private member's bill on repeal. Stansfeld, appropriately, won the ballot and the new debate was set for 20 April.

The repeal campaign's Parliamentary Committee now went into overdrive, focussing on undecided and hostile Liberal MPs. Josephine and her 'women workers' spent hours in the lobby of the House of Commons 'interviewing MPs'.[70] On 12 April, the National Liberal Federation agreed to press for immediate repeal, a major boost which enabled Henry Wilson to send a circular to every Liberal MP informing them that repeal was now Liberal policy.[71] The Cabinet was still divided over the issue, but agreed to allow ministers to vote freely according to their conscience. But still the outcome was in doubt.

On 20 April the prayer meetings resumed, and the ladies packed the gallery – there seems to have been no serious attempt to keep them out. In a rational, dispassionate speech, Stansfeld proposed the motion 'That this House disapproves of the compulsory examination of women under the Contagious Diseases Acts'.[72] He began by dismissing the majority report of the committee, which had flown in the face of the evidence presented to them. Its signatories would be happy to extend the Acts across the country, if they could. The minority report had produced better, more up-to-date, arguments, and had disproved statistics which claimed to show that the Acts reduced disease in the protected districts. The Acts did not aid the rescue of fallen women, but actually increased the time that women pursued 'this kind of life' and created 'a pariah class of prostitutes, under government supervision, for the public use'. He closed with a personal comment:

> I have had the weight of this question upon me now for some ten years past. I loathe its details ... What I have done I have done for conviction and for duty's sake, and never will I abandon a duty I have once undertaken to fulfil, not will I cease till I have proved the hygienic failure and imposture of these Acts; but no man knows, or ever can or will know, what to me has been the suffering, the burden and the cost.[73]

He was opposed by Osborne Morgan, a member of his own party. Morgan claimed to have joined the select committee with an open mind, but was actually highly partisan – he had consistently opposed Stansfeld's arguments and 'defended every official down to the meanest policeman engaged in the administration of the Acts'.[74] He made very disparaging remarks about the repealers, saying that they sent 'revolting letters and pamphlets' and stating that 'the very last thing they would desire to see is the stamping out of venereal disease. They regard it as a scourge sent by God to deter men from sin.' This was a gross misrepresentation of their views.

Like other supporters, Morgan believed that the Acts could only be wrong if innocent women had been hounded, since prostitutes were beneath contempt. The onus was on the repeal campaign to 'produce one authentic case of any respectable woman who had been molested under the Acts, or brought before a magistrate ... But there was not one case of this character brought before us which a lawyer would for a moment admit to be proved.'[75] He thus dismissed the case of Eliza Southey, and the 1875 scandal over Mrs Percy, which certainly did show the police operating cruelly and unfairly. However, it was true that very few cases of such women had been found and that repealers had overstated their number.[76] Morgan cited the strong support of most magistrates, doctors and clergy in the subjected districts, and dismissed those who opposed the Acts 'as all men of one type, and of one school of thought' because they had a religious point of view.[77]

The most impassioned speech against the examination came from Stansfeld's friend, George Russell:

> Under this Act we all but close the paths of regeneration against these women. We efface the divine stamp upon them; we stamp them with the signet of the State, which marks them as the common prey of animal desire; and we condemn them to continue there, practically to the end of their days, in the same bondage which the selfishness of man has reduced them to ... I desire, publicly and emphatically, to give the strongest protest of which I am capable against the doctrine that in a civilized State prostitution is to be recognized as a necessity, or that we can morally tolerate ... the degradation of our manhood and the degradation of womankind.

Russell's speech was immediately followed by a fickle and contemptuous outburst from the Tory, Cavendish Bentinck, who said that Russell 'did not appear aware that the Acts were applicable only to prostitutes, and that any woman might at any time relieve herself from consequences by a *bona fide* abandonment of prostitution, and without any difficulty being interposed by the authorities'.

The result of the debate hinged on the views of Liberal MPs, who had been given a free vote, so the speeches and the mailbags of letters and petitions had more influence than is normal in Parliamentary votes. Josephine went into the Lobby of the House several times, to be told that some MPs were embarrassed that 'all those women' should be praying for them and that Cavendish Bentinck, 'a man who foams at the mouth every time he speaks of us' was infuriated by all those who 'patronised that woman's praying'.[78] But the tide was turning. The division took place after midnight and, as the ladies continued to watch, Josephine recalled:

> Mr Gerard, the steward of the Ladies' Gallery, crept quietly in and whispered to me, 'I think you are going to win!' ... Never can I forget the expression on the faces of our M.P.'s in the House when they all streamed back from the division lobby ... We did not require to wait to hear their announcement of the division by the teller: the faces of our friends told the tale ... I thought of the words, 'Say unto Jerusalem that her warfare is accomplished' ... Then we ran quickly down from the gallery and met a number of our friends coming out from Westminster Hall.[79]

In scenes of high emotion, James Stansfeld grasped her hand, with tears trickling down his face.[80] The outcome was a rousing victory – MPs voted conclusively to suspend the CD Acts by a majority of seventy-two.

For James Stansfeld, it was 'a moral victory. My resolution appealed straight to the consciences of men, to all that is just and chivalrous, high, pure or manly in them: and it met with a response.'[81] It was equally a triumph for his own painstaking work on the facts and figures; he gained the support of the great majority of Liberal MPs because he had discredited the conclusions of the majority report. He persuaded Parliament to rule against the findings of its own select committee; a very rare outcome indeed.[82]

If Stansfeld was the hero of the hour in Parliament, it was the NA and LNA which had fought and won the battle in the country. Women who did not have the vote had wielded incredible moral power within the House of Commons, which could no longer debate this subject behind closed doors. Josephine herself never had any doubt that 'the avenging angel must be one of the sex which has been outraged'.[83] Without the 'avenging angel' the CD Acts would probably have remained a little discussed, regularly renewed, feature of the statute book. It was her willingness to speak out, in public, which made the difference.

If the 1883 result seems inevitable in retrospect, it is worth remembering that several other Liberal reform campaigns, with organisations and budgets far bigger than that of the LNA and the NA, did not succeed. Drinking was not outlawed, the Church of England was not disestablished, vaccination remained compulsory. The decision to outlaw the forced examination in 1883 was a triumph which might easily never have happened.

INTERLUDE

The Salvation Army in Switzerland

If any other Victorian woman bears comparison with Josephine Butler for her qualities of leadership, bravery, piety and devotion to the poor, it was Catherine Booth. She did not lead a political reform movement, but she founded a church, the Salvation Army, with her husband, William Booth. Originally the East London Mission, from 1865 the Army preached to the destitute and miserable, and gave them shelter and support. Its services featured simple gospel preaching and hearty hymn singing, led by a brass band, and the staff had military titles and wore uniforms.

The methods they used were often dismissed by the middle class as vulgar, but, while not keen on military titles, Josephine supported their work. Its mission buildings in the slums offered, she said, warmth, light, 'cheerfulness ... music, singing, and happy faces, earnest loving hearts, and affectionate hands held out to every comer'.[84] In the centre was 'the Divine Being, whose presence is invoked continually, to convert, comfort, heal and bless'. They achieved 'astounding success' in making converts and transforming desperate lives.[85] She was impressed by the 'Family Idea' of the Army which ensured that the Booths, and all their children, were utterly devoted to its work. 'The family,' she wrote, 'is remarkable for the united intensity of purpose ... for its oneness of heart and judgment in the pursuit of a single great object.'[86] Although she and George were equally as united, she must have compared the Booth family with her own, and hoped for more faith and commitment from their sons.

Catherine Booth was the matriarch of the Army – she and William believed in equality of the sexes. The Army trained and employed women, and encouraged them to keep their jobs after marriage, while William rebuked male officers who kept their wives at home.[87] Catherine, like Josephine, believed that women had the right to preach and was a powerful speaker. Both at times found this very difficult, but neither had any doubt that St Paul's 'supposed veto upon women preachers' must be challenged.[88] They pointed out that there were female prophets in his lifetime, and Josephine enjoyed Catherine's joke that 'St Paul must have had "a bad time of it" when he was staying in the house of Philip the Evangelist, for "Philip had four daughters, virgins, which did prophesy".'

Josephine seems to have found a spiritual home in the Army. She went to a meeting at its hall in Oxford Street, London, in 1882 before testifying to the select commission. 'It was lovely!' she told George. 'No Peeresses there, but the humblest people with faces radiant with happiness. I never saw *spiritual joy* like it.'[89] In a letter to a young Army preacher, she compared their work to a vision she had had of 'a vast evangelising army and a great outpouring of the spirit such as I have now lived to see, O! Praise and glory.'[90] She even said, 'Nothing would make me happier than to be a soldier in the Army, but I *am* one, though I wear no badge.' Her letters are confiding, as if she felt free to speak about her deepest feelings.

These letters were sent to the Booths' eldest daughter (Catherine, known as Katie) and her fellow officers, who were pioneering the Army's work in France and Switzerland. At the age of 24, Katie was already a powerful preacher. The Butlers were staying with the Humberts in Neuchâtel, Switzerland, in July 1883, when Josephine heard that Katie and her fellow officers had been expelled from Geneva for disturbing the public peace.[91] Their preaching against vice in the city had unleashed the violence of 'several noted traffickers' and three officers were stoned through the streets. Josephine was horrified that the police had not protected them and that the 'free expression of opinion' had been illegally suppressed.[92] Switzerland in theory enjoyed 'absolute religious liberty', but its governing authorities, as Josephine already knew, often acted with gross intolerance.[93]

Katie and her 17-year-old assistant, Maud Charlesworth, stayed with Josephine at Neuchâtel, where she was struck by the innocence of these 'girl warriors': 'it was difficult to realise that these were the instruments chosen of God to lead an attack on the kingdom of darkness with such a divinely inspired energy as to embarrass the governments of the world.'[94] Their youth, she was sure, enhanced their power.

Josephine helped them to make an appeal to the Federal Council of Berne, but it was dismissed. In Neuchâtel the persecution continued, even though the Army held its meetings in houses and on hillsides outside the towns. The police tracked them to a forest, where Katie was arrested again. She was granted bail but was then in a quandary since she had promised to return to Geneva to attend the funeral of one of her converts. It was at this point that Josephine took a bold step. After consulting lawyers, she advised Katie that her return to Geneva was not illegal.

Josephine attended the funeral herself, and 300 people followed the coffin to the graveside, where Katie spoke. As soon as she finished speaking she was arrested. Josephine followed her to the police station, where it was possible for her to hear the police interview with Katie from outside the door. Josephine advised her to persist with her claim that her original expulsion was illegal and a breach of the treaty of friendship between England and Switzerland. Later Josephine received a letter from Katie's mother, Catherine, thanking her, 'How remarkable that God should send her to you just then!'[95] Katie was released and deported from Geneva, but when she reached Neuchâtel she again refused to stop preaching. She was imprisoned in foul conditions, and quickly became ill.

By this time Josephine had left Switzerland to attend the Congress of the Federation at The Hague, which was a breath of fresh air. They received a 'cordial welcome', with a reception given by the Mayor and support from the royal family.[96] During her visit,

Josephine personally inspired Marianna Klerck-van-Hogendorp to set up the 'Dutch Women's Union for the Advancement of Moral Consciousness' which thereafter co-ordinated a women's campaign against regulated prostitution in the Netherlands.[97]

On her return to London, Josephine went straight to a prayer meeting at Exeter Hall held by Katie's supporters. Then she sat down and wrote, at breakneck speed, a vivid account of Katie's persecution in Switzerland, in 300 pages which were published later that year. Josephine felt she had to justify her own advice that Katie had been illegally expelled and imprisoned, and also prove the value of the Salvation Army's work to those who mistrusted it. She corresponded with Katie in prison and heard from her that, 'your sympathy and help, above all, your mother's heart towards me, are a great consolation ... You understand our aims; *your* work is our work – *one*.'[98]

Katie Booth was put on trial on 29 September, fully expecting to be found guilty. However, to ensure impartiality, the jury was composed of men who had not signed any petitions against the Salvation Army. They were 'all *good* men', Josephine rejoiced, and she was acquitted.[99] When Katie returned to France the following month, public opinion had changed and the work of the Army began to flourish.[100]

'The Maiden Tribute of Modern Babylon', 1885

Contie's Death and Charlie's Military Service

Josephine's niece, Constance (Contie) Grey, had been seriously ill with tuberculosis for two years.[1] In January 1884 it was obvious that she was dying. Adela brought her sister back to Winchester, to Josephine and George who had become their surrogate parents. Contie was only 25, and had been one of the first students at Newnham College, Cambridge, founded by Josephine's friend, Anne Clough.[2]

Josephine spent many hours 'in the room of my dear dying niece' and supporting Adela, who was three years younger, devoted to her sister and desperately upset.[3] They employed a day and a night nurse – 'lots of extra mouths to feed'.[4] The girls' father, Josephine's brother Charles, made a visit from Ireland before Contie died at The Close on 18 February. 'She did love her Saviour,' said Josephine. 'I feel sad tonight though I *rejoice* for Contie.'[5] But she admitted to her niece Rhoda Bolton that 'the last two days and nights have been a struggle and the last six hours terrible'. She told Stanley that she had tried to keep Adela out of the room as much as possible, because 'Contie was convulsed and her eyes turned back in her head'.[6] Even she found it hard to praise God.

When writing to Stanley, Josephine noted that 'a great fight is going on in the House over Egypt'. She wondered 'if poor "Gunner Butler" will be sent out'.[7] Charlie had enlisted in the army at a moment of crisis for the British Empire. British troops had occupied Egypt and its colony, Sudan, and were facing a native rebellion, led by the Mahdi, in Sudan. General Gordon had just been sent to the Sudan to evacuate the army, and was killed the following January, 1885, just before relief troops arrived. Charlie appears to have taken part in an expedition commanded by General Graham, which left England in March 1885 with the aim of constructing a railway from the Sudanese port of Suakin to the Nile.[8] The route was in enemy hands and skirmishes took place almost daily, under the relentless desert sun.[9] After two months ominous silence, Josephine heard the unsparing details of Charlie's terrible experiences, and recounted them to her friend Mrs Lundie – 'Sleeping out on the sand for three weeks ... every night ... recovering the bodies of the English who were killed, burying heaps of dead so corrupt that the strongest men were sick and vomited over the work ... The scenes and the stench were beyond description.'[10] Charlie had contracted a fever, and was invalided home, but he was plagued by recurrent malarial fever for the rest of his life.[11]

The 'Secret Commission', 1885

While she worried about Charlie, Josephine was again caught up in the campaign to raise the age of consent. After her exposure of the trafficking of young British girls to Belgium, the House of Lords select committee had recommended that it should rise to 16. There had been efforts since then to achieve this through a Criminal Law Amendment Act (CLAA), but all had failed. The third attempt was talked out in the House of Commons in May 1885. Too many MPs liked the *status quo*.[12] Some 'openly defended sexual access to working class girls as a time honoured prerogative of gentlemen'.[13]

'Ministers of the Crown and Members of Parliament' were among the customers of Mrs Mary Jeffries, a procuress with eight houses in London.[14] The perverted pleasures she offered included flogging and virgins. Just ten days before, she had been put on trial, but in order to protect her unnamed customers, she pleaded guilty and was let off with a fine of £200.

The outcome of this sensational trial was a great blow to Josephine's friends, Benjamin Waugh, Benjamin Scott and Alfred Dyer, of the London Committee against Trafficking. They had instigated the trial, by bringing a private prosecution against Mrs Jeffries when it was clear the police would not act against her. Josephine had fully supported this move, but now she declared that a different strategy was needed. As 'an old political agitator and the daughter of an old political agitator', she called for an 'appeal to the conscience of all England ... and now is the very time to do it'.[15]

Gladstone's government was falling apart, under the strain of his failure to save General Gordon, and a general election was imminent. The recent Reform Act meant that there would be around 6 million new working-class voters, who would be likely to support candidates pledged to raise the age of consent. Josephine's call was for publicity – to rouse the country's conscience by destroying the veil of secrecy which concealed the rape of 13-year-old virgins and the trafficking of deluded women to the Continent. Scott, Dyer and Waugh had come to the same conclusion.

So had Bramwell Booth, brother of Katie Booth, who ran the London headquarters of the Salvation Army. He had decided to 'do all I could to stop these abominations' after his encounter with Annie Swan, a pious young girl from the countryside who had been tricked into coming to London to take a job as a maid in a house which, to her horror, turned out to be a brothel.[16] She had escaped and walked across London during the night to seek the help of the Salvation Army.

It was Bramwell Booth who suggested contacting William T. Stead, the editor of the *Pall Mall Gazette*, who was a devoted friend of the Army. Aged 36, Stead had built the reputation of the *Pall Mall Gazette* as a campaigning paper, a pioneer of 'new journalism', with direct, confrontational, passionate and fearless prose.[17] He could be wrong headed (he had led the campaign for General Gordon to go to the Sudan), but the series of articles he had published in 1883 entitled 'The Bitter Cry of Outcast London' had roused consciences on the appalling conditions of life in slum housing. Stead had heard Josephine Butler speak at the Salvation Army meeting held at Exeter Hall in 1883 to campaign for Katie Booth's release. He was immediately smitten: 'She has a voice of great charm and softness, an intense but subdued earnestness and perfect simplicity in her style of speaking such as only the most accomplished orator possesses.'[18]

Earlier, he had wanted to publish Josephine's evidence about child prostitution in Belgium, but she had declined on the grounds that 'it is too horrible; no one would read it, no one would print it'.[19] However, Josephine had been forced to acknowledge the power of the press, since the conviction of Brussels brothel-keepers had been achieved through the revelations in *Le National*. She did not like the *Pall Mall Gazette*, indeed she had told Stanley '*I hate it*',[20] but now she saw that Stead might be their saviour.

Stead had been campaigning strongly for the raising of the age of consent through the CLAA, and was angry about the collapse of the Mrs Jeffries case. Booth began his campaign to enlist Stead's help by inviting him to his headquarters to meet some of the rescued girls there. Stead also went at Benjamin Waugh's request to meet children in the care of the NSPCC, including girls aged 4 and 7 who had been raped. The attacker of the 7-year-old had been brought to court, but the case was dismissed because during the long time delay 'the little memory had failed as to some of the details'.[21] (Children were required to swear an oath just like adults.) Stead was overcome with pity. When the younger girl said something 'that you needed only to hear to break your heart', he burst into tears. 'Mr Waugh,' he exclaimed, 'I will turn my Paper into a tub ... I will damn and damn.'[22]

Stead studied the tortuous history of the CLAA and 'saw at a glance that all that was needed to carry that measure ... was a vivid and graphic description of the actual evils'.[23] To achieve this, he decided to conduct his own investigation, with a team of hand-picked helpers. So Josephine became a member of Stead's so-called 'Secret Commission', which included journalists and Salvation Army officers. Georgie Butler also agreed to help. Given his lack of experience in this field, his discoveries must have been as traumatic for him as they were for Stead. Even Josephine found the next six weeks 'terrible', as she told Mary Priestman:

> I have been for ten days in London helping several friends in a most terrible investigation concerning the crimes (vice is too pale a word) of the aristocracy. It seems that all that goes on in Brussels and Paris goes on also in London ... I have been about the streets all day and sometimes late at night. O! What horrors we have seen ... My dear son has volunteered to go in disguise into one of the high class dens where there are *padded rooms*. We have had to assume disguises.[24]

She gave scarcely any more detail – then or later. Stead accomplished that task for her.

'The Maiden Tribute of Modern Babylon'

Stead was a journalist of genius. The title of his series of articles, 'The Maiden Tribute of Modern Babylon' has a haunting power which reached every nook and cranny of the capital.[25] Boys delivering the *Pall Mall Gazette* felt compelled, for the first time, to study its closely typed pages. Creased and dirty copies were passed round the poorest courts of the London slums. Second hand copies were sold hand to hand after supplies ran out. The newsagent W.H. Smith refused to stock it and many a *paterfamilias* tried to prevent his wife and daughters from reading it. It was sensation journalism at its most shockingly powerful, surfing a tidal wave of moral outrage.

In ancient times, wrote Stead, the defeated city of Athens was forced by her conqueror to pay a terrible tribute – the sacrifice of seven youths and seven maidens, every nine years, to be devoured by the Minotaur, 'a frightful monster, half man, half bull,' who prowled the Labyrinth of Daedalus seeking his prey.[26] This Labyrinth was so vast, and contained so many corridors and featureless rooms that those who entered it could never find their way out. The Athenians were so traumatised by the fate of their children that the young hero, Theseus, volunteered to risk his life in order to challenge and kill the monster. His victory freed the Athenians from their tribute and destroyed the threat of the Labyrinth forever. Yet in London, 'every night, year in and year out, not seven maidens only, but many times seven' are offered up as the Maiden Tribute:

> Maidens they were when this morning dawned, but tonight their ruin will be accomplished, and tomorrow they will find themselves within the portals of the maze of London brotheldom. Within that labyrinth wander, like lost souls, the vast host of London prostitutes ... The maw of the London Minotaur is insatiable, and none that go into the secret recesses of his lair return again.[27]

In London the 'cultured man of the world' shrugged his shoulders, so Stead cast himself (implicitly) as Theseus armed with the sword of truth to kill the monster through the glare of publicity. His interviewees included the senior Metropolitan policeman Howard Vincent, who told him that virgins were available in 'certain houses', and were very rarely 'consenting parties'. Stead responded:

> 'Do you mean to tell me that in very truth actual rapes, in the legal sense of the word, are constantly being perpetrated in London on unwilling virgins, purveyed and procured to rich men at so much a head by keepers of brothels?' 'Certainly,' said he, 'there is not a doubt of it.' 'Why', I exclaimed, 'the very thought is enough to raise hell.' 'It is true,' he said; 'and although it ought to raise hell, it does not even raise the neighbours'.[28]

One retired doctor, dubbed 'the Minotaur' by Stead, ordered three virgins every fortnight. The word 'order' was used by both buyers and suppliers, for this was a business, and a highly lucrative one for the suppliers who generally took 50 per cent of the fee. The business demanded constant fresh supplies and the suppliers, generally women, were skilled in seeking out attractive and naïve young girls. Two 'procuresses', 'Mesdames X and Z', boasted to Stead that 'at any time we can undertake to deliver a maid if we get due notice'.[29] They groomed nurse girls, who they encountered daily in the park with their young charges, and lured girls as young as 13 away from their poor families in return for fancy clothes and the promise of lucrative work. Once under their control, they took these girls to a brothel, where they were examined to prove their virginity and raped by a favoured customer. This crime was normally impossible to prove when the girl was of consenting age.

'Mesdames X and Z' told Stead that the girls 'sometimes kick and scream and make no end of a row'.[30] One girl 'wrapped herself up in the bed curtains and screamed and fought' so much that she had to be held down throughout the 'seduction'. 'It gave me such a sickening,' said one of them, 'that I was almost going to chuck up the business, but I got into it again.' After one too many of such conversations, Stead was overcome. Josephine encountered him in his office late one night, sobbing: 'Oh Mrs Butler, let me weep or my heart will break.'[31]

Rebecca Jarrett

To show how easy it was to buy a girl from her parents, Stead decided to do it himself and describe the entire process in his newspaper. He risked moral compromise, but the Secret Commission had already bought children in order to rescue them. Josephine and Georgie spent nearly £100 on this, from the 'joint purse'.[32] Josephine said later, 'I believe that it was understood amongst us, and it was my special wish ... that pure young girls were to be bought to prove that this was done for an immoral purpose.'[33] She, Stead and Bramwell Booth had agreed:

> ... that we had only to buy girls that were in the market, and that would otherwise in all probability be ruined ... I brought forward an analogy from the abolitionists in America appearing in the slave market and buying young girls who would otherwise have been sold into slavery, in order to set them free.

Crucial to Stead's plan was a believable woman who could act as procuress to buy the child. Josephine suggested Rebecca Jarrett, who was staying at her House of Rest in Winchester. A former brothel-keeper, Rebecca produced several versions of her life story and she probably never told the full truth to Josephine.[34] It is likely that she was seduced before the age of 13 and taken into prostitution due to the neglect of her mother, who drank in the evenings at the Cremorne Gardens, where gambling and prostitution was carried on openly. Rebecca's respectable version was that her mother had sent her to a private school and then into service, where she was seduced by 'one of the gentlemen visitors'.[35] However, Josephine did know that she had run several brothels in London, and possibly also that she had dealt in virgins.[36] Rebecca developed full-blown alcoholism and, at a time of deep misery while living in Northampton, she saw a Salvation Army poster and attended a meeting. There she was rescued and brought to a refuge in London's Whitechapel district run by Florence Booth, Bramwell Booth's wife. By 'pleading and praying' over many weeks, she was converted and persuaded to give up her way of life.[37] She was successfully treated for her alcoholism in the London Hospital, where one doctor said 'they had never seen such a bad drink case'.[38] When she was discharged Florence Booth decided to send her away from London, since her mother, brother and old associates were pressurising her to return to them. In January 1885 she asked Josephine to accept Rebecca in Winchester.

Rebecca was probably the most demanding and problematic of all the reformed prostitutes for whom Josephine cared. She was deceitful, in poor health, and emotionally unstable. Her drinking and lifestyle had damaged her to a degree which experienced officers of the Salvation Army found difficult to deal with, and Florence Booth may have been relieved to send her away. Josephine, characteristically, chose to believe only the best of Rebecca and gave her unstinting help and support.

In the House of Rest, which had been described to her as a 'faith healing place',[39] she was treated for a bad hip and embarked on a course of instruction in her new, often wavering, Christian faith. Josephine, George and Amelie Humbert spent many hours with her and, by April, allowed her to turn full circle and rescue girls she had previously seen as fair game. She went out at night with Amelie 'to try and undo some of the evil she had done, by speaking to her poor lost sisters in the streets and the public houses'.[40] Josephine was excited by Rebecca's success:

> She went straight into the worst and lowest dens of infamy ... [and] related to them what she herself had been and what God had done for her ... many faces turned to her in wonder, and the fact that she had been one of themselves and now ardently desired their salvation, seemed to have a power to win their hearts and overcome their incredulity, beyond any power which the words of a more blameless person might have had.[41]

The Salvation Army described this as 'sending class to class'. Josephine even suggested to Florence Booth that it was better than 'spending years reforming case after case inside our Homes ... old keepers of bad houses transformed by God's mighty grace as Rebecca has been ... might go out into the streets and gather in such a full and blessed harvest of those poor little girls'.[42] She raised money to rent a cottage where Rebecca could care for her 'harvest', which they called Hope Cottage. Rebecca proved an excellent nurse, not shrinking even from the tender care of a woman whose body became 'a mass of corruption' during her interminably long death. She went on a mission to Portsmouth, where the CD Acts had been enforced, and where prostitutes still abounded. Some were rescued and brought back to Hope Cottage.

When Josephine told her about Stead's request, Rebecca was reluctant, since she would have to return to London and her old haunts, play a role which now repulsed her, and might be found out. All these risks were clear to Josephine, who proposed Rebecca even though she was a new convert and very inexperienced. Did she know that Rebecca often doubted herself and was telling Florence Booth, 'I am not fully saved'?[43] Josephine later acknowledged her 'imprudence' but said that 'in an exceptional enterprise we were forced to use exceptional means'.[44] To persuade Rebecca she also used moral pressure: 'I urged upon her that to make reparation for her past life she should do what was required of her.'[45] Stead used the same argument when she met him. Rebecca reported that Bramwell Booth had instructed her, 'whatever Mr. Stead wanted me to do, I was to go and do it'.[46]

Eliza Armstrong

After one or two false starts, Rebecca decided to visit an old friend, Nancy Broughton, who lived in a single-room slum dwelling in Charles Street, a rough and insanitary backwater in the London borough of Marylebone.[47] The news that Nancy's visitor 'wanted a girl for a place' generated much interest on the street, and several promising girls were offered to her, including Eliza Armstrong, aged 13, who was nursing her baby sister. Her mother was drunk that day, as she was the next day when Rebecca returned and secured her permission for Eliza to take the 'place'. Eliza went off shopping with Rebecca and brought back a number of parcels. She emerged from Nancy's house wearing a complete set of new clothes, dress and necktie, boots and a hat, and departed with Rebecca. According to Rebecca's later account, when they left, Eliza's mother was in the public house drinking with the money she had just given her. She had 'told her I was a loose woman' so she had not obtained her child under false pretences.[48]

The sale of Eliza was to become the climactic article published by Stead on the first day of the Maiden Tribute campaign, with the arresting headline 'A child of thirteen bought for £5'. In this story Rebecca is anonymised as the 'agent of the purchaser' and Eliza is renamed 'Lily'. Stead is 'the purchaser' but does not acknowledge his own role, simply stating that 'I can personally vouch for the absolute accuracy of every fact in the narrative'.[49] In the story, the agent (Rebecca) takes Lily to be examined for virginity by a midwife, who says to her, 'She is so small, her pain will be extreme. I hope you will not be too cruel with her.'[50] To dull Eliza's trauma she offers 'a small phial of chloroform' which the agent buys, together with the statement of virginity. The midwife also offers to 'patch up' the child afterwards if she is badly injured. Lily is then taken to 'a house of ill-fame' in Regent Street, where despite her youth she is 'admitted without question'. The 'agent' puts her to bed and gives her the chloroform. Then she leaves and 'the purchaser' enters the bedroom and locks the door. 'There was a brief silence. And then there rose a wild and piteous cry ... the child's voice was heard crying, in accents of terror, "There's a man in the room! There's a man in the room! Take me home; oh, take me home!"'

The story ends with this cry – Stead had gone as far as he possibly could. In addition to entering the bedroom, his role included interviewing Eliza about her schooling and hovering outside the house of the midwife, Madame Mourez, with his colleague Sampson Jacques.[51] But Eliza, of course, was not assaulted by Stead and he even arranged for a doctor, Heywood Smith, to attest that she was still a virgin. The two intimate examinations of Eliza had not been agreed with Josephine and she was horrified when she found out. After her visit to the doctor, Elizabeth Combe of the Salvation Army took Eliza to one of their homes in France where, by Rebecca's account, she was cared for in 'a lovely home with a real titled lady'.[52] However, harm had been done, since Stead and Rebecca had frightened Eliza and caused her to be removed from her parents. They and the Salvation Army had no intention of returning her either, deeming her new home to be much better for her.

But Mrs Armstrong, Eliza's mother, wanted her daughter back and went looking for her.[53] She informed the local magistrate that Eliza was missing, and Inspector Borner from Scotland Yard arrived in Charles Street to interview Mrs Armstrong and Mrs Broughton. He discovered Rebecca's name and address in Winchester and her connection to Josephine Butler. Josephine herself was now a police target, as she explained in a high spirited letter to Stanley.[54] Describing herself as 'your hunted old Mother', she revealed that on 15 July, when she had returned to Winchester from London, detectives from Scotland Yard had followed her by the next train. They 'ransacked every corner' of The Close. Rebecca was being pursued by 'four brutal brothel-keepers' and had fled to the Continent. This was all due to 'the case of Lily whom we bought' but 'it is all coming out quite right of course'. The police had threatened her with 'six months prison' but she had laughed and said, 'We are detectives like yourselves.' She referred Inspector Borner to Bramwell Booth, who refused to reveal Eliza's location to him. However he reassured him that 'I know something of the case'.[55] Borner told Mrs Armstrong that 'her child was quite well and that she had now better let the matter drop'.

The Summer of 1885

The 'Maiden Tribute' articles were published in the week of 6–9 July. They galvanised public opinion to such an extent that Parliament felt compelled to act. MPs were being deluged with letters from constituents, and there were daily meetings and demonstrations. 'The crowds and scenes remind me of Revolution days in Paris,' wrote Josephine. 'It is a grand unveiling of hell, and a blessing it has come before the General Election.'[56] The CLAA was reintroduced on 9 July and debated for the next month. James Stuart, who had been elected to Parliament in 1884, was one of those working hard to ensure not only that the bill was passed but that unacceptable clauses were improved.

Josephine herself was now emotionally exhausted by 'the wrongs and sorrows we were forced deliberately to look upon and measure'. She had stood 'in the near presence of the powers of evil: what I see and hear are the smoke of the pit, the violence of the torture inflicted by man on his fellows, the cries of lost spirits, the wail of the murdered innocents, and the laughter of demons'.[57] Her distress was so great that it was probably at this time that she felt her faith faltering. 'I resembled the faint-hearted though loyal disciple, who when venturing to walk on the waters, in an evil moment looked away from Christ ... and immediately began to sink.'[58]

It was George who rescued her, as he:

> ... seemed to rise before me to a stature far above my level ... while he gently led me back to great first principles and to the Source of all Truth.[59]
>
> Turning from the contemplation of such unspeakable woes and depths of moral turpitude, it was a strength and comfort beyond description, through the years of strife, to look upon the calm face of my best earthly friend.[60]

George took Josephine and Georgie away on holiday – they left for Switzerland on 17 July.[61] The night before her departure, Josephine attended a 'great and true "Indignation meeting"' at Exeter Hall, addressed by prominent leaders of the purity campaign. She herself seconded the resolution, asking Parliament to pass 'a bill for the protection of young girls from the evil lusts of wicked men, which shall raise the age of protection'.[62]

In Geneva, the Butlers met up with other family members, including their niece Rhoda (the daughter of Josephine's youngest sister, Emily, by her second husband, Jasper Bolton) who was engaged to marry Stanley. This delighted Josephine; Rhoda was her favourite niece to whom she had become a spiritual mentor. She told her, 'It seems as if God has *put you* in my heart.'[63] Rhoda wrote to Stanley from Geneva, 'I do so admire Aunt Josey having the courage to find out these awful things ... what she has told me has quite sickened me.'[64]

Hatty and her family joined them in Grindelwald, a mountain village in the Bernese Alps which was so dear to George that he had started a project to build an Anglican church there. His friend, the mountaineer Emil Boss, wanted George to become the independent chaplain. Earlier that year, Boss had arrived in England with eight of his St Bernard dogs – who must have posed a considerable transportation challenge! Both Josephine and George loved St Bernards, and were delighted when Boss brought two of them on a visit to The Close. They bedded them down in the stable, and decided to keep one of them, Eiger.[65]

At the end of August, Stead came out to visit them there, and discovered an immediate rapport with Hatty.[66] He had come straight from a rally in Hyde Park to celebrate the passing of the Criminal Law Amendment Act (CLAA) on 14 August. The age of consent was now 16, and the requirement for child witnesses to understand the oath had been removed. The penalty for having sex with a girl aged 13–16, or keeping her on the premises for sex, was two years imprisonment. Abduction of a girl under 18 for sexual purposes would attract the same penalty. There were unprecedented scenes of jubilation in the House, and on Saturday 22 August the rally attracted a quarter of a million people. The ladies of the LNA drove in carriages; each dressed in black and carrying a bouquet of white flowers.[67] Josephine rejoiced in Switzerland.

The Consequences

During the summer, *Lloyd's Weekly* newspaper had been investigating the story of the lost girl, Eliza Armstrong.[68] Her mother still wanted to get her back to prove that she did not sell her. Under pressure from both the police and the press, Bramwell Booth caved in and Eliza was brought back from France. In a dramatic speech on 21 August, Stead came to the defence of his friends in the Salvation Army. He admitted publicly that Eliza was 'Lily' and stated that he alone was responsible for taking her 'from her mother's house' which he claimed was 'steeped in vice'.[69] This self-serving justification could not save him, however. While Stead was away in Switzerland, the police interviewed Eliza and her mother. After considering all the evidence, it was decided to prosecute him, along with others responsible for the abduction and detention of Eliza, including Rebecca Jarrett, Bramwell Booth and the midwife, Madame Mourez.

Stead's holiday was 'abruptly interrupted' and Josephine received a letter from Georgie (in London) telling her that Rebecca Jarrett was in prison.[70] Bramwell Booth had requested that she return to London to support them all. As she hurried back to help Rebecca, Josephine realised that, although not indicted herself, she would have to 'answer for her conduct'.[71]

The six defendants appeared at Bow Street Magistrates' court on 7 September, charged with taking Eliza against the will of her mother and father, detaining her, administering a 'certain noxious thing' (the chloroform) and committing an indecent assault on her (the examination).[72] During the six days of committal proceedings, the central issue became clear – did Mrs Armstrong know that Eliza was to be 'seduced'? Rebecca Jarrett said 'yes', but Mrs Armstrong, who made a good impression as 'a respectable woman doing the best for her children', maintained that Rebecca had said she wanted Eliza for 'cleaning and scrubbing'. The magistrate chose to believe the mother and committed five of the defendants to the Old Bailey for criminal trial.

The trial was a sensational epilogue to the 'Maiden Tribute' campaign. The court was packed and crowds thronged outside and rushed to read the transcript in the newspapers. The *Pall Mall Gazette* published a special supplement. Under close questioning, Stead was forced to admit that he had relied entirely on Rebecca's account of the sale of Eliza. He had not met Rebecca before her recruitment to the campaign, 'but she came to me with an emphatic testimonial as to her trustworthiness'.[73] Although unnamed, Josephine was implicated. When Mrs Armstrong was questioned again, her story began to unravel; it was most unusual for a girl to go away in new clothes, as Eliza had. The neighbours in Charles Street had noticed this and the story in the *Pall Mall Gazette* headlined 'A child of thirteen bought for £5' had aroused their suspicions. Their disapproval was most probably the spur goading Mrs Armstrong to find and recover Eliza.

Rebecca's testimony was now crucial, but could a former brothel-keeper convince the court? She gave a consistent account of events in Charles Street, but on her second day in the witness stand it was proved that she had deliberately given a false address for an 'improper house' she had kept in London. This was disastrous, it allowed the Judge to brand her a liar and conclude that 'Stead was misled by the lies Jarrett told him'.[74] She had told Stead that her crimes included buying and selling virgins, and so had pretended to buy a virgin in order to justify herself with him and keep 'her truthfulness ... in the eyes of Mrs Butler'. The Judge, who called the 'Maiden Tribute' articles 'disgusting and filthy', also ruled that, even if Rebecca was telling the truth, the consent of Eliza's father was required and had not been sought.

This objection, not raised until the tenth day of the trial, sealed the prosecution case. Stead and Rebecca had not dealt with Eliza's father at all. Although forced to admit that, 'I made many blunders and mistakes', Stead refused to be downhearted. Win or lose, the publicity was gold dust for his newspaper and his campaign. The jury found him guilty, but asked for his 'purest motive' to be taken into consideration. For Rebecca it had little sympathy and found her guilty, with Stead, of taking Eliza 'out of the possession of her father against his will'. They were also guilty of indecent assault. Stead was sentenced to three months imprisonment, while Rebecca received six months. Madame Louisa Mourez received the most severe sentence – six months with hard labour for the indecent assault.

Josephine's Defence

Bramwell Booth was exonerated and no criticism was attached to Josephine. However, both had encouraged Rebecca to help Stead, although Josephine did not know exactly what Rebecca would be required to do. She was in Winchester when Rebecca met Stead in London, and thus not able to support her. For this she undoubtedly felt guilty. She gave defence evidence at Rebecca's trial, going up to London eighteen times 'about the Trial alone, sometimes there and back in the same day'.[75] There she disclosed that she had wanted Eliza to come to live with Rebecca in Winchester: 'It was a very great disappointment to me that she did not come.'[76]

When Rebecca was in prison, Josephine took to her pen, dashing off a justification of their actions in a pamphlet simply called *Rebecca Jarrett*.[77] Rebecca's punishment, she wrote, was the greater because she was a 'fallen woman' and thus the 'scapegoat upon whom, justly or unjustly, the sins and miseries of society must be heaped', just like the outcast woman in the Temple.[78] In court she was an easy victim and was trapped into a lie by her promise to former friends not to reveal their address. While defending Rebecca, she revealed her own scars. The popular verdict of the London press was that she, Josephine, and the Salvation Army had been 'duped' by Rebecca. Josephine was incensed by this picture of herself as an innocent out of her depth – on the contrary, she knew all about Rebecca's past life and reminded her readers that Christ himself had been scorned for trusting prostitutes. She had trusted Rebecca to the extent that 'we were as sisters together, not "employer and employed"'.[79]

Rebecca's friends campaigned for a reprieve and presented a petition to the Home Secretary, Sir William Harcourt. He did not release her, but visited her in Milbank Prison and arranged for her to have a warmer cell.[80] Josephine also visited her regularly, and received messages from her via the chaplain, 'not to fret about her as she is well and happy'.[81] The chaplain offered to take Rebecca as his housekeeper when she was released, but Josephine wanted her back in Winchester. When Rebecca left prison in April 1886, however, Josephine was in France and she was met by Florence Booth, who took her to a restaurant for the cup of tea she had been longing for throughout her imprisonment. Captain Susan 'Hawker' Jones then took charge, taking Rebecca to lodgings in the country which Josephine helped to pay for.[82]

Rebecca was keen to resume her work in Winchester, but a visit there went very badly. Her nerves were in shreds. Josephine wrote to the Booths to tell them that 'poor Rebecca's brain is giving way' and she had been 'really insane' for several days.[83] Rebecca knew about this letter and it may be the reason why there is no further recorded contact with Josephine, although she sometimes gave her money. The Salvation Army decided to send Rebecca, accompanied by Susan Jones, to Canada but they fell out on the trip and returned to London within a few months.[84] Rebecca stayed in the Army throughout her long life, however, and was at times able to work in their homes. She received support through good times and bad from Florence Booth.

In Winchester, a year after the Maiden Tribute campaign, a highly agitated crowd objected volubly to a Salvation Army meeting on the Green and chased away the 'poor Army girls' leading it.[85] Hearing they had been hurt, Josephine went outside. The police told her the girls were safe but, seeing Josephine, someone in the crowd maliciously shouted 'Rebecca Jarrett' and so it turned on her. Josephine told Bramwell Booth, 'they were not wicked or violent in action but simply such a dense mass that I was almost borne down.' They pushed through The Close, where the 'awful howling of "Rebecca"' brought everyone to their windows. Georgie, who was visiting, lost his temper when he heard his mother insulted and 'knocked down the foremost man'. She feared that he would be charged with assault and the Dean was 'fearfully angry, with me of course, for being the occasion of such a disgraceful scene within the sacred precincts of The Close'. He had discovered for himself that life with Josephine was never quiet.

INTERLUDE

Ellice Hopkins, Purity and Vigilance

At a meeting to support the 'Maiden Tribute' campaign, Josephine was joined on the platform of the Prince's Hall in London by Jane Ellice Hopkins, a Purity worker who was just as committed, indeed obsessed, as she was.[86] The daughter of a Cambridge mathematician, Ellice Hopkins was a 'devout High Church spinster' who had committed her life to social purity.[87] Like Josephine, she had begun her philanthropic career as a rescue worker, and had become an inspirational speaker and campaigner. She too was brave enough to lecture undergraduates about purity, on one occasion facing down a daunting crowd of medical students at Edinburgh University.[88] She was extraordinarily energetic, producing pamphlets and articles constantly, and estimated to be responsible for the formation of 'well over two hundred rescue and moral reform charities'.[89]

In her heart of hearts, however, Ellice did not believe that moral change could be achieved by persuasion, or even Christian conviction, alone. Purity could, and must, be enforced by law – and deviation from morality must be punished. This should apply to both men and women. Ellice Hopkins was prepared to imprison immoral men and to make it impossible for prostitutes to carry on in business, by force.

This was not the voluntary approach in which Josephine believed so passionately, and nor was it feminist. Ellice 'did not connect prostitution to larger feminist issues, particularly to the economic and political disabilities of women'.[90] However, her objectives were close enough to the concerns of members of Josephine's LNA for many of them to be seduced by Ellice's eloquence into accepting her tactics.

The first time this happened was in Plymouth in 1879, where she had gone to establish an industrial school for girls.[91] The school was aimed at prostitutes' children, who were to be rescued from brothels and 'disorderly and immoral' homes.[92] The local branch of the LNA was struggling and leaderless at the time and Ellice quickly gained the members' support. Despite Josephine's urgent warnings, the ladies were enlisted into a cause which empowered the police to remove children forcibly from their homes and place them in the school. They thus formed common cause with the infamous Inspector Anniss, whose evidence had proved so harmful to the repeal campaign during the Royal Commission hearings in 1871.

The Plymouth branch of the LNA subsequently closed down, and its members followed Ellice Hopkins into a new rescue society. Her scheme to impound prostitutes' children became national policy in 1880, enshrined in law as the Industrial Schools Amendment Act. Josephine and her supporters dismissed them as 'large prison schools'.[93]

After the suspension of the CD Acts in 1883, Ellice Hopkins announced the formation of the 'White Cross Army'. Its name was carefully chosen – 'white' for purity, 'cross' for Christianity and 'army' for the rigorous, disciplined and relentless conviction of its 'troops'.[94] It advocated the same law of purity for both men and women. The programme included social purity training for young men and the pursuit of legal and institutional sanctions against working-class 'immorality'. Ellice hoped to 'take into custody every man and woman who were found publicly soliciting in the streets'.[95]

In 1883 her followers in Plymouth formed a 'vigilance committee' which held nocturnal patrols, described by the *Western Daily Mercury* as the 'demoralising spectacle of respectable ladies perambulating the town from twilight to midnight ... for the purpose of tracking young persons of both sexes whom they happen to observe about the streets of Plymouth after dark'.[96] Former metropolitan policemen were being employed to enforce a new moral regime with many of the features that should have disappeared with the suspension of the CD Acts. 'Control of the lives of accused prostitutes did not end with the repeal of the Acts: it was merely transferred to new agencies, often with similar personnel to those who had enforced the Contagious Diseases Acts.'[97]

The aim of Josephine's own Vigilance Association for the Defence of Personal Rights, formed in 1871, was very different. Its focus was on Parliament and keeping a 'vigilant' watch on its activities. When used by Ellice Hopkins and her supporters, the word 'Vigilance' had almost the opposite aim – of defining and controlling the moral behaviour of the people and punishing those who did not adhere to their standards. Josephine told Florence Booth that, in her opinion, the methods used by Ellice Hopkins were 'rather mechanical and without a mighty outpouring of the Spirit of God they will just pass on into the category of official remedies which merely touch the outside'.[98] After the passing of the CLAA in 1885, the contrast in their approaches became an increasing problem.

Time for George (1886–90)

～ℓ The National Vigilance Association

The passing of the CLAA in August 1885 was both a triumph and a setback for Josephine. She had campaigned hard for the raising of the age of consent, and was delighted by the success of the 'Maiden Tribute' campaign. Girls under 16 were now protected, and it was illegal to abduct a girl under 18 for the purposes of sex. Magistrates had powers to search premises where girls might be detained against their will 'for immoral purposes'.[1] On the whole, the Act criminalised those who abused women and girls, and avoided the 'legalised harassment' of prostitutes which had featured in previous versions of the Act, and which her Vigilance Association had campaigned against.[2]

However, the CLAA went much further than she had wished, in criminalising 'any person who keeps or manages or acts or assists in the management of a brothel'.[3] Josephine had no illusions that this would end prostitution – it would simply continue elsewhere. But the doors were now wide open for Purity activists like Ellice Hopkins to close down brothels and prosecute brothel-keepers. Vastly increased powers had been handed to the police, especially the Metropolitan police, which Josephine had denounced for its role in implementing the CD Acts as an 'organised body of woman-hunters'.[4] When the bill passed its first reading in the House of Commons, Josephine had hoped to 'strike out all the police clauses in committee!'[5]

An excited and enthusiastic rally to celebrate the passing of the CLAA was held at St James's Hall on 21 August, attended by members of rescue, purity and vigilance groups, the White Cross Army, the Salvation Army and the LNA. A new umbrella organisation, the National Vigilance Association (NVA), was formed to co-ordinate their efforts to implement the new Act. Josephine was now in a quandary. Only a few months earlier, she had described many of these groups as 'repressionists in our midst', because they wanted to abolish prostitution and improve morality through coercion, rather than free choice.[6] However, she hoped to win them over:

> These people are not our enemies. These repressionists, mistaken as we think they are in their methods, are still honestly desirous of getting rid of prostitution ... It is the fervent desire of my heart to win and gain over entirely to our side all that crowd of repressionists who are now, as I think, going in a distinctly wrong direction, but who may be won.[7]

For such reasons she decided to join the new National Vigilance Association, and encouraged her LNA followers to do the same. Their influence may, perhaps, have helped to ensure that in its early years the association focussed on assistance and rescue. It supported the victims of indecent assault, rape and kidnap, and provided them with a solicitor.[8] 'Many men were prosecuted for sexual offences against children and girls; servants were helped to find redress against masters who had made them pregnant and thrown them out into the street.'[9] The NVA campaigned for female magistrates and police, as well as educating schoolteachers, schoolgirls and managers about sexual danger.

However, the Vigilance Association increasingly abandoned the struggle to reform and educate, following the lead of its Secretary, William Coote, who argued:

> There is a very popular cant phrase that you cannot make men good by Act of Parliament. It is false to say so ... You can, and do, keep men sober simply by an Act of Parliament; you can, and do, chain the devil of impurity in a large number of men and women by the fear of the law.[10]

Josephine could not accept this view. She had been fighting against it all her life. She knew that attempts to enforce moral behaviour by law usually proved to be more socially harmful than the original problem. Evidence that this was happening quickly accumulated.

Groups of single women found it increasingly difficult to find housing, since landlords were reluctant to rent premises to them. It was not worth the risk of prosecution if the police decided that prostitution was taking place there.[11] The emphasis on rescuing and rehabilitating prostitutes gradually declined as they became 'public nuisances'. The Clapham Vigilance Association, for example, protested that not only was 'solicitation openly and offensively practised, but actual fornication is shamelessly committed on the numerous benches and in other places upon the Common'.[12]

Campaigns by vigilance groups, allied with residents' associations concerned about property prices, led to the arrest of prostitutes for soliciting, described as 'disorderly conduct'. Just as Josephine had feared, the CLAA was 'applied by the police in ways oppressive to women and girls rather than restraining the conduct of men (except male procurers and brothel keepers)'.[13] She did not mention that it also criminalised male homosexuals.[14] Her concern for them was aroused later, in 1894, when she felt 'so sorry for Oscar Wilde', who had been imprisoned for his homosexual affair, 'I hope they will treat him mercifully ... I pray for him constantly'.[15]

Prostitutes who were forced to leave brothels or lodgings moved elsewhere, and grew clever at disguising their new premises as massage parlours, manicure services, even nursing homes. A police raid on a so-called 'school', offering lessons in elocution and deportment, found 'several dog whips, 19 canes, some bearing marks of blood, four birches, a mask, three pairs of handcuffs, three padlocks, and books many of which were of a grossly obscene character'.[16]

Those with premises were the lucky ones – prostitute hunting and eviction caused destitution among women unable to find a new home. Many were forced to rely on pimps for protection, and put themselves at much greater risk of exploitation and ill treatment. The result of vigilance campaigns was, ironically, to put more women on the streets, where they were not only a greater nuisance to the public but also in far greater danger themselves. The most lurid example is the murder of prostitutes by 'Jack the Ripper' in the back streets of Whitechapel, London, in 1888. Four of the bodies were found in streets known as 'Do as You Please Street', where 'fourpenny knee tremblers' took their customers to dark corners to avoid the price of a room.[17] Such sensational and unusual murders might have happened at any time, but it is a fact that '[p]urity groups had closed down two hundred brothels in the East End in the year prior to the Ripper murders, rendering hundreds of women homeless, hence vulnerable to attack'.[18]

By then Josephine had lost most of her patience with the NVA. Her followers in the Vigilance Association for the Defence of Personal Rights were angry that the NVA had 'filched from us our good name' and had decided to change theirs to the 'Personal Rights Association' (PRA).[19] The PRA was incensed that the double standard was still thriving, the closure of brothels 'persecutes the women and leaves the men unmolested'.[20] When the NVA claimed to have rescued women from these houses, PRA members like Elizabeth Wolstenholme Elmy investigated and often found that they had been consigned to hospital or to prison. In 1886 she pointed out that under the Prisons Act they could still be forcibly detained and examined for sexually transmitted disease. 'Our mistaken friends' in the NVA 'have brought us back to that cruel oppression which they denounced and resisted'.[21]

The mistakes should not be exaggerated. Many of the women who worked for the NVA 'considered Josephine Butler their inspiration'.[22] She thoroughly approved of the achievements of some branches, which successfully prosecuted '[a] great many men (including police) ... for sexual offences against children and girls' and gained redress for servants 'against masters who had made them pregnant and thrown them onto the street'.

The Repeal of the CD Acts, 1886

Since the suspension of the CD Acts in 1883, there had been moves within Parliament to keep them in a modified form – a '"flank movement" of the enemy' which Joseph Edmondson had predicted.[23] The Liberal Minister Lord Hartington showed himself to be the 'enemy' by proposing a bill to retain the system of special police, police surgeons and compulsory detention in lock hospitals. He thought this could be done if the internal examination was voluntary.[24]

This bill was introduced in May 1883, to Josephine's horror. She said that it was simply the old CD Act, 'with the addition of the horrible insult to women of *forcing them to ask as a favour that the abominable outrage should be inflicted on them*'.[25] She feared that 'half of those who voted with Stansfeld are somewhat weak-kneed, or untaught, and would support a compromise framed by government'.[26] 'The traps laid for us are clever.'

James Stansfeld took the pragmatic view that it was better to amend the bill during the debate, but the NA publicly denounced it through *The Shield*. This was unfortunate for Stansfeld, whose sister-in-law Emilie Venturi was the editor.[27] The government quietly dropped Hartington's bill, but it left a lasting mark on the repeal movement. The NA decided to end its pro-Liberal policy, forcing Wilson, Stuart and the Butlers to cut their connections with the repeal society they had worked alongside since 1869.[28]

There was great instability in Parliament during the years 1885–86. The Liberals under Gladstone won the general election of November 1885, but the Irish Nationalists held the balance of power.[29] The Conservatives' attempt to run a minority government lasted three months and the Liberals returned to office, but Gladstone needed the support of all his MPs if he was to survive as Prime Minister.

Liberal repealers in the new House numbered 221, and Stansfeld was determined to use their bargaining power with the new government.[30] He was supported by James Stuart, now an MP who, Josephine said, was working 'with all his heart and might' to deliver repeal.[31] In March, a resolution that the Acts 'ought to be repealed' was carried in the House without a division. Stansfeld and Stuart went to see Gladstone and persuaded him to give government support to a repeal bill. As an unexpected bonus, he recalled Stansfeld to the Cabinet on 26 March 1886.

Time was running out. Gladstone had announced his conversion to Home Rule for Ireland. (Josephine enthusiastically supported him, indeed Stanley reminded her, 'you were in favour of Home Rule long before old Gladstone ever thought of it'.)[32] But before the General Election swept the Liberals from office, the Repeal of the Contagious Diseases Acts, a small but plucky ship on a stormy sea dotted with battered vessels, sailed through the Commons on 2 April and the Lords on 13 April.

Josephine was not in the Ladies' Gallery, or at the prayer meetings, or even in the country to witness the triumph of her seventeen year campaign. Not knowing that events would move so swiftly, and both 'in a very shakey condition', she and George had left for a holiday in Cannes, and gone on to Naples to stay with Hatty and Tell,[33] since a Federation Crusade was to be held in Naples that Easter. At the hour of repeal her mind was on the work in Europe.

Margaret Tanner was in the Ladies' Gallery when Stansfeld's initial resolution was passed, and sent Josephine this account:

> It was about 5 o'clock when, in full house, Mr Stansfeld rose to move his resolution. He was well received and the House listened with marked and almost reverent attention, to a speech, which for consummate tact and ability, exquisite diction, firm and high resolve, religious and moral fervour, clothed in earnest utterance, pathetic appeal, purity, grace and beauty; must ever remain in the memory of those who listened to it, as one of unrivalled eloquence ... Mr Stansfeld, Mr Stuart and Mr Wilson came up to the ladies gallery to receive our congratulations and share our joy – their faces were radiant.[34]

Telegrams arrived from both Stuart and Stansfeld on 16 April to tell Josephine of the Queen's Assent. She wrote to Stanley that she could scarcely believe it had happened: 'I feel inclined to do as Cromwell did when he saw poor King Charles lying dead. He just took hold of the head and shook it a little, to be quite sure that it was loose from the body!'[35] Despite the congratulations she received, her thoughts were of the agonising struggle they had endured, 'to us those seventeen years often seemed very long'.[36] To William Stead she wrote, 'now, when it has come at last, much of the triumph seems to have been lost in being deferred'; a response which he described as 'pathetic, but not unusual'.[37] She was reminded only 'at what a price the triumph has been won'.

George at Death's Door

Josephine had been struggling with illness – her own and George's. At the end of March she wrote a dramatic letter from Naples headed 'Middle of the night', to tell Georgie that his father had a serious fever.[38] The 'treacherous climate' of Naples 'with all its beauty' might be responsible. She was waking George regularly to give him beef tea, and Aunt Hatty had provided 'every possible comfort'. He made a slow recovery, and they met up with Charlie in Milan before George returned home to Winchester.

Josephine lingered on the Continent, and when she returned home in May, she found George seriously ill again, his illness now diagnosed as rheumatic fever. He was unable to attend the joyful Federation Congress in London, which celebrated the repeal of the CD Acts on 27 June with a 'praise meeting' and the shaking of hands among 'all the Societies and workers'.[39] He could not even see friends who came to his home, like William Shaen, the chairman of the NA, who had to settle for 'making the acquaintance of your charming house and garden and your magnificent dogs'.[40]

To their delight, they were joined at The Close by Stanley and his new wife, Rhoda.[41] Josephine and George had attended their wedding on 8 February before leaving for the Continent. The young couple spent the autumn at The Close, while they returned to Europe. George had recovered sufficiently for a journey to the medicinal spa at Bad Homburg, near Frankfurt, which doctors recommended.

Josephine's life was now centred on maintaining George's comfort and happiness. He was able to go to Grindelwald in September to preach in the little church he had founded, which had opened at Whitsuntide.[42] The 'bracing air' however did not improve his health and they were soon stranded at a pension outside Berne by a return of the rheumatic fever; a great setback for poor George, whom Josephine found with 'two large tears rolling down the side of his face'. Worried by the cost of their long exile, she took up cooking for possibly the first time in her life, reporting proudly that she had 'gathered a complete set of cooking apparatus in my own room, the gift of my dear sister Mrs Meuricoffre. At first I burnt my hands and made some sad messes, but now I can make beautiful cocoa, beef tea and several other things, an immense saving.'[43] Then 'a kind friend' lent Josephine her maid, 'who sleeps in my room, not to have the expense of another room'.

In the pension, a summer chalet without fireplaces, George was so ill that Josephine 'prayed earnestly for his dear life'.[44] As a chill, damp autumn settled, George struggled against pleurisy, pericarditis, and heart valve inflammation, all complications of rheumatic fever. For three weeks, according to his doctor, he was 'face to face with death'.[45] Hatty came to support Josephine, and all three sons made the journey to visit their father. Stanley reported to Rhoda that 'Father fidgets and can't sleep; Mother frets and can't eat'.[46]

Charlie was a great help, as Josephine reported, 'All that he had learned in the hospitals of Egypt of ambulance work, carrying and lifting wounded people etc. came in *so* usefully.'[47] As George began to recover, though so weak that his mind wandered, they were able to move him to more comfortable accommodation at a large hotel, the Bernerhoff, in Berne. The expenses were 'enormous', but Josephine's prayers were answered by a friend in Leeds, Emily Ford, who offered generous financial support.[48] She ensured that George's difficult journey home to Winchester was as comfortable as possible, with an 'invalid carriage' on the trains.[49] He was able to return despite a final relapse which, Josephine believed, was overcome by an answer to her prayers one night when her 'own strength was failing'. She was able to say confidently the next morning, 'You are going to be better today, beloved' – and he was.[50]

In the Grosvenor Hotel, London, on 20 December, she rejoiced that she had brought her husband back alive and that they would meet 'that dear little granddaughter who has now lived 3 months in our house without our ever seeing her'.[51] Rhoda had given birth to a baby girl, named Josephine, at The Close in September. Rhoda was so sure his new granddaughter would cheer George that she had offered to bring her to Switzerland to visit him.[52] Now she waited on the steps of The Close to greet their homecoming in time for Christmas 'with tears of joy'.[53]

India: the New 'Abolitionist Crusade'

During the months of anxiety about George, Josephine continued to think about her work. She discussed Federation issues with James Stuart when he came to visit George, and agreed with him that the battle against the CD Acts was not over. They had not been repealed in the British colonies, and the appalling situation in India had been a concern for many years.[54] The Indian CD Act enforced the registration and compulsory examination of prostitutes in the major cities, seaports and army camps.[55] The British Army stationed in India was vast, and most of the troops were single men on six year placements. The provision of healthy prostitutes was regarded as essential. Josephine wrote to the Priestman sisters:

> Mr Stuart has made my blood boil again with quite youthful wrath by what he has told me ... For 20 years Indian women have been oppressed and outraged ... and by a *Christian* nation ... Dear people, my heart is faint, but I can still denounce: will you help me somehow to stir up English women afresh? Please, I beg that we continue a separate *women's* organisation for at least a year.[56]

Shortly after returning home she wrote a 'Letter to the LNA', *The Revival and Extension of the Abolitionist Cause*, announcing 'a second chapter of our great Abolitionist crusade'.[57] The words 'Abolitionist' and 'crusade' deliberately evoked the anti-slavery campaign. Josephine argued that the LNA now had 'a decided vantage ground, as combatants after a first battle gained', and stuffed her pamphlet with detail (supplied by Stuart) about the enforcement of the CD Acts in the colonies. She concluded with a rallying call to her fellow Christians:

> I beseech you now, once more, to ... join hands with our sisters, of whatever colour, or race they may be, in order to wipe out the wrong done in that Beloved Name.

Josephine had done her homework, but knew that much of her information was out of date. She could not go to India herself, but Alfred Dyer, her Quaker publisher who investigated the Belgian trafficking scandal, spent several months there. In a series of articles for the *Sentinel*, Dyer described a system in which licensed prostitutes were officially attached to British regiments, with their living conditions and health carefully monitored to preserve the health of the troops. In Sitapur, for example, there were 'three bazaars of Government-certificated harlots' which the Army stated were 'well-kept and provided with requisites for the maintenance of cleanliness'.[58] The purpose of these houses was well known to the local inhabitants, destroying the idea that Christian Britain promoted a superior morality.

At Bareilly, the tents of the 'licensed harlots' were pitched right next to the Christian church and Christian village, set up by local missionaries. The system was so cosily arranged that the licensed prostitutes 'moved from place to place with British regiments on the march, under the sanction and direction of the Authorities'.[59]

Josephine was grateful for Dyer's typically thorough contribution, although she told the Priestman sisters that she disliked his attitude to the Indian women. He had no compassion for them, 'His expressions are those of disgust and reprobation only [while] ... [m]y heart is racked with pity for them.'[60]

In May 1888 Dyer published evidence which handed live ammunition to the Abolitionist campaign. A medical officer told him in confidence that, in order to obtain more women for the troops, officials went into the villages flourishing a government order for prostitutes. 'The poor people are afraid to refuse or resist; their daughters are delivered up; and thus virtuous girls are consigned to lives of infamy.'[61] The truth of this report was proved by 'secret official papers' obtained by Dyer.[62] These were orders sent to every cantonment (the areas controlled by the British Army in India), including a circular memorandum from the Quartermaster General who decreed: 'In the regimental bazaars, it is necessary to have a sufficient number of women [and] to take care that they are sufficiently attractive.'[63] The local women were described as 'convenient arrangements' for the troops. Dyer was horrified, 'but are they not among those for whom Christ died, and for whose salvation missionaries labour?'[64]

Josephine herself compared the girls to slaves – they were bought for 3 rupees and 'dragged into the *Chucklas* [sic], i.e. the camps of vice, in which they are held as complete slaves ... they are the women of a conquered race oppressed by their conquerors.'[65] She wrote to General Sir Frederick Roberts, Commander-in-Chief of the army, to denounce this treatment. He later repudiated this 'Infamous Memorandum' and claimed to have no prior knowledge of it, but in his reply to Josephine he said that the army's policy 'seemed necessary to preserve the health of their soldiers, who are surrounded in this country by far greater temptation than people in England have any idea of'.[66]

In the House of Commons, James Stuart had been addressing fruitless questions to Sir John Gorst, Under-Secretary of State for India, for several months. They were stonewalled with official denials that 'the Government of India was acting the part of a procurer'.[67] When the 'Infamous Memorandum' emerged there was outrage across Britain. It was 'denied point blank' in Parliament, until copies were issued to every MP and 'it could be denied no longer'. Josephine was in the Ladies' Gallery 'when Sir John Gorst had to confess that the ghastly story from India was true'.[68] Horrified, the House unanimously passed a resolution in June 1888 repealing the 'measures for the compulsory examination of women, and for licensing and regulating prostitution in India'.[69]

This swift success was a dazzling triumph for the Abolitionists. However, the army in India was a long way off and its need for healthy prostitutes undiminished. The India Office in London was giving private advice to the viceroy about how to evade the new rules.[70] A new Cantonment Act was passed the following year, 1889, which required anyone 'suspected of carrying a contagious disease' to submit to examination and be expelled from the cantonment for refusal.[71] This examination was not compulsory, but the poor women who followed the army and lived in the *chaklas* had no other home or livelihood. Through the 'sly intransigence' of the Indian authorities, the army was able to carry on abusing them almost as it had before.[72] The Abolitionist campaign had to continue.

George's Final Illness

The year 1887 was a happy one for the Butler family. George was able to return to his ministry at Winchester Cathedral and Josephine opened a new cottage home, with help from her ever supportive friends, the Priestman sisters.[73] They were proud that Charlie, who was still in Europe, was able to help the relief effort after an enormous earthquake struck the Riviera in February – he and an Irish friend, with two donkeys, distributed food and blankets to starving Italian villagers.[74]

George and Josephine returned to their beloved Switzerland and attended the Federation conference at Lausanne in September. George resumed his interest in politics, especially Irish Home Rule, and Josephine continued her India campaign. She never left him for more than a few hours, however, because he missed her. 'He was now less strong, and advanced in years, and these things seemed to me to constitute a most sacred claim to my personal and constant devotion to him.'[75] She refused invitations to attend meetings, despite the urgings of her fellow workers.

In November 1887 their son, Georgie, embarked for India on a trip that had been postponed at the last minute in 1886 when his father was ill.[76] Josephine hoped that he would gain 'a wide and statesmanlike grasp of our position there'.[77] Unfortunately, he contracted a fever on his way home, and was so delirious that Josephine had to nurse him in his 'little room' at Toynbee Hall in London's East End, where he taught classes for 'working men and poor schoolmistresses'.[78] In the February cold he slowly recovered.

That year, 1888, the Federation Congress was held in Copenhagen, Denmark, a country the Butlers had never visited. They set off in high anticipation. George had been commissioned to write an article on the famous Thorvaldsen sculptures and visited the art galleries in the company of Tell Meuricoffre. During his conference speech, George paid a heartfelt tribute to Josephine:

> It is sometimes said that women who take up a great cause for the benefit of their fellow creatures are in danger of neglecting the sacred duties of home ... I may tell you that had it not been for the constant and devoted care which my wife bestowed on me, during a long and very serious illness, I should not be standing here to speak to you today.[79]

After the conference, Josephine went to Malmo in Sweden to meet supporters there. They included the Crown Princess, with whom Josephine had a personal audience.[80] During the sea voyage back to England in September, the weather was cold and stormy but, to Josephine's dismay, George remained on deck throughout and was 'much chilled' by the time they disembarked.[81]

Stanley, Rhoda and their daughter, little Josephine, were at The Close when they returned. On 23 September, Rhoda gave birth to a son, Arthur Stanley George (always known as Bob). Hatty was visiting at the time and recalled that she and George sat in the cathedral, listening to an anthem, while they waited for news.[82] George's face was 'beaming with loving emotion' when Stanley came to tell him that his first grandson had arrived.

During the autumn, their lives were cheered by the presence of Rhoda and the children, even though George became ill again, with a severe form of jaundice (liver disease). Over the following months his appearance changed dramatically; he grew thin and his complexion became, in his own words, 'the colour of autumn leaves'. Both Josephine and Georgie believed that the cause was the chill he had received on the voyage back from Copenhagen. Later in the year a London specialist 'pronounced him to be very ill' and gave George only a few months to live. This frightened Josephine so much that she wrote to a friend: 'I am full of sorrowful anxiety about my husband. I should like so much to be permitted to go with him, if he has to go, out of this world. We have been so long together.'[83]

Georgie visited regularly from London, and on Christmas Day Charlie staged a surprise visit – from the South African Transvaal where he had taken work with a gold mining company. The journey home must have taken at least one month. Josephine rejoiced that, 'our little family was complete on this, probably the last Christmas in which we shall all be together'.[84] Her prediction proved true, but Charlie was so reluctant to leave his father that he did not return to South Africa until the following August.[85]

That Christmas was overshadowed by a new problem. Little Josephine developed a 'weakness of the spine' for which the treatment was to be kept 'quite flat at all times'.[86] It is hardly possible to imagine a less endurable regime for an active 2-year-old, and Rhoda, writing to Stanley in St Andrews, lamented that 'Baba' had reached 'such a charming age for running about. We will see none of that now.'[87] Josephine gave Rhoda devoted support and pronounced her granddaughter 'quite saint like in her patient cheerfulness, the dear little thing'.[88]

George's condition forced Josephine to take him abroad in the New Year (1889), when she kept a journal which she later transcribed for her sons.[89] At Cannes in the South of France George revived in the warmer weather. The Gladstones, the Governor of the Bank of England and the Prince of Wales were all staying there in February. Josephine reported to Stanley and Rhoda that Mrs Gladstone had visited them, ascending to their apartment in a lift which 'she must have nearly filled, for she is large'. At Easter they received a long visit from Hatty and Tell, and shortly afterwards travelled on to Switzerland, where George was well enough to accompany Josephine to a meeting on 'higher morality' and offer prayers.[90] Although George seemed better, Josephine knew this was borrowed time and rejoiced in every extra day they had together.

As summer beckoned, they returned home to Winchester, where George went 'bravely through the cathedral services, although he suffers a great deal in the effort'.[91] He had abdominal pain and diarrhoea. Josephine later recalled that George's dog, Carlo, used to wait at the door of the 'downstairs WC! His poor master used to have to frequent that corner *so much*'.[92] As he grew weaker and thinner, relatives and friends noted his deterioration. James Stuart was overcome with emotion when he visited in July, telling Josephine, 'I now fully realise that our dear, dear friend must leave us before long.'[93] During this summer, George preached his last sermon.

On medical advice, they went to Scarborough in August; a strange choice since, although a seaside town, it is much further north than Winchester. The trip was not a success – Josephine fell ill herself and hated the 'subtle east winds here which seem to search to one's bones'.[94] She was not able to complete the work she had taken with her, but she told her friends, 'I will never cease (please God) to do what work I can.'[95]

Unable herself to go to the Federation Congress in Geneva, Josephine urged her LNA friends to attend, and recommended an Indian representative, Mr Naoroji, to speak on 'the great question' of India.[96] She focussed on George, accepting Hatty and Tell's offer of ideal accommodation for the autumn – their summer home at Capo di Monti, near Naples. Georgie wrote to offer his father a fur coat for the trip, which George accepted, adding humorously that he would not have bought one for himself:

> ... as it might be regarded as a piece of self-indulgence ... but if the possession of such a garment will ... improve my chances of longevity, and give me a personal air of respectability, not to say distinction ... then I gladly accept it.[97]

The Meuricoffres' second son Fred met the Butlers in Naples at the end of October and took them to Capo di Monti, where the roses were in full flower in November.[98] The eldest son John, his wife Sophie and their two daughters had prepared the house for them. They found a typical note from Hatty. Knowing George would miss his dog, she offered substitutes:

I recommend to your protection and friendship Twiddle Dum and Twiddle Dee – they reside in a little courtyard below the South windows of the Living Room. Twiddle Dum is the largest with the finest hair and shortest nose – a little black bracelet in his fore wrists – Dee has the best bred head ... lovingest disposition, they must not come into the room for fear of Tell's Persian carpets! But will be flattered if you notice them in the garden.[99]

Josephine's bedroom faced Vesuvius 'and his perpetual fire, showing above the trees, gave light to my whole room'.[100] George had a separate bedroom, but Josephine often 'sat by him and rested my head on the same pillow'. Hatty and Tell arrived for a joyful reunion at the end of November, just before George had his first serious relapse, with bleeding from the mouth. The doctor said George's liver was 'much more enlarged' and the family's Swiss pastor prayed with him.

As the winter set in, Josephine and George left Naples for the even greater warmth of Amalfi, where George improved so much that Josephine allowed herself some hope of his recovery.[101] He could often walk a mile before breakfast and at Christmas wrote to his sons, 'I am getting better every day, thank God!'

Sadly, a nasty strain of flu arrived in Amalfi the following month; George caught the infection and 'from that time never rallied again'. He remained cheerful, but was missing his sons and grandchildren and wanted to return home, despite the risk.[102] Hatty showered them with presents as they left Naples by train on 13 February, and at 4 p.m. Josephine remembered the afternoon teas they had enjoyed together so often, 'my heart was very full'.[103] In Genoa, Josephine's sisters, Tully and Eliza, with some of their children, had gathered to cheer George on what was obviously his final journey.

By 18 February the Butlers were back in Cannes, where the doctor pronounced George to be 'much changed and weaker'.[104] As George deteriorated and was 'suffering much', Josephine prayed 'that we might reach home before he dies'.[105] At night she lay awake, wondering how she could live without him. But the next day, 'his bright "Good morning, darling!" ... used to dispel all clouds'.[106] In the evenings they prayed together and George was 'consciously in the presence of God'.

On 9 March Georgie arrived to support them, and they left Cannes two days later, travelling in reserved compartments to give George as much comfort as possible.[107] At the port of Boulogne George, wearing his fur coat, was carried on board ship by the superintendent of the St John Ambulance Association, who had crossed the Channel to help him.[108] When the steamer docked at Folkestone, George was transferred to an 'invalid compartment' on the train and arrived at the Grosvenor Hotel in London on the evening of 13 March. By then 'his exhaustion was extreme', but Josephine was buoyed up by the hope that after a night's rest she could take George home to Winchester. She stayed with him that night but, when she awoke, 'his sweet "Good morning" was not spoken, and a sense of great desolation came over me'. George was scarcely conscious and moaning sadly. His brothers and sister visited him and Stanley arrived, having travelled all night from Scotland. About 4 p.m. George grasped Josephine's hand and said, 'You will go with me, beloved, will you not?' She replied, '"Yes, I will!"'... For I knew that my heart would follow him whither he was going, and would dwell with him there.' Georgie and Stanley were with Josephine when George died, and 'an extraordinary beauty of expression' settled on his face.

George was buried in Winchester, after 'the brightest and the most beautiful' of funerals in the cathedral.[109] As friends and family visited The Close, they noticed George's dog, Carlo, 'outside the window looking wistfully in, as if searching for his master among us'. Josephine received many tributes to George's character, including from William Gladstone, who described George's career as 'no less blameless than useful and distinguished' and rejoiced that he had been able to offer the Winchester canonry which George had appreciated so much.[110] The tributes which most affected Josephine came from her sons – Georgie recalled 'those last few precious days I was with him' and wrote, 'You need never have any fear, dearest mother, that father's memory will ever grow dim to us. I shall remember many incidents of his life, and many of his sayings, as long as my own life lasts.'[111] Stanley treasured 'something beautiful in his calm faith and courage, and in his utter freedom from selfishness'.[112] From South Africa, Charlie sent a wreath of pure white and silver dried 'immortelles', which cheered Josephine, through her tears, at George's graveside.

INTERLUDE

The Queen's Daughters in India

Dr Kate Bushnell and Mrs Elizabeth Andrew were Americans, supporters of the Purity movement, and experienced ambassadors for the World's Women's Christian Temperance Union (WWCTU).[113] In the summer of 1890, Kate Bushnell was praying for guidance in her mission when she dreamed of crossing the sea to meet Josephine Butler. She wrote to Josephine, who replied that Kate might be the answer to her prayer for 'an English-speaking woman to go to [India] ... and make careful inquiry into the condition of things there'.[114] Josephine wanted a woman who would, effectively, act as a surrogate for investigations she could not conduct herself.

Kate's friend, Elizabeth Andrew, had heard about Josephine through William Stead, who had given her his 'Life Sketch', the biography of Josephine he wrote while in prison. As she read it, Elizabeth had 'a strong sense of the Divine will working within me' and changing her attitude to 'degraded' women who were 'not the utter outcasts from humanity that our ignorance and injustice would make them out to be'.[115]

Elizabeth and Kate decided to visit England together, and in London they met Josephine and other leaders of the campaign, including James Stansfeld and James Stuart. Talking to them, they became convinced that 'the native women ... are thrust down into the deepest abyss of degradation and slavery, and their necks are under the feet of their Christian (!) conquerors'.[116] They agreed to go to India as ambassadors for the abolitionists.

Their visit lasted four months. Unable to get any help from the army, Kate and Elizabeth went directly to the lock hospitals and *chaklas* and, through interviewing the wretched women kept there, found all the evidence they needed to prove that the 'healthy whores' system was still flourishing in India. They met many girls well below the age of consent in England, 'of the delicate oriental type', who were regularly served up to the soldiers.[117]

One orphan girl was taken by an Englishman to be his mistress at the age of 11 and, when deserted by him three years later, 'there was no door open to receive her but the *chakla*'.[118] Another had been sold by her husband to the '*mahaldarni*' – the madams employed by the army to run the *chaklas*. 'These bad women promise us everything and then betray us into this life', they were told many times.

Girls who came to the *mahaldarni* or to the soldiers in 'the agonies of slow starvation' found that the price of food was the sale of their body at the prescribed rate of 4 annas (a tiny sum, less than 4 English pennies). Escape was almost impossible, even when Kate and Elizabeth tried to help, because the girls had incurred debts to the *mahaldarni*. They endured 'periodical examinations' by a British medical officer, accompanied by an Indian doctor and nurse.[119] In theory these examinations were now voluntary, but if a prostitute did not attend she was threatened with arrest and could be fined, imprisoned or expelled from the cantonment.

Kate and Elizabeth concluded that the system of registering and regulating prostitutes had not changed since the repeal of the CD Acts in 1888.[120] Their proof positive was given to them in Meean Meer cantonment – a registration ticket for a prostitute named Begum, with signatures by the medical officer for regular examinations in January and February 1892.[121]

'The little women of India' had implored Kate and Elizabeth 'to help them to get deliverance from their oppression' – a trust which they regarded as sacred.[122] On their return they wrote up two volumes of evidence and sent them to Fanny Forsaith, the Secretary of the Federation. This report was the basis of the book they later wrote, *The Queen's Daughters in India*, a reference to the Indian women who told them 'it was a shame for *women* to be treated so when a woman was Queen'. The report was not published by Josephine and her Federation colleagues until after a Liberal government was returned to power and Stansfeld judged that Parliament might act on its shocking findings.

1 Delegates to the first Federation Congress, held in Geneva in 1877. Seated in the front row, first on the left, is Margaret Tanner, with Josephine Butler third. George Butler stands behind Josephine. In the second row, first on the left is Aimé Humbert with James Stuart next to him. (The Women's Library @ LSE)

2 A youthful Katie Booth, who led the Salvation Army mission to Switzerland in 1883. Josephine Butler gave her devoted support when she was arrested after defying a preaching ban. Katie was the eldest daughter of William and Catherine Booth, who founded the Salvation Army. (The Salvation Army International Heritage Centre)

3 Florence Booth, the wife of Bramwell Booth, instructs five of her children at home. The portrait above her head is the founding 'Mother of the Salvation Army', Catherine Booth. Bramwell and Florence Booth were leaders of the Salvation Army's mission in London and assisted Josephine during the 'Maiden Tribute' campaign. (The Salvation Army International Heritage Centre)

4 This photograph of Josephine Butler evokes Henry Scott Holland's description of her during the 'secret commission' into child prostitution in London in 1885: 'in passing up Holborn, a face looked at me out of a passing hansom ... It was framed on pure and notable and beautiful lines: but it was smitten, and bitten into, as by some East wind, that blighted it into grey sadness. It had seen that which took all colour out of it ... I knew that I had seen ... Mrs Butler in the thick of that terrible work that she had undertaken for God. She was passing through her martyrdom.' (Getty Images)

5 The intense, unflinching gaze of William Stead, editor of the *Pall Mall Gazette*, who exposed the 'Maiden Tribute' scandal. (Getty Images)

6 Stead and fellow members of the Secret Commission were prosecuted for buying 'a child of thirteen' for £5. This illustration commissioned by the *Pall Mall Gazette* shows them in the dock at Bow Street magistrates' court. *From left*: Bramwell Booth, Sampson Jacques, William Stead, Elizabeth Combe and Madame Mourez. *Above*: Rebecca Jarrett. ('The Eliza Armstrong Case', 1885)

7 George Butler and his retriever, Carlo, in the garden of 9 The Close, Winchester. The Butlers moved there in 1882 after George was appointed Canon of Winchester Cathedral. His health declined within a few years. Carlo was his faithful companion until George's death in 1890. (Johnsons)

8 The Butlers' substantial home in the cathedral close of Winchester. Josephine was delighted by 'the beautiful old house, with its thick walls, its picturesque gables, its antiquity ... its ample accommodation ... and its surroundings of fine ancestral trees and flowering shrubs, gorgeous in spring!' (Rev. Canon Gary Philbrick)

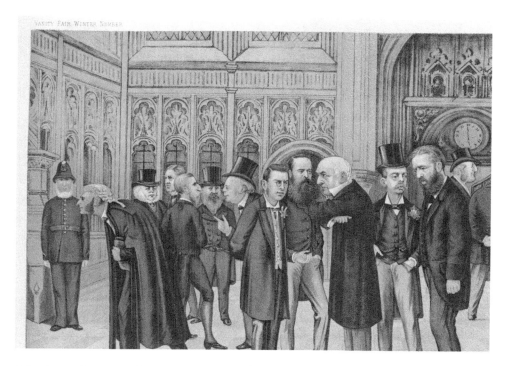

9 Leading politicians gather in the lobby of the House of Commons in 1886, the year the CD Acts were repealed. They include W.E. Gladstone, the prime minister and leader of the Liberal Party (*third from right*). Josephine Butler and her 'women workers' spent hours in the lobby 'interviewing MPs' during crucial stages of the vote to suspend the Acts in 1883. (Mary Evans Picture Library)

10 Josephine Butler in mourning, after George's death in 1890. She liked this photograph, by Elliott and Fry, telling her daughter-in-law Rhoda that it was 'really artistic'. (The Women's Library @ LSE/ Josephine Butler Society)

11 Josephine Butler at her desk, probably in her home in Balham, London, into which she moved in 1893. She loved her little study, where 'I have my books and papers in order around me ... I now feel as if I could write several books'. She started work on *Personal Reminiscences of a Great Crusade* the following year. (The Women's Library @ LSE/Josephine Butler Society)

SOCIAL QUESTIONS IN THE ORIENT.

MRS. ANDREW.

DR. BUSHNELL.

GREAT * MASS * MEETING

(Under the auspices of the Anti-Opium Urgency Committee, the Christian Union for the Severance of the connection of the British Empire with the Opium Traffic, and the World's W. C. T. U.),

IN THE

CENTRAL HALL, NEWCASTLE-ON-TYNE,

ON

Friday Evening, November 23rd, 1894,

AT **EIGHT O'CLOCK** (doors open at 7.15).

TO BE ADDRESSED BY

MRS. ELIZABETH ANDREW

AND

DR. KATE C. BUSHNELL.

(Round-the-World Missionaries of the Woman's Christian Temperance Union).

ALDERMAN W. D. STEPHENS, ESQ., J.P.

IN THE CHAIR.   [*A Collection towards Expenses.*]

SEAT RESERVED TILL 7.45.	RESERVED SEAT.	(OVER).

12 Ticket for a 'Great Mass Meeting' on 'Social Questions in the Orient', a euphemism for the campaign against the British Army's provision of regulated prostitutes in India. The speakers were Elizabeth Andrew and Katharine Bushnell, the authors of *The Queen's Daughters in India*. (Wellcome Library, London)

My dearest little Josephine

Aunt [fan] ny is here. She brought
with her a sweet little [cat] in a
[basket] and granny gives it [milk] in a
[dish] and it sleeps in granny's [bed]
at night. Twice we lost it, but soon
[Bella] found it again, sound asleep on a
soft [chair]. There are some very
pretty large [trees] now in
the gardens near which have
pink flowers on them.
Old [Carlo] dog went out with [Bella], & went
into a pond, and he went under the

13 A delightful illustrated letter sent by Josephine Butler to her granddaughter, 'little Josephine'. It was written in the house on Wimbledon Common, which Josephine shared with her son George. Josephine cared for her granddaughter there during a serious illness, and this letter was probably written after she returned home to her parents, aged almost 6, in the summer of 1892. 'Little Josephine' would have known 'Old Carlo', her grandfather's dog who now lived there, 'Bella' (presumably the cook or housekeeper) and 'Aunt Fanny' (Josephine's sister) who was a guest at the house. (John and David Thompson)

14 The Butler family at Ewart Park, George and Mia's home, where they all gathered for Christmas 1897. *From left*: Stanley and his wife Rhoda, Josephine, Mia (with George behind her) holding their daughter Hetha, and the newlyweds Margaret and Charlie. *In front*: Stanley and Rhoda's children, Bob and 'little Josephine'. Mia noted in her diary for 27 December 1897 that 'Gibson, photographer, came to take us all in a family group'. (Mary Margaret Butler Wray/Northumberland Archives)

15 Josephine Butler, aged 67, by the celebrated portraitist George Frederic Watts. Although the sittings with Watts, in 1895, went well, Josephine thought that the result was 'rather terrible. It bears the marks of storms and conflict and sorrow so strongly.' It certainly shows the drastic loss of weight she had suffered, most probably as a result of her serious illness in Rome the previous year. This emaciation can also be seen in the 1897 group photograph above. (© National Portrait Gallery, London

Struggle and Bereavement (1890–98)

India: The Campaign Continues

Only a month after George's death, Josephine bravely re-entered the battle for some of the poorest women of India. In *Dawn* she wrote, 'We have no less a job than that of *re*-conquering India in the matter of this vital question.'[1] A new Regulation issued by the Indian government was 'clearly capable of being worked so as to re-establish the whole system' of enforced examinations. Recent evidence must be found to prove that Indian officials were 'violating the Resolution of the House of Commons'.

After Kate Bushnell and Elizabeth Andrew produced the evidence, Josephine wrote a pamphlet, *The present aspect of the Abolitionist Cause*, in 1893, summarising their report. She concluded that nothing, not even the continuance of 'our military occupation of India', could justify 'this shameful system of oppression carried out on the helpless and unresisting daughters of a conquered people'.[2] James Stuart presented their unequivocal conclusions to Parliament, stressing that many of the prostitutes were 'very young (apparently 14 or 15 years of age)' and that they lived in 'abject poverty'.[3] Lord Kimberley, the Secretary of State for India, responded by setting up a departmental committee of inquiry under George Russell MP.

Kate and Elizabeth gave their evidence in person to this committee, while Russell instigated his own enquiries in India. Lord Roberts, the Commander in Chief of the Army, was vigorously disputing the picture presented to Parliament. Josephine told Stanley that 'things are rather "lively" at present, with Lord Roberts' hard swearing and our flat assertions, and though I am old and tired, I feel I must try and stand up at the guns a bit longer'.[4] Roberts was, she thought, 'a sincere man, but he has been extraordinarily disobeyed and gulled by his officers and surgeons in all the cantonments'.

Russell's enquiries in India supported Kate and Elizabeth's findings, and the majority report of the Russell Committee, whose members included James Stansfeld and Henry Wilson, concluded that the examination system 'amounted to compulsion'.[5] General Lord Roberts was forced to back down; he retracted his denials and admitted that 'the statements of the two American missionary ladies ... are in the main correct'. Josephine rejoiced in this 'good straightforward apology' but found it 'rather staggering' to discover that the orders of the Commander in Chief had not been obeyed implicitly.[6] Her belief, she told Stanley, was that Roberts had been betrayed by Chapman, the Quartermaster General who, although a member of the strict Plymouth Brethren, was 'a dark evil looking man ... a devil'.[7]

James Stansfeld prepared a parliamentary resolution which delighted Josephine – that 'official rape' should be 'punishable by law'.[8] She believed it would make any regulation system impossible, since 'long experience has taught us [this] is the central and necessary incident in the whole system'. This resolution did not succeed, but 'Stansfeld and his followers' were still in the ascendant; both Liberal and Conservative administrations found it impossible to resist them.[9] In 1895 the Indian government was persuaded by Westminster to pass a new Cantonment Act, outlawing the entire registration and examination system.[10] Another goal had been scored by the Abolitionists – but experience had taught them that this was likely to be a long game.

Josephine in Bereavement (1890–95)

'Oh Tully *what* a trial it is to live alone!' Josephine wrote to a sister who had also lost her husband.[11] 'Sorrow comes wave upon wave over my soul', but her consolation was 'that sweet old Cathedral near, which grew to be like a *person* to me!'[12] She had such happy memories of George there. Once, when she had felt faint during a service, she had tried to slip out unobserved but he had followed her, the flash of his white surplice like an 'angel's wing' as he took her in his arms.[13] The Psalms, which they had read together, became 'my delight, my daily food ... there is no difficult doctrine here, no conflict of apparently opposite truths ... as in some of St Paul's writings'.[14] However, the house 'seemed too silent and sad' to live in alone and she could not, in any case, stay at The Close, which was tied to George's job.[15] She made plans to find a home in London.

Margaret Tanner sent an invitation to stay at her home, Durdham Park in Bristol, which Josephine gratefully accepted, 'It is such peace to be with you.'[16] She could talk to Margaret about George, 'In talking of him, he seems almost to be present among us again.'

Family events curtailed her *tête a tête* with Margaret – Rhoda became seriously ill with rheumatic fever and had to join Josephine in Bristol. In August, Stanley took his wife to Switzerland to recuperate, leaving the two children with 'Grannie'.[17] By then, Georgie had found a substantial home to share with his mother, 8 North View, on Wimbledon Common. The house overlooked the common, a perfect location for horse-riding, which Georgie loved, and for the dogs to run around. Eiger, the St Bernard, had become Georgie's dog and Josephine brought Carlo from Winchester.[18] Although grateful to her 'kind son', Josephine was ambivalent about living with him.[19] She claimed to fear that it would prevent him finding a wife, but in reality she needed her independence.

By November, she was back in Switzerland, keen to 'find a quiet place to think and write'.[20] She had begun a biography of George, which was to be a tribute to his character and 'an act of justice and restitution'.[21] This phrase might suggest a degree of guilt about the effect of her campaign on his life and, particularly, his career prospects.[22] But it seems she simply wanted to give him credit for his contribution to the repeal cause, 'the world does not yet know how (next to God himself) my dear companion's inner life and heart were the fountain from which I drew so much life for myself and the work'.[23]

She must have taken many family letters with her to Switzerland, which she copied verbatim into the biography. This exercise consoled her even while, as she wrote to Rhoda, 'my longing to see him almost breaks my heart'.[24] She worried about whether 'I shall be able to write something worthy about him'.

By chance she met William Stead and his wife on the train from Paris to Basel, and their conversation led the impulsive editor to offer Josephine a 'large sum' to write her own biography.[25] She refused, saying 'I could not do it for anything – not for 50,000£ [sic]', because 'I hate the very appearance of egotism and I feel almost a *disgust* of speaking of myself.'[26] At this time she had severe money worries – she told Stanley that she was living on '10/6 a week board and lodging', and she was grateful to supporters who sent her cheques.

Her financial situation did not improve later. In 1896 she told friends that 'my dear husband left me very comfortably off, *as a widow living alone* ... But my life is not altogether allowed to be that.'[27] Her biggest expenses resulted from her work and travel abroad, and she was angry when the Federation seemed to expect her to work for nothing. This affected her relationship with James Stuart, who was the Treasurer.[28] Her financial worries would have ended had she accepted Stead's offer but nothing could persuade her, then or later, to write an autobiography.

It is ironic, therefore, that her biography of George reveals so much about her own life. Their love is revealed through their letters. Their family life, including the death of Eva, is described in detail. Her own career often takes centre stage, with a detailed account of her visits to the Liverpool Bridewell and her struggle to accept her call to lead the anti-CD Acts campaign. These accounts have been of great value to future generations who have sought to understand her, yet she received no payment for them and, indeed, struggled to find a publisher.

Josephine made several visits to her niece, Adela, who, like her sister Contie who died at The Close in 1884, had contracted TB and was suffering its final stages. Adela, now 29, was, Josephine said, 'like my own child'.[29] Adela was staying in the Jura Mountains, close to a pine forest which alleviated her laboured breathing. She 'had a terrible hollow cough' and was 'a perfect skeleton, though not thinner than my dear husband was'.[30] Poor Josephine was forced to 'watch death creeping on again'. Adela died at the end of December, having entrusted Josephine with carrying out her final wishes.

The year 1890 continued to 'fill up the measure of sadness to its last hour' when little Josephine was taken seriously ill in St Andrews – 'That darling is dearer to me than I can express'.[31] Stanley told his mother not to come back from Switzerland, and she acquiesced. By February, she was caught up in 'the most sustained and severe conflict I have ever had ... with the powers of evil'.[32] Stanley had said, 'Mother saw the Devil triumphant and she *went for him!*'

Josephine was always most disturbed when civic authorities connived at crimes against women and children. On a visit to the home in Geneva of her fellow Executive member of the Federation, Mme de Gingins, Josephine found the city on fire with anger over a recent court case, in which a magistrate had freed a man, Cougnard, who appeared to be guilty of enticing young girls to his house in order to violate them. The working-class parents of these victims demonstrated in the streets, despite the bitter cold which had frozen part of the lake. Mme de Gingins provided an indoor meeting place by 'removing the furniture from her suite of large apartments, and hiring some hundreds of chairs'.[33]

'The whole town was roused; they held meeting after meeting ... never at any Congress have I worked so hard', said Josephine.[34] She met the mothers of 'the poor little outraged girls' and a father, Merz, came to see her to tell his story. He had confronted the magistrate and was risking prosecution himself. Josephine offered to write to the London newspapers; she feared 'acts of violence and vengeance' and told him that only publicity could help.[35] However, her efforts to interest editors proved largely unsuccessful. In Neuchâtel, by comparison, she was a joyful witness to the Grand Council's decision to abolish the 'abomination of desolation', regulated prostitution.[36]

By February, she was keen to return home in time for the anniversary of George's death, writing to Stanley, 'I recall so vividly each day, what happened on the same day last year.'[37] On her return to London, Josephine was surprised and upset by the coldness of a Federation meeting in April when the Priestmans were absent and, she told them, 'no one spoke a friendly word' to her.[38] In compensation, the June meeting was packed with friends, who paid tributes to herself and George.

In Wimbledon, Josephine resumed the care of little Josephine (now 4), who was once again forced to stay prone at all times, under the care of a specialist doctor. By November she was able to tell Stanley that his daughter was 'well and frisky' but it was June the following year before she was able to return home to St Andrews. During that time, Josephine stayed at home, working on her biography of George. The final chapters were written 'in such pain and weakness', however, as she was unwell with influenza and pleurisy, a 'black cloud' which left her with only 'one sound lung'.[39]

Searching for a publisher, she encountered resistance to 'a book with so much Christianity in it'.[40] Josephine denied it was a 'religious biography', saying 'there is too much about dogs in it for that! And about fishing and shooting.' In truth, there is a great deal about George's love of the Bible and their shared prayers, especially during his last illness.[41] Ralph Butler, a younger cousin, described these sections as 'sanctimonious' and was glad George never saw them.[42] George's infectious sense of humour also struggles to emerge. After two publishers had declined, James Stuart suggested a more marketable title, *Recollections of George Butler by his wife Josephine E. Butler*, and J.W. Arrowsmith agreed to take it on.[43]

Josephine had recently been contacted by Mia St Paul, the 24-year-old granddaughter of her eldest brother, George. Mia was almost alone in the world – her grandparents and parents were dead and Josephine named her the 'orphan heiress' since from her father, Horace St Paul, she had inherited several properties in Northumberland (though all were in debt). Mia immediately took to Josephine, treating her as a surrogate mother. For her part, Josephine thought Mia 'a really lovable girl'.[44]

In July 1892 she invited Mia to go to Grindelwald with herself, Stanley and Georgie, to whom Mia had endeared herself by laughing at his jokes. Rhoda, who was visiting London, helped Josephine to buy a new wardrobe for the trip, since she felt herself to be 'so shabby and old' and 'all in rags'.[45] Her sister Fanny was living nearby in Wimbledon, alone and increasingly frail both mentally and physically. Josephine habitually spoke of her as a 'poor creature' and in July felt that she was 'leaving a helpless baby behind'. Fanny had retreated into a 'long silence' and for some reason chose this moment to leave Wimbledon and return to her previous home town, Cheltenham. Josephine could only pray for her.[46]

Grindelwald, that alpine resort of so many happy memories, held misery for her on this trip. A fire broke out, engulfing the wooden village, while they were there. Josephine and Mia were out riding, and for an hour did not know whether Stanley and Georgie were alive or dead. Mia was 'in great distress', but Josephine recalled the words spoken to St Paul in the shipwreck: 'Fear not, for I have given thee all those that are in the ship with thee.' Her sons had survived and were helping people from the burning chalets to save their goods, but the church founded by their father, containing an altar piece to his memory, was burnt to the ground.[47]

Josephine went on alone to Neuchâtel, Geneva and Cannes, for the first time since 1890, thinking of her husband with 'sweet, sweet memories' but sometimes overwhelmed by sadness.[48] In October, *Recollections of George Butler* was published and Josephine began to receive letters about it. William Stead wrote, 'I feel so grateful to you for writing this book ... I feel proud of my sex that such a man could be.'[49]

In the same month, she received the delightful news that Mia and George[*] were engaged to be married. George, now almost 40, had chosen to marry a Grey relative, just as Stanley had done. He was besotted with Mia, writing tender letters to her almost every day during their engagement, and she fully returned his love.[50] They planned a swift wedding, which took place the following January, 1893, at Kirknewton Church near Mia's ancestral home, Ewart Park, in Northumberland. Josephine did not return from the Continent, but sent a black diamond necklace and bracelet as her present. George's letter to her two days later rejoiced that they had 'the finest day of the whole winter to be married in'.[51] They had stayed in Northumberland for their honeymoon and George had taken Mia to see Dilston Castle, in the grounds of his mother's childhood home.

Before she left Cannes, Josephine was joined by Hatty and Tell, both very 'shaken' by grief at the loss of their son Conrad, who had succumbed to yellow fever in Brazil, aged 25.[52] Josephine had written movingly to Hatty: 'I know too well the strange moods and mysteries of sorrow, the ebb and flow ... It is still my cry "*I want my Love*" ... and you want your Connie and will always want him ... Darling, write freely when you feel you need to. I can never forget what your letters were to me all along in my sorrow.'[53]

When Josephine returned to London in March 1893 she went to stay with her sister, Emily, determined not to intrude on the newly-weds in Wimbledon. In May, their sister Tully died after a very short illness. A few days later Josephine was shopping for a wreath when she fell in the street and hit her head 'with great violence against a stone parapet'.[54] By June she was well enough to enjoy herself when Rhoda was in London, making calls with her in a hired coupé, dining at the House of Commons and going to the theatre to see the sell-out new farce *Charley's Aunt*. 'It is so long since I really laughed', said Josephine.[55]

Shortly afterwards, she moved into her own two-bedroom house in Balham, near Wandsworth where Emily lived. She had been worrying about Charlie, who had contracted fever in Rhodesia (now Zimbabwe), and endured 'weeks of silence and suspense', but on her first Sunday in the new house she heard that he was alive and feeling better.[56] Josephine loved her little study, where 'I have my books and papers in order around me ... I now feel as if I could write several books.'[57] She completed a rather lurid account of the life of St Agnes, a Christian fighting for her moral purity in the cruel decadence of imperial Rome, who is martyred as a 'magician' after converting the Prefect's son to Christianity.

Three years after the death of George, Josephine had achieved a new kind of equilibrium, but it was shadowed by loneliness and punctuated by long absences from her new home. Sometimes she was called away by her family – Rhoda endured the stillbirth of a premature baby in July 1893, and a few days later her son Bob fell from a cliff at St Andrews. Josephine went north to support the family and both recovered well.

Sometimes Federation work claimed her, and she went to the conference at The Hague in September, and in November set off for Italy with the ambitious aim of persuading the Pope to support 'the Cause'. In Rome, she met a priest, Père Rousseau, who had 'zeal' for reform, but was, she said, 'like all the rest, bowed and fettered by this great ecclesiastical tyranny'.[58] They talked of St Catharine and St Theresa, and he tried to convert her to Catholicism, telling her that she 'would be so comforted by the Sacrament'. When she replied that her Church also had the Sacrament, he objected that it did not have 'the *real presence* of the Saviour'. Her response was: 'Pardon me, Father, I think I have often been conscious of the real presence of my Saviour in receiving the Sacrament.' He invited her

---

[*] Georgie will be known as George from now on.

to meet the Pope, but she declined, knowing that if he asked her to share the Sacrament, she would have to refuse.

She lingered in Rome, anticipating the great joy of meeting Charlie, who had left Africa and came straight to see her after docking at Naples. They had not met since August 1889, a gap of four and a half years, but shortly after his arrival Josephine caught a nasty strain of malaria. This illness was so serious that George and Mia travelled from England to visit her, and she spent three months in a hotel in Rome, sometimes in great pain.[59] Her expensive medical bills were paid by James Stuart, who solicited donations from her friends.[60]

In March 1894, she told Fanny Forsaith in a letter, she began to feel angry, asking 'Why the God of Love *allows* a child of His to be so knocked down and stamped upon for such a long time'.[61] One morning God responded that He was 'all pity' and she was able to get up; her symptoms had vanished. This, she believed, was a miraculous cure, to be shared with a few 'bosom friends'. By the end of March she was at Hatty's home in Naples, and planning an issue of *The Dawn* which would feature her sister's work at the Sailor's Rest there. On her way home in April, she visited Charlie, who was convalescing 'up among the snows' in Switzerland.[62]

She returned to England to be greeted by the terrible news that George had fallen while horse riding, fracturing his skull, and had symptoms of brain damage. The family had gathered 'with aching hearts'; Mia had moments of 'broken-hearted weeping'.[63] Her son who 'always had such wonderful self-control' was 'quite changed', Josephine lamented to the Priestmans. 'He tries to throw himself out of the window, and has broken everything in his attempt at self-destruction.' Two male nurses could hardly control his violence.

After several anxious weeks, George began to recover. 'As I put my arms round him, I felt how kind and faithful God had been, to spare him to us.'[64] Josephine decided that 'God permitted but did not ordain that cruel accident. Evil things come from another source, not from God, but he overrules for good the work of the Enemy, the destroyer. He is the healer.'

George's recovery was slow, and in the future he was prone to depression and could be irascible and erratic (although the accident was not the only cause of this). The change in his personality was a source of pain to Josephine, even while she rejoiced at his survival. In the autumn she made her first visit to Ewart Park in Northumberland, Mia's family estate, which was close to Josephine's birthplace and first home, Milfield. She was delighted to find a Library '43 feet long, softly carpeted, with two fireplaces, seven writing tables and the walls lined with books' – even better than her own little study.[65]

She had begun writing *Personal Reminiscences of a Great Crusade*, a history of the anti-regulation campaign in Europe, and was completing *The Lady of Shunem*, a series of Bible studies aimed at Christian parents and dedicated to Hatty and Tell.[66] The title story portrays a devoted mother whose dead son is restored to life through her faith in the powers of the prophet Elisha. In 'Abraham as a Father', Josephine lambasts Abraham and his wife Sarai for their treatment of his mistress, Hagar, after she becomes pregnant. She faces destitution with her son in the wilderness, but God meets her there and gives her comfort. This was, Josephine noted, 'the first record of a direct communication from Jehovah to a woman'.[67] He had not chosen a 'Princess, or any other woman', but an outcast, 'an ill-used slave'. She found this fact 'a strength and consolation' in her work, and concluded that, 'It is only through conflict, and through trial of our integrity, that we can become in the highest sense sons and daughters of God. Christ himself was made perfect through suffering.'

Personal Reminiscences was harder to write and she found 'the mechanical labour of writing tires me much'.[68] When she returned to London, she found a shorthand writer.

However, the winter of 1894–95 was exceptionally bitter, the pipes froze and, even though Josephine's house was warmed by hot water pipes, 'the cold was terrible'.[69] She was conscious of 'the awful sufferings of the poor people ... men tapped at the window to see if they could do anything for us, for 6d or even 2d'.

Charlie was staying with her, and in March announced his engagement to Margaret Talbot. Josephine was delighted when she and Charlie sang duets together in her drawing room, playing her piano. This was an answer to prayer and a 'new door of hope'.[70] Charlie had no income to marry on, but found a new mining job in Australia, and left in April promising to return a year later for the wedding.

She was concerned about the health of Mia, who suffered a miscarriage in April and was in bed for six weeks. Josephine felt responsible since 'she has no mother or sister, and clings to me much'.[71] However, she was planning another Federation conference in Colmar, a German state which had abolished regulation but was threatened by policies of the German emperor which Josephine thought were 'cruel to women'.[72] She wrote a leaflet, *The Constitutional Iniquity involved in all forms of Regulation of Prostitution*, which had an initial print run of 10,000 copies.[73]

She left for Switzerland in May 1895, and there consulted a doctor, Professor Kocher, who cured her deafness. 'Suddenly, as if a heavy weight had been lifted off, I heard everything.'[74] For her lungs, he offered no dramatic cure – his opinion was that they were '*wasted*, almost to the last degree', and would 'not last above a short time in a town or low lying country, and above all in damp or among many trees'. She would have to spend winter in 'a high place with very pure air, like the Engadine'. She was sad about this, she told Stanley, because it meant separation from her children. 'Your love and companionship are life to my heart, as pure air is to my lungs. What are we to do? I must trust in God about it.'

Over the next few years, she spent more than half of her time in Europe, but longed for her family. Writing to Josephine and Bob on Ascension Day, she told them that she had seen them and their parents, and Uncle Charlie, Uncle George and Aunt Mia in a vision, saying, '"Pray for us" ... ever since then I hear those voices in the wind.'[75]

While Josephine was staying at Hatty's home on the shores of Lake Geneva in September, they heard that their sister Fanny had died in Cheltenham. Josephine returned home immediately, but was too late for the funeral. Before returning to Switzerland, she took the opportunity to move out of her house in Balham, since she no longer needed it. She sent all her furniture, her piano and paintings to Ewart Park. She also gave a final sitting to the celebrated portraitist G.F. Watts. He had asked to paint her for a series of nationally important figures.

The result is shocking – she looks emaciated, pale and expressionless. When she saw her portrait, Josephine was close to tears, overwhelmed by thoughts that the image was 'rather terrible. It bears the marks of storms and conflict and sorrow so strongly.'[76] In a letter, she told Watts that she 'felt so sorry for her. Your power has brought up out of the depths of the past, the record of a conflict which no one but God knows of.'[77] Surprisingly, the conflict she means is the 'years in which my revolt was not against man, but against God'. This was before her crusade began. Those years in which 'my soul went down to hell and dwelt there' were, to her, worse than anything that followed. She told Watts, 'Your picture has brought back to me all that I suffered and the sorrow through which the Angel of God's presence brought me out alive.' She was 'ready to go down to Hades again, if it were necessary for the deliverance of [my] fellow-creatures. But God does not require that descent more than once.'

Early in 1896 there was a chance to abolish the 'state patronised houses of shame' in Geneva when the Grand Council held a referendum on the issue. Josephine eagerly embraced the chance to use 'lawful means ... for the destruction of this iniquity'.[78] Just as in 1891, Mme de Gingins made her house available and a full scale abolitionist campaign was launched. Josephine travelled to other cantons to gather support. They were facing vicious opposition from brothel-keepers and had to suspend public meetings a week before the referendum, set for 22 March, when their speakers were shouted down. Josephine was afraid that the Federation offices would be attacked, and was personally abused in the local press. The referendum (of men only) was a 'crushing defeat' to their hopes – 4,000 for abolition and 8,000 against.

That night, the jubilant victors rampaged through the city, a terrifying situation for Josephine and her friends, who found sanctuary in a fortified house. She was consoled by the new supporters they gained in the following days, 'on whom the Spirit of the Lord has breathed, and these are the preservers of our onward victory, which may be quite in the future yet'.[79] That future battle was fought by others – Stanley was so concerned about the dangers his elderly mother had encountered that he asked her to stop campaigning in Switzerland.[80] Although Josephine was keen to continue, she proved unable to. State brothels were eventually abolished in Geneva in 1927.

Josephine came back to London in May to complete her book *Personal Reminiscences of a Great Crusade*, having given up any attempt to cover the history of the Federation beyond 1880. It is one of her least satisfactory books, because it is over reliant on official documents and episodic, but her subject was vast. At its best it offers vividly detailed glimpses of the European campaigns and conferences. In a moving section, she pays tribute to the loyalty of her LNA friends over many years, saying that the group was still 'full of life and energy'. They had been, for her, 'a kind of bodyguard, a *corps d'élite* on whose prompt aid, singleness of purpose, prudence, and unwearying industry I could and can rely at all times'.[81]

Mary Priestman later reflected that the Bristol group had gathered regularly for prayer and mutual support since 'the influence of religious fellowship and acquaintance is of great value, in overcoming the natural shrinking from a painful subject which cannot but be felt by everyone':[82]

> It has been often said that women are not loyal to women and that they do not work well together: the experience of [the LNA] has been contrary to this. I do not remember any disunion among the Branches; scattered widely as they were, they responded to every word from Josephine, and endeavoured to carry out every suggestion she made.[83]

Josephine stayed in London to support Mia, who was expecting a baby in July. This time, all went well for her. 'You would be delighted with little Hetha', Josephine wrote to her sister Emily, 'she is such a fine baby, with large dark eyes and a quantity of black woolly hair ... not the least like Eva, who was fair'.[84]

After the birth she returned to Switzerland to attend the Berne Federation Conference, which she had helped to organise. The size of the Federation Executive Committee had now reached the impressive extent of fifty-six members from fourteen countries (including USA and Russia).[85] Josephine spent the autumn and winter in Lausanne. She gave up editing *The Dawn*, but came back to London in March 1897 to deal with a serious crisis in the India campaign.

India: the Defection of Lady Somerset

A fight back against the Indian Cantonment Act of 1895 had begun the previous year. The British press reported, with hysterical passion, that the army was collapsing due to the number of soldiers invalided out by syphilis and gonorrhoea.[86] Many came home 'presenting a most shocking appearance', some had only a short time to live and 'others were unrecognisable from disfigurement'.

Another Secretary of State for India, Lord Hamilton, appointed another committee of inquiry which obligingly agreed that venereal diseases were 'spiralling out of control'.[87] Josephine returned to the fray when Hamilton proposed to repeal the Cantonment Act in favour of a regime which treated syphilis and gonorrhoea in the same way as other infectious diseases. She declared that it was 'a subtle and dangerous compromise'.[88] Her argument that it made no medical sense received welcome support from some seventy female doctors, who signed a 'Memorial' to Hamilton, stating their objections.[89] The Abolitionist and Purity organisations gathered an enormous 'Women's Memorial' with 61,437 signatures.[90]

It was impossible to curb the spread of sexually transmitted disease by regulation, as the campaign against the CD Acts in England had already shown. Henry Wilson in *The History of a Sanitary Failure* documented all the reasons for failure in India.[91] The solution was not the lock hospital, but a complete change in the army's attitudes toward sexual conduct. It assumed that soldiers required prostitutes, and there was no attempt to encourage them to lead a moral life. Josephine said that she was deeply troubled, as a mother, that the 'poor boys' sent out to India were 'subjected to every evil influence and to few good ones'.[92] They were 'carefully trained in the shameful doctrine of the necessity of sexual indulgence'.

In 1897, a spate of pamphlets and articles, inspired by the Purity movement, urged the army to promote better conduct, by offering 'healthy occupation and recreation'.[93] Dr Cleghorn, the Indian Sanitary Commissioner, proposed the most plausible, and pragmatic, solution – 'a large extension of the liberty to marry'.[94] Even the British government and the Indian Army was, according to *The Shield,* beginning to realise that regulation had failed to solve the problem and that it must appeal 'to the higher instincts of our soldiers to avoid vicious connections'.[95]

At this moment of consensus, Lady Henry Somerset, the British President of the WWCTU, took it upon herself to throw a spanner in the works by proposing a 'scientific' solution to infection.[96] In an open letter to Lord Hamilton, published in *The Times* in April 1897, she suggested that prostitutes and their male clients should both be examined, and quarantined if found to be diseased. To achieve this, soldiers wishing to visit the *chakla* should be certified as healthy, and logged by name in a register, with dates and houses visited. Lady Somerset wanted her system to be 'relentlessly strict' and 'as stringent for men as for women'. She gathered impressive support, in the form of a Memorial to Lord Hamilton signed by 122 women, including Florence Nightingale, Elizabeth Garrett Anderson and seventy titled ladies, headed by Princess Christian (daughter of Queen Victoria).[97] Josephine was predictably horrified. The proposals 'seem indeed to make the sexes equal, but it is an equality of unspeakable degradation for both'.[98] When Hatty heard about them, she wrote, 'does [Lady Somerset] really believe she will ever get men to do their fornications like going to a concert, with a ticket, name, date, place and their admissions to be registered in a book! Fool! Fool! Fool! *Indecent* fool!'[99]

Josephine had accepted the post of 'World's Superintendent' of the Social Purity department of the WWCTU in 1893. It was an honorary role, but she had spoken on public platforms with Lady Somerset and regarded her as a friend. Josephine had been her house guest, telling Stanley that she owned 'two big castles, three country houses, one town house, the "cottage" at Reigate and *100,000£* [sic] a year!!' But 'she had a monster for a husband [and] I would rather have darling father & *100£* [sic] a year. O *yes!*'[100] Now she was distraught because 'on such a vital question as this, womanhood is literally *cut in two*, publicly before the whole world'.[101]

In truth, this was not the first time – Elizabeth Garrett Anderson, for example, had never agreed with her and Josephine herself was at odds with the Purity movement over suppression of brothels – but this was a more public disagreement and therefore damaging to both the Purity and Abolitionist causes.

Josephine had been concerned for some time that the leaders of the WWCTU were taking on too much in tackling world purity as well as their core issue – temperance. They were inexperienced, and she knew how easily Purity campaigners could, in the name of vigilance, be persuaded to adopt extreme forms of regulation. Some WWCTU members had even defended the CD Acts.[102] She confessed to the Priestmans that 'our Cause has not gained but is suffering sadly from the union with it of the [WWCTU] and my own position is rendered painful and difficult'. At that time the WWCTU was expanding its purity work into Europe and looking to appoint a superintendent. Josephine was very upset when neither Kate Bushnell nor Elizabeth Andrew was selected, despite their experience and dedication. They were 'shamefully slighted' and 'Poor Mrs Andrew wept'.[103]

Lady Somerset's disastrous Indian scheme provoked the end game. Rather than minimise the split in the Purity movement, Josephine decided to tackle it head-on in a pamphlet, *Truth before Everything*, 'written on my sole responsibility'.[104] 'Purity', she wrote, was 'a beautiful word' that had become dangerously misleading, since some of the people adopting it were 'ready to accept any amount of inequality in the laws, any amount of coercive and degrading treatment of certain classes of their fellow creatures, in the fatuous belief that you can oblige human beings to be moral by *force*'.

The evidence from systems of regulation in many countries showed that this was impossible because its targets, both men and women, evaded it – 'it is of the essence of vice to refuse to be regulated ... You will never succeed in making disorderly passions well ordered in their gratification'. In addition it was an immoral, '*class* law, of the grossest kind', since only the lowest ranks of soldiers and the poorest of women were affected by it.

Having set out the moral case, Josephine proceeded to demolish Lady Somerset's arguments. Maurice Gregory, from the Quaker Abolitionist Association, had supplied her with proof that Lady Somerset had exaggerated the rate of 'hopelessly incurable' infections by a factor of sixty-five, and made many other elementary errors.[105] In her *Reply to Lady Somerset's Scheme*, published in August 1897, Josephine listed all her mistakes, pointing out that many of her statistics were 'monstrously incorrect'.[106] Six months later, Lady Somerset backed down, publishing a full retraction in the London papers. By then Josephine had decided to resign as 'World's Superintendent' of the WWCTU.[107] Kate Bushnell and Elizabeth Andrew resigned as well.

The opponents of Lady Somerset's scheme were vindicated, but dismayed by the harm she had caused, especially the 'division and discord' in the WWCTU.[108] Josephine was at times furiously angry with Lady Somerset and the 'idolatry' she inspired in some of her followers.[109] Underlying this was her fear that the next generation of Purity leaders was taking the movement in the wrong direction, and that her power to influence it was waning rapidly.

In 1897 a new Conservative government with a large majority repealed the Act of 1895, and reinstated the Indian Army's right to expel women who refused treatment for venereal disease from the cantons. Stansfeld, now nearing the end of his life, and Wilson had to admit defeat: Lord Hamilton reported that 'the feeling in the House of Commons is much against them'.[110] Jingoism in Britain was at its height and the Boer War just around the corner. There was no chance that the health of the army would be put at risk.

Purity: Josephine Vindicated

By 1897 Josephine had broken all her links with the Purity campaigns. *Truth before Everything* represents her final word on this subject.

One of the last straws for her was a campaign against immorality in the theatre led by Mrs Laura Chant of the NVA, and supported by Lady Somerset. Mrs Chant opposed the renewal of the licence of the Empire Theatre, a popular music hall in Leicester Square, on the grounds that it was not providing decent entertainment. There was a 'want of clothing in the ballet' and prostitutes, 'very much painted and more or less gorgeously dressed', were openly seeking customers among the audience.[111] Josephine found the issue difficult, because of the '*melancholy* of these poor women'.[112] But she decided 'to keep out of the Empire conflict' because 'I do not believe that any real reform will ever be achieved by outward repression'. In any case, the campaign failed miserably, since the music hall was popular with upper-class clients, including the young Winston Churchill, who made sure that the Empire's licence was renewed.

Josephine summarised her view of the NVA more in sorrow than in anger, since many of its members (such as the leaders of the Salvation Army) were her friends:

> I have *never* heartily sympathised with the work of the Vigilance Society, and yet undoubtedly they have done much good, many good things. But there is a constant tendency towards *external* pressure, and inside that a tendency to let the pressure fall almost exclusively on women because it is more difficult, they say, to get at men. It is dangerous work, in reference to personal liberty. But few people care for liberty or personal rights now.[113]

Josephine was correct. Repression failed dismally to achieve moral change, despite the most sustained purity campaigns ever seen in this country. If prostitution declined at all (and we have no means of knowing the true numbers) then it was due to women having better opportunities. 'The introduction of free and compulsory education, better job prospects, increased wages and improved working conditions' in the twentieth century were more important in freeing women from lives of vice.[114] The vision of Josephine Butler, whose first pamphlet called for better work conditions and opportunities for women, was vindicated.

The Boer War

Josephine's last campaign was conducted in a climate of passionate feeling about the Boer War (1899–1902). In Britain the mood was frenzied – passionate rejoicing at military success, such as the relief of Mafeking, and abject misery at reverses such as the 'Black Week' of December 1899. Jingoism had reached its height and the British government could do no wrong in the eyes of most of the population, even when it was the blatant aggressor.

The Boers were Dutch farmers who had migrated inland to the Transvaal to escape the British imperial rulers on the South African Cape. Gladstone had guaranteed its self-government in 1881. However, gold was discovered in the Transvaal in 1886, making the Boers rich and creating the city of Johannesburg. Cecil Rhodes, incensed at Britain's loss of this wealth, annexed land to the north and encircled the Transvaal, hoping to destabilise its government, led by the formidable Kruger. He failed, but Kruger began to arm himself with German weapons against the threat. The British leaders, Joseph Chamberlain and Lord Salisbury, declared war. Thousands of young soldiers joined the army and set off for the Transvaal. Despite the 'David and Goliath' nature of the struggle, it took three years before peace was declared.

Most of Josephine's friends opposed the war, especially Henry Wilson, who declared that it was 'a crime against humanity and a great political blunder'.[115] The British Empire was stamping on a small independent nation with no justification. He became a leader of the so-called 'Pro-Boer' faction, which was supported by Quakers (who were pacifist) and many Liberals. On the Continent, there was deep antipathy to Britain, especially from Germany and the Netherlands, which actively supported the Boers. Josephine was in Switzerland when the war broke out, and was deeply affected by the 'bitter feelings of hatred to England' which she felt even among her friends.[116] She foresaw, then, that there would one day be a 'great European War'.[117]

Josephine had taken an interest in South Africa since her cousin, Sir Charles Grey, was Governor of the Cape in the 1850s.[118] She had read its history, followed its development, and noted a fact which the 'Pro-Boers' had overlooked. The Boers had, in effect, enslaved the native African people since their earliest days of settlement. Josephine had campaigned against white slavery in Europe, and now she felt called to return to the campaign of her father, 'one of the energetic promoters of the Abolition of Slavery in the years before 1834, a friend of Clarkson and Wilberforce', from whom she had inherited the 'horror of slavery in every form'.[119] Josephine saw an analogy between the Boer War and the American Civil War (1861–65) when she and George, by supporting the North, had been out of step with their friends. Gladstone, for example, during a speech they heard him give in Liverpool, had spoken of the struggle of the Southern States, 'as one on behalf of liberty and independence'. He 'had not even taken in the fact of the existence of those four millions of slaves'. Only afterwards had it become clear to everyone that the Civil War was about slavery. Josephine thought the same might be true of the Boer War. That was why she felt able to support the British side, since although:

... the English have also been guilty of cruelty to native races ... this fact does not touch the far more important and enduring fact that *wherever British rule is established, slavery is abolished, and illegal.*

Josephine began sending letters to the press and collecting evidence for a book.[120] While she was in Switzerland, her son George sent her important material. After she returned to London, she studied Blue Books, Parliamentary papers and the accounts of South African missionaries and travellers. The book she produced, *Native Races and the War*, is a model of careful research, with witness evidence for all her arguments, a 'most remarkable' achievement, especially considering her age and failing health.[121]

She argues that the Boers left the Cape so that they could continue to practise slavery outside the boundaries of the British Empire. She quotes the reports of missionaries, such as David Livingstone, who had met native children in the Transvaal, captured from their parents at a very young age and forced into service in Boer houses.[122] During his time in Bechuanaland (adjacent to the Transvaal), Livingstone had observed native children being taken from their parents.

Josephine argued that the British constitution and its laws had, in the past, saved the Transvaal 'from anarchy and confusion, and its native populations from bondage or annihilation'.[123] Privately she stated that Britain 'is the only really just and successful colonising power'.[124] This seems inconsistent with her Indian campaign, and especially with her stated view in 1886 that 'annexation and conquest are morally wrong'.[125] However, it could be argued that she never condemned the idea or the institutions of British rule, but simply adopted 'a special imperial mission' of campaigning for poor colonial women.[126] Now the focus of her mission was the African slaves in Boer territory.

When *Native Races and the War* came out in July 1900, Josephine was attacked by the Pro-Boers. W.T. Stead was the most outspoken; she declared that he had 'gone clean mad'.[127] Mrs Sheldon Amos published a 'Criticism' of the book and distributed it to the members of the Abolitionist Federation. Henry Wilson told Fanny Forsaith that most of them were 'astounded' at the line Josephine was taking.[128] Millicent Fawcett was one of the few who agreed with her.

This was a lonely time for Josephine, and her relations with some friends, like the Wilsons, never fully recovered. Her willingness to overlook outrages perpetrated by the British made her unpopular, although *Native Races* appeared before General Kitchener began rounding up Boer women and children and incarcerating them in the first concentration camps. It is possible to argue that she justified aggression and war, but also that she was in tune with 'high-Victorian liberalism of the imperial expansionist variety'.[129]

For these liberals, imperial expansion was justified by the motive of moral, social and religious reform in the colonised countries. Josephine believed that the Empire could promote civilisation, especially when it aimed to improve the conditions of slaves and native women. Her final comment was about the dangers of racism:

Race prejudice is a poison which will have to be cast out if the world is ever to be Christianized, and if Great Britain is to maintain the high and responsible place among the nations which has been given to her.[130]

The Storm-Bell

Family Time 1897–99

From May 1897 to May 1899, Josephine spent most of her time either at Ewart Park, with Mia and George, or at St Andrews with Stanley's family. She went to Switzerland for a few months each year, and returned to London for Charlie and Maggie's wedding in August 1897. They were so short of money that in their new home they did 'everything for themselves', employing no servants – a situation Josephine clearly found novel.[1] George and Mia planned a family gathering at Ewart Park for Christmas that year, a unique occasion to which they invited a photographer. One shot shows the Butlers in evening clothes in the drawing room, framed by large and rather gloomy oil paintings, and another was taken outside the house, Stanley and George in country tweeds and Charlie wearing a splendid dark double breasted suit and bowler hat.[2] Rhoda and Margaret wear close fitting dresses and stylish hats, while Josephine looks very frail. Mia was heavily pregnant, and gave birth the following month to a son, named Horace after Mia's father.

At Ewart, Josephine carried on writing in her favourite place, the library, where she returned to some of her favourite topics. In *Prophets and Prophetesses*, published in 1898, she explains that prophecy does not mean 'the foretelling of future events ... but ... "to show forth the mind of God" on any matter'.[3] Prophets were badly needed at this time of imperialism and 'the influence of wealth', and they could be women, since the apostles Peter and Paul had believed that 'women as well as men were destined by God to be prophets'.[4]

This theme of the call of women to leadership had been constant in her work since *Woman's Work and Woman's Culture* (1869), but now she felt she had more to add from her own experience. For the prophet, 'It is in the solitude of the soul, alone with God, that his thoughts are revealed'.[5] The Church had not yet called women forward but in these 'latter days' they were more than ever needed.

In 1898 Josephine launched a new magazine with the title *The Storm-Bell*, taken from a poem by Whittier – 'The Storm-Bell rings – the Trumpet blows/ ... Wherever Freedom's vanguard goes/ ... I know the place that should be mine.'[6] *The Storm-Bell* was officially linked to the LNA and the Federation, but was in reality a vehicle for her own concerns. Most of the articles were written by her, and some are autobiographical reflections, including the account of her religious crisis at the age of 17.[7]

Often sixty pages long, and published monthly, *The Storm-Bell* was a huge labour which she undertook purely because she wanted to. She hoped that it would be read by 'poor and humble people' rather than educated people and that it would be used as a campaign leaflet.[8] Amelie Humbert came to Ewart Park to act as Josephine's assistant and Fanny Forsaith in the London office arranged for the printing and distribution. The first editions were ordered in the tens of thousands, particularly the second, February 1898, which reported the death of Sir James Stansfeld.[9] She described him as 'a born *forlorn hope* leader' who always encouraged her, even at the 'darkest times'.

While working on the magazine, Josephine and Amelie also helped to organise the London conference of the Federation, planned for July. Josephine was in London in May 1898 for the funeral of Gladstone. 'Mr Gladstone's "going home" and his Burial, and the nation's homage are a grand awe-inspiring sight', she told Stanley.[10] She rejoiced to see solemn testimony given to 'a man who represented so much of what is best in English character and tradition ... his greatness rested on the strong foundation of his *goodness*'. She had not always been so enthusiastic about Gladstone, and still sometimes lamented that he 'never *openly* took up our cause'.[11]

Demand for *The Storm-Bell* decreased, but Josephine continued to produce it, mostly unaided and often during illness. She went to Switzerland in the autumn of 1898, but was in St Andrews by December. While staying there she inspired her grandson Bob with the desire to become an architect. She showed him the 'delicately-coloured plates' in John Ruskin's *The Stones of Venice* which convey 'the excitement of architecture, of lines creating form, of the function of ornament, and the value of colour in material'.[12] He came to feel that 'this was my Thing' and she maintained her interest, fussing over his school reports for drawing. 'Grannie' gave him her paint box, a 'large walnut box' with lots of compartments and a thrilling 'secret drawer in the false bottom containing a variety of china palettes and the finest sable brushes'.[13] Bob treasured the box and used the brushes throughout his career. Ironically, his 'Grannie' had not used them. Bob observed that her drawing was 'very swift, rarely rubbed out' – a comment which could also apply to her writing. Josephine gave generous and imaginative presents to her grandchildren – she once sent Hetha a pair of lovebirds.[14]

Josephine returned to Ewart in March 1899 and began to keep a diary which provides us with a very intimate account of life there: Mia and George singing together after dinner; Mia and George walking hand in hand to see their children asleep in bed.

Horace (aged 12 months) slept in a crib in his parents' bedroom, an unusual practice then. Josephine asked 'if he did not disturb them with early waking and child's noises'. 'Yes', said George, ' ... but then *we love him so much*, that we don't mind.'[15]

In May, Josephine fell down the stairs and sustained nerve damage which caused her such pain that she took opium pills to help her sleep for three nights, but then gave them up, fearing addiction.[16] Although it was 'the worst pain I ever had', she was 'unwilling to let anyone know how great' it was – a habit of concealing the true level of her suffering from her family which had become engrained.[17]

After Mia and George had stayed up half the night to copy an article on the history of Finland which Josephine needed for her journal, she left Ewart in June for London and Switzerland. While she was in Geneva attending another Federation conference, Charlie telegraphed the joyful news that Maggie had given birth to a daughter, Rosalind – 'another dear grandchild'.[18]

Her sister Hatty was now in need of her, since her husband Tell had terminal cancer. As the Meuricoffre family gathered round his bedside in Berne, Josephine was forcibly reminded of 'the gradual passing away of my beloved husband, the alternations of hope and fear, and the pitifulness of it all'.[19] She saw her own strain mirrored in the face of her sister. Like George, Tell struggled for months and lingered until the spring, dying in March 1900.

While she was in Switzerland, Josephine corresponded with her sons about the Boer War. Charlie, now safely back in England, had personal experience of the Transvaal and of Cecil Rhodes, whom he detested. She sympathised with Stanley, who had told her of the wounded and missing among his acquaintance, 'you must feel very grave and sad, knowing so many of the brave Highlanders and other regiments'.[20] When she heard of the defeat of General Buller in December 1899, she admitted, 'I got quite faint and had to lie down on my bed. I was sleepless and bewildered all night'. To Rhoda, she wrote of her 'gratitude that there was a heart which so echoed my own thoughts' because she had suggested 'a day of national prayer and humiliation' to ask God to 'save our armies, the lives of our dear ones and our national honour'.[21]

She was lonely in Montreux over the winter and too ill to go out, but was able to depart for England in February. She stayed for a few weeks at Charlie and Maggie's new home in St Ives in Cornwall, before returning to Ewart. There she completed a little book, entitled *Silent Victories*, about 'the wonderful spiritual work being done in our army'.[22] This is a collection of reports from missionaries at the front, and testimonies to the conversion of soldiers. It is quite unlike *Native Races and the War*, or indeed any other book she produced, in being unselective and largely unmediated by her own comments. It is sentimental and uses conventional Evangelical language, such as 'winning Harry for Christ'.[23] The book shows her emotional identification with the soldiers and her hope that Christian belief would sustain and comfort them in the face of so much death and destruction.

Josephine and Hatty, 1900–01

By August, Josephine felt herself pulled '*four* ways, to my three sons with their families, and to my dear sister, now a widow and sorrowful, and, like myself, growing old'.[24] Hatty's need, and her own desire to be with her, triumphed, and she crossed the Channel again early in August 1900, kindly accompanied by Charlie who returned to Dover by the next boat. She found Hatty at La Gordanne, very subdued and 'much thinner', but the sisters had 'some sweet talks' as they walked together around the estate.[25] Hatty showed her the 'Book of Testimonies' to Tell's character, collected in Naples, and they read it aloud, Josephine taking over when her sister was overcome by weeping. On the last day of her visit, they consoled themselves with plans for Hatty to visit England and 'stay a good while' at Ewart Park. As Josephine boarded the train Hatty asked, 'Will May be too early for me to come to England?' and she replied, 'You cannot come too early, my Beloved.'[26]

Josephine arrived in London on 14 September.[27] Checking in at her hotel, she was handed a telegram from Hatty's daughter Thekla: '*Mother died this morning*'.[28] Hatty's illness had been very sudden and only two of her children reached her before she died. Josephine could never have anticipated that her robust and normally healthy younger sister would die before her. She managed to reach her room before collapsing on the floor, but was unable to leave it for many days as she agonised over her loss. Charlie visited her, deeply grieved himself by the death of an aunt who had hospitably cared for him on many occasions. Josephine tried to explain the depth of her feelings: 'She was more than a sister; she was my first, earliest, closest friend.'[29] Even after Hatty had married and left for Italy, they had kept in close touch; they had grieved together at the deaths of their young daughters and Hatty had wholeheartedly supported her crusade. Josephine once wrote to her, 'You are the only living, *except God*, who knows by *intuition* all I feel, all the pain etc. of the work, and the hope and the inward motive. I dread to think what the blank would be to *me* if you were gone.'[30] Mia told George, 'I think Mother loved her better than anyone else in the world.'[31]

The Meuricoffre children, broken hearted at the loss of both their parents within a few months, begged Josephine to write a memoir of their mother. Boxes of her letters began to arrive and the task helped her recovery, as it had done after the death of George. She focussed on it obsessively, giving up other activities, including *The Storm-Bell* which never appeared again, and visits to her family. She did not move from London until it was finished.[32]

In January 1901, Queen Victoria died, and Josephine was touched by the 'worldwide mourning' and by the Queen's 'courage to endure and to be strong under grief and trouble'.[33] Her coffin was borne on a gun carriage through the streets of London during her state funeral on 2 February. Josephine was probably not among the crowds lining the route, however, since she had been taken ill again.

In mid-February she was feeling 'exceedingly weak after several days of constant heart attacks', and hoping she would live long enough to finish the memoir.[34] She had heard in January that Mia was 'seriously ill in pregnancy' and that the doctor doubted whether she would 'get through her confinement', and considered going north to Ewart.[35] Instead, probably because she felt too ill to help Mia, she accepted an invitation from Charlie to stay at his new home in Devon. She travelled there in an invalid carriage, accompanied by her servant, Annie. Before she left she heard that Mia had given birth to a second daughter, Irene, on 14 March.

Mia, who was only 33, did not recover from the difficult pregnancy and labour, and died on 26 April. During those weeks of desperate anxiety after the birth, George wanted his mother to go north to visit Mia (a journey of some 400 miles) but Josephine's doctor would not allow it.[36] Josephine did not tell George how seriously ill she was, however, with the result that his bitterness at Mia's loss was intensified by feeling that his mother had deserted them.[37] Over the next few years, he expressed his anger in heartbreaking letters, showing that he and Mia had hoped that she would live with them permanently, and were dismayed by the decreasing time she had spent at Ewart – '13 weeks ... in 1898, 8 weeks in 1899, 3 weeks in 1900, and in 1901 she only came after her "daughter" was no longer there to welcome her.'[38] Josephine unfortunately tried to justify her behaviour by saying she did not know of the pregnancy until very late, but George knew this was not true.[39] She even found it difficult, afterwards, to convince him of the severity of her illness.

Charlie attended Mia's funeral, while Josephine and Maggie, in tears, read the burial service together at their home.[40] Concerned for his mother's physical and emotional health, and angered at the Federation's unrelenting demands on her energy, Charlie took action. He wrote to James Stuart, 'Most of my mother's friends ... have no idea how very weak and frail her general condition is ... Now if my mother was too ill to go to see her dying daughter-in-law, of whom she was *very* fond, it is not likely she is either able or willing just now to receive visitors from the Continent.'[41] On 11 May Josephine resigned as an 'active member' of the Federation.[42] In June she was finally able to visit Ewart, where she did her best to console George, who was 'very brave and restrained, but he suffers much'.[43] When the family moved out of Ewart for a summer let, Josephine went on to Stanley and Rhoda's home in St Andrews.[44]

Josephine Alone

While in Scotland, she planned a journey into her past, starting with Corbridge, where she arrived in mid-October and was delighted to meet 'a very few old people' who had been tenants of her father.[45] She was dismayed by the changes to her childhood home, Dilston House. Major extensions had changed it beyond recognition and were 'a huge mistake'.

She went south to Winchester to see George's grave, feeling so weak that she wished she could 'go to him at once. But the promise of the Resurrection and future glad meeting keeps me going.'[46] After a visit to her oldest friends the Priestman sisters in Bristol, she arrived in Cheltenham by late November. And there she stayed, for almost two years.

This is the surprising fact of Josephine's final years. She decided to remain in a place where she had no friends or family, only 'dear old associations'.[47] Eva's grave was there, and her sister Fanny's, but the reality of her daily life was solitude. She lived in a boarding house, having decided that 'I don't think I should care to go to a Home or Retreat, so long as I can take care of myself'.[48] Even her maid Annie did not join her immediately. George and Stanley and their families lived too far away to visit easily. Charlie was slightly nearer, and he, Maggie and Rosalind visited for a week in December. It was, Josephine said, 'so cheerful to hear their voices, and to see little dollies and untidy bits of pictures and toys lying about'.[49] She spent Christmas alone in 1901 and 1902, waiting for letters from her grandchildren and feeling the bitter cold.[50]

She needed to retreat from the world and its demands. Much of her time was spent in contemplation, prayer and reminiscence. She wrote a memoir of her early religious experiences, especially those relating to the Irvingite church, and its millennial belief in the imminent Second Coming of Christ.[51] She and Hatty had attended its services with their governess. Now, in her declining years she wrote passionately of her desire for 'the outpouring of the Holy Spirit which is promised for the latter times, and through which alone can the materialism, the incredulity and the other great evils of the times be successfully opposed and overcome'.[52] She awoke crying, 'Pentecost! Come again, O! Come again',[53] and was later greatly heartened by news of an Evangelical revival in Wales. 'Sober Quakers' told her 'it is Pentecost continued, beyond the shadow of a doubt'.[54] The accounts of spontaneous services and conversions and an 'ethical revival' led her to conclude, 'what we now see is the "Second Advent" begun, blessed, welcome Advent; of which His personal appearance will be the crowning Act'.

During this time of retreat she produced her important final work, *The Morning Cometh*, a set of reflections on the Bible which had been her 'constant companion' for many years.[55] She begins by arguing that eternal punishment is an 'unscriptural' doctrine, proving this by quoting original Greek and Hebrew texts to show that they were mistranslated.[56] This is an argument she must have discussed with George. She notes that the name El Shaddai, given to God in the Book of Genesis, derives from 'a nursing mother's breast ... the One who pours forth, satisfies like a mother ... the Mother God'.[57] Proclaiming this gender equality made Josephine ahead of her time, theologically.[58] Her approach to scientists and biblical critics, however, was conservative – she had 'great respect' for their work but advised them to seek the guidance of the Holy Spirit.[59] She concludes with her hope of 'a new Pentecostal era', but warns, 'There will be tribulation in the last times'.[60]

The Morning Cometh was intended solely for her sons and a few friends, and partly inspired by a conversation she had with Stanley about contentious passages in the Bible.[61] She expected that 'the Higher critics will scorn it, because it holds to the *whole* Bible as a

Revelation from God'. This was the faith she wanted to pass on to her children, although she had little indication that they had come to share it.

During the warm weather of August 1902, Josephine visited Charlie and Maggie with Rosalind and their new son John.[62] She enjoyed giving him his bottle: 'When he was well filled up, he used to look at me, and smile with that wide mouthed toothless smile of a young baby which is so bewitching.'[63] Charlie had now moved his family again, to Malvern in Worcestershire, a pattern of repeated uprootings which continued until the family emigrated to Canada in October 1904. Charlie's health was still subject to regular breakdown and, unhappily, did not improve in Canada. Josephine sometimes received news which made her anxious about him.[64] It is possible that she did not see him or his family again after this visit.

'Correctly evangelical Cheltenham' aroused all her righteous anger when a 'distinguished' prostitute living in rooms below Josephine was asked to leave.[65] She followed her to a 'house of ill-fame' and discovered 'an atmosphere of French vice' and that Cheltenham harboured 'low-class brothels ... and slums which would be a disgrace to London or New York'. The churches were doing nothing to help, but the 'godly people have numerous "Conferences for the deepening of Spiritual Life" from which they come away gorged with spiritual "sweet stuff"'. What was the use of that? She would like to 'lay a train of gunpowder here, and perhaps God will put a spark to it one day'.

In the spring of 1903, she developed 'a mysterious and severe internal pain' which gave her 'nights like Hell. Demons were all around my bed.'[66] One specialist doctor diagnosed cancer, and spoke of 'necessary operations. I decided I would rather die than suffer this.' Her prayers appeased the pain more than any doctor she consulted, until finally she shut her door and 'elected to be alone here with God'.

Writing to Katie Booth, she reaffirmed her belief in divine healing, 'a part of that large and rich "inheritance" in Christ which is ours, but which we have never yet claimed or entered into'.[67] By August, she had improved and, amazed by her continuing resilience, decided that 'my whole life has been a miracle ... like St Paul out of weakness I was made strong'.[68]

Her sons, however, could no longer endure her being 'away from us and recording her sufferings by post'.[69] George wrote a distressed and angry letter, reminding her of the three grandchildren she had not seen for two years.[70] Although she 'dreaded leaving this quiet retreat', she agreed to go back to Northumberland.[71] On the journey north in September, she spent a few days with Stanley in York, before George arrived to conduct her to her new home, a bungalow called Galewood on the Ewart Park estate.

The following day the three children came to see her, 'all much grown and a joy to my eyes'.[72] But George was resentful in his behaviour towards Josephine. Shortly after her arrival she wrote about 'differences and some estrangement' in her family, which caused her to turn to the Bible and the story of Catharine of Siena, 'a great peacemaker' and to ask for the gift of 'assured prayer' to help her family.[73] George believed his mother's public role had caused her to neglect his family:

> When a character has been through intense excitement, in public life, it is as though a furnace had blazed at white heat, and becomes calcined [sic], and cannot afterwards work at a dull red glow, and the character having endured the high tension and stress, cannot thereafter thrill to less intense emotions, such as the delight in young children's ways and voices and life.[74]

This deeply hurtful comment is disproved by a diary she kept at this time, with lovingly detailed observations of her grandchildren's behaviour.[75] They came to visit her on Sundays and sang hymns, 'as Grannie cannot get to church or hear music'.[76] The youngest, Irene, was 'very loving to me; throws her arms round my neck and almost stifles me with kisses ... one would think there was little to attract a child in a faded skeleton old Grannie'.[77]

Josephine was cheered by a visit from James Stuart in April 1904, after a week of 'more acute pain than I have ever had', which flared up repeatedly throughout the year.[78] She described her condition to Fanny Forsaith in excruciating detail: 'chronic ulceration of the bowels' causing constipation and the need for 'a powerful enema' every two days with effects as painful as childbirth.[79] She asked her friends to pray for her pain to be relieved but 'not to pray too much that I may have a prolonged life'.[80] She prioritised unfinished tasks, including arrangements for her diary of their father's final months to be copied for her sons, and the disposition of her family heirlooms and property stored at Ewart Park.[81]

She wrote to friends asking them to destroy all letters which 'have any allusions to my family or private life'.[82] (Some did, but many did not do so.) In her Will, she told them, she had 'charged my sons not to allow any biography of me ever to be published' – she knew that obituaries were inevitable but she 'disliked and deprecated' the kind of biography which probed the 'inner life' and often produced an untrue or overly flattering picture. These were the same objections she had made to Stead after George's death. She had previously explained to Fanny Forsaith that her biographies of her father, husband and sister, together with the history of their crusade, gave enough information:

> My children and grandchildren would be grieved if any life of me were written as uniquely and solely connected with our Abolitionist work. It would be very one-sided and ... it would be most unpleasant to my children to have a book written which identified me with the crusade and with nothing else. We have had so much bright family life ... that the Abolitionist crusade seems to become, in comparison, quite secondary to *us.*[83]

This shows Josephine's determination to acknowledge the role of her family, and her husband in particular. She feared that no biographer would maintain the same balance. However, by requesting the destruction of family papers, she tried to ensure that no one could even try. That may be why neither George nor Stanley destroyed their letters, or even Josephine's private diaries.[84]

Josephine decided not to spend another winter at Galewood, it was 'completely isolated' among trees.[85] She made plans to move to lodgings in Wooler, a small market town in the foothills of the Cheviots, less than 4 miles from Ewart. This was her last place of residence. Her pain continued, and her eyesight was often poor, so that she found it difficult to read anything except her large print Bible. But she kept up an astonishing flow of correspondence, describing herself as 'this old person, who is writing nearly all day'.[86] She recalled that St Paul had written many of his Epistles at the end of his life, 'this aged disciple did more for the world when he was, as it were past work'.[87]

She sent a forty-four page letter to Stanley with her thoughts on spiritual issues like the Second Coming, science and the Book of Revelation.[88] She reveals her sympathy with Polish Anarchists who were avenging 'centuries of horrible misrule and cruelty' by Russia, and rejoices at the recent Russian Revolution.[89] Despite her retirement from the Federation, she was unable to resist dabbling in its affairs.[90] In March 1905 she sent a formal request for expenses, since she was spending 'five to seven shillings a week' on postage.[91] She was advising on the thirtieth anniversary celebrations to be held in Neuchâtel and sending 'such heaps of letters to Switzerland'. Fanny Forsaith, who was to represent Josephine there, came to Wooler to consult her and received many suggestions for her speech.[92]

George was writing a memoir of Mia, and consequently read through his mother's letters to her. Unfortunately, this reinforced his belief that 'Mia did not receive that response to her love for you that she might have had.'[93] This charge was made in a series of painful letters which George sent to Josephine in June 1905.[94] She tried to make amends. That year she sent him 'a beautiful cross of alum lilies and other white flowers' on the anniversary of Mia's death.[95] She also wrote for him a detailed account of Eva's death, entitled 'A Memory of Child Sorrow'.[96]

Thoughts of Eva crowded upon her as she finalised her bequests – three pages are devoted to the relics, such as locks of her hair, which she had treasured.[97] Writing her final instructions with characteristic thoroughness and clarity in her copperplate handwriting, she asked to be buried beside George at Winchester, and that her funeral 'may be of the very simplest kind, inexpensive, and without any show of deep mourning'.

Early in 1906, after a 'terrible attack ... such pain as I have seldom endured', she bravely noted that Jesus suffered 'at the *close* of his earthly life. If some of us ... find the way of the Cross rather hard at the end, we cannot complain.'[98] The doctor ordered her to stop writing and stay in bed, advice which, surprisingly, she found 'marvellous'.[99]

She retired from Federation work for the second time, and accepted the title of Hon. President. In March she was carried to her last lodgings, 2 Victoria Villas, where the landlady, Miss Moodie, and nurse, Mary Cockburn, took good care of her. The LNA collected £884 'to add to her comforts in her last years' and presented her with a beautiful album of signatures, which touched her deeply.[100] Her grandson Bob and a school friend, Noel Russell, visited her at the end of their summer holidays. Noel never forgot:

> ... the tiny figure with wrinkled ivory skin stretched, as it seemed, straight over the bones ... the beautiful and serene face, with the vital intensity of the eyes. I can't remember what we talked about, but I fancy it was Faith and Guidance and Purpose in life. I know that I was intensely moved by the experience.[101]

During the final month of her life, Josephine wrote two letters to Rhoda which upset her a great deal.[102] The originals have not been found, but the likely reason is that both Rhoda and her daughter had converted to Catholicism the previous year and Josephine (then 18) had entered a convent school.[103] Her Grannie had given spiritual advice to Josephine in 1904, when she was 'going through a religious experience just as I did at her age', but it had a very different outcome in her case, one which the elder Josephine was bound to find very hard to accept.[104]

In October she was well enough to have several teeth removed, in preparation for 'lovely artificial teeth to smile with!'[105] She soon had to take to her bed again, however, and on 27 December wrote, 'I am holding on in faith. The Eternal Hand is holding mine.'[106] A fever, possibly pneumonia, took hold of her suddenly and on 28 December she wrote to Stanley, 'I think I may have to die. Don't mourn too much.'[107] When her breathing became difficult, on the morning of Sunday 30 December, she thanked her landlady and nurse, 'whispered a prayer or two' and passed peacefully away.[108]

She died as she had lived – fiercely independent, and close to her God.

O friends! with whom my feet have trod
The quiet aisles of prayer,
Glad witness to your zeal for God
And love of man I bear.

But still my human hands are weak
To hold your iron creeds:
Against the words ye bid me speak
My heart within me pleads.

I see the wrong that round me lies,
I feel the guilt within;
I hear, with groan and travail-cries,
The world confess its sin.

Yet, in the maddening maze of things,
And tossed by storm and flood,
To one fixed trust my spirit clings;
I know that God is good!

The wrong that pains my soul below
I dare not throne above,
I know not of His hate, – I know
His goodness and His love.

I know not what the future hath
Of marvel or surprise,
Assured alone that life and death
His mercy underlies.

And so beside the Silent Sea
I wait the muffled oar;
No harm from Him can come to me
On ocean or on shore.

I know not where His islands lift
Their fronded palms in air;
I only know I cannot drift
Beyond His love and care.

And Thou, O Lord! by whom are seen
Thy creatures as they be,
Forgive me if too close I lean
My human heart on Thee!

Verses from the hymn by J.G. Whittier,
selected by Josephine Butler as her epigraph
to *The Morning Cometh*

Epilogue

Josephine's sons were not with her when she died. Stanley was ill in St Andrews, under doctor's orders not to travel, Charlie was far away in Canada, and she does not appear to have summoned George. He now took charge, deciding immediately to disregard her request to be buried in Winchester. This decision has been criticised, but it was deepest winter with heavy snow in northern England. Few trains were running. Reaching Winchester, 355 miles away, with a coffin would have been very difficult. Even Josephine had recently told Stanley that 'if it involved great expense and trouble ... she would much rather be buried quietly at Kirknewton among her relations'.[1] This is what George did, with Stanley's full support. A simple funeral took place on 3 January at the tiny Anglican church of Kirknewton in the heart of Glendale, where Josephine's brother, George, and their grandparents were buried. It is less easy to defend George's treatment of his mother's colleagues and friends. Determined that this should be a family funeral, with no acknowledgement of his mother's public role, he did not invite any of them.[2] However, the only family member who managed to travel was Bob. He found the funeral 'very cold and dreary; it also seemed pathetic'.[3] Josephine did not want a grand funeral, but a 'pathetic' one was less than she deserved.

In the aftermath of Josephine's death, George received some very touching sympathy letters.[4] Amelie Humbert said that it was a 'high privilege to have been allowed to live with dear Mrs Butler in such near friendship, and the lessons I have learnt in the contact with such a noble soul, have been the most precious in my life'.[5] Mrs G.F. Watts, widow of the portraitist, sent a laurel wreath for her grave and wrote: 'she was the greatest woman of her time *or any*. Surely no woman so crucified herself for suffering souls as she did.'[6] Maud Garston, Josephine's niece by marriage, said, 'she seemed to be as *beautiful* as it was possible for anyone to be', and spoke of 'the wonderful grace and charm of her voice and manner'.[7] The vivid impression of her beauty was mentioned by many correspondents.

Her leadership qualities stand out from the reminiscences of her colleagues, some of which were published in *The Shield*. George Howell wrote, 'her nobleness and purity and character and her high objects and aims, inspired the Committee in their work. Many of the London ladies would have shrunk from the task but for her.'[8] Florence Booth said, 'The beauty and simplicity, and yet the indomitable courage of her spirit, helped me years ago – a young and hesitating woman – to attack forms of evil which seemed to me at the time to be so horrible, as well as so powerful, that I might have been excused if I had left them to others.'[9] Josephine herself believed that 'a leader should always be *most* full of hope and courage in the darkest hour'.[10] James Stuart emphasised how cosmopolitan she was, 'like most of the very great people of the world'.[11]

George received several immediate offers to write Josephine's biography, and refused them all. Her friends George and Lucy Johnson cleverly edited quotations from her publications in order to produce an *Autobiographical Memoir* in 1909. Josephine's centenary in 1928 was marked by tributes and Millicent Fawcett's biography, based on published sources.[12]

However, her memory languished once all her contemporaries were dead, despite the publication of Bob's affectionate portrait of his grandmother, the first to use the family's collection of letters, in 1954. An Anglican priest, Father Joseph Williamson, described Josephine in 1977 as 'The Forgotten Saint' in a heartfelt pamphlet, and succeeded in having her named in the Anglican Calendar of Saints.[13] It was not until the advent of women's history in the early 1980s that a significant number of publications began to appear.

There is another reason why Josephine was forgotten – as Elizabeth Longford pointed out, 'she did not champion the right women' and her campaigns were so disturbing and disruptive to Victorian convention that she could never be honoured by her country.[14] Once she had gone, her disturbing ideas, inconvenient truths and outstanding ability to inspire support could be swept under the carpet, except by those who shared her beliefs. Her followers created the Josephine Butler Society, which still exists, and the societies she founded continued their work. The Abolitionists claimed success in abolishing regulation and closing licensed houses in ten European countries in the years 1911–27.[15] (Ten countries still regulated, including France, Belgium and Italy.)[16] Inspection of prostitutes servicing the British Army briefly returned during the First World War, but almost entirely disappeared from the Empire when peace was restored. The 'tolerated houses' in Indian cantonments were closed in 1918.

Although the CD Acts have disappeared, trafficking of women and young girls for the purposes of prostitution has become a far greater problem than in Josephine's day, facilitated by easy air travel and the growth of organised crime.[17] Just as in Belgium in the 1870s, their passports are confiscated and they are imprisoned in brothels without hope of escape. If Josephine was alive today, these are the outcast women she would be fighting for. Her work is not over, and the legacy she hoped for was that others would follow the trail she blazed. As James Stuart concluded – 'the world as a whole is better, because she lived; and the seed that she has sown can never die'.[18]

Josephine Butler's Siblings

George Annett Grey, 1815–86

Josephine's eldest brother was born and raised at Milfield Hill and educated at King's College, London. He returned to Northumberland at the age of 17 when his father passed the management of Milfield to him, following his appointment to run the Greenwich Hospital estates. George recalled that, at this tender age, he was trusted with 'the charge of a farm of near 1,000 acres on which I lived; one adjoining of about 600 acres; one of 1,200, and one near it of about 500'.[1] He acquitted himself superbly, using innovative techniques to develop the land, just as his father did. George's passion for hunting induced him, he said, 'to rise early and take long rides before many were up'. Josephine and Hatty loved to join his hunts and were known to be fearless riders.

George took on more land agencies, and in 1853 was appointed as an inspector under the Enclosure Commissions for England and Wales. He lost 'a very large sum of money' in the Northumberland Bank failure of 1858 which also cost his father, John Grey, all his savings. Josephine attributed their losses to 'that dreadful *unlimited* liabilities system'.[2]

George married Elizabeth Boyd Neil in 1839 and the couple had nine children, before she died after the birth of the youngest, Mary, in 1856. His second wife, Elizabeth Jane Morton, survived him. His son George succeeded him as the owner of Milfield Hill.

John Henry Grey, 1817–44

John Henry was brought up at Milfield and appears to have been healthy until he suffered a punctured lung in an accident. At the age of 26, he set out on a sea voyage to visit his sister Eliza in Hong Kong in the hope of improving his health. However he died 'off the Cape', to the great sadness of the family back in Northumberland.[3]

Hannah Eliza Grey (Eliza), 1819–1900

Josephine's eldest sister was married at the age of 17, in 1836.[4] Her husband was William Morrison, a surgeon, aged 24, who was the first licensed lecturer in anatomy and physiology at the Newcastle School of Medicine. The Morrisons had four children, Edith, William, Constance and Anna Mary. In 1847 the family sailed to Hong Kong, where Morrison had been offered the post of senior surgeon. Morrison became seriously ill in 1853, and was nursed devotedly by Eliza, but he died at the age of 41.

Eliza brought the children back to England, and was living in Cheltenham, where she kept a school, at the time the Butlers moved there. In 1861, Eliza married Norman Ramsay Masson, who she must have met through her brother George. Masson's father, a great friend of George's, died when he fell from his horse in 1850. George took his children under his protection, and described Norman, as 'a steady deserving fellow'.[5] The Massons appear to have left England for northern Italy after Eliza's daughter, Edith, married Ludwig Leupold, a Swiss banker based in Genoa, in 1862.[6] Eliza was living in the Coronata, a district of Genoa, at the time of George Butler's last journey in 1890.

Mary Ann Grey (Tully), 1821–93

Tully was living nearby when the Butlers moved to Liverpool in 1867. She had married Edgar Garston, a former volunteer in the Greek fight for independence from Turkey, who later settled in the Liverpool area where he followed his father's trade as a merchant. There he built a substantial house, The Mount, at Aigburth.

Tully waited eleven years after their marriage for the birth of a daughter, Ethel, in 1853. A son, Edgar, followed in 1856. Tully's husband, who was considerably older than her, died in 1880. She left The Mount and lived in Westmorland until her death in 1893.

Frances Hardy Grey (Fanny), 1823–95

Fanny's life was consistently unhappier than that of any of her sisters. In later years, Josephine often referred to her as 'poor Fanny'. Most of her problems were caused by an unsuccessful marriage, to George Hunt Smyttan in 1848, when she was 25. Smyttan was ordained Deacon within two weeks of the wedding and they made their home at Charlton Hall in Northumberland.[7]

After two years, her husband took on the living of Hawksworth in Nottinghamshire, where he stayed until 1859. He is the author of the well-known hymn 'Forty Days and Forty Nights'. However, the couple separated before 1860, when Fanny was living alone in Cheltenham.

George Smyttan gave up his parish. He attended her mother's funeral in 1860, but little more was heard from him. He died in Frankfurt, Germany, in 1870, aged 48.

Fanny, who had no children, became 'her widowed father's companion'.[8] They moved to Lipwood House together after his retirement in 1863. Fanny later helped Josephine with her rescue work in Liverpool, but after her father's death she lived alone in London and Cheltenham, dying there at the age of 72. Josephine described her later life as 'many years of lonely, childless widowhood, and much physical pain and weakness'.[9]

Charles Grey Grey, 1825–1915

Charles graduated from Durham University with a degree in mathematics in 1846, and later took his MA.[10] He was the only graduate in the family. He moved to Ireland in the late 1840s, and in 1853 became land agent to Lord Derby on his Tipperary estates, following his father and brother's profession. Josephine and Hatty visited him in Ireland, and the Butlers holidayed in Tipperary in 1858.

When John Grey retired in 1863, Charles took over the management of the Greenwich Hospital Estates and lived at Dilston with his family. However, in 1865 the Estates were transferred to the Lords of the Admiralty, who began selling them to private owners.[11]

Dilston House was sold in 1874, and Charles returned to Ireland a few years later, where he stayed for the rest of his long life. Charles was married twice, first to Emily Mary Bolton, by whom he had six children. Two of these, Constance and Adela, became very close to Josephine and George after their father's second marriage to Eliza Jemfrey, by whom he had three more children.

Harriet Jane Grey ('Hatty'), 1830–1900

As the sister to whom Josephine was closest, most of Hatty's story has already been told. Her husband, Tell Meuricoffre, belonged to the fourth generation of a family of Swiss Protestant bankers which established the Bank Meuricoffre in Naples.[12] He and his brother Oscar ran the bank after their father, Achilles, died.

The family were celebrated for their liberalism and philanthropy in the city. For example, when a cholera epidemic broke out in 1884, Hatty and Tell cut short a trip to England and returned to Naples, where Hatty nursed in the hospital for six weeks.

Hatty and Tell had four sons, John, Frederic, George and Conrad, and three daughters, two of whom died very young. Conrad also died in 1892, aged 25, from yellow fever while working for a bank in Brazil. He was 'of such a sweet and loveable nature, a good deal like [Hatty] in sweetness of mind and geniality of nature, a son full of promise and hope', wrote Josephine.[13]

Both Tell and Hatty died in 1900, and four years later the Bank Meuricoffre was sold, after accumulating debts (largely due to embezzlement) which caused the sale of most of the family properties.

Emily Georgina Grey, 1836–1922

Josephine's youngest sister was the longest lived and most resilient, giving birth to eleven children. She was married three times, and endured the loss of all three husbands. Widowed first at the age of 24, after four years of marriage, and left with three children, she remarried two years later, to Jasper Bolton. Emily met Jasper in Ireland through her brother Charles; his first wife Emily Bolton was Jasper's sister. Charles succeeded their father as the land agent on Lord Derby's Tipperary estates.[14] When Charles moved to Dilston in 1863, Jasper became the land agent and the family moved into Charles's home, Ballykisteen House. There were five children, including Edith Rhoda, the future wife of Stanley Butler. Tragically, Jasper died in 1871, aged only 30.

Emily was still only 35, and went on to have three more children with her third husband, F.W. Thomas. She divorced him for adultery and desertion in 1906. In later life, she lived in Wandsworth, London, and was sympathetic to Josephine in her bereavement. She was an active supporter of Josephine's campaign and lived long enough to see women get the vote.

Josephine Butler's Homes: An Update

～～ Milfield Hill, near Wooler, Northumberland, 1828–35

Josephine's birthplace, Milfield, was a farmhouse on a large estate adjacent to Flodden Field, where 'the flower of Scotland' perished in battle against the English in 1513. Her father, John Grey, farmed it as a tenant of Earl Grey, and he passed the tenancy to his eldest son, George, when the family moved to Dilston. George bought the estate and improved and extended it, passing it to his son on his death in 1886. It remained in Grey hands until after the Second World War, but the land had been sold by 1958 and the house was demolished in the 1960s. Claire Grey's website – http://milfieldgreys.co.uk – contains photos, information and a family tree.

～～ Dilston House, near Corbridge, Northumberland, 1835–52

Dilston House was built by Josephine's parents, John and Hannah Grey, when John took over the administration of the Greenwich Hospital estates in Northumberland. Its site above Devil's Water was striking and beautiful, and its grounds contained the ruins of the fifteenth-century Dilston Castle and chapel.

Josephine's brother, Charles, lived at Dilston House after their father's retirement, but it was sold to W.B. Beaumont (later Lord Allendale) in 1874 and the name was changed to Dilston Hall.[1] Josephine was dismayed, on a return visit in 1901, to find that its appearance had been changed by the addition of a new wing.

The house and grounds have been occupied since 2014 by the Cambian Dilston College. Access to the site is restricted.

～～ Oxford, 1852–57

After their marriage, Josephine and George had lodgings in several buildings, including 124 High Street and 34 Beaumont Street. Their final home, in St Giles Street, was 'Butler House', which no longer has that name. The 'Museum in the Parks', which George did so much to develop, is now the Oxford University Museum of Natural History.

～～ Cheltenham, The Priory, London Road, 1857–66

The Priory was a 'gorgeous bow-fronted Regency house', built about 1820, and was a boarding house for Cheltenham College when the Butlers lived there.[2]

Later it became part of St Paul's Teacher Training College, and was used as a VA Hospital during the Second World War. It was unfortunately demolished in 1967 and 'replaced by an exceptionally ugly concrete office block, which was itself derelict for many years and eventually replaced (in 2000) with luxury residential flats in the same style as the original Priory building'.[3] The flats have a blue plaque recording the residence of Josephine Butler on the site.

Liverpool, 280 South Hill, Park Road, 1866–82

The house in which the Butlers lived while George was Principal of Liverpool College, and in which they accommodated 'dying Magdalens', was a large villa with a garden opening onto South Hill Grove, at that time a 'verdant pasture'.[4] The Dingle was known as 'one of the most lovely bits of scenery in the neighbourhood'. However, the area went downhill in the twentieth century and the house was demolished, probably as a result of the major clearance schemes of the 1960s.

Liverpool College

Founded in 1840, this is now an 'Independent IB [International Baccalaureate] World School for boys and girls aged 3 to 18'.[5] Its site has moved from Sefton Park, where it was located in George's day, to Queen's Drive, Mossley Hill.

Brownlow Hill Workhouse

Erected 1769–72, it was demolished in 1931. Liverpool's magnificent Catholic cathedral now stands on the site. Jane Jordan comments, 'only a row of the original redbrick outbuildings, laundry rooms, survive, standing opposite the University College building'.[6]

Winchester, 9 The Close, 1882–90

The house in the cathedral close still stands, looking very similar to its appearance in the Butlers' day. So does Hamilton House, Canon Street, which Josephine used as a House of Rest.

London, Wimbledon, 8 North View, 1890–93

The house which Josephine shared with her son, George, and in which he started his married life with Mia, stands immediately opposite Wimbledon Common. Even today the location feels almost rural. A blue plaque erected by English Heritage records – 'Josephine Butler, 1828–1906, Champion of Women's Rights, lived here 1890–93.'

London, Balham, 29 Tooting Bec Road, 1893–95

Josephine's 'little retreat' was a two-bedroom terraced house, certainly the smallest she had ever lived in. It was in a less exclusive part of London, but she loved her independence there. Balham was a typical London suburb built up during the second half of the nineteenth century following the building of a local railway line. Josephine's house has been demolished and modern flats now occupy the site, but houses further down the road are identical to the one she had. She gave it up in 1895, when it was clear she would have to spend a great deal of time abroad.

After 1895

Josephine had no permanent home, but stayed in a succession of boarding houses in England, and hotels on the Continent, supplemented by visits to her sons and to relatives, especially her sister Hatty. She spent the final three years of her life, 1903–06, in Northumberland, staying at Galewood, a bungalow on the Ewart Park estate of her son George, and then in lodgings in Wooler. She died there at 2 Victoria Villas.

Josephine sent her property, including her paintings, piano and furniture, to Ewart Park when she left Balham. Ewart Park was a stately home, built in 1787–90 by Mia Butler's great-grandfather, Colonel Horace St Paul. George Butler inherited it from Mia and left it to their son Horace, who sold the house in 1937. It was listed by English Heritage but reported as 'empty and partly derelict' in 1951.[7] It is still standing but still empty and derelict.

Josephine Butler's Grave

Her grave is in St Gregory the Great Church, Kirknewton, Northumberland, a small peaceful churchyard deep in the countryside, enfolded by hills. Sited to the west of the church tower, the grave is full-size and topped by a horizontal cross. The lettering is much eroded, but it is marked by a plaque erected by the Josephine Butler Society. Inside the church is the Centenary Window and Sculpture in memory of Josephine Butler, by artist Helen Whittaker.

None of Josephine Butler's homes has been preserved as a museum to her life and work. The University of Durham named its newest college 'Josephine Butler College' in 2005.

Notes

Abbreviations

ASB – Arthur Stanley Butler, Josephine and George's second son, known as Stanley.
ASGB – Arthur Stanley George Butler, Stanley's son, known as Bob.
JB – Josephine Butler.
JEB – Josephine Elizabeth Butler.
JG – Josephine Grey (JB's maiden name).
John Grey – JEB, *Memoir of John Grey of Dilston*, London, Henry S. King, 2nd ed. 1874.
GB – George Butler (Josephine's husband).
GGB – George Grey Butler (Josephine and George's eldest son, known as 'Georgie' until his father's death.)
George Butler – JEB, *Recollections of George Butler*, Bristol, J.W. Arrowsmith, 1892.
Harriet Meuricoffre – JEB, *In Memoriam. Harriet Meuricoffre*, London, Horace Marshall, 1901.
HCPP – *House of Commons Parliamentary Papers.*
Johnsons – George W. and Lucy A. Johnson (ed.), *Josephine E. Butler: An Autobiographical Memoir*, Bristol, J.W. Arrowsmith, 1909.
Jordan – Jane Jordan, *Josephine Butler*, London, John Murray, 2001.
Jordan and Sharp (I–V) – Jane Jordan and Ingrid Sharp (ed.) *Josephine Butler and the Prostitution Campaigns: Diseases of the Body Politic*, Volumes I–V, London, Routledge, 2003.
LUL – Liverpool University Library Archives.
McHugh – Paul McHugh, *Prostitution and Victorian Social Reform*, London, Croom Helm, 1980.
NRO – Northumberland Record Office (now known as Northumberland Archives) at Woodhorn, Ashington, Northumberland.
ODNB – *Oxford Dictionary of National Biography*, Oxford University Press, online edition.
Personal reminiscences – JEB, *Personal reminiscences of a Great Crusade*, London, Horace Marshall, new edition 1898.
Petrie – Glen Petrie, *A Singular Iniquity: The Campaigns of Josephine Butler*, New York, Viking Press, 1971.

Portrait – A.S.G Butler, *Portrait of Josephine Butler*, London, Faber and Faber, 1954.

RIBA – Royal Institute of British Architects study rooms, Victoria and Albert Museum, London.

SAHC – Salvation Army Heritage Centre, at William Booth College, Denmark Hill, London.

UP – University Press.

WL – The Women's Library, which moved to the London School of Economics in 2013.

NB Transcriptions of all letters have '&', 'wh.' and other abbreviations rendered in full in my quotes. Underlining is indicated by italics.

Many letters have no date. I have accepted the dates proposed by WL, NRO and LUL, so all dates in square brackets indicate my own suggestion.

A quotation without a note comes from the same source as the previous quote.

Chapter End Notes

INTRODUCTION
1   Millicent Garrett Fawcett and E.M. Turner, *Josephine Butler. Her Work and Principles, and their meaning for the Twentieth Century*, Association for Moral & Social Hygiene, London, 1927, p.1. Fawcett was the leader of the NUWSS which was also ultimately successful in securing its object, votes for women.
2   Benjamin Jowett, letter to Florence Nightingale, quoted E. Moberley Bell, *Josephine Butler. Flame of Fire*, London, Constable & Co, 1962, p.79.
3   Maud Royden, 'Josephine Butler', pamphlet issued by Josephine Butler Fellowship, nd, WL, 7AMR/2/01, p.1.

PROLOGUE
1   These quotes are based on Butler's revised account in *Personal Reminiscences*, pp.47–50. Her original account is included in W.T. Stead, *Josephine Butler. A Life Sketch*, London, Morgan & Scott, 1886, pp.59–63. Petrie, pp.133–4, tells us that this account was written at Stead's request and presumably not for publication.
2   In this first account, in relation to the threats of the men, JB writes, 'as what would have been to any of us *worse than death*; for the indecencies of the men, their gesture and threats, were what I would prefer not to describe'. In *Personal Reminiscences* she substitutes, 'so much as the mental pain inflicted by the rage, profanity and obscenity of the men, of their words and their threats'. In her own published account she therefore plays down the physical, sexual, threat.
3   *Personal Reminiscences*, p.49.

CHAPTER 1
1   *John Grey*, p.5.
2   *John Grey*, p.3; 'we'ed' is Scots for 'withered'.
3   *John Grey*, p.1.
4   *John Grey*, p.11.
5   E.A. Smith, 'Grey, Charles, second Earl Grey (1764–1845)', *ODNB*, Oxford UP, online ed., May 2009, http://www.oxforddnb.com/view/article/11526.
6   This story is told in the 2008 film *The Duchess* starring Keira Knightley. Eliza was brought up on Grey's estate in Howick. Claire Grey points out that the two branches of the Grey family had become, over the previous 300 years, quite distantly connected and Josephine was not a first cousin of Charles Earl Grey.
7   *John Grey*, p.13.
8   This estate remained in the family until 1865 when it was lost due to 'very adverse circumstances in this neighbourhood'. *John Grey*, speech quoted p.45.

9   200,000 Huguenots left France after the Revocation of the Edict of Nantes in 1685.
10   The Huguenot Society, 'Huguenot Settlements outside London', http://www.huguenotsociety.org.
     uk.
11   *John Grey*, p.25.
12   *John Grey*, p.26.
13   *John Grey*, pp.77–9.
14   *John Grey*, p.132.
15   *John Grey*, p.133.
16   The date was probably early in 1834, but I have not been able to locate a death certificate.
17   September 1834, quoted *John Grey*, p.148.
18   See Appendix 2 for information on Dilston House, and Frances Dickinson, *Historic Dilston: Guide
     and History*, North Pennines Heritage Trust, 2009.
19   *John Grey*, p.140.
20   *John Grey*, pp.162–3.
21   JEB to Fanny Forsaith, 11 August 1903, WL, 3JBL/47/21. JB describes herself as 'shy' in letter to
     Rhoda ref. 63, p.30.3.
22   Jordan, p.8.
23   Jordan, p.8; *Harriet Meuricoffre*, pp.293–4.
24   *Harriet Meuricoffre*, quoted Johnsons, p.9.
25   Quoted Johnsons, p.10.
26   Jordan, p.15.
27   Quoted *John Grey*, pp.297–98.
28   *Harriet Meuricoffre*, quoted Johnsons, p.9.
29   JB to her granddaughter, quoted Jordan, p.14, *John Grey*, p.294.
30   Quoted *John Grey*, p.166.
31   Quoted *John Grey*, p.147.
32   Bolton, *The Six Brides of Dilston*, Bognor Regis, New Horizon, 1984, p.34.
33   Quoted *John Grey*, p.167.
34   *John Grey*, pp.166–9.
35   *John Grey*, p.71.
36   Quoted Jordan, p.116.
37   Quoted Johnsons, p.14
38   Letter written 1905, quoted Johnsons, p.14.
39   Letter written 1905, quoted Johnsons, p.14.
40   Johnsons, p.15.
41   Johnsons, p.16.
42   Memories recorded in 1900, Johnsons, p.15.
43   Letter to Fanny, quoted Jordan, p.303.
44   JB to H.J. Wilson, 1 June 1873, WL, 3JBL/07/40. Judith R. Walkowitz, *Prostitution and Victorian
     Society: Women, Class and the State*, Cambridge UP, 1980, pb. 1982, p.116, and Petrie, p.133, also
     refer to this illness, describing it as a 'lesion on the lung'.
45   Jordan, p.20.
46   JEB, *Our Christianity Tested by the Irish Question*, London, T. Fisher Unwin, nd [1886–90], p.44.
47   Quoted Jordan, p.19. Jordan explains in a footnote that book-muslin was: 'A very fine, and thus
     expensive, muslin, so-named because it was folded like a book when sold.'
48   JG to Eliza Morrison, quoted Jordan, p.19.
49   JB to ASB, quoted Jordan, p.20.
50   *Portrait*, p.36; Bolton, *Six Brides*, p.26.
51   Hatty to 'Lee' (Eliza Morrison), 12 August 1850, NRO, ZBU/E3/C1.
52   *Ibid.*
53   *John Grey*, pp.25–6.
54   Jordan points this out, p.8. Josephine also believed this story and retold it in her biography of her
     father.
55   *George Butler*, p.209.
56   JB to Miss Priestman, 17 January 1883, quoted Jordan, p.16.
57   Letter to Eliza, 15 January 1851, quoted GGB, *Some Recollections of Josephine Butler*, p.5, NRO,
     ZBU/E3/E3.
58   Quoted Johnsons, p.15.

59   Quoted Kristine Frederickson, 'Josephine Butler and Christianity in the 19th-century British Victorian Feminist Movement', University of Utah PhD, 2008, chapter 4, section 1.
60   JB, 'Private Thoughts' diary, p.27, NRO, ZBU/E3/A2.
61   JEB, *Woman's Work and Woman's Culture*, London, Macmillan, 1869, p.lxiv. I am now convinced by Alison Milbank's argument, supported by Kristine Frederickson, that eschatology was important to JB from the start and not just in later life. See Alison Milbank (ed.), *Beating the Traffic: Josephine Butler and Anglican Social Action on Prostitution Today*, Winchester, George Mann, 2007, pp.92–102.
62   Bolton, *Six Brides*, p.25.
63   Quoted Johnsons, p.13. Miss Tidy is named by Bolton, *Six Brides*, p.25, and as the teacher of Emily by JG writing to Eliza Morrison, 12 April [1851], NRO, ZBU/E3/C1.
64   Quoted Johnsons, p.13.
65   Previous assumptions that Josey was also there for only two years are wrong according to Bolton, *Six Brides*, p.26.
66   Johnsons, pp.12–3.
67   *John Grey*, p.14
68   *John Grey*, p.290
69   Jane Robinson, *Bluestockings: The Remarkable Story of the First Women to Fight for an Education*, London, Viking, 2009, p.36.
70   Diary entry of 1853, quoted *John Grey*, pp.288–9 (footnote).

CHAPTER 2

1   *John Grey*, p.163.
2   See Pat Starkey, 'Saints, Virgins and Family Members: Exemplary Biographies? Josephine Butler as Biographer', in Jenny Daggers and Diana Neal (eds), *Sex, Gender and Religion: Josephine Butler Revisited*, New York, Peter Lang, 2006, pp.47–8.
3   *George Butler*, p.14.
4   *George Butler*, p.20.
5   *George Butler*, p.38.
6   *George Butler*, p.34.
7   *George Butler*, p.35.
8   *George Butler*, p.64.
9   *George Butler*, p.63; Timothy Larsen, *A People of One Book: The Bible and the Victorians*, Oxford UP, 2011, pp.222–3.
10   She only records that the date of their meeting was in the 'latter part' of George's time in Durham, which lasted from 1848–51, *George Butler*, p.53.
11   She visited Durham twice, in 1848 and 1849, Jordan, p.21.
12   GGB quotes a letter from Hatty (since lost) which describes her return in November 1849, *Some Recollections of Josephine Butler*, p.7. In a letter to Eliza Morrison, March 15 [1851], NRO, ZBU/E3/C1, JG says, 'I detest London … I have not a single pleasant experience of it – all my pleasures having been poisoned by illness and other annoyances.'
13   Louisa Butler to H.M. Butler, 23 January [1851], Sir James Ramsay Montague Butler Papers, Trinity College Library, Cambridge, M 3/1/91. I am grateful to the Archivist of Trinity College for suggesting that these papers contained letters relevant to my research.
14   *Ibid.* The word transcribed as 'June' is scrawled and hard to decipher, but it fits the known facts.
15   JB gives the date of 1851 in *George Butler* (p.65), but this is clearly incorrect. George's poems about Dilston were written the previous year.
16   Volume of poems by GB, p.1, NRO, ZBU/E2/12. This poem is dated, in pencil, October 1850.
17   Poems by GB, pp.6–8, *ibid.*
18   Poems by GB, 'The Early Morn. To Josephine', pp.9–10, *ibid.*
19   Poems by GB, 'To Josephine', pp.11–2, *ibid.*
20   JG to Eliza Morrison, 15 March [1851], NRO, ZBU/E3/C1.
21   *Ibid.* As Jordan says, pp.25–6, it is surprising that she chose Eliza for the role of confidante since she was so remote. Both Hatty and Josey were in the habit of writing very long and detailed letters to Eliza.
22   Jordan, p.26
23   JG to Eliza Morrison, 15 March [1851], NRO, ZBU/E3/C1.

24 *Ibid.*
25 JG to Eliza Morrison, April 12 [1851], NRO, ZBU/E3/C1.
26 *The Storm-Bell*, 1898, quoted in Johnsons, pp.251–2.
27 GB to JG, Sunday, nd [1851], NRO, ZBU/E3/B1.
28 See Jordan, p.29. The reason why she was painted by such a famous artist is not revealed in any letters.
29 Jordan, p.29.
30 JG to Eliza Morrison, nd [May 1851], NRO, ZBU/E3/C1.
31 The first visit is described in JG to Mrs Spring Rice, May 22 1851, WL, 3JBL/54/1.
32 JG to Eliza Morrison, nd [June 1851], NRO, ZBU/E3/C3.
33 *Ibid.*
34 JG to Mr Spring-Rice, 27 June 1851, WL, 3JBL/54/3.
35 JG to Mr Spring-Rice, 9 July [1851], WL, 3JBL/54/4.
36 *George Butler*, pp.70–1.
37 *George Butler*, pp.72–3.
38 Harriet Grey to 'Lee' (Eliza Morrison), 19 September [1851], NRO, ZBU/E3/C1.
39 Harriet Grey's diary, December 1851–January 1853, NRO, ZBU/E3/A1.
40 *Ibid.*
41 'Visitor's Guide to St Andrew's Parish Church, Corbridge, Northumberland', pamphlet.
42 Harriet Grey's diary, December 1851–January 1853, NRO, ZBU/E3/A1.
43 1851 census, Township of Dilston, PRO H.O. 107 2414.
44 Harriet Grey's diary, December 1851–January 1853, NRO, ZBU/E3/A1.

CHAPTER 3

1 *George Butler*, p.114.
2 Described by A.S.G. Butler, p.42, from a sketchbook kept by Hatty and Josephine. This appears to be their first sitting room, as suggested by Jordan, p.34, but the piano in it was not Josephine's new one, which arrived in October.
3 Harriet Grey to Eliza Morrison, Oxford, 17 November 1852, quoted in George Grey Butler, *Some Recollections*, p.7. The sketch is reproduced in Bolton, *Six Brides of Dilston*.
4 JB to Bob (ASG Butler), *c.* 1900, WL, 3JBL/58/01.
5 Harriet Grey's diary, December 1851–January 1853, NRO, ZBU/E3/A1.
6 Arthur Butler to GGB, 1907, quoted Jordan, p.34, f.2.
7 Harriet Grey's diary, December 1851–January 1853, NRO, ZBU/E3/A1.
8 Quoted Jordan, p.38.
9 He paid £5,000 to the settlement, see contract dated 19 December 1851, NRO, ZBU/E2/24. John Grey's contribution is not mentioned.
10 For this account, see *George Butler*, pp.110–3.
11 John Ruskin to GB, *c.* 1852, WL, 3JBL/01/06.
12 History of the Oxford University Museum of Natural History, http://www.oua.ox.ac.uk/holdings/MU%20Introduction.pdf.
13 Philippa Toogood, 'Josephine Butler (1828–1906) as depicted by Alexander Munro in sculpture (1855) and obituary (1907)', University of Oxford Department of Continuing Education, open resources, 2013, http://open.conted.ox.ac.uk/resources/documents.
14 *George Butler*, p.81. JB dates this as the winter of 1852/53, but the lectures were published by November 1852 when a friend wrote to thank George for a copy. Chevalier Bunsen to GB, 11 November 1852, WL, 3JBL/01/08.
15 *George Butler*, pp.77–8.
16 *George Butler*, p.93.
17 *George Butler*, p.91.
18 JB to Eliza Morrison, 18 September [1852] NRO, ZBU/E3/C3. This fragment has not been previously cited.
19 *Ibid*; Harriet's diary 16 October–13 November 1852.
20 Harriet Grey to Eliza Morrison, Oxford, 17 November 1851, quoted in GGB, *Some Recollections*, p.7. The date may be wrong, or the letter written over several days, as this section clearly dates from before Georgie's birth on 15 November.
21 JB to Albert Rutson, 22 February 1868, WL, 3JBL/02/07.

22   This is also the assumption of Lisa Severine Nolland, *A Victorian Feminist Christian: Josephine Butler, the Prostitutes and God*, Milton Keynes, Paternoster, 2004, p.30.
23   See Edward Shorter, *History of Women's Bodies*, London, Allen Lane, 1982, pp.130–8.
24   JB to Albert Rutson, 22 February 1868, WL, 3JBL/02/07.
25   JB to Montagu Butler, 26 December 1852, NRO, ZBU/E3/C8.
26   Jordan, illustration 13.
27   JB to Mr Spring-Rice, 2 January 1853, WL, 3JBL/54/06.
28   Harriet Grey's diary, December 1851–January 1853, NRO, ZBU/E3/A1; JB to Montagu Butler, 26 December 1852, NRO, ZBU/E3/C8.
29   JB to Mr Spring-Rice, 2 January 1853, WL, 3JBL/54/06.
30   This episode is described in *George Butler*, pp.103–4.
31   Jordan, p.38.
32   Catherine Butler, 'Memories of George Butler', Trinity College Library, Cambridge, Sir J.R.M. Butler Papers, M/2/5/2; the obituary of George Butler, M/2/5/7, mentions his heart condition.
33   Quoted *George Butler*, p.104.
34   *George Butler*, p.64.
35   *George Butler*, p.105.
36   *George Butler*, p.94.
37   The first to do so, Lady Margaret Hall, did not open until 1878.
38   JB letter, quoted *Portrait*, p.43.
39   *George Butler*, p.90.
40   *George Butler*, p.95.
41   *George Butler*, p.98. Jowett is not named here, but it is clear from her letter to him (see below) that he made this remark.
42   *George Butler*, p.99.
43   *George Butler*, p.99.
44   JB to B. Jowett, nd (*c*. 1865–68), WL, 3JBL/01/20.This long letter is the only one known to have been preserved from either side.
45   *Ibid*.
46   *George Butler*, p.96.
47   *George Butler*, p.101.
48   *George Butler*, p.96.
49   *George Butler*, p.97.
50   *George Butler*, pp.97–8.
51   *George Butler*, p.98.

INTERLUDE – A Victorian Obsession: Rescuing Prostitutes
52   Michael Mason, *The Making of Victorian Sexual Attitudes*, Oxford UP, 1994, p.108.
53   When the 1851 Religious census was taken, 41 per cent of the total population went to church, and 58 per cent of the population was actually able to attend on that day.
54   Matthew 25:35–36.
55   John 8:11, Authorised version.
56   Quoted F. Prochaska, *Women and Philanthropy in Nineteenth Century England*, Oxford UP, 1980, p.201.
57   See Annemieke Van Drenth and Francisca de Haan, *The Rise of Caring Power: Elizabeth Fry and Josephine Butler in Britain and the Netherlands*, Amsterdam UP, 1999, pp.101–4.
58   Quoted Janet Murray, *Strong-Minded Women and Other Lost Voices from 19th-century England*, New York, Pantheon, p.415.
59   Prochaska, *Women and Philanthropy*, p.197.
60   Mason, *Victorian Sexual Attitudes*, p.93.

CHAPTER 4
1   JB to Mr Spring-Rice, 13 August 1853, WL, 3JBL/54/10.
2   JB to Edith Leupold, 8 March 1867 in Jordan and Sharp (I), pp.82–3.
3   *Ibid*.
4   JB to Albert Rutson, February 22 1868, WL, 3JBL/02/07.
5   This letter also mentions their cook, who was paid 10s a week.
6   JB to GB, 1854, nd, NRO, ZBU/E2/7. The 'machine' was a bathing machine, like a caravan, which was driven into the water.

7   E.g. Harriet Grey to Fanny Smyttan, 4 August [1853], NRO, ZBU/E3/C1, in which she rhapsodises about a number of other young men.

8   Garston's meeting with the Meuricoffres is described in a catalogue note to WL, 3JBL/02/49. I have found no other source for this information.

9   Bolton, *Six Brides*, p.72.

10 'Meuricoffre – The most important Swiss family lived in Naples: the Meuricoffre.' http://it.wikipedia.org/wiki/Meuricoffre (automatic translation from Italian).

11 Quoted Jordan, p.39.

12 Letter from Hatty quoted JB, *Harriet Meuricoffre*, p.27.

13 JB, *Harriet Meuricoffre*, p.30; Jordan, p.39.

14 Quoted *George Butler*, p.115.

15 *George Butler*, p.108; Jordan, pp.46–7.

16 *George Butler*, p.108.

17 *George Butler*, p.118.

18 Diana Neal supports my interpretation: 'Flirting with the Catholic Other' in Daggers and Neal, *Sex, Gender and Religion*, p.160.

19 JB, 'Private Thoughts', February 1856, NRO, ZBU/E3/A2.

20 *Ibid*.

21 JB to GB, nd [1856], NRO, ZBU/E2/7.

22 JB, 'Private Thoughts', 22 July [1856], NRO, ZBU/E3/A2.

23 *George Butler*, p.123.

24 GB to JB, Saturday, nd 1856, NRO, ZBU/E3/B1.

25 *George Butler*, p.124.

26 *George Butler*, p.126.

27 JB, 'Private Thoughts', Oxford, 8 December 1856, NRO, ZBU/E3/A2.

28 JB, 'Private Thoughts', 8 December 1856, NRO, ZBU/E3/A2.

29 JB to Albert Rutson, 22 February 1868, WL, 3JBL/02/07.

30 The date of this visit is unclear, since JB suggests in George Butler, p.126 that the visit was in the autumn. It resulted in her immediate dispatch to Clifton and therefore cannot have been before December, when she notes in her diary that she was still in Oxford. See also JB to Albert Rutson, 22 February 1868, WL, 3JBL/02/07.

31 *George Butler*, p.128.

32 Jordan suggests that he was named after Charles Vaughan, who succeeded George's father as head of Harrow, p.50.

33 *George Butler*, p.128.

34 *Portrait*, facing p.50.

35 Baron Sandford to GB, 29 August 1854, WL, 3JBL/01/13.

36 M.C. Morgan, *Cheltenham College: The First Hundred Years*, published for the Cheltonian Society by Richard Sadler, 1968, p.8.

37 He published a selection in 1862.

38 Jordan, p.49. She quotes an 1828 advertisement describing the interior.

39 The Priory had eight servants in 1861, including a butler, housekeeper and nurse – Cheltenham census, 1861, www.ancestry.co.uk.

40 11 in 1861 – Cheltenham census, 1861, www.ancestry.co.uk.

41 JB to Mr Spring-Rice, 8 February [1858], WL, 3JBL/54/08.

42 This is my assumption – Eva was christened Evangeline Mary, which is an unusual name and not one used by the Butler or Grey family for any other child.

43 *John Grey*, p.277.

44 *George Butler*, p.150 (quoting letter to JB in May 1860); GGB to JB, nd [May 1860], WL, 3JBL/01/19. Both these letters were written to Josephine while she was at Dilston at the time of her mother's death.

45 *George Butler*, p.153, quoting letter from JB to a friend, August 1864.

46 JB to H. Montagu Butler, 30 June [1859], J.R.M. Butler papers, Trinity College, Cambridge, M3/1/377.

47 Jordan, p.50, suggests that she may have sustained a serious injury during Eva's birth which left her unable to have more children. However, this is an unlikely and life-threatening outcome for which there is no evidence. A series of difficult labours would lead to medical advice to avoid another pregnancy, which would anyway be complicated by JB's other health problems.

48   JB to Mr Spring-Rice, 3 August 1858, WL, 3JBL/54/09.
49   *George Butler*, p.140. No date is given for this visit, but 1860 is most likely.
50   *George Butler*, p.144. For this account, see pp.143–8.
51   *George Butler*, p.147.
52   *Ibid.*
53   *George Butler*, p.148.
54   JB, 'Private Thoughts' diary, nd (1858–62), NRO, ZBU/E3/A2. This entry is discussed in more detail
      by Lisa Nolland, *A Victorian Feminist Christian*, p.283.
55   *The Hour Before the Dawn*, p.96.
56   JB to Florence Booth, 26 March 1885, SA RJ/1/13.
57   *The Hour Before the Dawn*, p.96.
58   *The Hour Before the Dawn*, p.87.
59   For this account, see *George Butler*, pp.141–2.
60   JB, 'Private Thoughts' diary, 18 April 1865, NRO, ZBU/E3/A2.
61   *George Butler*, p.150.
62   Fanny's diary, quoted Jordan, p.52.
63   See Jordan, pp.52; 309, f.12, referring to Fanny's diary, which I have not been able to see due to
      unknown current location.
64   The Massons were married in Cheltenham in 1861, and Edith the following year. Bolton, *Six Brides*,
      says that the Massons moved to Northern Italy, p.53. The exact date they moved is unclear but Eliza
      certainly lived there in later life. See Appendix 1.
65   GGB to GB, nd, NRO, ZBU/E2/18.
66   Jordan, p.51.
67   Fanny's diary, quoted Jordan, p.51.
68   Diary in Boulogne, 1861, NRO, ZBU/E2/18, quoted Jordan, p.51.
69   Fanny's diary, quoted Jordan, p.54.
70   *George Butler*, p.152.
71   Description by Jordan, p.57, based on inquest evidence by the butler and Eva's governess. Eva's
      death has been recounted many times using JB's accounts, but Jordan has used the inquest report to
      give some objectivity. Her account of Eva's death is more detailed than mine, see pp.55–8.
72   These include Portrait, p.52.
73   Jordan, p.57.
74   JB, letter dated August 1864, in *George Butler*, p.153.
75   This account is JB to GGB, 'A Memory, which is still living in my mind' (usually known as 'A
      Memory of Child Sorrow'), nd [c. 1904], NRO, ZBU/E3/A10. Jordan believes it was written
      in 1895, see p.310, ref. 27. It is possible that both dates are correct, since there is a postscript
      'added later'.
76   'A Memory of Child Sorrow', *ibid.*
77   'A Memory of Child Sorrow', *ibid.*
78   *George Butler*, p.155.
79   JB, letter dated August 1864, in *George Butler*, p.154.
80   JB, prayer, September 25 1864, WL, 3JBL/01/26.
81   John Grey, p.277.
82   Letter from Mr Powles, quoted *George Butler*, p.159.
83   Quoted George Butler, p.158.
84   JB to Stanley Butler, 1901, quoted Jordan, p.55.
85   'A Memory of Child Sorrow', NRO, ZBU/E3/A10; Jordan, p.61.
86   *Portrait*, p.53.
87   *John Grey*, p.269.
88   JB to GB, nd [late 1864] NRO, ZBU/E2/7.
89   *George Butler*, p.159.
90   JB to GB, quoted *George Butler*, p.162.
91   *Harriet Meuricoffre*, p.103.
92   *Harriet Meuricoffre*, p.105. The letters were written to Hannah's eldest daughter Eliza, who was
      Edith's mother.
93   This account is taken from a letter Harriet wrote to Edith, quoted in *Harriet Meuricoffre*, pp.105–
      19.

94 *Harriet Meuricoffre*, pp.119.
95 *Harriet Meuricoffre*, pp.109.
96 *Harriet Meuricoffre*, pp.117.
97 JB to Albert Rutson, 22 February 1868, WL, 3JBL/02/07.
98 M. Gelder, D. Gath, R. Mayou, *Oxford Textbook of Psychiatry*, 2nd ed., Oxford UP, 1989, p.204.
99 *George Butler*, pp.163–4. Josephine does not mention the voyage in George's biography but only in the later one she wrote of Hatty.

INTERLUDE – Victorian Prostitutes by Day and Night
100 William Acton, *Prostitution, Considered in Its Moral, Social and Sanitary Aspects*, 2nd ed., London, Frank Cass, 1870 ed., p.4.
101 For example, the historian of one small city, York, identified 1,400 women sex-workers in the years 1837–87. Frances Finnegan, *Poverty and Prostitution: A Study of Victorian Prostitutes in York*, Cambridge UP, 1979.
102 Walkowitz, *Prostitution*, p.24.
103 *Ibid.*
104 Acton, *Prostitution*, pp.4–7.
105 Quoted Finnegan, *Poverty and Prostitution*, p.6.
106 This information and subsequent data quoted by Walkowitz, *Prostitution*, pp.18–20.
107 *The Unknown Mayhew: Selections from the Morning Chronicle*, E.P. Thompson and E. Yeo (eds), London, Merlin Press, 1971, pp.147–9.
108 This is the view of Judith Walkowitz, *Prostitution*, pp.14–5.
109 Quoted Walkowitz, *Prostitution*, p.26.
110 Although in the first edition Dickens wrote in the introduction, 'Nancy is a prostitute', http://www.victorianweb.org/authors/dickens/rogers/6.html.
111 Charles Dickens, *Oliver Twist*, (1837–39), chapters IX, XIII.
112 Quoted Murray, *Strong-minded Women*, pp.398–9.

CHAPTER 5
1 JB, 'Private Thoughts', 10 March 1865, NRO, ZBU/E3/A2.
2 JB, 'Private Thoughts', 18 April 1865, NRO, ZBU/E3/A2.
3 Jordan, p.65, points out that this is her first written reference to prostitutes.
4 Beverley Grey suggests this, 'Sin is Contagious: Josephine Butler's Mission to Reform', Bristol University MA thesis, 1997, p.38.
5 M.C. Morgan, *Cheltenham College: The First Hundred Years*, Cheltonian Society, 1968, p.33; *Reminiscences of Cheltenham College by an Old Cheltonian*, London, Benrose & Sons, 1868, p.161.
6 Morgan, *Cheltenham College*, pp.17–8. Two boys who contracted scarlet fever at The Priory in 1864 were moved to another house by the butler, p.16.
7 In 1863 GB tried to apply for the headship of Charterhouse School, but his testimonials (see NRO ZBU/E2/3) arrived too late. Since he had collected thirteen of these, he must have been disappointed.
8 Both have a claim to be the first of this kind: Cheltenham opened first but Liverpool was founded earlier – David Wainwright, *Liverpool Gentlemen: A History of Liverpool College, an Independent Day School, from 1840*, London, Faber and Faber, 1960, p.67.
9 Wainwright, *Liverpool Gentlemen*, p.114.
10 *George Butler*, p.165.
11 *George Butler*, p.167.
12 *George Butler*, p.182.
13 *George Butler*, p.183.
14 M.W. Royden, 'The 19th Century Poor Law in Liverpool and its Hinterland: Towards the Origins of the Workhouse Infirmary' (1999), http://www.btinternet.com/~m.royden/mrlhp/local/poorlaw/poorlaw.htm. Florence Nightingale said of Agnes Jones, 'In less than three years she reduced one of the most disorderly populations in the world to something like Christian discipline. She converted the Liverpool Select Vestry to the conviction, as well as the humanity; of nursing the pauper sick by trained nurses, the first instance of its kind in England'.
15 Jordan, p.67.

16   *George Butler*, pp.183–6. Quotes in this paragraph are taken from these pages.
17   *George Butler*, p.184. Other quotes in this paragraph are from p.185.
18   JB to Fanny Smyttan, 27 February 1867, WL, 3JBL/01/31.
19   JB to 'my dear A', 7 March 1867, WL, 3JBL/01/31. I take 'dear A' to be Albert Rutson, to whom she
     was close at this time and who took a keen interest in her Home. She wrote to Rutson in the same
     style the following year, 1868, and they were definitely friends in 1867, since Emily Davies mentions
     him as 'a friend of Mrs G. Butler's' in a letter written 1 August 1867, Ann B. Murphy and Deirdre
     Raftery (eds), *Emily Davies: Collected Letters, 1861–1875*, Charlottesville, Virginia UP, 2004, p.244.
20   JB to Miss Priestman, 24 January 1873, quoted Jordan, p.69. See also p.70.
21   JB to Edith Leupold, 8 March 1867, in Jordan and Sharp (I), p.87.
22   JB to 'my dear A', 7 March 1867, WL, 3JBL/01/31. For the identity of 'A', see note 19.
23   JB, *Harriet Meuricoffre*, pp.179–80, quoting a letter from Harriet to herself.
24   See Jordan, p.74. She notes that at the 1871 census there were thirty-seven inmates.
25   George Butler, p.185. Alison Milbank explains that JB's view of Anglican rescue homes had been
     strongly influenced by the work of Felicia Skene, who she met in Oxford. *Beating the Traffic*,
     pp.18–21.
26   JB to Fanny Smyttan, 12 February 1867, WL, 3JBL/01/31.
27   *George Butler*, p.185.
28   *George Butler*, pp.185–6.
29   JB letter to Edith Leupold, 8 March 1867, in Jordan and Sharp (I), p.86.
30   JB to Fanny Forsaith, 1 January 1905, quoted Jordan, p.71.
31   JB to Fanny Smyttan, quoted Jordan, p.71.
32   Jordan, p.71, suggests that 'Josephine was endangering not only the career of her husband but the
     moral well-being of her three schoolboy sons'.
33   JB to Fanny Smyttan, quoted Milbank, *Beating the Traffic*, p.25.
34   JB to Edith Leupold, 8 March 1867, in Jordan and Sharp (I), p.86. This is the main source for the
     following account. Quotes in this paragraph are taken from this letter, pp.82–8. See also Jordan,
     pp.70–3; 83–4.
35   *George Butler*, p.190.
36   JB to Fanny Forsaith, quoted Jordan, p.72.
37   JB to Edith Leupold, 8 March 1867, in Jordan and Sharp (I), p.84.
38   This paragraph from JB to Edith Leupold, 8 March 1867, in Jordan and Sharp (I), pp.84–6.
39   Jordan, p.72.
40   JB to 'my dear A', nd [March 1867], WL, 3JBL/01/31. JB tells him that Mary had died the previous
     evening. See note 19 for identity of 'A'.

INTERLUDE – The Dark Side of English Life
41   JEB, 'The dark side of English life, illustrated in a series of true stories. No.I – Marion', *The Methodist
     Protest*, January 1877. The first two stories were sent to the editor of *The Torch* in 1868 but may not
     have been published (no copies survive).
42   Jane Jordan, '"Trophies of the Saviour": Josephine Butler's biographical sketches of prostitutes', in
     Daggers & Neal (eds), *Sex, Gender and Religion*, p.23.
43   JEB, 'The dark side of English life, illustrated in a series of true stories. No.I – Marion': see Jordan,
     '"Trophies of the Saviour"', pp.21 & 32, note 1.
44   JEB, 'The dark side of English life, illustrated in a series of true stories. No.I – Marion'. Other quotes
     in this paragraph are from this story. This published version differs in some respects from the first
     version of the story, intended for *The Torch*. (See WL, 3JBL/02/01.)
45   JEB, 'The dark side of English life, illustrated in a series of true stories. No.I – Marion'. Other quotes
     in this paragraph are from this story.
46   Jordan, '"Trophies of the Saviour"', p.25.
47   This was first noted by Jordan, '"Trophies of the Saviour"', pp.21–32. Her analysis has informed my
     discussion here.
48   Judith R. Walkowitz, *City of Dreadful Delight: Narratives of Sexual Danger in Late-Victorian
     London*, Chicago UP, 1992, p.89.
49   Cited by Walkowitz, *City of Dreadful Delight*, pp.89–90.
50   Walkowitz, *City of Dreadful Delight*, p.90.
51   JEB, 'The dark side of English life. Illustrated in a series of true stories. No.III – Margaret', *The
     Methodist Protest*, March 1877.

52   Jordan, '"Trophies of the Saviour"', pp.31–2.

53   JEB, 'The dark side of English life, illustrated in a series of true stories. No.III – Margaret'. Jordan, '"Trophies of the Saviour"', p.23, states that the original for Margaret has not been found.

54   JEB, 'The dark side of English life, illustrated in a series of true stories. No.III – Margaret'.

55   Elizabeth Barrett Browning, 'The Runaway Slave at Pilgrim's Point', 1848, in D. Karlin (ed.), *The Penguin Book of Victorian Verse*, London, 1997, pp.93–102. See Helen Mathers, ''Tis dishonour done to *me*: Self-representation in the writings of Josephine Butler', Daggers & Neal (ed.), *Sex, Gender and Religion*, pp.43–4.

56   JEB, 'The dark side of English life, illustrated in a series of true stories. No.III – Margaret'.

57   Jordan, '"Trophies of the Saviour"', in Daggers & Neal (eds), p.26.

CHAPTER 6

1   This story is told in *George Butler*, pp.187–9. Josephine Meuricoffre's death took place at Ormskirk, Lancashire, in September 1866, http://www.freebmd.org.uk.

2   *George Butler*, p.189.

3   Harriet Meuricoffre to JB, quoted Johnsons, p.137.

4   Thekla's birth date has not been found, but on 18 June 1869, JB sent her mother-in-law a photograph of 'sweet Thekla, 3 years old', WL, 3JBL/02/49. This puts her birthday between July 1865 and May 1866. So baby Thekla must have been at home in Italy when Hatty and Tell came to England. 'Thecla' was a Meuricoffre family name – Tell's sister was named Sophie Thecla. For some reason the Butlers and Greys always spelled the name with a 'k'.

5   *Harriet Meuricoffre*, p.181.

6   JB to 'My dear A', nd, WL, 3JBL/01/31. See ch.5, note 19, for identity of 'A'.

7   JB to Edith Leupold, 8 March 1867, in Jordan and Sharp (I), p.83.

8   JB to Fanny Smyttan, 12 February 1867, WL, 3JBL/01/31.

9   *Ibid*; JB to Edith Leupold, February 1867, WL, 3JBL/01/31.

10   JB to Mrs Myers, February 26 [1867], WL, 3JBL/01/31. She was Eva's godmother and lived in Cheltenham.

11   Two of these had moved into the House of Rest by the following day, see JB to 'Dear A' 27 February 1867, WL, 3JBL/01/31.

12   JB to Fanny Forsaith, quoted Jordan, p.71.

13   JB to Fanny Smyttan, 27 February [1867], WL, 3JBL/01/31.

14   JB to Miss Wallace, 14 February 1873, WL, 3JBL/56/05.

15   JB to 'Dear A', 7 March 1867, WL, 3JBL/01/31.

16   *George Butler*, p.187.

17   JB to Fanny Smyttan, 27 February [1867]; JB to 'Dear A', 27 February 1867, WL, 3JBL/01/31.

18   JB to 'Dear A', 7 March 1867, WL, 3JBL/01/31.

19   *George Butler*, p.186.

20   Quoted Jordan p.137.

21   JB to Mrs Myers, 26 February 1867; JB to Fanny Smyttan, 12 February 1867, WL, 3JBL/01/31.

22   Jordan, p.85.

23   Anne Clough's diary, quoted Margaret Simey, *Charity Rediscovered: A Study of Philanthropic Effort in Nineteenth-Century Liverpool*, first published 1951, republished by Liverpool UP, 1992, p.67.

24   Gillian Sutherland, 'Clough, Anne Jemima (1820–1892)', ODNB, Oxford UP, 2004, http://www.oxforddnb.com/view/article/5710.

25   See Kathryn Hughes, *The Victorian Governess*, London, Hambledon, 1993.

26   JEB, *The Education and Employment of Women*, T. Brakell (printer), Liverpool, 1868, and London, Macmillan, 1868, p.7, accessed via Victorian Women Writers Project, http://www.indiana.edu/~letrs/vwwp.

27   This was the number counted in the census of 1861, which Josephine studied carefully.

28   JEB, *The Education and Employment of Women*, p.13.

29   JEB, *The Education and Employment of Women*, p.22.

30   JEB, *The Education and Employment of Women*, p.18.

31   JB to Albert Rutson, 7 May 1868, WL, 3JBL/02/18–19.

32   JB to Frederic Harrison, 9 May 1868, in Jordan and Sharp (III), pp.17–20.

33   JB to Albert Rutson, 22 May 1868, WL, 3JBL/02/25a–b. See also Jordan, pp.94–5.

INTERLUDE – A Victorian Brand of Feminism
34   It first appeared in dictionaries in 1897.
35   Quoted *John Grey*, pp.288–9 (footnote).
36   *George Butler*, p.101.
37   *George Butler*, pp.57–8.
38   I am grateful to Kris Frederickson for this phrase and her insights on this topic.
39   *George Butler*, p.98.
40   Galatians 3:28, the Bible, Authorised version.
41   1 Timothy 2:12. In 1 Corinthians 14:34, he writes 'let your women keep silent in the churches: for it
      is not permitted unto them to speak; but they are commanded to be under obedience'.
42   This section is derived from two articles by Helen Mathers, 'The Evangelical Spirituality of a Victorian
      Feminist: Josephine Butler 1828–1906', *Journal of Ecclesiastical History*, Vol. 52, April 2001,
      pp.302–6, and "Tis dishonour done to me': Self-representation in the writings of Josephine Butler' in
      Daggers & Neal (ed.), *Sex, Gender and Religion*, pp.40–2.
43   JEB, *Woman's Work and Woman's Culture*, London, Macmillan, 1869, p.li (footnote).
44   *Woman's Work and Woman's Culture*, p.lvii.
45   John 20:16 (New English Bible version). The other gospel references are Matthew 28:1–8, Mark
      16:1–8; Luke 24:1–12.
46   JB, 'Private thoughts', February 1856, NRO, ZBU/E3/A2.
47   Luke 7:36–50, Authorised version of the Bible.
48   JEB (ed.), *Woman's Work and Woman's Culture*, p.lix.
49   The first conference of the Women's Liberation Movement was held at Oxford in 1970.
50   See further discussion in Eileen Janes Yeo (ed.), *Radical Femininity: Women's Self-Representation in
      the Public Sphere*, Manchester UP, 1998, pp.136–8.

CHAPTER 7
1   This paragraph taken from Wainwright, *Liverpool Gentlemen*, pp.113–127; *George Butler*,
     pp.169–75.
2   *George Butler*, p.26.
3   *George Butler*, p.15.
4   GB to JB, 3 December 1867, WL, 3JBL/01/32.
5   *George Butler*, p.196.
6   *George Butler*, p.177.
7   *George Butler*, p.43: Wainwright, *Liverpool Gentlemen*, p.125.
8   Ruth Schwartz Cowan, 'Galton, Sir Francis (1822–1911)', *ODNB*, Oxford UP, online ed. October
     2005, http://www.oxforddnb.com/view/article/33315. Galton later pioneered eugenics, which
     he intended to have a positive effect, not the negative racist applications it had in the twentieth
     century.
9   'The first meeting was held 1–2 November 1867 in the Heaton's drawing room at Leeds. Mrs Butler
     was elected President and Miss Clough Secretary of the Council', WL catalogue entry, 3JBL/02/48.
10   Emily Davies, August 1867, in Murphy and Raftery (ed.), *Emily Davies: collected letters, 1861–
     1875*, p.245.
11   James Stuart, *Reminiscences*, London, Cassell, 1912, p.165. The following account is taken from
     this book. See also H.C.G. Matthew, 'Stuart, James (1843–1913)', ODNB, Oxford UP, 2004,
     http://www.oxforddnb.com/view/article/38025.
12   In *Reminiscences,* Stuart says that the course was astronomy but Kelly has shown by reference
     to local newspapers that his memory is at fault on this point. Thomas Kelly, *A History of Adult
     Education in Great Britain*, Liverpool UP, 1992, p.220.
13   Quoted Jordan, p.87.
14   Quoted E. Moberly Bell, *Josephine Butler: Flame of Fire*, London, Constable, p.61.
15   Kelly, *History of Adult Education*, p.219.
16   Helen Mathers, *Steel City Scholars: the Centenary History of the University of Sheffield*, London,
     James & James, 2005, p.6.
17   Quoted Kelly, *History of Adult Education*, p.227.
18   *George Butler*, p.180; *John Grey*, pp.306–7.
19   *John Grey*, pp.301–2.
20   *George Butler*, p.180.

21   These were recognised at the time, to the extent that the biography had three editions, and was translated into Italian as an example of 'the life of a true English gentleman ... whose character and life have proved to be a power for good in his country'. Preface to the Second Edition, *John Grey*, 1874.

22   JB to Albert Rutson, 10 February 1868, 22 February 1868, WL, 3JBL/02/07.

23   Albert Rutson (1836–90) attended Rugby school, Oxford student 1855–60, Fellow of Magdalen College, 1860–70, barrister at law, Lincoln's Inn 1864. 'Oxford University Alumni, 1500–1886', www.ancestry.co.uk. His father owned Nunnington Hall near York.

24   JB to Albert Rutson, 22 February 1868, WL, 3JBL/02/07.

25   JB to Albert Rutson, 10 February 1868, WL, 3JBL/02/03.

26   JB to Albert Rutson, 17 February 1868, WL, 3JBL/02/05.

27   JB to Albert Rutson, 9 May 1868, WL, 3JBL/02/20. JB points out that her father had been called the 'Black Prince' by local newspapers during election hustings, *John Grey*, p.91.

28   JB to Albert Rutson, 5 March 1868, WL, 3JBL/02/09.

29   Sara Delamont, 'Davies, (Sarah) Emily (1830–1921)', *ODNB*, Oxford UP, online ed. May 2007, http://www.oxforddnb.com/view/article/32741.

30   Delamont, 'Davies, (Sarah) Emily (1830–1921)', p.4.

31   JB to Albert Rutson, 23 May 1868, WL, 3JBL/02/26a–c.

32   Jordan, p.98.

33   Delamont, 'Davies, (Sarah) Emily (1830–1921)', p.4.

34   Henry Sidgwick was a Professor of Philosophy at Cambridge whose 'dedication to the cause of university access for women was unstinting', Jane Robinson, *Bluestockings*, p.46. He planned Newnham College with Anne Clough and his wife Eleanor.

35   Matthew Cragoe, 'Bruce, Henry Austin, first Baron Aberdare (1815–1895)', *ODNB*, Oxford UP, online ed. January 2008, http://www.oxforddnb.com/view/article/3732; Jordan, p.89.

36   JB to Albert Rutson, 27 April 1868, WL, 3JBL/02/14.

37   JB to Albert Rutson, 22 May 1868, WL, 3JBL/02/25a–b. She was still reeling from Frederic Harrison's attack on her pamphlet supporting women's employment, described in chapter 6.

38   JB to Albert Rutson, nd (June 1868), WL, 3JBL/02/30a–b.

39   JB to Albert Rutson, 2 June 1868, WL, 3JBL/02/29a–b.

40   JB to Albert Rutson, 28 May 1868, WL, 3JBL/02/27a–b.

41   JB to Albert Rutson, 1 June 1868, WL, 3JBL/02/28a–b.

42   JB to Albert Rutson, 2 June 1868, WL, 3JBL/02/29a–b.

43   JB to Albert Rutson, 8 June 1868, WL, 3JBL/02/31b.

44   Jordan, p.96.

45   The law gradually adjusted in the direction of equality, but women were not able to sue for divorce under the same terms as men until 1923.

46   Patricia Branca, *Silent Sisterhood: Middle Class Women in the Victorian Home*, Carnegie-Mellon UP, Pittsburgh USA, 1975, p.47.

47   JB to Frederic Harrison, 9 May 1868, in Jordan and Sharp (I), p.17.

48   JB to Frederic Harrison, 9 May 1868, in Jordan and Sharp, (I), p.17.

49   *John Grey*, p.291.

50   Mary Lyndon Shanley, *Feminism, Marriage, and the Law in Victorian England, 1850–1895*, Princeton UP, 1989, p.52.

51   Shanley, *Feminism, Marriage, and the Law*, p.51.

52   Lydia Becker to JB, 19 October 1868, Manchester Central Library, GB127, M50/1/2.

53   Sylvia Pankhurst, *The Suffragette Movement*, London, Longman, 1931, p.35.

54   JB to Albert Rutson, 8 & 19 June 1868, WL, 3JBL/02/31 & 32.

55   JB to Albert Rutson, 26 July & 10 August 1868, WL, 3JBL/02/34 & 35.

56   JB to Mrs George Butler, 11 January 1869, WL, 3JBL/02/39a.

57   JB to Albert Rutson, 26 July 1868, WL, 3JBL/02/34.

58   JB, letter to GB, 21 July 1871, in WL, 'JB and her contemporaries', p.11.

59   JEB, Introduction to *Woman's Work and Woman's Culture*, p.xvi.

60   *Woman's Work and Woman's Culture*, p.xix. The source of this statistic is not given.

61   *Woman's Work and Woman's Culture*, p.xxi.

62   *Woman's Work and Woman's Culture*, p.xxxi.

63   *Woman's Work and Woman's Culture*, p.xxxii.

64　　*Woman's Work and Woman's Culture*, p.xxxv.
65　　John Stuart Mill, *The Subjection of Women*, quoted Jordan, p.100.
66　　Jordan, p.100.
67　　Victoria, Crown Princess of Prussia, to JB, 7 December 1868, WL, 3JBL/02/38a–b.
68　　J.S. Mill to JB, 22 March 1869, WL, 3JBL/02/42.
69　　Princess Louise to JB, 27 March 1869, WL, 3JBL/02/43.
70　　Jordan, p.103.

INTERLUDE – Dr Acton and the Lock Hospitals
71　　Quoted Frank Mort, *Dangerous Sexualities: Medico-Moral Politics in England Since 1830*, London,
　　　Routledge and Kegan Paul, 1987, p.79.
72　　William Acton, *The Functions and Disorders of the Reproductive Organs: In Childhood, Youth,
　　　Adult Age and Advanced Life, Considered in their Physiological, Social and Moral Relations*,
　　　6th ed., 1875, pp.212–4.
73　　See chapter 10, note 24.
74　　For this account, see Judith Walkowitz, *Prostitution*, pp.50–1. I am grateful to Dr Nigel Mathers for
　　　medical advice.
75　　Linda Mahood, *The Magdalenes. Prostitution in the Nineteenth Century*, London & New
　　　York, Routledge, 1990, p.29. Walkowitz has a slightly different explanation, taken from Acton,
　　　Prostitution, p.59.
76　　For this paragraph, see Ivan Crozier, 'William Acton and the history of sexuality: the medical and
　　　professional context', in *Victorian Culture*, 5 (2000), pp.7–10.
77　　William Acton, *Prostitution*, 2nd ed. 1870, p.85.
78　　Acton, *Prostitution*, p.81.
79　　Acton, *Prostitution*, p.88. This was actually true, since there is no internal pain in this area.
80　　Quoted Roy Porter and Lesley Hall, *The Facts of Life: The Creation of Sexual Knowledge in Britain,
　　　1650–1950*, New Haven & London, Yale UP, 1995, p.135.
81　　Sir Samuel Solly, quoted Porter and Hall, *The Facts of Life*, p.134.
82　　Acton, *Prostitution*, p.88.

CHAPTER 8
1　　JB to Mrs G. Butler, February 1869, WL, 3JBL/02/40.
2　　*Ibid.*
3　　JB to Mrs G. Butler, 18 June 1869, WL, 3JBL/02/49.
4　　*Ibid.*
5　　JB to Anne Clough, 7 July 1869, WL, 3JBL/02/52.
6　　JB to Anne Clough, 13 July 1869, WL, 3JBL/02/54 & 57.
7　　JB gives the date of 1871 in *The Dawn*, but Anne Clough's niece prefers 1873, as do most other
　　　sources, see Jordan, p.317, note 70.
8　　GB to Mrs G. Butler, quoted *George Butler*, p.199.
9　　For this paragraph, see Jordan, p.106. This decision must have been short-lived, since JB found little
　　　evidence of them when she visited Europe in 1874–75.
10　　Walkowitz, *Prostitution*, p.49.
11　　Jordan, p.107. In her account in *George Butler*, pp.217–8, JB does not say who it was from. This
　　　was in late September or early October, not December, as stated by Walkowitz, *Prostitution*,
　　　p.93.
12　　*George Butler*, p.218.
13　　*Personal Reminiscences*, p.7.
14　　*George Butler*, p.217.
15　　Quoted Jordan, p.110 (My added emphasis).
16　　*George Butler*, p.219.
17　　Larsen, *A People of One Book*, p.239.
18　　*George Butler*, p.218.
19　　*George Butler*, pp.219–20.
20　　*Personal Reminiscences*, p.7.
21　　*George Butler*, p.219.
22　　JEB, 'Emancipation – as I learned it', *The Storm-Bell*, 19 January 1900.

23   *George Butler*, p.218.
24   *Personal Reminiscences*, pp.8–9.
25   Nolland, *A Victorian Feminist Christian*, answers the question of JB's motivation for the campaign in great detail in chapter 7, pp.240–64. She sees it as 'five-fold' – 'Prostitution seen as cruel oppression and slavery'; 'a Liberal's fear for the future of England'; 'her antagonism to materialistic science and bad science'; 'her sense of divine destiny' and 'her concern for sons'.
26   *George Butler*, p.221.
27   Reprinted in Jordan and Sharp (II), pp.33–44; R.K. Webb, 'Martineau, Harriet (1802–1876)', *ODNB*, Oxford UP, 2004; online ed. October 2006, http://www.oxforddnb.com/view/article/18228.
28   Jordan and Sharp (II), p.36.
29   Reported to JB by a sympathetic MP and quoted in *Personal Reminiscences*, p.11.
30   Florence Nightingale to JB, 22 November & 20 December 1869, WL, 3JBL/55/30 & 31.
31   *Personal Reminiscences*, p.10.
32   *Personal Reminiscences*, p.11.
33   *George Butler*, p.228.
34   *British Medical Journal*, 29 January 1870, reprinted Jordan and Sharp (I), p.80.
35   See JB to Albert Rutson, 22 February 1868, WL, 3JBL/02/07.
36   20 March 1870, quoted *Personal Reminiscences*, p.13.

INTERLUDE – Steel Rape

37   E.I. Carlyle, 'Wilkinson, (James John) Garth (1812–1899)', rev. Logie Barrow, ODNB, Oxford UP, 2004; online ed. October 2005, http://www.oxforddnb.com/view/article/29427.
38   James John Garth Wilkinson, *The Forcible Introspection of Women for the Army and Navy by the Oligarchy*, London, F. Pitman & Glasgow, John Thomson, 1870, p.3.
39   Letter from Josephine Butler to Garth Wilkinson, reprinted in *Forcible Introspection*, p.23, and Jordan and Sharp (I), p.22.
40   Quoted Kelly Lynn Trumble, '"Her body is her own"': Victorian feminists, sexual violence, and political subjectivity', Florida State University PhD, 2004, p.42.
41   Wilkinson, *Forcible Introspection*, pp.10–1.
42   Quoted Trumble, '"Her body is her own"', pp.44–5.
43   Wilkinson, *Forcible Introspection*, pp.10–1.
44   See Walkowitz, *Prostitution*, pp.56–7, f.55.
45   Letter to Wilkinson reprinted in *Forcible Introspection*, p.25.
46   Quoted Trumble, '"Her body is her own"', p.45. Mrs Lewis was testifying to the Royal Commission on the Administration of the CD Acts, 1871.
47   Wilkinson, *Forcible Introspection*, p.15.
48   *The Shield*, 2 May 1870, quoted Walkowitz, *Prostitution*, p.109.
49   This signed deposition was taken in 1881 when the CD Acts were still in force. Reprinted from Parliamentary papers in E.O. Hellerstein, L.P. Hume and K.O. Offen (ed.), *Victorian Women*, Stanford UP, 1981, pp.423–8.
50   Hellerstein et al, *Victorian Women*, p.427.

CHAPTER 9

1   McHugh, p.57.
2   JB, Speech to working men's meeting at Liverpool, in Jordan and Sharp (II), p.73.
3   *Personal Reminiscences*, p.37.
4   JB, Speech to working men's meeting at Liverpool, in Jordan and Sharp (II), p.67.
5   Quoted Petrie, p.90. Symonds had a tortured fascination with Butler, described by Anne Summers, *Female Lives, Moral States: Women, Religion and Public Life in Britain 1800–1930*, Newbury, Threshold Press, 2000, pp.71–75.
6   Speech to Women's Meeting, Nottingham, 8 March 1870, in Jordan and Sharp (II), p.118.
7   L. Hay-Cooper, *Josephine Butler and her Work for Social Purity*, London, Society for Promoting Christian Knowledge, 1922, p.21.
8   James Stuart, 'Introduction' to Johnsons, p.ix.
9   *Autobiographical Memoir*, pp.305–6. There is a conflict between JB's account and Mary Priestman's 'Reminiscences' (see note 10), in which she says that she first saw JB at the Birmingham meeting in 1870. Possibly Miss Priestman meant that it was the first time she saw her speak.

10   Mary Priestman, 'Reminiscences of Mrs Butler by an early member of the L.N.A.', MS, WL, 3JBL 53/45.
11   *Ibid.*
12   Mary Priestman, MS sent to H.J. Wilson, 21 February 1907, WL 3JBL 53/43.
13   Mary Priestman, 'Ladies' Branch Associations', *National League Journal*, 1 December 1881, quoted by Walkowitz, *Prostitution*, p.134.
14   JB to Mrs G. Butler, 3 January 1870, WL, 3JBL/03/05.
15   Quoted McHugh, p.59.
16   JB to GB, 6 May [1870], WL, 3JBL/03/13.
17   *Ibid.*
18   JB to Mr R. Ryley, 17 February 1871, LUL, JB 1/1 1871/02/17 II. See also JB to H.J. Wilson 5 November 1870, WL, 3JBL/03/19.
19   *Personal Reminiscences*, p.27.
20   JB to H.J. Wilson, 5 November 1870, in Jordan and Sharp (II), p.106.
21   *Personal Reminiscences*, p.30.
22   *Personal Reminiscences*, pp.29–30.
23   *Portrait*, p.74.
24   *Personal Reminiscences*, pp.32–3.
25   Petrie, p.142.
26   *Personal Reminiscences*, p.28.
27   *The Standard*, 4 November 1870, cited McHugh, p.83.
28   Kingsley Kent argues that Butler's campaign led many women into the suffrage movement, *Sex and Suffrage in Britain*, p.9.
29   The full title was JEB, *An Appeal to the People of England, on the Recognition and Superintendence of Prostitution by Governments, by an English Mother*, 1st ed. 1869, 2nd ed. 1870.
30   *Appeal to the People of England*, p.17. Other quotes in this paragraph are from p.12 and p.13.
31   'The Garrison Towns of Kent', Letters to *The Shield* from Josephine Butler, in Jordan and Sharp (II), pp.88–9.
32   'The Garrison Towns of Kent', p.90. The other quote in this paragraph is from p.87.
33   'The Garrison Towns of Kent', p.87. The other quote in this paragraph is from p.88.
34   'The Garrison Towns of Kent', p.91. The other quote in this paragraph is from pp.81–2.
35   *Portrait*, p.74.
36   'The Garrison Towns of Kent', p.92.
37   'The Garrison Towns of Kent', p.93. Walkowitz points out that this is 'a denunciation that conveniently incorporated the entirety of Butler's brief against the acts', *City of Dreadful Delight*, p.92.
38   'The Garrison Towns of Kent', p.96. The other quotes in this paragraph are from p.97.
39   *George Butler*, p.229.
40   *George Butler*, p.229.
41   *George Butler*, p.231.
42   Petrie, p.105. The following story is derived from this book.
43   *Constitution Violated*, reprinted in Jordan and Sharp (II), p.217. The other quote in this paragraph is from p.224.
44   *Constitution Violated*, reprinted in Jordan and Sharp (II), p.227. The other quote in this paragraph is from p.252.
45   *Constitution Violated*, reprinted in Jordan and Sharp (II), p.228.
46   *Constitution Violated*, reprinted in Jordan and Sharp (II), p.271.
47   *Constitution Violated*, reprinted in Jordan and Sharp (II), p.241.
48   *Hansard*, 24 June 1884, Vol. 289, cc.1208-23.
49   JB, *The Constitution violated: An Essay*, Edinburgh 1871.
50   *George Butler*, p.231.
51   Quoted Jordan, p.120.
52   Wainwright, *Liverpool Gentlemen*, p.126. The next quote is from p.129.
53   For this paragraph, see Wainwright, *Liverpool Gentlemen*, pp.139–44.

INTERLUDE – Speaking on Public Platforms about Unmentionable Subjects
54   Quoted by Stead, p.54.
55   JEB, 'The Lovers of the Lost', *Contemporary Review 1870*, in Jordan and Sharp (I), p.119.

56   JEB, *Sursum Corda: Annual Address to the Ladies National Association*, London, World's Women's Temperance Union, nd [1871], p.14.
57   C.W.S. Deakin, lecture to the Medical Society of University College, London, quoted Walkowitz, *Prostitution*, p.88.
58   Petrie, p.141.
59   JEB, 'The Lovers of the Lost' in Jordan and Sharp (I), p.119.
60   JEB, *Sursum Corda*, p.23.
61   JEB, Address delivered at Croydon, 3 July 1871, in Jordan and Sharp (ed.), Vol. II, p.163.
62   JB, 'Letter to an MP', February 1883, quoted Kent, *Sex and Suffrage in Britain*, pp.73–4.
63   JB, 'The Duty of Women', speech to audience of ladies in Carlisle, 25 November 1870, in Jordan and Sharp (II), p.125. Further quotes in this paragraph are taken from this speech – p.125, 132 (capitals in original), 128.
64   She never used this word to the Royal Commission, for example – see Trumble, '"Her body is her own"', pp.60–2.
65   JB to Charlotte Wilson, 26 August 1872, WL, 3JBL/05/42. The term 'medical rape' was used by the Dean of Carlisle when introducing Josephine Butler's speech to a public meeting there in November 1870, see Jordan and Sharp (II), p.135.

CHAPTER 10
1   JB to Anna Maria Priestman, 12 December 1871, in Jordan and Sharp (II), p.317.
2   LNA, *Annual Report for 1870*, quoted McHugh, p.60. The Commissioners who opposed the Acts were A.J. Mundella MP, Peter Rylands MP, and Robert Applegarth, the first working man to sit on a Royal Commission.
3   The full report of the Commission was 'Royal Commission upon the administration and operation of the CD Acts, PP1871 (408 and 408-1)'. Page numbers below are from the 'House of Commons Parliamentary Papers Online' (HCPP), PDF.
4   Contagious Diseases Commission (CDC) 1871 – Analysis of Evidence, p.xxvi (PDF p.53).
5   CDC 1871 – Analysis of Evidence, p.vi–vii (PDF pp.33–4).
6   CDC 1871 – Analysis of Evidence, pp.xxii–xxiii (PDF pp.49–50).
7   CDC 1871 – Analysis of Evidence, p.xxxvi (PDF p.63).
8   CDC 1871 – Analysis of Evidence, p.xii (PDF p.39).
9   CDC 1871 – Analysis of Evidence, Miss Green, p.xxvi; Miss Farrow, p.xxxi (PDF pp.53, 58).
10   JEB, *Vox Populi*, in Jordan and Sharp (II), p.325. *Vox Populi* is an edited selection of the letters, published in April 1871.
11   CDC 1871 – Minutes of Evidence, p.438–39 (PDF pp.527–8).
12   CDC 1871 – Analysis of Evidence, p.xii (PDF p.39).
13   CDC 1871 – Minutes of Evidence, p.441 (PDF p.530).
14   CDC 1871 – Minutes of Evidence, p.442 (PDF p.531).
15   Quoted Jordan, p.19.
16   CDC 1871 – Minutes of Evidence, p.440 (PDF p.529).
17   CDC 1871 – Minutes of Evidence, p.439 (PDF p.528).
18   McHugh, pp.64, 65.
19   Letter quoted *George Butler*, p.234.
20   CDC 1871 – Minutes of Evidence, p.744 (PDF p.833).
21   Quoted Walkowitz, *Prostitution*, p.95.
22   JB to Margaret Tanner, 4 April 1871, in Jordan and Sharp (II), pp.352–3.
23   JB, LNA circular, 8 July 1871, in Jordan and Sharp (II), p.355.
24   CDC 1871 – Report, p.11 (PDF p.11).
25   CDC 1871 – Report, p.17 (PDF p.17).
26   CDC 1871 – Report, clause 59, p.17; clause 65, p.19 (PDF pp.17, 19).
27   CDC 1871 – Report, clause 67, p.20 (PDF p.20).
28   JB, LNA circular, 8 July 1871, in Jordan and Sharp (II), p.356.
29   JB to GB, 21 July 1871, WL, 3JBL/03/39. See also Jordan, p.133.
30   Quoted McHugh, p.80.
31   Speech delivered by JB at the 4th Annual Meeting of the Vigilance Association for the Defence of Personal Rights, 15 October 1874, in Jordan and Sharp (II), p.137.
32   JEB, 'A Vigilance Committee', in Jordan and Sharp (II), p.124.
33   JEB, 'A Vigilance Committee', in Jordan and Sharp (II), p.125. The next quotes are from p.125 and 126.

34   Speech delivered by JB at the 4th Annual Meeting of the Vigilance Association for the Defence of Personal Rights, 15 October 1874, in Jordan and Sharp (II), p.134. The next quote is from pp.136–7.
35   Quoted McHugh, p.75.
36   Quoted Petrie, p.124.
37   JB, open letter to repealers on Mr Bruce's Bill, 12 March 1872, WL, 3JBL/04/08, p.27.
38   JB, 'A few words addressed to true hearted women', 18 March 1872 in Jordan and Sharp (II), p.362.
39   JB, open letter to repealers on Mr Bruce's Bill, 12 March 1872, WL, 3JBL/04/08, p.6.
40   Ibid., p.28.
41   The commissioner Peter Rylands MP, see McHugh, pp.78–9.
42   JEB, 'A few words addressed to true hearted women', 18 March 1872 in Jordan and Sharp (II), p.361.
43   JB to Hatty Meuricoffre and Fanny Smyttan, c. June 1872, in Jordan and Sharp (II), pp.368–9.
44   JB to Charlotte Wilson, 2 June 1872, WL, 3JBL/04/24.
45   JB to Hatty Meuricoffre and Fanny Smyttan, c. June 1872, in Jordan and Sharp (II), p.368.
46   For example, Bruce received a petition from 1,000 physicians and surgeons supporting the CD Acts – far more than the fifty doctors who had signed the NA's petition for repeal.
47   JB to Hatty Meuricoffre and Fanny Smyttan, c. June 1872, in Jordan and Sharp (II), p.368.
48   It was her 'most satisfactory apologia against her critics', Petrie, p.128.
49   George Butler, p.205.
50   W.S. Fowler, A Study in Radicalism and Dissent: The Life and Times of Henry Joseph Wilson, 1822–1914, London, Epworth Press, 1961, p.24.
51   Quoted M. Hewitt, 'Wilson, Henry Joseph (1833–1914)', ODNB, Oxford UP, September 2004; online ed. October 2009, http://www.oxforddnb.com/view/article/50958.
52   JB to Charlotte Wilson, 8 October 1873, WL, 3JBL/08/20.
53   'Memoir of Mrs Henry J. Wilson', Sheffield Archives, Wilson Collection, MD 2469-17.
54   McHugh, p.84.
55   The following account is taken from Personal Reminiscences, pp.46–52. Quotes are from pp.48 and 49.
56   Letter to JB, quoted Personal Reminiscences, p.53.
57   JB to H.J. Wilson, 23 August 1872, WL, 3JBL/05/36; 24 August 1872, WL, 3JBL/05/40.
58   Quoted McHugh, p.93
59   JB to Mary Priestman, 24 September 1872, WL, 3JBL/06/09; Jordan, p.144.
60   For example, the Liberation Society (which campaigned for disestablishment of the Church of England), see McHugh, p.94.
61   JB to Charlotte Wilson, 3 December 1872, WL, 3JBL/06/32.
62   Interview in 1894, quoted Walkowitz, Prostitution, p.121.
63   George Butler, p.241.
64   George Butler, p.243.
65   George Butler, p.244. The next quote is from p.245.
66   JB, Sursum Corda, p.18.
67   Diary entry by JB, quoted Portrait, p.150.
68   Portrait, p.50.
69   James Stuart, Reminiscences, p.232.
70   Petrie, p.143.
71   GGB to GB, 28 March 1873, NRO, ZBU/E2/18.
72   JB to H.J. Wilson, 1 April 1873, WL, 3JBL/07/40.
73   JB to H.J. Wilson, 16 October 1872, WL, 3JBL/06/15.
74   GB to GGB, 27 October 1872, quoted Jordan, p.143. See note 68 explaining the terms of John Grey's will.
75   GGB to JB and GB, 15 August 1875, 17 January 1876, NRO, ZBU/E3/B2. 'Fives' was played in a court similar to a squash court, with the ball being struck by hand.
76   GGB to JB, 22 July nd [1873–76], NRO, ZBU/E3/B4.
77   JB, LNA Circular, 8 July 1871 in Jordan and Sharp (II), pp.356–7.
78   JB to H.J. Wilson, 23 December 1872, WL, 3JBL/06/38.
79   Jordan, p.142, points out that this was unfair since she was actively involved in rescue work.
80   JB to H.J. Wilson, 23 December 1872, WL, 3JBL/06/38.

81   Jordan, p.142.
82   JB to H.J. Wilson, 23 December 1872, WL, 3JBL/06/38.
83   JB to Mary Priestman, 6 January 1873, WL, 3JBL/07/09.
84   JB to H.J. Wilson, 1 April 1873, WL, 3JBL/07/40.
85   Jordan, pp.144–5.
86   JB to H.J. Wilson, 26 May 1873, WL, 3JBL/07/60.
87   JB, 'Grannie Diary', June–July 1873, WL, 3AMS/J/01.
88   *George Butler*, p.209.
89   Johnsons, p.127.
90   McHugh, pp.96, 98; JB to R. Martineau, 27 May 1873, WL, 3JBL/07/61.
91   JB to M. Priestman 28 February 1874, WL, 3JBL/08/39.

INTERLUDE – The Attack on Women's Bodies
92   JB to Joseph Edmondson, 28 March 1872, in Jordan and Sharp (II), pp.364–5.
93   JEB, 'Some thoughts on the present aspect of the Crusade against the State Regulation of Vice',
     Jordan and Sharp (III), p.59.
94   Wilkinson, *Forcible Introspection*, p.22.
95   JEB, 'Some thoughts on the present aspect of the Crusade ...' Jordan and Sharp (III), p.53.
96   Anne Summers, '"*The Constitution Violated*": The Female Body and the Female Subject in the
     Campaigns of Josephine Butler', *History Workshop Journal*, 48, 1999, p.8.
97   JB, 'A few words addressed to true-hearted women', 18 March 1872, in Jordan and Sharp (II),
     p.362.
98   See Pat Jalland and John Hooper (ed.), *Women from Birth to Death: The Female Life Cycle in
     Britain 1830–1914*, Harvester Press, Brighton, 1986, pp.250–63.
99   Kent, *Sex and Suffrage*, pp.47–9.
100 Quoted Jalland and Hooper, *Women from Birth to Death*, p.42.
101 Mary Catherine Hume-Rothery, *Women and Doctors* (1871), p.5, quoted Anne Summers, '*The
     Constitution Violated* ...' p.15, f.45.
102 Hume-Rothery, *Women and Doctors*, quoted Summers, '*The Constitution Violated* ...' p.12.
103 Carlyle, 'Wilkinson, (James John) Garth (1812–1899)', *ODNB*, http://www.oxforddnb.com/view/
     article/29427.
104 JB to Maurice Gregory, 16 March 1902, quoted Larsen, *A People of One Book*, p.226.
105 Quoted Walkowitz, *Prostitution*, p.131. This discussion is informed by Anne Summers' article, '*The
     Constitution Violated* ...'

CHAPTER 11
1   Nigel Scotland, *Apostles of the Spirit and Fire: American Revivalists and Victorian Britain*, Milton
    Keynes, Colorado Springs & Hyderabad, 2009, pp.157–8.
2   JEB, 'Some thoughts on the present aspect of the Crusade against the State Regulation of Vice',
    Jordan and Sharp (III), p.55. She does not name Moody, but it is clear she is talking about the revival
    he led. The next quotes are from pp.57 and 55.
3   JB, 'Some thoughts on the present aspect of the Crusade against the State Regulation of Vice',
    Jordan and Sharp (III), p.58. The next quotes are from pp.58 and 57.
4   For Stansfeld, see McHugh, pp.101–2; Petrie, pp.146–9, Alan Ruston, 'Stansfeld, Sir James (1820–
    1898)', *ODNB*, Oxford UP, September 2004; online ed., May 2006, http://www.oxforddnb.com/
    view/article/26288.
5   JB to LNA, 8 July 1871, in Jordan and Sharp (II), p.356.
6   Petrie says this is how he became popular among Liberals, p.147.
7   Quoted McHugh, p.102.
8   Petrie, p.148.
9   C. Butler to JB, nd [autumn 1874], NRO, ZBU/E3/B4. See also C. Butler to JB, nd [September 1874],
    NRO, ZBU/E3/B2.
10 See various letters to 'Meelchis', c. 1874–78 in NRO, ZBU/E3/B4. These letters are undated but
    appear to have continued after Charlie went up to Trinity College, Cambridge.
11 Petrie, pp.148–9.
12 J. Stansfeld to JB, 21 October 1874, WL, 3JBL/08/58.
13 McHugh, pp.100–1. This book is the source for unattributed information in this section.

14   JB to H.J. Wilson, 1 June 1873, WL, 3JBL/07/66.
15   This account is taken from Petrie, pp.159–62.
16   JB, *Appeal to the People of England*, [1869], p.12. Golgotha was a burial ground in Jerusalem, often cited in the Bible.
17   Harriet Martineau, 'The CD Acts, Letter III', in Jordan and Sharp (II), p.43.
18   *Personal Reminiscences*, p.62 (JB does not name the organisation).
19   Moberley Bell, *Josephine Butler*, p.112.
20   James Stuart (ed.), *The New Abolitionists*, London, Dyer Brothers, 1876, p.5.
21   Quoted Johnsons, p.132.
22   'Private Record', September 1874, NRO, ZBU/E3/A4.
23   'Private Record', *ibid*.
24   *Personal Reminiscences*, p.66.
25   Stuart, *New Abolitionists*, p.7.
26   Maria Richardson to Maurice Gregory, 22 February 1907, WL, 3JBL/53/47.
27   JB, letter to a friend, quoted Johnsons, p.132.
28   This account is based on Petrie, pp.162–70, *Personal Reminiscences*, pp.70–7 and Jordan, pp.147–56. Some of the details have been corrected, using her correspondence at the time.
29   JB, 'Women and Politics', speech to Portsmouth Women's Liberal Association, 11 April 1888, WL.
30   Jordan, p.147.
31   Quoted *Personal Reminiscences*, p.13.
32   Petrie, p.164.
33   JB to GB, quoted Petrie, p.163.
34   JB to GB, 13 December 1874, WL, 3JBL/09/05.
35   JB to J. Stansfeld, quoted Petrie, p.165; see also Jordan, pp.148–9.
36   JB to J. Stansfeld, 20–22 December 1874, WL, 3JBL/09/09.
37   Jordan, pp.149–50.
38   JB to J. Stansfeld, 20–22 December 1874, WL, 3JBL/09/09; Jordan, p.156.
39   JB to J. Edmondson, 15 December 1874, WL, 3JBL /09/07.
40   The original appears to have been lost, but in a letter to Joseph Edmondson sent on 21 December (see note 43), she says 'of that scene, and that conversation, I must write to all of you more fully from the South of France'. The copied letter is in *Personal Reminiscences*, pp.70–7. All the quotes in this section are taken from these pages.
41   *Personal Reminiscences*, p.77.
42   Petrie, p.170.
43   JB to J. Edmondson, 21 December 1874, Sheffield Archives, H.J. Wilson MSS, MD 2548.
44   JB to J. Edmondson, *ibid.*, says that the visit happened that day.
45   JB to GB, 16 December 1874, WL, 3JBL/09/08.
46   JB to GB, 13 December 1874, WL, 3JBL/09/05.
47   Harriet Meuricoffre to JB, New Year's Eve 1874–75, quoted Johnsons, p.136.
48   JB to J. Stansfeld, 1 January 1875, quoted Petrie, p.171.
49   JB letter quoted in Stuart, *New Abolitionists*, p.33.
50   JB to GB, 13 January 1875, quoted Johnsons, p.137.
51   *Personal Reminiscences*, p.95.
52   *Personal Reminiscences*, p.89.
53   G. Garibaldi to JB, 16 December 1874, WL, 3JBL/08/62.
54   *Personal Reminiscences*, p.86.
55   JB to Hannah Ford, quoted Jordan, p.158.
56   Jordan, p.158.
57   JB to Harriet Meuricoffre, 29 January 1875, quoted Stuart, *New Abolitionists*, p.56.
58   JB to Harriet Meuricoffre, 29 January 1875, quoted Johnsons, p.140. JB was likening herself again to Mary, 'the most solitary woman of the sword-pierced heart', *Sursum Corda*, p.30; Larsen, *A People of One Book,* p.239.
59   JB to GB, quoted Stuart, *New Abolitionists*, p.46.
60   JB to Hatty Meuricoffre, 5 February 1875, WL, 3JBL/09/18.
61   Pastor Borel, quoted Petrie, pp.175–6.
62   JB, letter to Hatty Meuricoffre, quoted Stuart, *New Abolitionists*, pp.64–5.
63   The Genevan paper, *La Semaine Religieuse*, quoted Stuart, *New Abolitionists*, p.61.

64 Père Hyacinthe to JB, 4 February 1875, WL, 3JBL/09/17; JB to J. Edmondson, February 1875, Sheffield Archives, MD2548/2.

65 *Personal Reminiscences*, p.96.

66 *Personal Reminiscences*, pp.99–100.

67 JB to GB, 13 February 1875, WL, 3JBL/09/21. Her visit is described most fully in her letter to 'a friend' dated March 1875, quoted Stuart, *New Abolitionists*, pp.89–95.

68 Paul Blum, 'The Hôpital Saint-Lazare in Paris: Its Past and Present History', in *British Journal of Venereal Disease*, 24, 1948, pp.151–2. This is factual, not critical of the regime.

69 JB to J. Edmondson, 15 December 1874, WL, 3JBL/09/07.

70 *Personal Reminiscences*, p.78. Other quotes in this paragraph from pp.78–81.

71 The following account is taken from Petrie, pp.180–2. See also Yves Guyot, *Prostitution Under the Regulation System French and English*, (transl. French into English), George Redway, London, 1884.

72 The last quote is Josephine's comment on extracts from Grandpre's diary which she published in *The Storm-Bell*, February 1899, No. 12. Quoted by Jordan, ref.29, p.325.

73 Quoted Jordan, p.162.

74 JB to GB, quoted Johnsons, pp.146–7. This visit is also described in JB to J. Edmondson, February 17 1875, Sheffield Archives, Wilson MSS, MD 2548/4.

75 Quoted Petrie, p.165.

76 JB to Hatty Meuricoffre, 19 February 1875, WL, 3JBL/09/22.

77 JB to H.J. Wilson, quoted Jordan, p.165.

78 H.J. Wilson to Federation Executive, 22 March 1875, WL, 3JBL/10/26.

79 JB recommended Stansfeld in letter to H.J. Wilson, 16 March 1875, WL, 3JBL/10/23.

80 JB to H.J. Wilson, 8 March, 14 March 1875, WL, 3JBL/10/16 & 22; Jordan, p.165.

81 Quoted Moberley Bell, p.128.

82 JB to Edith Leupold, quoted Jordan, p.167.

83 JB to H.J. Wilson, 10 May 1875, WL, 3JBL/11/16.

84 JB to H.J. Wilson, 11 May 1875, WL, 3JBL/11/19.

85 Quoted Jordan, p.173.

86 JB to Charlotte Wilson, 19 May 1875, WL, 3JBL/11/31; H.J. Wilson to 'Mrs Butler's friends', 20 May 1875, WL, 3JBL/11/34.

87 JB to the Wilsons, 7 June 1875, WL, 3JBL/11/68.

88 JB to Mary Priestman, 15 June 1875, WL, 3JBL/11/73. Mary collected Charlie and arranged his train journey home.

89 JB to H.J. Wilson, 28 June 1875, WL, 3JBL/11/88.

90 The title of the book is a quotation from Isaiah 40:3 – 'The voice of one crying in the wilderness. Prepare ye the Way of the Lord'.

91 JEB, *The voice of one crying in the wilderness. Being her first appeal, made in 1874–75, to continental nations against the system of regulated vice* (English translation by Osmund Airy), Bristol & London, J.W. Arrowsmith, 1913, p.13.

92 Helen Mathers, "Tis dishonour done to Me.' Self-representation in the writings of Josephine Butler' in Daggers and Neal (eds), *Sex, Gender and Religion*, p.46.

93 JB to A. Humbert, quoted Johnsons, p.150.

94 JEB, *The voice of one crying in the wilderness …*, p.17.

95 JEB, *Prophets and Prophetesses. Some Thoughts for the Present Times*, nd [1898], p.13.

96 JEB, *The Voice of one crying in the wilderness …*, p.31.

97 JEB, *The Voice of one crying in the wilderness …*, p.31. The quote is from Matthew 25:40.

INTERLUDE – The Hour Before the Dawn

98 Anne Summers, 'Introduction: the International Abolitionist Federation', *Women's History Review*, Vol. 17, April 2008, p.10.

99 J. Stuart to H.J. Wilson, 4 September 1875, WL, 3JBL/12/64.

100 JEB, *The Hour Before the Dawn. An Appeal to Men*, Published for the Social Purity Alliance, 2nd ed., London, 1882, p.35. The next quotes are from p.64 and p.35.

101 JEB, *The Hour Before the Dawn*, pp.5, 13.

102 JEB, *The Hour Before the Dawn*, p.7.

103 JEB, *The Hour Before the Dawn*, p.95. See chapter 4, note 53.

104   JEB, *The Hour Before the Dawn*, p.97.
105   JEB, *The Hour Before the Dawn*, p.109.
106   I am indebted to Kristine Frederickson, 'Josephine Butler and Christianity …', Chapter 4, for her insights into JB's millennialism.
107   'Private Thoughts', nd, p.27, NRO, ZBU/E3/A2.
108   JEB, *The Hour Before the Dawn*, p.107.
109   JEB, *The Hour Before the Dawn*, p.111.

CHAPTER 12

  1   For the Percy story, see Jordan and Sharp (III), pp.1–3 and 17–48. The letter to the *Daily Telegraph* is reprinted on pp.18–9.
  2   Letter to Edith Leupold, 9 April 1875, Jordan and Sharp (III), p.42.
  3   JB to Charlotte Wilson, 15 April 1875, WL, 3JBL/10/56. They later found a domestic servant job for her in Liverpool, see Jordan, p.170.
  4   Jordan comments on this article and transcribes quotations, p.170; for George's role, see pp.170–1.
  5   JB to H.J. Wilson, 1 April 1873, WL, 3JBL/07/40.
  6   1879, in Jordan and Sharp (III), pp.71–111. Quotes in this paragraph are from pp.92, 97, and 104–5.
  7   'Report of the Commissioner of Police of the Metropolis for the year 1872, Devonport Division', HCPP online, pp.112–3.
  8   Quoted Walkowitz, *Prostitution*, p.202.
  9   Walkowitz, *Prostitution*, p.184. The case of Harriet Hicks is described in detail, pp.181–3.
 10   JB to Charlotte Wilson, 14 October 1875, WL, 3JBL/13/13.
 11   JB to Mary Priestman, *c*. 30 October 1875, WL, 3JBL/13/23.
 12   Jordan, p.179, quoting *Shield*, 1 December 1875, p.304.
 13   Sandra Stanley Holton, 'Elmy, Elizabeth Clarke Wolstenholme (1833–1918)', *ODNB*, Oxford UP, 2004; online ed. May 2007, http://www.oxforddnb.com/view/article/38638.
 14   JB to Millicent Fawcett, 8 December 1875, WL, 3JBL/14/04.
 15   JB to Millicent Fawcett, *ibid*. See also JB to H.J. Wilson, 19 December 1875, WL, 3JBL/14/10. This was not true, as these letters show.
 16   JB to Mary Priestman, 5 September 1875, WL, 3JBL/12/65.
 17   H.J. Wilson to Charlotte Wilson, 31 May 1876, WL, 3JBL/15/11.
 18   GGB to GB, 28 January 1876, NRO, ZBU/E2/18. I am grateful to Jonathan Smith, Trinity College archivist for information about Georgie's results. He came top of his year in his first year, in the next year he was second.
 19   GGB to JB, nd [*c*. 1877], NRO, ZBU/E3/B4.
 20   JB, *Personal Reminiscences*, p.132.
 21   *Ibid*., p.135.
 22   JB to Hatty Meuricoffre, 11 September 1876, WL, 3JBL/15/15.
 23   JB, Address to Annual Meeting of LNA, 19 October 1876, in Jordan and Sharp (III), p.69.
 24   This account based on Petrie, pp.190–4.
 25   Quoted Petrie, p.191. Other quotes are from p.191 and 192.
 26   JB, *Personal Reminiscences*, p.139.
 27   Some of the following account taken from *George Butler*, pp.304–12.
 28   JB to Hatty Meuricoffre, 31 January 1877, NRO, ZBU/E3/C2.
 29   *George Butler*, p.306.
 30   Alain Courbin (Transl. Alan Sheridan), *Prostitution and Sexuality in France after 1850*, Harvard UP, 1990, p.233.
 31   JB to J. Edmondson, May 1877, WL, 3JBL/16/06; JB to Mrs Clark, 28 April 1877, WL, 3JBL/16/05.
 32   JB, *Personal Reminiscences*, pp.167–78.
 33   For this paragraph, see Jordan, p.182, Moberley Bell, *Josephine Butler*, p.141.
 34   McHugh, p.107. This book is the source for unattributed information in this section.
 35   JB to H.J. Wilson, 28 June 1875, WL, 3JBL/11/88. This was partly because the case of Mrs Percy was misrepresented in the debate, see Jordan, p.171.
 36   Quoted McHugh, p.108.
 37   Quoted McHugh, p.108.

38   JB, *Personal Reminiscences*, p.165.

39   JB to Hatty Meuricoffre, 10 November 1877, WL, 3JBL/16/18.

40   This part of the diary is at the rear of the 'Private Record' volume, NRO, ZBU/E3/A4. See Wednesday 27 March in particular.

41   'Private Record', Monday 4 [March, 1878]. Josephine was staying at Sestri, near her niece Edie Leupold's home at Genoa.

42   'Private Record', Tuesday 19 [March, 1878].

43   'Private Record', Wednesday 27 March [1878].

44   'Private Record', Easter Sunday [1878].

45   'Private Record', 25 August [1878].

46   'Private Record', 14 September 1878; GGB to JB, nd [September 1878], NRO, ZBU/E3/C3.

47   JB to SB, 15 September 1878, LUL 1878/09/15 (I), quoted Jordan, p.180.

48   JB to Federation Committee, 11 January 1879, WL, 3JBL/18/02.

49   JB to Fanny Smyttan, 15 March 1879, LUL JB 1/1 1879/03/15 (II). Quotes in this paragraph are taken from this letter.

50   *Personal Reminiscences*, p.198. The following account is taken from pp.193–205.

51   Quoted Jordan, p.185.

52   Jordan, p.185, quoting JB's long account in a letter to Mary Priestman (29 August 1879).

53   Jordan, p.186.

54   Moberley Bell, *Josephine Butler*, p.151.

55   *Ibid.*, p.150.

56   *George Butler*, p.334.

57   *Personal Reminiscences*, p.216. The following account and quotes are taken from pp.214–21.

58   The son is not named and could also be Stanley.

59   *Personal Reminiscences*, p.86.

60   JB to Mrs Chambers, June 1876, NRO, ZBU/E3/C3.

61   JEB, 'Social Purity', 1879, in Jordan and Sharp (III), p.316.

62   W.T. Stead, *Josephine Butler: A Life Sketch*, p.44, cites a boy at Harrow School who read and was deeply affected by it at the age of 17.

63   JEB, 'Social Purity', 1879, in Jordan and Sharp (III), p.311.

64   *Ibid.*, p.319.

65   Moberley Bell, pp.161–2. She gives the date as autumn 1882, but the collected letters JB wrote came from Liverpool and so have been dated 1881 by WL, *c.* 4 November 1881, WL, 3JBL/20/12.

66   JB to ASB, 4 March 1883, WL, 3JBL/22/19.

67   This account is based on Alfred Dyer, *The European Slave Trade in English Girls*, 1880, reprinted in Jordan and Sharp (IV), pp.25–54, 'The deposition on oath of Josephine Butler' in Jordan and Sharp (IV), pp.58–79 and *Personal Reminiscences*, pp.221–36. These accounts sometimes conflict and when they do I have relied on the deposition, as a sworn statement by JB. The account in Petrie, pp.209–22 contains some inaccuracies; Jordan, chapter 11, is more accurate. Witness testimony to the House of Lords select committee, 1881, gives the names of the girls.

68   JB, *A Letter to the Mothers of England*, in Jordan and Sharp (IV), p.87.

69   Dyer, *European Slave Trade*, in Jordan and Sharp (IV), p.28.

70   He may have visited her at the conference in Liège, as suggested by Petrie, p.209.

71   George Gillett was a member, together with Joseph Edmondson, of the Quaker Association for Abolishing the State Regulation of Vice, which paid Josephine's expenses on her trip to Europe, 1874–75. The title of the committee, in its later simplified form, was 'The London Committee for Suppressing the Traffic in British girls, for Purposes of Continental Prostitution'.

72   Yves Guyot, *Prostitution Under the Regulation System*, p.134.

73   The following account is taken from Dyer, *The European Slave Trade*, in Jordan and Sharp (IV), pp.36–43.

74   The traffickers are named by Bridget O'Donnell, *Inspector Minahan Makes a Stand: The Missing Girls of England*, London, Picador, 2012, pp.69–70. She gives a detailed account of the abduction of the three girls, pp.67–74. The abduction of Louise Hennessey is described by Susan Mumm, 'Josephine Butler and the International Traffic in Women' in Daggers and Neal (eds), *Sex, Gender and Religion*, pp.65–6.

75   JB, letter to Dr Carter, 1 April 1880, in Jordan and Sharp (IV), p.18.

76   See Adeline's account quoted by Dyer, *The European Slave Trade*, in Jordan and Sharp (IV), p.43.

77   Dyer, *The European Slave Trade*, in Jordan and Sharp (IV), p.39.

78   JB, *The Modern Slave Trade*, in Jordan and Sharp (IV), pp.20–4.

79   *Ibid*. She did not name this house, but several are noted in her deposition (see note 83).

80   The Belgian detective's written statement is reproduced in Jordan and Sharp (IV), pp.74–9, as part of JB's deposition. She met him in Paris, probably in October 1880, see letter from JB to unknown recipient, Jordan and Sharp (IV), pp.55–6.

81   JB to Elizabeth Lundie, 2 November 1880, WL, 3JBL/19/10.

82   *Personal Reminiscences*, p.222. Other quotes in this paragraph are from pp.22, 231, 223–4.

83   The deposition is reprinted in Jordan and Sharp (IV), pp.58–79. Quotes in this and the next paragraph are taken from pp.59–60, 68.

84   *Personal Reminiscences*, p.230.

85   Petrie, p.222

86   *Personal Reminiscences*, p.228.

87   This story is told in *Personal Reminiscences*, pp.228–9.

88   *Personal Reminiscences,* p.210.

89   Quoted *Personal Reminiscences*, p.211.

90   The Home Secretary received her deposition through official channels, but JB also sent him the letter from the whistle-blower, De Rudder.

91   Snagge's report to select committee of House of Lords, 1881, 'House of Commons Parliamentary Papers Online' (HCPP), PDF, pp.121–52. This is the source for the following account.

92   JB, *A Letter to the Mothers of England*, reprinted in Jordan and Sharp (IV), pp.80–94. Quotes in this paragraph are taken from pp.85, 87, and 89.

93   The following account is taken from Jordan, p.119.

94   Dyer's evidence to select committee of House of Lords, 1881, PDF, pp.105–113.

95   Petrie, p.227.

INTERLUDE – Catharine of Siena

This 'Interlude' is based in part on Helen Mathers, 'The Evangelical Spirituality of a Victorian Feminist: Josephine Butler, 1828–1906', in *Journal of Ecclesiastical History*, 52, 2001, p.306.

96   'Private Record', May–July 1878, Northumberland RO, ZBW E3 A4. Moberley Bell, p.147, expresses astonishment that JB had the time to write this book, but Anne Summers, like myself, has noted that she took time out for reflection in 1878, *Female Lives, Moral States*, pp.75–7. David Scott, 'Josephine Butler and St. Catharine of Siena' in Milbank, *Beating the Traffic*, p.55 suggests the books she may have read.

97   Summers, *Female Lives*, p.76.

98   Moberley Bell, p.306; this section of the biography has many helpful insights.

99   J.E. Butler, *Catharine of Siena*, 4th ed., London 1885, p.67.

100   Butler, *Catharine of Siena*, p.329.

101   Butler, *Catharine of Siena*, p.47.

102   This is the conclusion of Beverley Grey, 'Sin is Contagious …', p.32.

103   Summers, *Female Lives*, p.75.

104   Diana Neal, 'Flirting with the Catholic Other' in Daggers and Neal (eds), *Sex, Gender and Religion*, pp.157–8, 164.

105   'Private Record', 1878 nd, p.29.

106   JB to SB, 22 April 1877, WL, 3JBL/16/04; 'Private Record', 1878 nd, p.29.

107   'Private Record', 1878 nd, p.29.

108   Summers, *Private Lives*, pp.76–7.

109   This practice started with the 'Private Record, 1874' and continued for the rest of her life. One indication of her purpose is that George is usually 'Papa' in the later diaries.

110   Butler, *Catharine of Siena*, p.239.

111   GB to Hatty, 29 December 1880, NRO, ZBU/E3/C3.

112   Moberley Bell, p.172.

113   Moberley Bell, p.173.

CHAPTER 13

1   Information supplied by Trinity College, Cambridge.
2   See letters between GB, JB and Hatty from the summer of 1880, NRO, ZBU/E3/C3.
3   Wainwright, *Liverpool Gentlemen*, pp.153–4.
4   Thomas Kelly, *For Advancement of Learning: The University of Liverpool 1881–1981*, Liverpool UP, 1981, p.42. George's contribution is noted on pp.37 and 44.
5   JB to Rhoda Bolton, 13 November [1881], RIBA, BuFam, 2/3/1.
6   GB to Mrs Clark, 9 October 1879, WL, 3JBL/18/14.
7   Moberley Bell, *Josephine Butler*, p.166.
8   JB to Hatty, nd [1881], NRO, ZBU/E3/C3.
9   Quoted *George Butler*, p.356.
10   JB to Rhoda Bolton, 13 November [1881], RIBA, BuFam, 2/3/1.
11   JB diary, 17–27 July 1881, WL, 3JBL/20/07; JB to GB, 5 & 6 August 1881, NRO, ZBU/E2/7; *George Butler*, pp.349–52.
12   *George Butler*, pp.350–1.
13   A paper written by Robert Martineau in May 1915, headed 'Butler Fund – 1882' gives more details, WL, 3JBL/21/03. See also Jordan, p.204.
14   JB to R. Martineau, 22 May 1882, WL, 3JBL/21/05.
15   Letter to GB, Christmas 1881, quoted *George Butler*, p.358.
16   Letter to JB, quoted *George Butler*, p.358.
17   Quoted *George Butler*, p.359.
18   JB to GB, 17 August 1882, WL, 3JBL/21/14.
19   JB to Mary Priestman, 22 June 1887, quoted Jordan, p.206.
20   Jordan, p. 206, has a full account of Mrs Gelling's letters.
21   JB to Hatty Meuricoffre, 18 October 1882, WL, 3JBL/21/36.
22   *Ibid*.
23   Jordan, p.207; *George Butler*, pp.370–2.
24   JB to Miss Priestman, 10 November 1882, WL, 3JBL/21/43.
25   *George Butler*, p.374.
26   Adela, in particular, had 'never known her mother and she seems to have regarded her Aunt Josey and Uncle George as her closest family', Jordan, p.259.
27   *George Butler*, p.374; Jordan, p.207.
28   *George Butler*, p.375.
29   Jordan, p.208. This is based on a letter dated January 1883 from JB to the Priestmans referring to the hospital and the arrival of Miss Humbert (WL, 3JBL/22/02). Moberley Bell, *Josephine Butler*, p.175, says that the House of Rest opened in February 1884 which seems more realistic, but the dating of the letter appears correct.
30   See Jordan, p.209. JB thanks the Priestman sisters for their 'kind interest', January 1883, WL, 3JBL/22/02.
31   McHugh, p.172.
32   She first mentions this fear in a letter to Edmondson in April 1875, quoted Jordan, p.188.
33   JB to Charlotte Wilson, 3 October 1881, WL, 3JBL/20/09. Jordan, pp.200–1, gives a full account of the meeting.
34   JB to LNA, *c.* 1882, WL, 3JBL/21/01.
35   JB to ASB, 3–4 March 1883, WL, 3JBL/22/17.
36   McHugh describes its development, pp.112–9. See also Jordan, pp.175–6.
37   McHugh, p.119.
38   This section derived from McHugh, pp.128–34.
39   Letter to H.J. Wilson, quoted McHugh, p.132.
40   JB to Margaret Tanner, 30 October 1882, WL, 3JBL/21/37.
41   1881 (351) *Report from the Select Committee on the Contagious Diseases Acts: Together with the Proceedings of the Committee, Minutes of Evidence, and Appendix*, HCPP online, pp.72–126. See also McHugh, p.216.
42   McHugh, p.216.
43   The proceedings relating to Eliza Southey: 1882 (340) *Report from the Select Committee on the Contagious Diseases Acts …*, HCPP online, pp.388–435.
44   JB to GB, 4 May 1883, WL, 3JBL/21/07. Jordan, p.209.

45 Josephine Butler's evidence: 1882 (340) *Report from the Select Committee on the Contagious Diseases Acts …*, HCPP online, pp.336–48. Quotes in this section are from questions 5269-70, 5330, 5350, 5368, 5395, 5416, 5415.
46 Jordan, p.209.
47 JB to Mary Priestman 28 February 1874, WL, 3JBL/08/39.
48 J.L. Hammond and Barbara Hammond, *James Stansfeld: A Victorian Champion of Sex Equality*, London, Longmans, Green and Co., 1932, p.221.
49 McHugh, p.213. She had an incurable long-term illness affecting both her mental and physical health which lasted from 1881 until her death in 1885. Hammonds, *James Stansfeld*, p.259.
50 McHugh, p.216.
51 McHugh, p.216.
52 Hammonds, *James Stansfeld*, p.228.
53 Quoted McHugh, p.217.
54 Quoted McHugh, p.217. This episode is described on pp.217–20.
55 JB to Robert Martineau, 2 October 1882, WL, 3JBL/21/34; Jordan, p.210.
56 Quoted McHugh, p.220.
57 JB and GB attended a meeting mentioned in JB to Miss Priestman, 20 November 1882, WL, 3JBL/21/48.
58 JB to A.M. Priestman, 17 January 1883, in Jordan and Sharp, (III), p.197.
59 This issue is discussed further in Nolland, pp.42 & 45, and Larsen, *A People of One Book*, p.221. Kristine Frederickson, while agreeing that JB was Evangelical, believes she would be happiest with the simple description 'disciple of Christ', because that is, above all, what she tried to be (correspondence with the author).
60 Lisa Nolland, *A Victorian Feminist Christian: Josephine Butler, the Prostitutes and God*, Paternoster, 2004, p.285.
61 *The Times*, 26 January 1883. The convention was on 24 January, at Devonshire House.
62 JB to A.M. Priestman, 17 January 1883, in Jordan and Sharp, (III), p.198.
63 Jordan, p.211.
64 3 March 1883, *George Butler*, p.389.
65 In the period 1870–86, 18,068 petitions for repeal were sent to Parliament, with 2,657,348 signatures. Only eighty-three petitions, with 3,883 signatures, were sent in defence of the Acts, McHugh, p.127.
66 Letter to ASB, 3 March 1883, in *George Butler*, p.388.
67 McHugh, p.221; *George Butler*, p.390.
68 Letter to ASB, 4 March 1883, in *George Butler*, pp.390–1.
69 JEB, 'Ought women to be in the Gallery of the House of Commons on the 27th? Letter to an MP', *c*. 20 February 1883, in Jordan and Sharp, (III), pp.217–9.
70 JB to Stanley Butler, 3 March 1883, WL, 3JBL/22/17.
71 McHugh, p.222.
72 All quotes from the debate taken from *Hansard*, 20 April 1883, vol. 278, cc 749-858.
73 Quoted Hammonds, *James Stansfeld*, p.230.
74 Hammonds, *James Stansfeld*, p.222.
75 *Hansard*, 20 April 1883, vol. 278, cc 749-858.
76 Morgan cited Mr Wheeler, who had told the Committee, that 'there were hundreds of cases in which "terrified", and, I presume, innocent girls had to submit to examination; but, when pressed, he could only name one case – that of Caroline Wybrow'. *Hansard*, 20 April 1883, *ibid*.
77 *Hansard,* 20 April 1883, *ibid.*
78 Quoted Moberley Bell, *Josephine Butler*, p.163.
79 *George Butler*, pp.393–4. The 'Jerusalem' quote is from Isaiah 40:2.
80 JB to Fanny Forsaith, 5 March 1903, in Jordan and Sharp (III), p.230.
81 J. Stansfeld to Emile de Laveleye, 5 September 1883, in Jordan and Sharp (III), p.233.
82 Hammonds, *James Stansfeld*, p.228.
83 Letter to members of LNA 1877, quoted McHugh, p.184.

INTERLUDE – The Salvation Army in Switzerland
84 JB, 'Catherine Booth', *Contemporary Review*, 58, November 1890, p.641.
85 JEB, *The Salvation Army in Switzerland*, London, Dyer Bros, 1883, p.7.

86   JB, 'Catherine Booth', p.640.
87   Norman H. Murdoch, 'Female Ministry in the Thought and Work of Catherine Booth', *Church History*, 53, 1984, p.358.
88   JB, 'Catherine Booth', p.649.
89   JB to GB, 4 May 1882, WL, 3JBL/21/07.
90   JB to Miss Cox, 27 July [1883], SAHC, BC/1/1/65.
91   The following account is taken from JEB, *The Salvation Army in Switzerland*, passim; Moberley Bell, pp.169–72.
92   JEB, *The Salvation Army in Switzerland*, pp.31, 37.
93   *Ibid.*, p.3.
94   *Ibid.*, p.201, 202.
95   *Ibid.*, p.233.
96   *George Butler*, p.384.
97   Van Drenth and de Haan, *The Rise of Caring Power*, pp.149–52.
98   Quoted JEB, *The Salvation Army in Switzerland*, p.231.
99   *Ibid.*, p.267.
100 L.E. Lauer, 'Clibborn, Catherine Booth (1858–1955)', *ODNB*, Oxford UP, online ed., September 2012, http://www.oxforddnb.com/view/ article/49017.

CHAPTER 14

1   JB told Rhoda Bolton, 23 July [1882], RIBA, BuFam 2/3/4, that Contie was 'mortally attacked' and spending time in Switzerland.
2   1881 Census, Newnham College, Cambridge. With thanks to David Thompson for this information.
3   JB to Mrs Hinde Smith, 31 January 1884, WL, 3JBL/23/04.
4   JB to Rhoda Bolton, 11 February [1884], RIBA, BuFam 2/3/5.
5   JB to Rhoda Bolton, nd [18 February 1884], RIBA, BuFam 2/3/6.
6   JB to ASB, 19 February 1884, 3JBL/23/06.
7   JB to ASB, 19 February 1884, *ibid*; 26 March 1884, WL, 3JBL/23/08.
8   The date fits the information in JB's letters and Gen. Graham is mentioned in JB to Mary Priestman, 5 May 1885, WL, 3JBL/24/12. I have not located Charlie's military service record.
9   '1st Battalion KSLI in the Eastern Sudan 1885–86', http://www.shropshireregimentalmuseum. co.uk/regimental-history/shropshire-light-infantry/1st-battalion-ksli-in-the-eastern-sudan-1885-86/.
10 JB to Mrs Lundie, 26 June 1885, WL, 3JBL/24/16. This description fits the battlefield of Tofrek, described in '1st Battalion KSLI in the Eastern Sudan 1885–86', *ibid*.
11 JB to M. Butler, 23 February [1904], NRO, ZBU/E3/C8, reports that Charlie went to Liverpool to consult Dr Carter about the 'lingering effects of S. African malarial fever'. In 1887 she told Mary Priestman that, 'He still has internal attacks, arising from an enlargement of the spleen contracted in that horrid climate,' 5 January 1887, WL, 3JBL/26/02.
12 This was Stead's suggestion – G.S. Railton (ed.), *The Truth about the Armstrong Case and the Salvation Army*, Salvation Army, nd [1885/6] pp.7–8.
13 Walkowitz, *Prostitution*, p.250.
14 'Stead's defence' in G.S. Railton, *The Truth about the Armstrong Case* …, p.8. This story is told in detail in O'Donnell, *Inspector Minahan* …, Picador, 2012, pp.11–135.
15 Letter to B. Booth, quoted W.B. Booth, *Echoes and Memories*, London, Hodder & Stoughton, 1925, p.122.
16 Booth, *Echoes and Memories*, p.120. This story is told by Roy Hattersley, *Blood and Fire: William and Catherine Booth and their Salvation Army*, London, Little, Brown & Co., 1999, pp.304–7.
17 Joseph O. Baylen, 'Stead, William Thomas (1849–1912)', *ODNB*, Oxford UP, 2004; online ed. September 2010, http://www.oxforddnb.com/view/article/36258.
18 Quoted A. Stafford, *The Age of Consent*, Hodder and Stoughton, 1964, p.116.
19 *The Shield*, 3 October 1885, quoted Jordan, p.222, the source for this paragraph.
20 JB to ASB, 27 February 1885, WL, 3JBL/24/09.
21 Benjamin Waugh, *William T Stead: A Life for the People*, London, Vickers, nd [c. 1904], p.10.
22 Booth gives a similar account of Stead's words during his visit to the HQ, with Scott present. *Echoes and Memories*, p.121. He also says Stead met Rebecca Jarrett there.

23   'Stead's defence' in G.S. Railton (ed.), *The Truth about the Armstrong Case*, p.9.

24   JB to Mary Priestman, 5 June 1885, WL, 3JBL/24/13.

25   This account is derived from text of *The Maiden Tribute of Modern Babylon*, reprinted in Jordan and Sharp (IV), pp.115–234.

26   *Ibid.*, p.115.

27   *Ibid.*, pp.116–7.

28   *Ibid.*, p.122. Vincent is not named.

29   *Ibid.*, p.158.

30   *Ibid.*, p.156.

31   Pearson, *Age of Consent*, quoted O'Donnell, *Inspector Minahan*, p.165.

32   JB to Mary Priestman, 5 June 1885, WL, 3JBL/24/13. JB mentions the 'joint purse' in her evidence to the trial of Rebecca Jarrett, William Thomas Stead, Sampson Jacques, William Bramwell Booth, and Elizabeth Combe (t.1031), *Old Bailey Proceedings Online* (www.oldbaileyonline.org, version 6.0, 17 April 2011), 2 November 1885.

33   JB, evidence to trial of Jarrett et al, *Old Bailey Proceedings Online*, 2 November 1885.

34   Josephine wrote a biography, *Rebecca Jarrett*, which differs in some respects from three versions of Rebecca's autobiography in the Salvation Army archives, which comprise a manuscript and two typescripts, all written in old age. The manuscript is transcribed by Pamela Walker in 'The Conversion of Rebecca Jarrett', in *History Workshop Journal*, 58 (1), 2004, pp.254–8.

35   'The History of a Rescued Woman', in Josephine Butler, *Rebecca Jarrett*, reprinted in Jordan and Sharp (IV), p.245. JB represents this as being Rebecca's own account of her life (see p.244), written in her own handwriting. However, it is written in the third person and contains judgements which can only have been made by her rescuers, almost certainly Salvation Army officers. So this is a more complex document than Josephine makes out. The original has been lost.

36   This was stated at her trial, see Alison Plowden, *The Case of Eliza Armstrong: 'A child of 13 bought for £5'*, London, BBC, 1974, p.99.

37   JB, *Rebecca Jarrett*, in Jordan and Sharp (IV), p.248.

38   Walker, 'The Conversion of Rebecca Jarrett', p.255.

39   Rebecca Jarrett to Florence Booth, 29 January [1885], SAHC, RJ/1/10.

40   JB, *Rebecca Jarrett*, in Jordan and Sharp (IV), p.249.

41   *Ibid.*, p.250.

42   JB to Florence Booth, 26 March 1885, SAHC, RJ/1/13.

43   Rebecca Jarrett to Florence Booth, nd [1885], SAHC, RJ/1/12.

44   JB, *Rebecca Jarrett*, in Jordan and Sharp (IV), p.255.

45   JB, evidence to trial of Jarrett et al, *Old Bailey Proceedings Online*, 2 November 1885.

46   Rebecca Jarrett, evidence to trial of Jarrett et al, *Old Bailey Proceedings Online*, 30 October 1885.

47   This account is based on Plowden, *The Case of Eliza Armstrong*, pp.7–11.

48   Quoted Walker, 'The Conversion of Rebecca Jarrett', p.255.

49   'The Maiden Tribute of Modern Babylon', in Jordan and Sharp (IV), p.136.

50   *Ibid.*, p.138. The following quotes are taken from this page.

51   O'Donnell, *Inspector Minahan*, pp.152–4.

52   Rebecca's autobiography reprinted by Walker, 'The Conversion of Rebecca Jarrett', p.255.

53   This account is taken from Plowden, *The Case of Eliza Armstrong*, pp.9–10.

54   JB to ASB, [17 July 1885], LUL, JB 1/1/1885/07/00 (II).

55   O'Donnell, *Inspector Minahan*, p.190, quoting trial of Jarrett et al, October–November 1885.

56   JB to H.J. Wilson, 10 July 1885, Sheffield Archives, Wilson MSS, MD2548/8.

57   JB, *George Butler*, p.343. This is a quote from an undated letter to a friend, but it fits her experience at this time. It certainly relates to the 1880s. Alison Milbank points out that the language evokes the Book of Revelation 9, *Beating the Traffic*, p.97.

58   JB, *George Butler*, p.340. See Matthew 14:28–33.

59   JB, *George Butler*, p.342.

60   JB, *George Butler*, p.344.

61   JB to Mr Naish, 26 July 1885, WL, 3JBL/24/18.

62   JB to ASB, [17 July 1885], LUL, JB 1/1/1885/07/00 (II).

63   JB to Rhoda Bolton, Ash Wednesday [1884]; RIBA, BuFam, 2/3/7; also 11 February [1884], 2/3/5, 13 November [1881], 2/3/1.

64   Rhoda Bolton to ASB, 16 July [1885], RIBA, BuFam, 3/4/1.

65   JB to ASB, 27 February 1885, WL, 3JBL/24/09. See also note in WL online catalogue, which notes
      that quarantine rules were not introduced until 1901. This visit is also described in *George Butler*,
      p.399, but JB dates it incorrectly as April.
66   W.T. Stead, *Josephine Butler. A Life Sketch*, London, Morgan & Scott, 1886, p.6.
67   Jordan and Sharp (IV), pp.235–6.
68   Plowden, *The Case of Eliza Armstrong*, p.10; O'Donnell, *Inspector Minahan*, pp.188–201.
69   Quoted Plowden, *ibid.*, p.10.
70   Stead, *Josephine Butler*, p.6; GGB to JB, 3 September 1885, WL, 3JBL/24/26.
71   JB, *George Butler*, p.402.
72   Plowden, *The Case of Eliza Armstrong*, p.11. Subsequent quotes from pp.24, 50.
73   Quoted Plowden, p.41. Next quote from p.65.
74   Trial transcript, quoted Plowden, p.121. Other quotes in this and the next paragraph are from
      pp.121, 119, 132–3, 135.
75   JB to [Miss Priestman] requesting payment of expenses, 17 December 1885, WL, 3JBL/24/29.
76   JB, evidence to trial of Jarrett et al, *Old Bailey Proceedings Online*, 2 November 1885.
77   JB, *Rebecca Jarrett*, London, Morgan and Scott, 1885.
78   JB, *Rebecca Jarrett*, in Jordan and Sharp (IV), p.238.
79   *Ibid.*, p.254.
80   Jordan, p.233.
81   JB to [Miss Priestman], 17 December 1885, WL, 3JBL/24/29.
82   Rebecca Jarrett to Florence Booth, 27 April 1886, SAHC, RJ/1/21.
83   JB[?] to B. Booth[?], nd [1886], SAHC, RJ/1/22. This is an unsigned note in pencil.
84   Susan 'Hawker' Jones to B. Booth, 26 February 1887, SAHC, RJ/1/27.
85   JB to B. Booth, 28 June 1886, SAHC, RJ/1/26. Quotes in this paragraph taken from this letter.

INTERLUDE – Ellice Hopkins, Purity and Vigilance

86   *The Shield*, 18 July 1885. For Hopkins, see also Sue Morgan, 'The Power of Womanhood – Religion
      and sexual politics in the writings of Ellice Hopkins', in Anne Hogan and Andrews Bradstock (eds),
      Women of Faith in Victorian Culture: Reassessing the Angel in the House, Basingstoke, Macmillan,
      1998, pp.209–24.
87   Sue Morgan, 'Hopkins, (Jane) Ellice (1836–1904)', *ODNB*, Oxford UP, 2004. http://www.
      oxforddnb/view/article/33978.
88   Mort, *Dangerous Sexualities*, pp.121–2.
89   Prochaska, *Women and Philanthropy*, pp.204–5.
90   Walkowitz, *Prostitution*, p.238.
91   The following account is based on Walkowitz, *Prostitution*, pp.238–45.
92   Paula Bartley, *Prostitution: Prevention and Reform*, London, Routledge, 2000, p.84.
93   *Ibid.*, p.84; Mort p.125.
94   Bartley, *Prostitution: Prevention and Reform*, p.184.
95   Walkowitz, *Prostitution*, p.242.
96   *Ibid.*, p.243.
97   Jeffrey Weeks, *Sex, Politics and Society: The Regulation of Sexuality Since 1800*, London, Longman,
      1981, p.90. See also Walkowitz, *Prostitution*, p.245.
98   JB to Florence Booth, 26 March 1885, SAHC, RJ/1/13.

CHAPTER 15
1   The Criminal Law Amendment Act, 1885, http://www.lawindexpro.co.uk.
2   Lesley Hall, *Sex, Gender and Social Change in Britain Since 1880*, Basingstoke, Macmillan, 2000,
     p.36.
3   The Criminal Law Amendment Act, 1885, http://www.lawindexpro.co.uk.
4   JEB, *Government by Police*, London, Dyer Brothers, 1879, 2nd ed., 1880, p.97.
5   JB to Mary Priestman, 1885, quoted Walkowitz, *Prostitution*, p.247.
6   Lucy Bland, *Banishing the Beast: English Feminism and Sexual Morality, 1885–1914*, London,
     Penguin, 1995, p.98. The quote is from JB's speech at Exeter Hall, reported in *Shield*, 11 April 1885.
7   JB's speech at Exeter Hall, reported in *Shield*, 11 April 1885.
8   Bland, *Banishing the Beast*, p.99.
9   Anne Summers, *Female Lives, Moral States*, p.128.

10   Quoted Mort, *Dangerous Sexualities*, pp.104–5.
11   Bland, *Banishing the Beast*, p.101; Bartley, *Prostitution: Prevention and Reform*, p.169. Both point out that self-contained flats were exempt from the CLAA, but Bland says many landlords did not know about this distinction.
12   Quoted Bartley, *Prostitution: Prevention and Reform*, p.158.
13   Hall, *Sex, Gender and Social Change*, p.38.
14   An additional clause of the CLAA bill made indecent acts between consenting male adults illegal.
15   JB to ASB, 4 June 1895, WL, 3JBL/34/29.
16   Quoted Bartley, *Prostitution: Prevention and Reform*, p.169.
17   Walkowitz, *City of Dreadful Delight*, p.194.
18   Walkowitz, *City of Dreadful Delight*, p.213. Bartley disputes the significance she attaches to this, *Prostitution: Prevention and Reform*, p.168.
19   Bland, *Banishing the Beast*, p.100.
20   Quoted *ibid.*, p.102.
21   Elizabeth Elmy, quoted *ibid.*, p.102.
22   Summers, *Female Lives, Moral States*, p.128.
23   J. Edmondson to H.J. Wilson, 21 April 1883, Sheffield Archives, Wilson Papers, MD 2546/3.
24   This was introduced May–June 1883, see NA, 'Historical Review of the Present Crisis', 23 July 1883, in Sheffield Archives, Wilson MSS, MD 2544/5. See also Jordan, pp.216–7; Hammonds, *James Stansfeld*, p.255.
25   Quoted Jordan, p.216.
26   JB to Mrs Hind Smith, 7 May 1883 & nd [May 1883] Sheffield Archives, Wilson Papers, MD2548/6&7.
27   Hammonds, *James Stansfeld*, pp.238–9.
28   McHugh, p.227.
29   The result was Liberals 335, Conservatives 249 and Irish Nationalists 86.
30   Figure given by McHugh, p.227.
31   *George Butler*, p.395.
32   ASB to JB, 22 April 1887, NRO, ZBU/E3/B2.
33   JB to the Misses Priestman, 4 February 1886, WL, 3JBL/25/03; Jordan, p.236.
34   Margaret Tanner to JB, nd [17 March 1886], WL, 3JBL/25/08.
35   JB to ASB, 25 April 1886, in Jordan and Sharp (III), p.238.
36   *George Butler*, p.397.
37   Stead, *Josephine Butler*, p.97.
38   JB to GGB, 26 March 1886, WL, 3JBL/25/10.
39   JB to M. Tanner [?] 6 May 1886, WL, 3JBL/25/21, JB to M Priestman, 11 May 1886, WL, 3JBL/25/23. This Federation Congress incorporated the meetings of the NA and LNA.
40   *George Butler*, p.423.
41   The date they arrived is not recorded but by August they regarded The Close 'as home'. *George Butler*, p.425.
42   *George Butler*, pp.421, 426, and 427.
43   JB to M. Estlin, 31 October 1886, WL, 3JBL/25/40.
44   *George Butler*, p.429.
45   JB to Emily Ford, 15 November 1886, WL, 3JBL/25/42.
46   ASB to Rhoda Butler, 13 August [1886], RIBA, BuFam 2/2/1. See also JB to Priestman sisters, 19 October 1886, in Jordan and Sharp (V), pp.65–7.
47   JB to Mary Priestman, 5 January 1887, WL, 3JBL/26/02.
48   JB to Emily Ford, 15 November 1886, WL, 3JBL/25/42. Emily was the daughter of Josephine's friend, Hannah Ford, who had recently died. Hannah had often given money to help Josephine and Emily carried on the tradition.
49   JB to Emily Ford, 29 November 1886, WL, 3JBL/25/45.
50   *George Butler*, p.435.
51   JB to M. Tanner and M. Priestman, 19–20 December 1886, WL, 3JBL/25/50.
52   Rhoda Butler to ASB, 8 November 1886, RIBA, BuFam 2/5/2.
53   JB to Emily Ford, 24 December 1886, WL, 3JBL/25/51; *George Butler*, p.143.
54   Letters about the effects of the CD Acts in India were published in *The Shield* as early as 1870, see *New Abolitionists*, p.193.

55   Philippa Levine, 'Venereal Disease, Prostitution, and the Politics of Empire: The Case of British India', in *Journal of the History of Sexuality*, 1994, Vol. 4, p.581.

56   JB to Priestmans, 19 October 1886 in Jordan and Sharp (V), p.66.

57   JB, *The Revival and Extension of the Abolitionist Cause: A Letter to the Members of the Ladies' National Association*, 1887, in Jordan and Sharp (V), p.13. The next quote is from p.60.

58   Dyer, article in *Sentinel*, March 1888, Jordan and Sharp (V), p.120. See sketch of Bareilly, p.122.

59   Dyer quoting Hugh Price Hughes, in *Sentinel*, February 1888, Jordan and Sharp (V), p.112.

60   JB to Priestmans, 27 February 1888, in Jordan and Sharp (V), p.110.

61   Dyer, article in *Sentinel*, May 1888, Jordan and Sharp (V), p.142.

62   Dyer in *Sentinel*, May 1888, Jordan and Sharp (V), p.139.

63   Copy of a circular memorandum by the Quartermaster General in India dated 17 June 1886, Jordan and Sharp (V), p.152.

64   Dyer in *Sentinel*, May 1888, Jordan and Sharp (V), p.140.

65   JB in *Sentinel*, May 1888, Jordan and Sharp (V), pp.133–4. The camps were actually called 'chaklas'.

66   From *Dawn*, August 1888, Jordan and Sharp (V), pp.135–6.

67   James Stuart, interview to *Christian Commonwealth*, 18 May 1893, in Jordan and Sharp (V), p.224.

68   JB to Margaret Tanner, 12 May 1888, quoted Jordan, p.243.

69   House of Commons, 5 June 1888, in Jordan and Sharp (V), p.159.

70   Philippa Levine, *Prostitution, Race and Politics: Policing Venereal Disease in the British Empire*, London, Routledge, 2003, p.102.

71   Introduction by Ingrid Sharp, Jordan and Sharp (V), p.3.

72   Levine, *Prostitution, Race and Politics*, p.102.

73   JB to Priestmans and Mrs Tanner, 24 March 1887, WL, 3JBL/26/15.

74   JB, *George Butler*, pp.440–1.

75   JB, *George Butler*, p.448.

76   JB, *George Butler*, p.429; GGB to JB, 30 September 1886, NRO, ZBU/E3/B2.

77   JB to 'dear sons and daughter', 25 April [1886], WL, 3JBL/25/18.

78   GGB to JB, 27 February 1890, NRO, ZBU/E3/B2; JB to Miss Priestman, 17 February 1888, WL, 3JBL/27/03.

79   Quoted Jordan, p.252.

80   JB to Mary Priestman, 4 September 1888, WL, 3JBL/27/27.

81   JB, *George Butler*, p.450.

82   JB, *George Butler*, p.453. The following quotes are from p.459 & 450. See Jordan, p.250.

83   JB to Helen Clark, 10 November 1888, quoted Jane Jordan, p.252.

84   JB letter quoted *George Butler*, p.453.

85   JB to Priestmans, 28 August 1889, WL, 3JBL/28/19.

86   JB to Mrs Bright, 5 December 1888, WL, 3JBL/27/41.

87   Rhoda Butler to ASB, nd [December 1888], RIBA, BuFam, 3/4/4.

88   JB to Emily Ford, 25 December 1888, WL, 3JBL/27/43.

89   JB Diary (1889–1890), NRO, ZBU/E3/A5. This copy was given to GGB. See also JB to ASB, 17–23 February 1889 (journal letter), WL, 3JBL/28/06.

90   JB, *George Butler*, p.458.

91   JB letter, quoted *George Butler*, p.460.

92   JB to Tully Garston, fragment nd [June 1890], NRO, ZBU/E3/C1.

93   JB letter, quoted *George Butler*, p.460.

94   JB, undated fragment, nd, [c. August 1889], NRO, ZBU/E3/C3; Jordan, p.255.

95   JB to Priestmans, 28 August 1889, WL, 3JBL/28/19.

96   JB to Priestmans and LNA Committee, 29 May 1889, WL, 3JBL/28/12.

97   GB to GGB, 9 October 1889, WL, 3JBL/28/21.

98   *George Butler*, p.464.

99   Hatty Meuricoffre to GB, 17 October nd [1889], NRO, ZBU/E3/C3.

100 JB Diary (1889–1890) 28 November 1889, NRO, ZBU/E3/A5.The following quotes are 23 & 22 November 1889.

101 JB, *George Butler*, pp.465. Next quotes are pp.466, 467.

102 GB to Dean Kitchin of Winchester, 9 March 1890, WL, 3JBL/29/13. JB mentions the risk in a PS.

103 JB to Hatty, in *George Butler*, p.470.

104 JB Diary (1889–1890) 19 February 1890, T/S, ZBU/E3/A5.
105 JB Diary (1889–1890) 4 March 1890, T/S, ZBU/E3/A5.
106 *George Butler*, p.474.
107 JB letter, quoted *George Butler*, p.478.
108 *George Butler*, p.478. The following quotes are from pp.477, 478, and 479.
109 Letter from Charles Parker, quoted *George Butler*, p.480.
110 W.E. Gladstone to JB, 18 March 1890, WL, 3JBL/29/14.
111 Letter from GGB, quoted *George Butler*, p.485.
112 Letter from ASGB, quoted *George Butler*, p.485.

INTERLUDE – The Queen's Daughters in India
113 This account is taken from JB, 'The Present Aspect of the Abolitionist Cause in Relation to British India. A Letter to my Friends' in Jordan and Sharp (V), pp.182–86. JB quotes the accounts of both women.
114 JB quoting Dr Kate Bushnell, *ibid.*, p.183.
115 JB quoting Mrs Elizabeth Andrew, *ibid.*, p.184.
116 JB quoting Mrs Elizabeth Andrew, *ibid.*, p.186.
117 JB quoting Dr Kate Bushnell, *ibid.*, p.195.
118 Elizabeth Andrew and Kate Bushnell, *The Queen's Daughters in India*, in Jordan and Sharp (V), p.260. Other quotes in this paragraph are taken from pp.260–1.
119 JB quoting Dr Kate Bushnell, Jordan and Sharp (V), p.195.
120 Their conclusions are summarised in Jordan and Sharp (V), pp.240–3.
121 Reprinted in Jordan and Sharp (V), pp.321–2.
122 Andrew and Bushnell, *The Queen's Daughters in India*, in Jordan and Sharp (V), p.294. The next quote is from p.279.

CHAPTER 16
1 JB, *Dawn*, April 1890 in Jordan and Sharp (V), pp.164–5.
2 JB, 'The Present Aspect of the Abolitionist Cause …' in Jordan and Sharp (V), p.200.
3 'East India Cantonments Acts and Regulations. Statement of Facts' in Jordan and Sharp (V), p.242.
4 JB to ASB, 20 May 1893, in Jordan and Sharp (V), p.228.
5 'Report of the Committee appointed by the Secretary of State for India', in Jordan and Sharp (V), p.347. The next quote is from p.367.
6 JB in *Dawn*, October 1893, in Jordan and Sharp (V), p.386.
7 JB to ASB, 24 August 1893, in Jordan and Sharp (V), p.382.
8 JB in *Dawn*, October 1893, in Jordan and Sharp (V), p.389.
9 Lord Kimberley, India Secretary in the Liberal government 1892–94, quoted Levine, *Prostitution, Race and Politics*, p.113.
10 For details, see *ibid.*, pp.112–6.
11 JB to Tully Garston, fragment [June 1890], NRO, ZBU/E3/C1.
12 JB diary, June 1890, NRO, ZBU/E3/A12; JB to Tully Garston, *ibid.*
13 *George Butler*, pp.344–5.
14 JB diary, June 1890, NRO, ZBU/E3/A12.
15 JB to Margaret Tanner, 30 March 1890, WL, 3JBL/29/15.
16 *Ibid.*
17 JB to Margaret Tanner, 19 June 1890, WL, 3JBL/29/16; JB to Mary Priestman, 4 August 1890, WL, 3JBL/29/19. The trip was supposed to last a month but the children were still with JB on 18 October.
18 Carlo died in 1892 and Eiger in 1893. JB records her grief at Eiger's death (which was attended by George, Mia and the North View servants, all crying) in her diary. NRO, ZBU/E3/A12, p.19.
19 JB to Priestman sisters, 18 October 1890, WL, 3JBL/29/24; *c.* 4 January 1891, WL, 3JBL/30/02.
20 JB to Rhoda Butler, 4 November 1890, WL, 3JBL/29/26.
21 JB to Priestman sisters, *c.* 4 January 1891, WL, 3JBL/30/02.
22 There is a belief among George's descendants that he could have done much better. Beverley Grey, *Sin is Contagious*, pp.30–1.
23 JB to Priestman sisters, *c.* 4 January 1891, WL, 3JBL/30/02.
24 JB to Rhoda Butler, 4 November 1890, WL, 3JBL/29/26.

25   Jordan, p.260.
26   JB to Rhoda Butler, 4 November 1890, WL, 3JBL/29/26: JB to Priestman sisters, c. 4 January 1891, WL, 3JBL/30/02.
27   JB to Mrs Ryley, 30 April 1896, LUL, JB 1/1 1896/04/30 (ii).
28   JB to ASB, 3 February 1991, WL, 3JBL/30/05.
29   JB to Annie Priestman, 30 December 1890, WL, 3JBL/29/36.
30   Ibid. JB to Priestmans, 13 November 1890, WL, 3JBL/29/27.
31   JB to Priestman sisters, c. 4 January 1891, WL, 3JBL/30/02.
32   JB to Priestman sisters, 4 February 1891, WL, 3JBL/30/06.
33   JB, 'Familiar Letter to my Friends', The Dawn, 1 April 1891.
34   JB to Priestman sisters, 4 February 1891, WL, 3JBL/30/06.
35   JB, 'Geneva', The Dawn, 1 April 1891.
36   JB, 'Familiar Letter to my Friends', The Dawn, 1 April 1891.
37   JB to ASB, 3 February 1891, WL, 3JBL/30/05.
38   JB to Priestman sisters, c. 26 April 1891, WL, 3JBL/30/20.
39   JB to Mary Priestman, 29 July 1892, WL, 3JBL/31/26; JB to Mr Johnson, 14 July 1892, WL, 3JBL/31/25.
40   JB to Mary Priestman, 8 June 1892, WL, 3JBL/31/20.
41   Larsen, A People of One Book, pp.229–30.
42   Quoted Beverley Grey, Sin is Contagious, p.31.
43   JB to Mary Priestman, 8 June 1892, WL, 3JBL/31/20; Jordan, p.260.
44   JB to ASB, 16 November 1891, WL, 3JBL/30/42.
45   JB to Mary Priestman, 29 July 1892, WL, 3JBL/31/26.
46   JB diary, NRO, ZBU/E3/A12, p.9. The next quote is from p.7.
47   This 'reredos' was made of 'English oak with a centre of rich damask and two wings of excellent carved panelling surmounted by an ornamental cross'. It was inscribed 'In memory of George Butler DD, Canon of Winchester, who died 14 March 1890, aged 70 years'. (G.W. Kitchin, Dean of Winchester, 'Memorial to the late Canon Butler', 8 August 1891, NRO, ZBU/E2/15.)
48   JB diary, NRO, ZBU/E3/A12, p.8.
49   JB to Rhoda Butler, 31 October 1892, WL, 3JBL/31/32.
50   These letters were copied by GGB into volumes available in NRO, ZBU/F1/1 & F1/12.
51   GB to JB, 21 January 1893, supplied by Claire Grey.
52   JB diary, NRO, ZBU/E3/A12, p.9.
53   JB to Hatty Meuricoffre, nd [February 1892], NRO, ZBU/E3/C3.
54   JB to Mary Priestman, 6 May 1893, WL, 3JBL/32/23.
55   JB to ASB, 7 June 1893, WL, 3JBL/32/30; 17 April 1893, WL, 3JBL/32/17.
56   JB diary, NRO, ZBU/E3/A12, pp.15–6.
57   JB to Mary Priestman, 18 July 1893, WL, 3JBL/32/36.
58   JB to 'Sons', 23 December 1893, WL, 3JBL/32/61. Further quotes in this paragraph are taken from this letter.
59   JB to Fanny Forsaith, 8 April 1894, WL, 3JBL/33/15.
60   JB to Stanley Butler, 7 March 1894, WL, 3JBL/33/11.
61   JB to Fanny Forsaith, 10 March 1894, quoted Jordan, p.271.
62   JB to Fanny Forsaith, 8 April 1894, WL, 3JBL/33/15.
63   JB to Priestman sisters, 7 May 1894, WL, 3JBL/33/24; JB to Emily and Gertrude Butler, 19 May 1894, NRO, ZBU/E3/C1.
64   JB diary, ZBU/E3/A12, p.26. The next quote is from p.27.
65   JB to Mary Priestman, 20 September 1894, WL, 3JBL/33/40.
66   See Larsen, A People of One Book, pp.240–2, for an illuminating discussion of this book.
67   JEB, The Lady of Shunem, London, Horace Marshall, 1895, p.82; also p.128; Larsen, ibid., p.242.
68   JB to Mary Priestman, 20 September 1894, WL, 3JBL/33/40.
69   JB to Mary Priestman, 2 March 1895, WL, 3JBL/34/12.
70   JB diary, NRO, ZBU/E3/A12, p.33.
71   JB to Mary Priestman, 9 April 1895, WL, 3JBL/34/17. Judging from oblique references in Josephine's diaries, Mia may have had other miscarriages. She seems also to have had one later in 1895, since Josephine mentions Mia being pregnant in June 1895 (3JBL/34/29), but her first child was not born until July 1896.

72   JB to Mary Priestman, 2 March 1895, WL, 3JBL/34/12.

73   JB to Mary Priestman, 9 April 1895, WL, 3JBL/34/17.

74   JB to ASB, 23 June 1895, WL, 3JBL/34/34.

75   JB to Josephine and Bob Butler, 24 May 1895, supplied by John Thompson.

76   JB to ASB, 14 October 1895, WL, 3JBL/34/54.

77   JB to G.F. Watts, quoted in letter from Winifred Coombe Tennant to the Editor, *The Times*, 7 July 1928.

78   JB, 'The conflict in Geneva and its lessons', *The Dawn*, 1 February 1896. The campaign is documented in a series of eight letters from JB to Fanny Forsaith, titled 'The Geneva Struggle', January–May 1896: WL, 3JBL/35/12-19.

79   Circular letter from JB to Federation members, 13 May 1896, WL, 3JBL/35/31.

80   See Jordan, p.276.

81   *Personal Reminiscences*, p.104.

82   Mary Priestman, 'Ladies' Branch Associations', in *National League Journal*, 1 December 1881, quoted by Walkowitz, *Prostitution*, p.134.

83   Mary Priestman, 'Reminiscences of Mrs Butler by an early member of the L.N.A.', WL, 3JBL/53/45.

84   JB to Emily Thomas, 19 August 1896, NRO, ZBU/E3/C1. Hetha was born on 26 July. George mentions 'The brown withered bracken on Yeavering & Hetha' which he and Mia passed on their wedding day, so this could be the origin of the name, GGB to JB, 21 January 1893, supplied by Claire Grey.

85   List dated 18 September 1896, WL, 3HJW/E/2.

86   Figures reported in 'Lord Hamilton's Despatch', Jordan and Sharp (V), pp.449–56. The next quote is from p.451.

87   Jordan and Sharp (V), p.6.

88   JB, Letter to a friend, 20 April 1897, in Jordan and Sharp (V), p.486.

89   Memorial of Medical Women, Jordan and Sharp (V), pp.565–77.

90   Jordan and Sharp (V), pp.545–7.

91   H.J. Wilson, *The History of a Sanitary Failure*, 4th ed., 1898, in Jordan and Sharp (V), pp.419–45.

92   JB, Letter to a friend, 20 April 1897, in Jordan and Sharp (V), pp.486–7.

93   'The British Soldier in India', in *Review of Reviews*, 1897, in Jordan and Sharp (V), pp.415–6.

94   Quoted by H.J. Wilson, Jordan and Sharp (V), p.444.

95   *Shield*, October 1897, in Jordan and Sharp (V), p.548.

96   Lady Henry Somerset's letter to *The Times*, in Jordan and Sharp (V), pp.482–4.

97   Jordan and Sharp (V), pp.476–80.

98   *Shield*, May 1897, in Jordan and Sharp (V), p.498.

99   Quoted by JB, letter to Miss Priestman, in Jordan and Sharp (V), p.500.

100 JB to ASB, 20 May 1893, in Jordan and Sharp (V), pp.227–8.

101 Open letter from JB, 30 May 1897, in Jordan and Sharp (V), p.503.

102 JB to Priestmans, 4 April 1895, WL, 3JBL/34/16; 3 May 1895, WL, 3JBL/34/22 (next quote).

103 JB to Mary Priestman, 26 July 1895, WL, 3JBL/34/39.

104 JEB, *Truth Before Everything*, 1897, in Jordan and Sharp (III), p.334. Other quotes in this paragraph from pp.340–1, 349 and 354. In fact, James Stuart insisted on offering Federation support, see Jordan, p.280.

105 He published the full details in *Sentinel*, September 1897, see Jordan and Sharp (V), pp.535–42.

106 JB, *Reply to Lady Somerset's Scheme for Dealing with Disease in the Indian Cantonments*, Jordan and Sharp (V), p.526.

107 See Frances Willard's announcement of JB's resignation, *Chicago Tribune*, 8 December 1897.

108 *The Christian*, 17 February 1898, in Jordan and Sharp (V), p.324.

109 See JB to Fanny Forsaith, 1 February 1898, in Jordan and Sharp (V), pp.578–9.

110 Lord Hamilton, quoted Levine, *Prostitution, Race and Politics*, p.118.

111 This account taken from Bland, *Banishing the Beast*, pp.95–7, 115.

112 JB to Anna Maria Priestman, 5 November 1894, in Jordan and Sharp (III), pp.140–2.

113 JB to Anna Maria Priestman, *ibid.*, p.141. It was probably at this time that she left the NVA; no precise date has been discovered.

114 Bartley, *Prostitution: Prevention and Reform*, p.169.

INTERLUDE – The Boer War

115 Fowler, *A Study in Radicalism and Dissent*, p.108.
116 JB to ASB, 20 January 1900, WL, 3JBL/44/19.
117 JB to GGB, 23 December 1899, LUL, JB 1/1/1899/12/23 (II).
118 Jordan, p.283.
119 JEB, *Native Races and the War*, 1900, http://www.gutenberg.org/files/14299/14299-h/14299-h. htm, Ch. 8 (this edition does not have page numbers). Other quotes in this paragraph are from Ch.1 and Ch.4.
120 See press cuttings in LUL, JB/1/5.
121 Moberley Bell, *Josephine Butler*, p.244.
122 JEB, *Native Races and the War*, Ch.3.
123 *Ibid.*, Ch.6.
124 JB to ASB, 19 December 1899, WL, 3JBL/43/61.
125 JEB, 'A Grave Question', quoted Jo-Ann Wallace, '*A Class Apart: Josephine Butler and Regulated Prostitution in British India, 1886–1893*', p.80.
126 Judith R. Walkowitz, 'Butler, Josephine Elizabeth (1828–1906)', *ODNB*, Oxford UP, 2004; online ed. May 2006, http://www.oxforddnb.com/view/article/32214.
127 JB to Mia Butler, 19 November 1900, LUL, JB 1/1/1900/11/19 (II); *Portrait*, p.192.
128 H.J. Wilson to Fanny Forsaith, 7 January 1901, quoted Jordan, pp.283–4.
129 Antoinette Burton, 'States of Injury: Josephine Butler on Slavery, Citizenship, and the Boer War', in *Social Politics*, 1998, Vol. 5, No.3, p.345.
130 JB, *Native Races and the War*, Ch.8.

CHAPTER 17

1 JB to Priestmans, 10 November 1897, WL, 3JBL/38/52.
2 The outdoor photo is reproduced in this book; the indoor picture is Plate 30 in Jordan.
3 JEB, *Prophets and Prophetesses: Some Thoughts for the Present Times*, Newcastle-upon-Tyne & London, 1898, p.4. This book was originally a series of articles for the magazine *Wings* in 1897.
4 JEB, *Prophets ...*, pp.5–6, 11. Lucretia Flammang calls this theology of women's prophecy, by now associated with the Second Coming, 'apocalyptic feminism', '"And your sons and your daughters will prophesy". The voice and vision of Josephine Butler', in Julie Melnyk (ed.), *Women's Theology in Nineteenth-Century Britain: Transfiguring the Faith of their Fathers*, New York, Farland Publishing, 1998, p.161.
5 JEB, *Prophets ...*, p.11.
6 Printed on the masthead of *The Storm-Bell*, nos 1–24, January 1898–July 1900.
7 *The Storm-Bell*, January 1900. See pp.19–20 of this book.
8 JB to Fanny Forsaith, 15 December 1897, WL, 3JBL/38/69.
9 JB to Priestman sisters, 1 March 1898, WL, 3JBL/40/01.
10 JB to ASB, 31 May 1898, WL, 3JBL/41/17.
11 JB to 'Dear friends', 26 May 1906, WL, 3JBL/58/05. In this letter she also criticises his faulty judgement in allowing the import of opium to China, with disastrous results.
12 *Portrait*, pp.22–3.
13 *Portrait*, p.22. This box was a present from George.
14 JB to Hetha Butler, LUL, JB1/1/1902/05/26(II); JB1/1/1902/03/28(II).
15 JB, 'A few dates and notes from my occasional diary' [1 March 1899–26 April 1901], NRO, ZBU/E3/A8.
16 She states that she had never used them before, but her Cheltenham diary records her using opiates, see Chapter 4, note 53.
17 JB, 'A few dates ...' (see note 15), May 1899. She did the same thing the following winter in Switzerland, when she was ill for three months and told Stanley that 'all this time I have tried to conceal from all my dear ones how bad I felt'. 20 January 1900, WL, 3JBL/44/19.
18 *Ibid.*, 23 September 1899.
19 *Ibid.*, 30 October 1899.
20 JB to ASB, 18 December 1899, WL, 3JBL/43/61.
21 JB to Rhoda Butler and ASB, 27 December 1899, WL, 3JBL/43/65.
22 JB to Fanny Forsaith, 12 July 1900, WL, 3JBL/44/24.
23 JEB, *Silent Victories*, p.37.

24   JB, 'A few dates ...' (see note 15), August 1900.

25   *Ibid.*, 2 September 1900. (This date is the day she left La Gordanne; the visit began in August.)

26   *Ibid.*, [September] 1900.

27   She visited Stanley and family on holiday in Grindelwald on her way home, see WL catalogue note
       to 3JBL/44/28.

28   JB, 'A few dates ...' (see note 15), 14 September 1900. For this account, see also JB to unknown
       recipient, March 1901, WL, 3JBL/45/12.

29   *Ibid.*, 14 September 1900.

30   JB to 'My own, own Darling' [Hatty Meuricoffre], 23 April [1877 or 1880], WL, 3JBL/57/13.

31   Mia Butler's letter book, 15 September 1900, NRO, ZBU/F1/12. George was in Canada at the time.

32   She stayed with friends, particularly Mrs Terrell, who lived in West Ealing.

33   JB to Maud Garston, 24 January 1901, LUL, JB 1/1 1901/24/2(II); JB to ASB and Rhoda Butler,
       23 January 1901, WL, 3JBL/45/05.

34   JB to Priestman sisters, 14 February 1901, WL, 3JBL/45/10.

35   JB to Rhoda Butler, 29 January 1901, WL, 3JBL/45/07.

36   JB, 'A few dates ...' (see note 15), [March] 1901. GGB kept a diary of those weeks which was being
       catalogued at Woodhorn at my last visit.

37   She told this to the Ewart housekeeper, Jane Grey, and that she regretted not telling him. JB to Jane
       Grey, Sunday [1901], NRO, ZBU/E3/B1/10.

38   GGB to JB, 15 June 1905; GGB notes for letter to JB, 17 June 1905, NRO, ZBU/E3/B4.

39   See GGB's annotations to JB, 'A few dates ...' (see note 15), nd [March] 1901; GGB to JB, 24 June
       1905, NRO, ZBU/E3/B4.

40   JB, 'A few dates ...' (see note 15), 26 April 1901.

41   Charles Butler to James Stuart, 7 May 1901, WL, 3JBL/45/17.

42   JB to Chairman of Federation, 11 May 1901, WL, 3JBL/45/18. See also Charles Butler to James
       Stuart, 7 May 1901, *ibid.*

43   JB to Montague Butler, 14 June 1901, NRO, ZBU/E3/C8.

44   See JB to Hetha Butler, 17 July 1901, LUL, JB 1/1 1901/07/17(II). Ewart was regularly let,
       presumably to pay off some of the outstanding debt on the estate.

45   JB to GGB, 12 October 1901, LUL, JB 1/1/1901/10/12 (II).

46   JB to 'Dear Friend' [Margaret Tanner], WL, 3JBL/45/31.

47   JB to Priestman sisters, 21 December 1901, WL, 3JBL/45/35.

48   JB to Rhoda Butler, 30 October 1901, LUL, JB 1/1/1901/10/30 (I).

49   JB to Margaret Tanner, 8 December 1901, WL, 3JBL/45/34. For the family visit to Eva's grave, see
       Jordan, p.289.

50   In a letter to Catherine (Katie) Booth-Clibborn, 18 January [1902], SAHC, BC/1/1/65, JB says she
       will only go north in the summer.

51   This memoir is in the form of a letter to Maurice Gregory, 16 March 1902, WL, 3JBL/46/04.

52   JB to Maurice Gregory, 16 March 1902, WL, 3JBL/46/04. See Kristine Frederickson, 'Josephine
       Butler and Christianity ...', pp.128–40, for an extended discussion of JB's millennialism. Lisa Nolland
       discusses whether she was an 'apocalyptic', p.272, coming to a different conclusion from both
       Frederickson and Alison Milbank. This is an unresolved debate on whether JB believed that Christ
       would come before or after the Millennium. I suggested in 'Evangelical Spirituality', p.301, that
       she was postmillennial, but Frederickson has a convincing argument that she was premillennial. It
       is possible to find support for both positions in her writings. It is certain that she did not believe the
       date could be predicted, she quoted Christ saying, 'of the day and hour knoweth no man' in a letter
       to Catherine Booth-Clibborn, 3 February 1902, SAHC, BC/1/1/65.

53   JB to Maurice Gregory, 16 March 1902, WL, 3JBL/46/04.

54   JB to ASB, 3 March 1905, WL, 3JBL/49/17. The revival began in 1904.

55   Larsen, *A People of One Book*, p.243. I have found Larsen's analysis, pp.243–5, helpful in writing
       this section.

56   Philalethes (JEB), 'The Morning Cometh': A Letter to my Children, Newcastle 1903, pp.2, 9–12.

57   *Ibid.*, p.22.

58   Larsen makes this point in relation to 'The Lady of Shunem', which speaks of God as 'the Great
       Father–Mother', in *A People of One Book*, p.241.

59   JEB, 'The Morning Cometh', pp.33–34. Larsen comments, 'this marked her as an evangelical of the
       old school', p.244.

60   JEB, 'The Morning Cometh', pp.49–50.
61   JB to GGB, February 1903, LUL, JB 1/1 1903/02/00.The conversation with Stanley is described in JB to Montague Butler, 6 December 1903, NRO, ZBU/E3/C8. It took place during a visit to Cheltenham in 1902. The book was later published more widely.
62   He was born in June 1902.
63   JB to Fanny Forsaith, quoted Jordan, p.289.
64   She mentions concerns about Charles's health in JB to Montague Butler, 6 December 1903 & 23 February [1904], NRO, ZBU/E3/C8; JB to Fanny Forsaith, 25 December 1905, WL, 3JBL/50/35.
65   This account is taken from Portrait, pp.210–1. ASGB quotes JB to Fanny Forsaith, 13 December 1902, WL, 3JBL/46/30.
66   JB to Fanny Forsaith, 25 June 1903, WL, 3JBL/47/19.
67   JB to Catherine (Katie) Booth-Clibborn, 25 January [1902], SAHC, BC/1/1/65. Katie and her husband had just left the Salvation Army to follow a healer, Dr Dowrie. JB sympathised but suggested he might be a charlatan. Her objections appear to have terminated the correspondence.
68   JB to Fanny Forsaith, 11 August 1903, WL, 3JBL/47/21.
69   Notes by GGB, 1905, NRO, ZBU/E3/B4.
70   GGB to JB, 29 August 1903, NRO, ZBU/E3/B4. This letter is scrawled in pencil and headed 'Dr Mr'.
71   JB to Fanny Forsaith, 11 August 1903, WL, 3JBL/47/21. She was actually speaking of a hillside house outside Cheltenham which she used during the summer and the need to move back to the town centre.
72   JB, 'A few impressions of my dear Ewart grandchildren', NRO, ZBU/E3/A9.
73   JB to Fanny Forsaith, 11 November 1903, WL, 3JBL/47/33; 21 November 1903, WL, 3JBL/47/34.
74   GGB to JB, 20 June 1905, NRO, ZBU/E3/B2.
75   JB copied up this diary, 'A few impressions of my dear Ewart grandchildren', and gave it to GGB in June 1905.
76   JB, 'A few impressions of my dear Ewart grandchildren', Sunday 1 November [1903], NRO, ZBU/E3/A9.
77   JB to Montague Butler, 31 December 1903, NRO, ZBU/E3/C8.
78   JB to Fanny Forsaith, 5 April 1904, WL, 3JBL/48/09; see 23 April 1904, WL, 3JBL/48/11 for James Stuart's visit.
79   JB to Fanny Forsaith and Harriet Allan, 6 November 1904, WL, 3JBL/48/30.
80   JB to Fanny Forsaith, 8 October 1904, WL, 3JBL/48/26.
81   JB to ASB, 16 September 1904, WL, 3JBL/48/21.
82   JB to 'Kind Friends, the Winter of 1904–5', NRO, ZBU/E3/C2/2.
83   JB to Fanny Forsaith, 5 March 1903, WL, 3JBL/47/15. Part of this letter is quoted by Jordan, p.5, in a sympathetic discussion of this issue. The letter was dictated but the words 'to us' were added by JB.
84   Most of Charlie's adult letters to his mother have not been archived, which suggests that he asked George to destroy them. He wrote to her every week from Canada.
85   JB to Fanny Forsaith, 14 July 1904, WL, 3JBL/48/18. See also 24 June 1904, WL, 3JBL/48/16 when she invites Fanny to visit her 'at Wooler in my winter rooms'.
86   JB to Fanny Forsaith, 10 March 1905, WL, 3JBL/49/19.
87   JB to Fanny Forsaith, quoted Portrait, p.216.
88   JB to Fanny Forsaith, 11 February 1905, WL, 3JBL/49/08; JB to ASB, 3 March 1905, WL, 3JBL/49/17.
89   JB to ASB, ibid.
90   This goes back to 1903: see for example, JB to Mr Johnson, 24 January 1903, WL, 3JBL/47/07.
91   JB to Fanny Forsaith, 10 March 1905, WL, 3JBL/49/19.
92   JB to Fanny Forsaith, 28 March 1905, 3JBL/49/23. The visit took place at the beginning of March. JB sent her a lovely letter detailing instructions for the journey, quoted Portrait, p.215. Fanny Forsaith was prevented by illness from attending the conference, held in September 1905, but she sent her paper. See JB to Fanny Forsaith, 6 August 1905, WL, 3JBL/50/04.
93   GGB to JB, 24 June 1905, NRO, ZBU/E3/B4.
94   See GGB to JB, 15 June 1905; notes on his reply 16 June; 20 June 1905; 24 June 1905; 25 June 1906, NRO, ZBU/E3/B4. Josephine's side of the correspondence is not included.
95   Notes by GGB, 1905, NRO, ZBU/E3/B4.

96 See Chapter 4, note 74. It is undated but the comments about George are consistent with other writings at this time, e.g. 'A few impressions of my dear Ewart grandchildren' which he received in June (see 24 June 1905, ZBU/E3/B4). The 'Memory of Child Sorrow' is mentioned in JB's will and may not have come to George until after her death.

97 JB, 'Directions for my sons to be read after my death', c. 1905, NRO, ZBU/E3/C4/2.

98 JB to Fanny Forsaith, 21 January 1906, LUL, JB1/1 1906/01/21(I); Portrait, quoting letter to unnamed recipient, p.216.

99 JB to Fanny Forsaith et al, 1 February 1906, WL, 3JBL/51/05.

100 JB to LNA, 7 April 1906, WL, 3JBL/51/11. She arranged for a printed message of thanks to all her supporters, but decided that she did not like the photo by Emily Ford which Millicent Fawcett chose to accompany it. See Jordan, p.293 for details.

101 Letter to ASGB, quoted Portrait, p.217.

102 ASGB to GGB, 30 December 1906, Rhoda Butler to GGB, 2 January [1907], NRO, ZBU/E3/C5.

103 His daughter wrote to ASB, nd [1905], from the school, St Joseph de Cluny, Fontainebleau, France. RIBA, BuFam 3/3/1.

104 JB to ASB and RB, 26 April 1905, WL, 3JBL/49/30.

105 JB to Fanny Forsaith, 5 October 1906, WL, 3JBL/51/34.

106 JB to Mrs Terrell, 27 December 1906, WL, 3JBL/51/38.

107 JB to 'Beloved ones, my Stanley', 28 December 1906, LUL, JB 1/1/ 1906/12/28 (I).

108 Portrait, pp.217–8.

EPILOGUE

1 ASB to GGB, 2 January 1907, NRO ZBU/E3/C5.

2 Jordan, p.296, shows that James Stuart, Henry Wilson and Fanny Forsaith were notified too late to be able to attend.

3 ASG Butler to James Stuart, 10 February 1907, RIBA BuFam 3/17/1.

4 They are archived at LUL, JB3, and WL, 3JBL/53.

5 Amelie Humbert to GGB, 4 January 1907, WL, 3JBL/53/28.

6 Mrs Watts to GGB, 3 January 1906 [07] 3JBL/53.

7 Maud Garston to GGB, 2 January 1907, 3JBL/53.

8 George Howell to H.J. Wilson, 18 February 1907, WL, 3JBL/53/27.

9 'In Memory of Mrs Josephine Butler', The Deliverer, June 1907, p.83.

10 JB to Miss Priestman, 4 November 1896, WL, 3JBL/36/43.

11 James Stuart, Introduction to Johnsons, p.ix.

12 Fawcett and Turner, Josephine Butler, 1927. NRO, ZBU/E3/D2 is a collection of newspaper cuttings from the Centenary.

13 Joseph Williamson, Josephine Butler: The Forgotten Saint (1977). The date has recently been changed to 30 May.

14 Elizabeth Longford, (1981), 'Josephine Butler' in Eminent Victorian Women, London, Weidenfeld and Nicholson, p.109.

15 Fawcett and Turner, Josephine Butler, pp.vi–vii.

16 Daniel Gorman, 'Empire, Internationalism, and the Campaign against the Traffic in Women and Children in the 1920s', Twentieth Century British History, 2008, p.212. Netherlands is the tenth country, not mentioned here.

17 Mumm, 'Josephine Butler and the International Traffic in Women', p.69; Carrie Pemberton, 'Josephine Butler and the trafficking of women today', in Milbank (ed.), Beating the Traffic, p.169.

18 James Stuart, Introduction to Johnsons, p.xi.

APPENDIX 1

1 G.A. Grey, 'An Agricultural Education', and biography, http://milfieldgreys.co.uk/5_george_annett/george_annett.html.

2 JB to Mr Spring-Rice, 8 February [1858], WL, 3JBL/54/08.

3 Bolton, Six Brides, p.33.

4 The main source for this account is Bolton, Six Brides, pp.48–53; Jordan, pp.38, 50, 53, 187.

5 Letter from George Grey copied in JG to Mr Spring-Rice, 27 June 1851, WL, 3JBL/54/3.

6 She was married in Cheltenham, according to JB to ASB, 23 December 1901, WL, 3JBL/45/36. Jordan says that the Massons went to China after Eliza's marriage, p.53. If so, they later settled in Genoa.

7   Josephine's sepia drawing of this house is reprinted in Bolton, *Six Brides*, p.62.
8   Jordan, p.52, based on Fanny's diaries. Jordan, pp.51–2 and Bolton, *Six Brides*, pp.61–2, are the sources for my account of Fanny's marriage.
9   *Harriet Meuricoffre*, p.295.
10   Jordan, p.21.
11   Frances Dickinson, *Historic Dilston: Guide and History*, North Pennines Heritage Trust, 2009.
12   Daniela Luigia Caglioti, 'Meuricoffre, Tell', in *Biographical Dictionary of Italian*, Vol. 74, 2010 (in translation).
13   *Harriet Meuricoffre*, p.292.
14   Bolton, *Six Brides*, pp.77–8.

APPENDIX 2

1   Information from Frances Dickinson.
2   http://www.angelfire.com/az/garethknight/redcross/priory.html.
3   *Ibid*.
4   http://www.historic-liverpool.co.uk/toxteth.
5   http://www.liverpoolcollege.org.uk.
6   Jordan, p.67.
7   http://www.britishlistedbuildings.co.uk/en-237633-ewart-park-ewart.

Bibliography

Archives

The main archives containing letters and papers relating to Josephine Butler's life and campaigns are the Women's Library (formerly the Fawcett Library) now housed at the London School of Economics, the Sydney Jones Library at the University of Liverpool, and Northumberland Archives at Woodhorn, Ashington, Northumberland.

The majority of her correspondence held at the Women's Library and the University of Liverpool was microfiched in the early 1980s – both libraries hold this fiche and encourage researchers to use that. I have referenced letters from the fiche using the Women's Library online catalogue. I have used Liverpool's online catalogue for its collection of letters which are not on the fiche. The Northumberland Archives were engaged, in 2013, in listing and separately numbering all the items in the 'ZBU' catalogue. I have not been able to use these item numbers in my references, but the file numbers are correct.

In addition there are important collections of letters at St Andrews University Library, Salvation Army Heritage Centre at William Booth College, London; Royal Institute of British Architects study rooms at the Victoria and Albert Museum, London; Sheffield Archives (H.J. Wilson Collection); Trinity College, Cambridge (James Ramsay Montague Butler Collection) and Brotherton Library, University of Leeds (Emily Ford letters).

Major Works by Josephine Butler

An Appeal to the People of England, on the Recognition and Superintendence of Prostitution by Governments, by an English Mother, 1869.
Catharine of Siena: A Biography, 1878.
'Catherine Booth', *Contemporary Review*, 58, November 1890, pp.639–54.
The Constitution Violated, 1871.
The Duty of Women in Relation to Our Great Social Evil, 1870.
The Education and Employment of Women, 1868.
A Few Words Addressed to True-Hearted Women, 1872.
Government by Police, 1879.
The Hour Before the Dawn: An Appeal to Men, 1876.
In Memoriam: Harriet Meuricoffre, 1901.
The Lady of Shunem, 1895.
A Letter to the Mothers of England, 1881.
Life of Jean Frederic Oberlin, Pastor of the Ban de la Roche, 1882.

Memoir of John Grey of Dilston, 1869.
The Moral Reclaimability of Prostitutes, 1870.
'The Morning Cometh': A Letter to my Children, 1903.
Native Races and the War, 1900.
The New Abolitionists (ed. James Stuart), 1876.
The New Era, 1872.
The New Godiva: A Dialogue, 1883.
Our Christianity Tested by the Irish Question, 1887.
Personal Reminiscences of a Great Crusade, 1896.
Prophets and Prophetesses: Some Thoughts for the Present Times, 1898.
Rebecca Jarrett, 1885.
Recollections of George Butler, 1892.
The Salvation Army in Switzerland, 1883.
Silent Victories, 1900.
Social Purity, 1879.
Some Thoughts on the Present Aspect of the Crusade Against the State Regulation of Vice, 1874.
Sursum Corda, 1871.
Truth before Everything, 1897.
*The Voice of One Crying in the Wilderness: Being her First Appeal, Made in 1874–5, to
     Continental Nations Against the System of Regulated Vice*. English translation by
     Osmund Airy, 1913.
Vox Populi, 1871.
Woman's Work and Woman's Culture, 1869.

NB I have given the original date of publication, but not the publisher, since many
     books were reissued. The Notes indicate the edition I used. A complete bibliography
     of all Josephine Butler's works would include her journal articles, of which there
     are hundreds in the ones she wrote for regularly: *The Shield, Sentinel, Dawn* and *The
     Storm-Bell*.
     I have made full use, as indicated in the Notes, of the transcriptions of selected
     letters, pamphlets and books in Jane Jordan and Ingrid Sharp (eds), *Josephine Butler
     and the Prostitution Campaigns: Diseases of the Body Politic*, Vols I–V, Routledge,
     London and New York, 2003. A Bibliography of Josephine Butler's works is included
     in Vol. I, pp.24–6.

Writings on Josephine Butler

Bell, Enid Moberley, *Josephine Butler: Flame of Fire*, London, Constable, 1962.
Boyd, Nancy, *Three Victorian Women Who Changed Their World: Josephine Butler, Octavia
     Hill, Florence Nightingale*, New York & London, OUP & Macmillan, 1982.
Burton, Antoinette, 'States of Injury: Josephine Butler on Slavery, Citizenship, and the
     Boer War', *Social Politics*, 1998, Vol. 5, No. 3, pp.338–61.
Butler, A.S.G, *Portrait of Josephine Butler*, London, Faber and Faber, 1954.
Butler, George Grey (nd [*c.* 1929]), *Some Recollections of Josephine Butler*, NRO ZBU/E3/
     E3.
Caine, Barbara, 'Josephine Butler' in *Victorian Feminists*, pp.150–95, Oxford UP, 1992.
Daggers, Jenny and Neal, Diana (eds), *Sex, Gender and Religion: Josephine Butler Revisited*,
     New York, Peter Land, 2006.

Dickinson, Frances, *The Rose of Dilston: Josephine Butler 1828–1906*, Historic Dilston, 2006.

Fawcett, Millicent Garrett and Turner, E.M., *Josephine Butler: Her Work and Principles, and their Meaning for the Twentieth Century*, London, Association for Moral & Social Hygiene, 1927.

Flammang, Lucretia, '"And your sons and your daughters will prophesy". The voice and vision of Josephine Butler', in Julie Melnyk (ed.), *Women's Theology in Nineteenth-Century Britain: Transfiguring the Faith of their Fathers*, New York, Farland Publishing, 1998.

Frederickson, Kristine, 'Josephine Butler and Christianity in the 19th-century British Victorian feminist movement', University of Utah PhD, 2008.

Forster, Margaret, 'Josephine Butler' in *Significant Sisters: The Grassroots of Active Feminism 1839–1939*, 2nd ed., London, Penguin, 1986.

Grey, Beverley, 'Sin is Contagious: Josephine Butler's Mission to Reform', MA dissertation, Bristol University, 1997.

Hay-Cooper, L., *Josephine Butler and her Work for Social Purity*, London, Society for Promoting Christian Knowledge, 1922.

Holmes, Marion, *Josephine Butler: A Cameo Life Sketch*, Women's Freedom League, nd [1913].

Johnson, George W. and Lucy A. (eds), *Josephine E. Butler: An Autobiographical Memoir*, Bristol, J.W. Arrowsmith, 1909.

Jordan, Jane, *Josephine Butler*, London, John Murray, 2001.

Levine, Philippa, 'Josephine Butler' in *Victorian Feminism 1850–90*, Florida UP, 1994.

Longford, Elizabeth, 'Josephine Butler' in *Eminent Victorian Women*, London, Weidenfeld and Nicholson, 1981.

Mathers, Helen, 'The Evangelical Spirituality of a Victorian Feminist: Josephine Butler, 1828–1906', *Journal of Ecclesiastical History*, 52 (2001), pp.282–312.

Milbank, Alison, 'Josephine Butler: Christianity, Feminism and Social Action' in J. Obelkevich, L. Roper and R. Samuel (eds), *Disciplines of Faith: Studies in Religion, Politics and Patriarchy*, London, Routledge & Kegan Paul, 1987, pp.154–64.

Milbank, Alison (ed.), *Beating the Traffic: Josephine Butler and Anglican Social Action on Prostitution Today*, Winchester, George Mann, 2007.

Nolland, Lisa Severine, *A Victorian Feminist Christian: Josephine Butler, the Prostitutes and God*, Milton Keynes, Paternoster, 2004.

Petrie, Glen, *A Singular Iniquity: The Campaigns of Josephine Butler*, New York, Viking Press, 1971.

Rappaport, Helen, 'Josephine Butler (1828–1906)' in *Encyclopedia of Women Social Reformers* Vol. 1 (A–L), ABC-Clio, 2001, pp.119–23.

Royden, Maud, 'Josephine Butler', pamphlet issued by Josephine Butler Fellowship, nd.

Stead, W.T., *Josephine Butler: A Life Sketch*, London, Morgan & Scott, 1886.

Summers, Anne, '"The Constitution Violated": The Female Body and the Female Subject in the Campaigns of Josephine Butler', *History Workshop Journal*, 48, 1999, pp.1–15.

Toogood, Philippa, 'Josephine Butler (1828–1906) as depicted by Alexander Munro in sculpture (1855) and obituary (1907)', University of Oxford Department of Continuing Education, open resources, 2013 http://open.conted.ox.ac.uk/resources/documents.

Uglow, Jenny, 'Josephine Butler: from Sympathy to Theory' in Dale Spender (ed.), *Feminist Theorists: Three Centuries of Women's Intellectual Traditions*, London, Women's Press, 1983.

Van Drenth, Annemieke and de Haan, Francisca, *The Rise of Caring Power: Elizabeth Fry and Josephine Butler in Britain and the Netherlands*, Amsterdam UP, 1999.

Walkowitz, Judith R., 'Butler, Josephine Elizabeth (1828–1906)', *Oxford Dictionary of National Biography*, Oxford University Press, September 2004; online ed., May 2006.

Wallace, Jo-Ann, '"A Class Apart": Josephine Butler and Regulated Prostitution in British India 1886–1893', in Leigh Dale and Simon Ryan, *The Body in the Library*, Rodopi, 1998, pp.73–85.

Williamson, Joseph, *In Honour Bound*, pamphlet, 1977.

Williamson, Joseph, *Josephine Butler, the Forgotten Saint*, London, pamphlet, 1971.

Wilson, A.N., 'Josephine Butler' in *Eminent Victorians*, BBC Books, London, 1989, pp.164–202.

Other Works Cited

Contemporary Sources

Acton, William, *The Functions and Disorders of the Reproductive Organs, in Childhood, Youth, Adult Age and Advanced Life, Considered in their Physiological, Social and Moral Relations*, 6th ed. London, J. and A. Churchill, 1875.

Acton, William, *Prostitution, Considered in Its Moral, Social and Sanitary Aspects*, 2nd ed. London, Frank Cass, 1870.

Booth, William Bramwell, *Echoes and Memories*, London, Hodder & Stoughton, 1925.

Dyer, Alfred, *The European Slave Trade in English Girls*, London, Dyer Brothers, 1880.

Guyot, Yves, *Prostitution Under the Regulation System French and English* (English translation), George Redway, 1884.

Holland, Henry Scott, *A Bundle of Memories*, London, Wells, Garner, Darton & Co., 1915.

Railton, G.S.(ed.), *The Truth about the Armstrong Case and the Salvation Army*, London, Salvation Army, nd [1885/6].

Reminiscences of Cheltenham College by an Old Cheltonian, London, Benrose & Sons, 1868.

Waugh, Benjamin, *William T Stead: A Life for the People*, London, Vickers, nd [c. 1904].

Secondary Sources

Bartley, Paula, *Prostitution: Prevention and Reform in England, 1860–1914*, London & New York, Routledge, 2000.

Bland, Lucy, *Banishing the Beast: English Feminism and Sexual Morality, 1885–1914*, London, Penguin, 1995.

Blum, Paul, 'The Hôpital Saint-Lazare in Paris: Its Past and Present History', *British Journal of Venereal Disease*, 24, 1948, pp.151–2.

Bolton, A.R.C., *The Six Brides of Dilston*, Bognor Regis, New Horizon, 1984.

Courbin, Alain (Translated Sheridan, Alan), *Prostitution and Sexuality in France After 1850*, Harvard UP, 1990.

Crozier, Ivan, 'William Acton and the history of sexuality: the medical and professional context', *Victorian Culture*, 5 (2000), pp.1–27.

Dickinson, Frances, *Historic Dilston: Guide and History*, North Pennines Heritage Trust, 2009.

Finnegan, Frances, *Poverty and Prostitution: A Study of Victorian Prostitutes in York*, Cambridge UP, 1979.

Fowler, W.S., *A Study in Radicalism and Dissent: The Life and Times of Henry Joseph Wilson, 1822–1914*, London, Epworth Press, 1961.

Gallant, Mary (ed.), *A Feminist Case Study in Transnational Migration: The Anne Jemima Clough Journals*, Cambridge, Scholars Publishing, 2009.

Gelder, M., Gath, D. and Mayou, R., *Oxford Textbook of Psychiatry*, 2nd ed., Oxford UP, 1989.

Gorman, Daniel, 'Empire, Internationalism, and the Campaign against the Traffic in Women and Children in the 1920s' in *Twentieth Century British History*, 2008, pp.186–216.

Hall, Lesley, *Sex, Gender and Social Change in Britain Since 1880*, Basingstoke, Macmillan, 2000.

Hall, Lesley, 'Hauling Down the Double Standard: Feminism, Social Purity and Sexual Science in Late Nineteenth-Century Britain', *Gender and History*, 16, 2004, pp.36–56.

Hammond, J.L. and Hammond, Barbara, *James Stansfeld: A Victorian Champion of Sex Equality*, London, Longmans, Green and Co., 1932.

Hattersley, Roy, *Blood and Fire: William and Catherine Booth and their Salvation Army*, London, Little, Brown & Co., 1999.

Hellerstein, E.O., Hume, L.P. and Offen, K.O. (eds), *Victorian Women*, Stanford UP, 1981.

Hughes, Kathryn, *The Victorian Governess*, London, Hambledon, 1993.

Jalland, Pat and Hooper, John (eds), *Women from Birth to Death: The Female Life Cycle in Britain 1830–1914*, Harvester Press, Brighton, 1986.

Karlin, D. (ed.), *The Penguin Book of Victorian Verse*, London, 1997.

Kelly, Thomas, *A History of Adult Education in Great Britain*, Liverpool UP, 1992.

Kent, Susan Kingsley, *Sex and Suffrage in Britain, 1860–1914*, Princeton, NJ, UP, 1987.

Larsen, Timothy, *A People of One Book: The Bible and the Victorians*, Oxford UP, 2011.

L'Esperance, Jean, 'Doctors and Women in Nineteenth Century Society: Sexuality and Role', in John Woodward and David Richards (eds), *Health Care and Popular Medicine in 19th Century England: Essays in the Social History of Medicine*, London, Croom Helm, 1977, pp.105–27.

Levine, Philippa, *Prostitution, Race and Politics: Policing Venereal Disease in the British Empire*, London, Routledge, 2003.

Levine, Philippa, 'Venereal Disease, Prostitution, and the Politics of Empire: The Case of British India', *Journal of the History of Sexuality*, 1994, Vol. 4, pp.579–602.

McHugh, Paul, *Prostitution and Victorian Social Reform*, London, Croom Helm, 1980 (republished 2013).

Mahood, Linda, *The Magdalenes: Prostitution in the Nineteenth Century*, London & New York, Routledge, 1990.

Mason, Michael, *The Making of Victorian Sexual Attitudes*, Oxford UP, 1994.

Mathers, Helen, *Steel City Scholars: The Centenary History of the University of Sheffield*, London, James & James, 2005.

Morgan, M.C., *Cheltenham College: The First Hundred Years*, published for the Cheltonian Society by Richard Sadler, 1968.

Morgan, Sue (ed.), *Women, Religion and Feminism in Britain, 1750–1900*, Palgrave, Macmillan, 2002.

Morgan, Sue, 'The Power of Womanhood – Religion and sexual politics in the writings of Ellice Hopkins', in Anne Hogan and Andrew Bradstock (eds.), *Women of Faith in Victorian Culture: Reassessing the Angel in the House*, Basingstoke, Macmillan, 1998, pp.209–24.

Morgan, Sue and de Vries, Jacqueline (eds), *Women, Gender and Religious Cultures in Britain*, London, Routledge, 2010.

Mort, Frank, *Dangerous Sexualities: Medico-Moral Politics in England Since 1830*, London, Routledge and Kegan Paul, 1987.

Murdoch, Norman H., 'Female Ministry in the Thought and Work of Catherine Booth', *Church History*, Vol. 53 (September 1984), pp.348–62.

Murphy, Ann B., and Raftery, D., *Emily Davies: Collected Letters, 1861–1875*, Charlottesville, Virginia UP, 2004.

Murray, Janet, *Strong-Minded Women and Other Lost Voices from 19th-century England*, New York, Pantheon, 1982.

O'Donnell, Bridget, *Inspector Minahan Makes a Stand: The Missing Girls of England*, London, Picador, 2012.

Pankhurst, Sylvia, *The Suffragette Movement*, London, Longman, 1931.

Plowden, Alison, *The Case of Eliza Armstrong: 'A child of 13 bought for £5'*, London, BBC, 1974.

Porter, Roy and Hall, Lesley, *The Facts of Life: The Creation of Sexual Knowledge in Britain, 1650–1950*, New Haven & London, Yale UP, 1995.

Prochaska, F., *Women and Philanthropy in Nineteenth Century England*, Oxford UP, 1980.

Robinson, Jane, *Bluestockings: The Remarkable Story of the First Women to Fight for an Education*, London, Viking, 2009.

Royden, M.W., 'The 19th Century Poor Law in Liverpool and its Hinterland: Towards the Origins of the Workhouse Infirmary', lecture, 1999, http://www.btinternet.com/~m.royden/mrlhp/local/poorlaw/poorlaw.htm.

Scotland, Nigel, *Apostles of the Spirit and Fire: American Revivalists and Victorian Britain*, Milton Keynes, Colorado Springs & Hyderabad, Paternoster, 2009.

Shorter, Edward, *A History of Women's Bodies*, London, Allen Lane, 1982.

Simey, Margaret, *Charity Rediscovered: A Study of Philanthropic Effort in Nineteenth-Century Liverpool*, first published 1951, republished by Liverpool UP, 1992.

Stafford, A., *The Age of Consent*, London, Hodder and Stoughton, 1964.

Summers, Anne, *Female Lives, Moral States: Women, Religion and Public Life in Britain 1800–1930*, Newbury, Threshold Press, 2000.

Thompson, E.P. and Yeo, E. (eds), *The Unknown Mayhew: Selections from the Morning Chronicle*, London, Merlin Press, 1971.

Trumble, Kelly Lynn, '"Her body is her own": Victorian feminists, sexual violence, and political subjectivity', Florida State University, PhD, 2004.

Wainwright, David, *Liverpool Gentlemen: A History of Liverpool College, an Independent Day School, from 1840*, London, Faber and Faber, 1960.

Walker, Pamela, 'The Conversion of Rebecca Jarrett', *History Workshop Journal*, 58 (1), 2004, pp.254–8.

Walkowitz, Judith R., *Prostitution and Victorian Society: Women, Class and the State*, Cambridge UP, 1980, pb. ed. 1982.

Walkowitz, Judith R., *City of Dreadful Delight: Narratives of Sexual Danger in Late-Victorian London*, Chicago UP, 1992.

Weeks, Jeffrey, *Sex, Politics and Society: The Regulation of Sexuality Since 1800*, London, Longman, 1981.

Yeo, Eileen Janes (ed.), *Radical Femininity: Women's Self-Representation in the Public Sphere*, Manchester UP, 1998.

Oxford Dictionary of National Biography (ODNB)

Baylen, Joseph O., 'Stead, William Thomas (1849–1912)', *ODNB*, Oxford UP, 2004; online ed., September 2010, http://www.oxforddnb.com/view/article/36258.

Carlyle, E.I., 'Wilkinson, (James John) Garth (1812–1899)', Rev. Logie Barrow, *ODNB*, Oxford UP, 2004; online ed., October 2005, http://www.oxforddnb.com/view/article/29427.

Cowan, Ruth Schwartz, 'Galton, Sir Francis (1822–1911)', *ODNB*, Oxford UP, online ed., October 2005, http://www.oxforddnb.com/view/article/33315.

Cragoe, Matthew, 'Bruce, Henry Austin, first Baron Aberdare (1815–1895)', *ODNB*, Oxford UP, online ed., January 2008, http://www.oxforddnb.com/view/article/3732.

Delamont, Sara, 'Davies, (Sarah) Emily (1830–1921)', *ODNB*, Oxford UP, online ed., May 2007, http://www.oxforddnb.com/view/article/32741.

Hewitt, M., 'Wilson, Henry Joseph (1833–1914)', *ODNB*, Oxford UP, September 2004; online ed., October 2009, http://www.oxforddnb.com/view/article/50958.

Holton, Sandra Stanley, 'Elmy, Elizabeth Clarke Wolstenholme (1833–1918)', *ODNB*, Oxford UP, 2004; online ed., May 2007, http://www.oxforddnb.com/view/article/38638.

Lauer, L.E., 'Clibborn, Catherine Booth (1858–1955)', *ODNB*, Oxford UP, 2004; online ed., September 2012, http://www.oxforddnb.com/view/ article/49017.

Matthew, H.C.G., 'Stuart, James (1843–1913)', *ODNB*, Oxford UP, 2004, http://www.oxforddnb.com/view/article/38025.

Morgan, Sue, 'Hopkins, (Jane) Ellice (1836–1904)', *ODNB*, Oxford UP, 2004, http://www.oxforddnb.com/view/article/33978.

Ruston, Alan, 'Stansfeld, Sir James (1820–1898)', *ODNB*, Oxford UP, September 2004; online ed., May 2006, http://www.oxforddnb.com/view/article/26288.

Smith, E.A., 'Grey, Charles, second Earl Grey (1764–1845)', *ODNB*, Oxford UP, online ed., May 2009, http://www.oxforddnb.com/view/article/11526.

Sutherland, Gillian, 'Clough, Anne Jemima (1820–1892)', *ODNB*, Oxford UP, 2004, http://www.oxforddnb.com/view/article/5710.

Walkowitz, Judith R., 'Butler, Josephine Elizabeth (1828–1906)', *ODNB*, Oxford UP, 2004; online ed., May 2006, http://www.oxforddnb.com/view/article/32214.

Webb, R.K., 'Martineau, Harriet (1802–1876)', *ODNB*, Oxford UP, 2004; online ed., October 2006, http://www.oxforddnb.com/view/article/18228.

Parliamentary Papers and Online Sources

Hansard

House of Commons Parliamentary Papers online (HCPP).

Old Bailey Proceedings Online (www.oldbaileyonline.org, version 6.0, 17 April 2011).

The Criminal Law Amendment Act, 1885, http://www. lawindexpro.co.uk.

Acknowledgements

M y debts in relation to this book go back many years. I was introduced to Josephine Butler by Professor Clyde Binfield during the 1970s, in my third year as a history undergraduate at Sheffield University. How many student lectures launch a lifetime's research? This one did.

I returned to Josephine Butler in the late 1990s when I was teaching an Open University course on 'Women and Evangelicalism in the Nineteenth Century', led by Professor John Wolffe. One of my students, Janet Heywood, discovered Josephine's spiritual diaries in the Northumberland Record Office, and I was hooked. I embarked on my own research and published an article about her religion in 2001. Sue Morgan, as well as John Wolffe, were very helpful in developing my ideas at this stage. I also had the pleasure of meeting Jane Jordan, who made a comprehensive survey of Josephine Butler's writings for her biography, published in 2001. Together with Ingrid Sharp, she also edited five volumes of her letters, pamphlets and books. These contributions have been invaluable aids to my own research.

Beverley Grey, a granddaughter of Josephine's brother, Charles, kindly gave me a copy of her MA thesis on her great-aunt. In the run-up to Josephine Butler's centenary in 2006 I enjoyed working with a number of scholars on a volume of essays edited by Jenny Daggers and Diana Neale of Liverpool Hope University.

In my early research, I had encouraging aid from David Doughan of the Fawcett Library, in the old days when the collections were kept in a cramped and dingy basement at London Guildhall University. Renamed the Women's Library, it moved to its own building and has now been relocated again, to the London School of Economics. I am grateful to the staff there and also at Liverpool University Library, where Katy Hooper's knowledge has been very helpful.

The Northumberland Archives, now housed at Woodhorn, contain a treasure trove of family letters and diaries. Here I have had assistance from Carol Scott and her staff. The British Library, Sheffield University Library, Sheffield Archives, Salvation Army Heritage Centre, St Andrews University Library, Liverpool Record Office and Trinity College, Cambridge Archives have all provided me with valuable information. By suggesting that I look at the papers of J.R.M. Butler, the Trinity archivist directed me towards a previously unnoticed letter describing how Josephine met George!

Since my own article on Josephine Butler's religion appeared, there has been an encouraging increase in publications about it. The work of Lisa Nolland, Alison Milbank and Timothy Larsen has deepened my own understanding. Kristine Frederickson gave me new insights through her PhD thesis, which I supervised, and I also thank her for reading and commenting on the entire final draft of this book. Frances Dickinson talked me through the history of Dilston and gave me copies of her own pamphlets.

The Josephine Butler Society, which faithfully continues her work, gave me permission to reproduce photographs held in its extensive collection at the Women's Library. Calum Cheape advised me on the use of www.ancestry.co.uk, which led me to contact David and John Thompson, descendants of George Grey, who are responsible for the Thompson family tree. They kindly gave me permission to use the Grey and Butler sections of the tree in this book, and supplied family photos. They have patiently answered my frequent queries. So has Claire Grey, the creator of the website www.milfieldgreys.co.uk, who also gave me some invaluable photos. Ann Lewin supplied photos and local knowledge from Winchester, together with her own insights on Josephine Butler.

Early draft chapters of this book were read by a number of friends, including Catherine Annabel, Rosie Hunt and Alison Twells, to whom I am grateful. My son Kieran Mathers not only read them, but completely reworked them. He also came up with the title for this book. Roger Harper and Peter Mason, who worked with me on a previous book, have supplied maps and photos for this one. My dear friends Celia and Simon Gibbs gave me accommodation at their London home on countless visits to the Women's Library from my home in Sheffield.

The History Press had faith in this project, and I am grateful to Mark Beynon, Lindsey Smith and Christine McMorris in particular. Finally, I want to thank my father Keith, my stepmother Pat, my other children Ellie and Joe and my sisters Pat and Ruth for being so supportive to me over the years. My mother-in-law Dr Patricia Mathers, who is writing a book about another great and underrated Victorian, Alfred Russell Wallace, is an inspiration. Above all, my husband Dr Nigel Mathers has been encouraging and interested from day one, and a ready and indispensable source of advice on all matters medical. It is to him that I dedicate this book.

Helen Mathers
August 2014

 Postscript

When *Patron Saint of Prostitutes* came out in hardback, I was invited by the Josephine Butler Society to hold a book launch at Westminster, in the House of Lords. It was a wonderful occasion, with friends and family present, as well as many devoted JBS members. It seemed entirely appropriate that the Lords were holding a debate that day on the motion that women should be allowed to become Anglican bishops. I thought about the many hours Josephine herself spent in this building – in the Lobby, accosting MPs and demanding their support, and in the Ladies Gallery, watching debates. She was never allowed to follow the MPs into the Chamber of the House of Commons, and yet her presence was felt there and her efforts succeeded.

I have told Josephine Butler's story many times since then, in lectures across the country. I never tire of it and it never fails to stir strong emotions – in me as well as my audience. I want to thank the colleges and universities, history and civic societies, women's groups and other organisations who hosted me, gathered large audiences for me, listened intently and asked challenging questions. Future invitations are welcome! I can be contacted through my website – josephinebutlerpage.com. This also contains Josephine Butler news and updates to my Bibliography.

January 2021

Index

Nightingale, Florence 80, 179
North of England Council for Promoting
the Higher Education of Women
(NECPHEW): formation and aims 67,
69, 76
Northern Counties League (NCL) 100, 121

Oberlin, Pastor J.F. 134
Oxford/Oxford University: Butlers study
there 24, 103, 122; GB's work there
26–8, 31–2; Butlers' life there 30–6,
39–42, 52, 198; 'seamy side' 36, 128;
campaigns involving JB 67–8, 69, 70,
84, 128

Pall Mall Gazette 81, 148–55
Paris, France. *See* France/Police des
Moeurs/St Lazare Hospital
Parliament. *See* House of Commons
Percy, Jane and Jenny 120, 143
Personal Rights Association. *See* Vigilance
Association for the Defence of Personal
Rights
Pimps. *See* brothel-keepers
Playfair, Dr Lyon, MP 86
Police administering CD Acts. *See*
Metropolitan Police
Police des Moeurs (French Morals Police)
108–12, 114–5, 123–4
Pontefract by-election (1872) 13–4,
99–100, 101
Portsmouth 152
Powles, Rev. 46, 78
Preston by-election (1872) 100–1
Priestman, Mary 85, 109, 121–2, 137,
140, 165, 174, 178, 188
Priestman, Anna Maria 85, 140, 165, 188
Pro-Boers. *See* Boer War
Prostitute rescue 37–8, 54, 56–8, 60–1,
71, 79, 93, 102, 115, 121, 139, 142,
149–52, 157, 160–1, *see also* House of
Rest, Winchester and Liverpool
Prostitutes and 'fallen' women: Victorian
myths and views 73–4, 143, 156;
Different types in Victorian period
49–50; Risk of disease 74; Liverpool
women and girls 54; Experiences and
implications of CD Acts 77, 81–2, 88–9,
90–1, 95, 96; enslaved/'white slaves' 51,
56, 58, 81, 84, 90, 93, 106, 110, 111,
114, 119, 123, 128, 131–2, 137, 151,
165, 169; evidence to Parliamentary
inquiries 95, 96, 97, 138–9; treatment
under CLAA 160–1; treatment in France
108, 111, 114–5; treatment in Brussels
128–32; treatment in Switzerland
108, 113–4; treatment in Berlin 99;
treatment in India 164–5, 169–70, 194

Puerperal fever 33
Purity campaign 118, 127–8, 154,
157–60, 169, 175, 179–81

Quakers (Society of Friends) 85, 99, 109,
116, 128, 133, 182, 188; 'Christian
Convention' 140–1, 142
Queen's Daughters in India, The 170

Rees, Rowland 139
'Regulated prostitution' in Europe. *See*
Prostitutes, treatment
Rescue Society 77, 96
Rhodes, Cecil 182, 186
Richmond, George 27
Roberts, General Sir Frederick (later Lord)
165, 171
Roger, Edouard 129, 131
Rome, Italy 112–3, 175–6
Ruskin, John 31, 185
Russell, George MP/Russell Committee
143, 171
Russell, Noel 191
Ruth by Elizabeth Gaskell 35–6, 57
Rutson, Albert 63, 68–9, 70, 72, 210

Sallecartes, John 129
Salvation Army 144–6, 159, 181;
involvement in Maiden Tribute campaign
148–56; rescue work 151–2; attacks on
their preachers 145–6, 156–7
Schroeder, chief of Brussels Morals Police
129, 130, 131
Scott, Benjamin 128, 130, 132, 148
Seamstresses 49–50, 57
Sexually transmitted diseases (syphilis
and gonorrhoea) 49, 74–5, 77, 80,
115, 127
Shaen, William 140, 163
Shield, The 86, 130, 140, 161
Sidgwick, Prof. Henry 69
Slavery/slaves 36, 51, 52, 58, 73, 183,
see also Prostitutes – 'white slaves';
anti-slavery campaign 15, 19, 44,
101, 151, 164, 182–3
Sloggett, Dr W.H. 88, 95
Smyttan, Frances Hardy *née* Grey (sister,
known as Fanny) 22, 44–5, 47, 60,
68, 174, 177, 196
Smyttan, Rev. George Hunt (husband of
Fanny Grey) 45, 196
Snagge, Thomas 131, 132
Social Purity Alliance 127, 128, *see also*
Purity campaign
Somerset, Lady Henry 179–81
Southey, Eliza 138–9, 143
Speculum: use of 74–5, 82, 89, 90, 105,
121, 161; 'steel rape'/'outrage' 81–2,